DATE DUE

DEMCO 38-296

Charles Wuorinen

Photo by Anne Dowie. Courtesy Howard Stokar Management.

Charles Wuorinen

A Bio-Bibliography

Richard D. Burbank

Bio-Bibliographies in Music, Number 49
Donald L. Hixon, Series Adviser

Greenwood Press
Westport, Connecticut • London

Library of Congress Cataloging-in-Publication Data

Burbank, Richard.
    Charles Wuorinen : a bio-bibliography / Richard D. Burbank.
      p. cm.—(Bio-bibliographies in music, ISSN 0742-6968 ; no.
  49)
    Discography: p. 95.
    Includes index.
    ISBN 0-313-25399-4
    1. Wuorinen, Charles—Bibliography. 2. Wuorinen, Charles—
Discography. I. Title. II. Series.
ML134.W86B87 1994
780'.92—dc20
  [B]   93-28492

British Library Cataloguing in Publication Data is available.

Library of Congress Catalog Card Number: 93-28492
ISBN: 0-313-25399-4
ISSN: 0742-6968

First published in 1994

Greenwood Press, 88 Post Road West, Westport, CT 06881
An imprint of Greenwood Publishing Group, Inc.

Printed in the United States of America

The paper used in this book complies with the
Permanent Paper Standard issued by the National
Information Standards Organization (Z39.48-1984).

10 9 8 7 6 5 4 3 2 1

To my mother, Hazel Lillian Burbank

Contents

Preface

This bio-bibliography is a chronicle, a lexicon, a manual, a narrative, and a testament to the life and work of an American musical genius. The book is a comprehensive reference tool for accessing information by and about the composer Charles Wuorinen. It conforms to the Greenwood Press *Bio-Bibliographies in Music* series requirements for content, format, and style, and simultaneously stands as the only monographic work on the life and work of this composer. My primary aims have been to collocate information about Wuorinen's creative activity, to provide annotations summarizing the intellectual content of the materials identified, and, also, to refer the reader to things that have been written or said about Charles Wuorinen's life and music, pro or con, friendly or otherwise.

My research took me to many places and libraries, to clipping and personal files, public and private. Some visits were more successful than others, though I would point out that from the beginning, Charles Wuorinen was consistently helpful and supportive. I have sought out domestic and foreign, journalistic and scholarly, sophomoric and learned commentary about Wuorinen and his music.

During the summer of 1986, I was fortunate enough to stay at Wuorinen's Manhattan residence for three weeks to begin my research. I spent most of that time sifting through files in his composing studio, going through batches of material in cabinets on the lower level of the house, and sorting through many piles and cartons of material in his basement. The latter was a particularly odd experience since there was but one naked light bulb to illuminate a dark, dank area, and since I had the company of at least one large *Periplaneta Americana* (New York City water bug).

By the end of that period, however, I had come across a number of early fragments — partially composed works or early compositions that had later been completed. These materials consisted of the following: sketches of an unfinished piano concerto dated June-September 1960; a violin sonata dated 21 July 1957 (dedicated to Max Pollikoff, with movements titled "Rhapsody," "Scherzo," "Elegy," and "Finale"); and a work called *Improvisation for Eleven Players*, dated 1955 and written in Gardner, Massachusetts, which appeared to be an aleatoric work. Wuorinen told me that all of these compositions are *dead* and that they were simply early attempts at composition, or juvenilia. He does not consider them to be part of his catalog of works, nor do they consist of enough substance to warrant inclusion in the *Works and Performances* section of this book.

I was also fortunate enough to have Wuorinen's permission to consult his *Register of Works*, a detailed group of notebooks he has maintained since his earliest days as a composer. The notebooks provide information on various aspects of each work, from its source of commission to the date of its premiere. Some of the information is of a personal nature, and is not included in this book. Other writings consist of such information as Wuorinen's own annotations about premiere performances or his observations of famous performers. I have occasionally included such notations, most commonly in the form of what I have termed a "historical note" at the end of an entry.

Most of my library research was carried out at the Music Library of the University of Illinois at Urbana-Champaign. This magnificent collection offered me the opportunity to go on a research expedition in one of the most fertile resource centers in the nation, which happened to be right in my own backyard. Other important work was done at the Music Division of the Library of the Performing Arts at the New York Public Library at Lincoln Center, in New York City — another familiar, great haunt of the music researcher. Additional important collections were consulted at the Farber Creative Arts Library, Brandeis University (Waltham, Massachusetts), the Newspaper Annex of the New York Public Library, and the Newspaper Library of the University of Illinois at Urbana-Champaign. Clipping files at other libraries, such as the San Francisco Public Library, were consulted with the help of friends and colleagues in those locations.

Concert reviews and articles were tracked through the many music indexing and abstracting tools available. Online databases were also searched. A great deal of material was obtained through the mail, especially materials from symphony orchestra publicity departments and artist management firms. In some cases foreign consulates and overseas clearinghouses for music proved to be helpful. The most time-consuming aspect of my research was the examination of hundreds of reels of microfilm, necessary because I went back to the original articles to make sure review quotes and other comments were not taken out of context and to verify bibliographic citations. Wherever possible, I have included page numbers for articles published in the major newspapers. Many of the citations for articles from the lesser-known tabloids also include page numbers. Further, I have deliberately listed *all* page numbers for articles which have non-consecutive pagination because I indicate in the annotation the individual page number of the article from which a particular quotation was taken.

This bio-bibliography consists of several sections: a biographical overview, an interview, a listing of works and performances, a discography (sound and video), a catalog of writings about Wuorinen as well as one of writings by Wuorinen, appendices, and an index. Each section of the book has its own organization and purpose, and each contains links, or references, to related entries in other sections, so that the reader can move back and forth without losing track. The different sections of the book have their own mnemonic numbering schemes, with consecutive numbers.

The section entitled *Biography* is a brief biographical sketch of the composer. It includes some personal recollections of my own encounters with Wuorinen as well an overview of his work. It is intended to function as a succinct and general introduction to the annotated bibliography. Similarly, the *Interview* section is introductory. It sets forth Wuorinen's professional and personal views on issues directly related to my research — issues which are subsequently addressed by music critics, musicologists, and others cited in the annotated bibliography.

The *Works and Performances* section lists Wuorinen's works by instrumental or vocal medium, progressing from the large to the small: orchestra; chamber orchestra; instrumental and chamber music; piano; harpsichord; organ; percussion; electronic tape; stage works; chorus and orchestra; choral; vocal. Each entry is numbered consecutively beginning with **W1**. Noteworthy performances (or other performances I decided to list for various reasons) appear immediately following each main entry, with an alphabetical indication, such as **W27a** or **W49f**.

Entries in the *Works and Performances* section contain the following categories of information: title, instrumentation, dates of composition and place(s) where Wuorinen composed the work, duration, publisher information, dedicatee, individual or corporate body from whom the work was commissioned, premiere information (ensemble, performers, concert hall, concert series [if any], location), and, in some cases, a historical note that for the most part provides information pertinent to the composition or its premiere event. Entries in this section are linked, or cross-referenced, to relevant entries in other sections of the bio-bibliography.

Instrument abbreviations are as follows: **Picc** = Piccolo; **Fl** = Flute; **Rec** = Recorder; **Ob** = Oboe; **EH** = English Horn; **Cl** = Clarinet; **Bcl** = Bass Clarinet; **Cbcl** = Contrabass Clarinet; **Bsn** = Bassoon; **Cbsn** = Contrabassoon; **Sax** = Saxophone; **Horn** = French Horn; **Trp** = Trumpet; **Trb** = Trombone; **Tba** = Tuba; **T** = Timpani; **Bar Hrn** = Baritone Horn; **Perc (P)** = Percussion; **Glsp** = Glockenspiel; **Vibr** = Vibraphone; **Mar** = Marimba; **Xyl** = Xylophone; **Hp** = Harp; **Gtr** = Guitar; **Mand** = Mandolin; **Pf** = Piano; **Cel** = Celesta; **Org** = Organ; **Harm** = Harmonium; **Vn** = Violin; **Va** = Viola; **Vc** = Violoncello; **Cb** = Contrabass; **Str** = Strings; **Cemb** = Cembalo; **Sop (S)** = Soprano; **Mezzo-Sop (M)** = Mezzo-Soprano; **Alto (A)** = Alto; **Ten (T)** = Tenor; **Bar** = Baritone; **Bass (B)** = Bass.

Instrumentation is indicated by the common code listing the number of instruments in each section, according to their sequence in a full score. The first four numbers represent the woodwinds, the next four numbers represent the brass, and all remaining instruments are shown by the abbreviations. *Ad libitum* instruments are listed in parentheses. Numbers following "Perc" or "P" indicate the number of players required (not including Timpani when it is listed separately). Alternating or substitute instruments are listed in parentheses after the appropriate number. Players either alternate between instruments or may play the substitute instrument throughout the composition, unless Wuorinen specified otherwise in the score.

The dates and place(s) of composition category contains the chronological and geographical information relating to a work's creation. This information is usually expressed as a range of dates during which the composer worked on the piece, and his whereabouts as well. Wuorinen takes work with him almost any place he goes — compositional activity does not stop for a day or two while he travels long distances to perform or lecture. This information was often found in the colophon of a manuscript or score. In recent years, Wuorinen has stopped including this information in his published scores. Thus, I was not able to determine this information in every case, but included it wherever I could. I believe this chronological and geographical information will prove important to musicologists at a future time, when they begin comparing Wuorinen's musical sketches to his published scores and discover how the composer continuously used and transformed his musical materials from work to work, especially in terms of pitch and rhythm content.

The durations of compositions are expressed as in the following example: 7:32 = seven minutes, thirty-two seconds. The other categories of information are self-evident and appear consistently from entry to entry, depending on whether the information is appropriate, relevant or available for any given composition. Historical notes accompany some entries and include information not commonly known about the piece or the circumstances under which the premiere performance took place.

Wuorinen's publishers are: **C.F. Peters Corporation**/373 Park Avenue South/New York, NY 10016/(212)686-4147; **McGinnis & Marx Music Publishers**/236 West 26th Street #11S/New York, NY 10001-6736/(212)675-1630; **American Composer Alliance (American Composers Edition, Inc.)**/170 West 74th Street/New York, NY 10023/(212)362-8900; **Plymouth Music Co., Inc. (Music for Percussion)**/170 Northeast 33rd Street/Fort Lauderdale, FL 33334/ (305)563-1844; **Lawson-Gould Music Pub., Inc.**/250 West 57th Street #932/New York, NY 10107/(212)247-3920; and **Theodore Presser Company**/Presser Place/Bryn Mawr, PA 19010/(215)525-3636. Works with an asterisk attached to publisher number indicate that the work is available on a rental basis, not for purchase.

The *Discography* section is arranged chronologically, and then alphabetically by title of work. It includes commercial releases of Wuorinen's music and recordings that feature him as a performer (conductor or pianist). In addition, some non-commercial sound and video recordings are included, either because they have been cataloged and appear in the Online Computer Library Center (OCLC) shared-cataloging international bibliographic database, or because they were noteworthy for some other reason, e.g., foreign non-commercial studio recordings. Thus, the categories for this section of the book are as follows: Commercial Releases; Commercial Releases — Wuorinen as Performer; Non-Commercial Sound Recordings; Non-Commercial Sound Recordings — Wuorinen as Performer; Non-Commercial Sound Recordings — Video Recordings.

Wuorinen has in his possession sound tape recordings, reel-to-reel and cassette, of most of his works, especially first performances and subsequent renditions taped and sent to him (or to his manager, Howard Stokar) by the performers themselves. These recordings vary in both quality of musicianship and of sound. Since they are part of Wuorinen's personal, private sound archive they are not included in the discography.

Categories of information for each discographical entry are self-evident. Data was taken from many sources of information on each physical piece: label, container, etc. Historical notes appear when I have obtained relevant information concerning the creation of the recording or when other important information was available from the composer. Entries in this section of the book are linked to entries in the bibliography (in which a given recording is reviewed or discussed in print) as well as to its corresponding main entry in the *Works and Performances* section.

The annotated bibliography portion of this book consists of two major sections — *Writings About Wuorinen* and *Writings by Wuorinen*. The first major section (and the longest) consists of almost everything written about Wuorinen that I could find. Some writings, such as bibliographies of printed music, are only included if there is something important or unusual about the publication, e.g., one of the few European bibliographies containing entries or comments on Wuorinen. The 1,059 entries in this, the largest part of the book, contain summaries and/or brief quotations from concert reviews, essays, books, journal articles, masters theses and doctoral dissertations, editorials, textbook references, etc. The first portion of this section contains writings on specific musical works by the composer, and is arranged alphabetically by title of work, then chronologically within each work. (If two or more entries within this section bear the same chronological information, the entries are then arranged alphabetically by author and/or article title). Not every musical composition is represented in this part of the bibliography since a number of Wuorinen's works were never performed, published, recorded, or discussed. I chose this arrangement so that the reader could obtain a critical perspective of how the work has been viewed or assessed by critics and musicologists since the premiere performance. I felt that this was especially important since the vast majority of comments by music critics were negative, and since the vast majority of scholarly comments in journal articles, music monographs, and non-concert reviews were positive. Given these findings, in conjunction with Wuorinen's assessment of music critics and criticism as expressed in the *Interview* section of this book, it is apparent that composer and critic view each other in very different terms. I have tried to quote the briefest possible portion of the writings cited, selecting the most salient and pithy comments.

The remaining categories for this section of the book were created in an attempt to sort all other writings on Wuorinen into meaningful groups. Some of these categories are self-evident; others need a collective title to pull them together. These categories are arranged alphabetically by collective category, then alphabetically by author or title of article. The categories are as follows: Academia; Awards; Compositional Theory and Analysis; Ensembles — Group for Contemporary Music; Ensembles — Other Ensembles; Fromm Music Foundation; Genre — Electronic Music; Genre — Sacred Music; References — General Citations; References — Scholarly Citations; *Simple Composition*; Viewpoints; Wuorinen as Performer.

The other major section of the bibliography, *Writings by Wuorinen*, is arranged alphabetically by title. Note that Wuorinen's book, *Simple Composition*, is entered here, not in the *Works and Performances* section, since it is a textbook on musical composition, not a musical work. Writings about *Simple Composition* appear in their own subsection of the *Writings About Wuorinen* section, as described in the above paragraph, not in the alphabetically arranged portion of the bibliography devoted to writings about Wuorinen's musical compositions.

Entries in all parts of the annotated bibliography are linked to other, related entries within the annotated bibliography itself, as well as to entries in the

Discography and *Works and Performances* sections of the book. Thus, the reader can flip back and forth to track what was written about a particular performance, recording, or controversy.

Appendix I is a chronological list of works; Appendix II is an alphabetical list of works. The index features an explanatory note at the beginning.

I prepared this camera-ready book using WordPerfect 5.1 in conjunction with Hewlett-Packard's Type Director 2.0 (CG Times typeface, 17, 13, and 11 point fonts), and produced the text on a Northgate Slimline 386DX microcomputer and HP LaserJet IIP printer.

ACKNOWLEDGMENTS

It would be impossible to thank every individual who helped in various ways. The following individuals provided generous assistance throughout the research and writing of the book.

University of Illinois at Urbana-Champaign and environs: Robert Wedgeworth, Barton Clark, Sharon Clark, David Bishop, Arnold Wajenberg, Rhoda Engel, Robert Burger, Donald W. Krummel, Paul Zonn, William McClellan, Jean Geil, Leslie Troutman, Marlys Scarbrough, William Brockman, Nancy Anderson, Gail Hueting, Paul Keith, Steven Schaufele, David Bade, Joan Edwards, Walter Allen, Frank Davis, Merrill Eskew, Jerry Wray, Shirley Evosovich, Col. Ken Kolster, and the Library Research and Publication Committee, which was generous in funding two research travel expeditions to New York City.

Greenwood Press: Alicia Merritt, Marilyn Brownstein, Maureen Melino, Ann LeStrange, and Andrea Morgan.

Music Library Association: Susan T. Sommer, Deborah Campana, Ralph Hartsock, Don L. Hixon, Don Hennessee, Michael Colby, Calvin Elliker, and Monica Slomski.

New York City and environs: Charles Wuorinen, Howard Stokar, Jeffrey Kresky, Coburn Britton, Robert G. Zack, Jack Theurer, Harvey J. Satty, Tata Sato, Fr. James F. Schneipp, Hazel L. Burbank, George F. Burbank Sr., and George F. Burbank Jr. Also, I would like to thank Jacques Barzun for permission to reprint excerpts from his January 2, 1968 letter to Charles Wuorinen, and his April 28, 1993 letter to me.

Brandeis University: Robert L. Evensen.

Simmons College: Sheila S. Intner.

McMaster University: Professor John Clinard.

The photograph of Charles Wuorinen, by Ann Dowie, is a pun on the several photographs of Igor Stravinsky in which Stravinsky wears two pairs of eyeglasses. I am grateful to Howard Stokar Management for permission to reproduce it in this book.

The following journals and publishers granted me permission to quote excerpts from the copyrighted materials below, taken from the specific page numbers listed:

Wuorinen, Charles. "Notes on the Performance of Contemporary Music." *Perspectives of New Music* 3, no. 1 (Fall/Winter 1964): pp. 10, 14, 21.

Kresky, Jeffrey. "The Recent Music of Charles Wuorinen." *Perspectives of New Music* 25 (1987): pp. 416-417.

Julius, Ruth. "Edgard Varese: An Oral History Project, Some Preliminary Conclusions." *Current Musicology* 25 (1978): pp. 43, 45, 48.

Wuorinen, Charles. "We Spit On the Dead." *High Fidelity/Musical America* 24, no. 12 (December 1974): p. MA16. (Copyright © 1974 Hachette Magazines, Inc. All rights reserved. Reproduced from *High Fidelity/Musical America*, December 1974, with permission.)

Tawa, Nicholas, *A Most Wondrous Babble: American Art Composers, Their Music, and the American Scene, 1950-1985.* Copyright © 1987 by Nicholas Tawa. Published by Greenwood Press, an imprint of Greenwood Publishing Group, Inc., Westport, CT. Reprinted with permission. Excerpts from pages 24, 45, 49, 64-65, 69, 99, and 100.

To these and other people with whom I came in contact during the course of the work, I offer my sincere thanks and gratitude.

Charles Wuorinen

Biography

This biographical sketch offers an outline of Charles Wuorinen's career and accomplishments. It does not analyze his music or assess its importance — I leave that to the composers, musicians, musicologists, and critics listed in the bibliography section of this book. I have included, however, some of my personal impressions and recollections of encounters with Charles Wuorinen.

Charles Peter Wuorinen was born on 9 June 1938 in Physicians and Surgeons Hospital, Manhattan, New York City. His parents were John Henry Wuorinen and Alfhild (Kalijarvi) Wuorinen. He was their second son and last child. (His older brother, John, is an electrical engineer.) Nothing has been written about Charles Wuorinen's childhood or adolescence. During our interview sessions he was reluctant to talk about that period of his life, preferring instead to discuss his music.

According to Charles, John Wuorinen Sr., his father (born 1897), ran away from an insecure life in Finland in the middle of a winter night. He took a steamer across the Atlantic Ocean and arrived in Boston, a young man and an illegal alien. He then worked as a grocery clerk and in factories before deciding to pursue his education. After a long struggle, he earned his doctorate in history at Columbia University. The senior Wuorinen subsequently taught at Columbia for forty years.

Charles began taking piano lessons early in childhood. His piano teachers were Vladimir Ussachevsky and Jack Beeson. Given the cultural milieu of New York City, Charles had access, as a child, to many of the best concert activities and influences. By the age of five he was tinkering with musical composition. He attended the Trinity School, an Episcopalian middle school (then only for boys) located on the upper west side of Manhattan. While there (at age sixteen), he was awarded the New York Philharmonic Young Composers' Award (1954). In addition to his piano playing and composing, he performed as a countertenor with various choral groups in New York City. He graduated from Trinity School in 1956 and pursued his undergraduate studies at Columbia University. During this period and throughout his education, Wuorinen's parents discouraged him from pursuing a career in music. (See the interview for Wuorinen's comments on his parents' response to his career choice.) Jacques Barzun has written to me:

"I do not how much detail you supply in the biographical part of your book, and whether you go into his parents' fierce opposition to Charles's becoming a professional musician. But it may interest you to know that Charles's father was a colleague and good friend of mine in the Columbia [University] History department and that when the rift came between father and son, I stood up for Charles in a couple of vehement conversations — all in vain: John Wuorinen gave no entry to my reasons and thought he had Reason on his side."

There is a section in Wuorinen's *Register of Works* notebook called *Resonant Facts*. I noticed bits of biographical information there, especially for the early years, that I found nowhere else. From 1952-1956 Wuorinen was president of the Trinity School Glee Club. He was pianist, librarian, and general manager of the Columbia University Orchestra (1956-1957). He managed the *New Music Edition* in the spring of 1957, while Vladimir Ussachevsky was in Europe. He was a countertenor at the Church of the Heavenly Rest, New York City during the 1956-1957 season, then countertenor at the Church of the Transfiguration (Little Church Around the Corner), New York City, 1957-1958. He was the rehearsal pianist for the world premiere production of Carlos Chavez's opera *Panfilo and Lauretta*, given at Columbia University during the spring of 1957. During the summers of 1955 and 1956 he was organist at Saint Paul's Church in Gardner, Massachusetts, where his parents stayed during the summer months. He studied conducting with Rudolf Thomas at Columbia University, 1957-1959. In 1958 Douglas Moore nominated Wuorinen for a Woodrow Wilson Fellowship. Wuorinen was a special assistant to Ussachevsky at Columbia University, 1958-1959.

An entry in the notebook states Wuorinen was a Festival Fellow, Santa Fe Opera Festival honoring Igor Stravinsky's 80th birthday (25 July-21 August 1962), with the annotation "Kicked out." Yet another entry states Edgard Varèse nominated Wuorinen for an Arts and Letters award in the fall of 1964; the entry has the annotation "Rejected." A noteworthy event took place on 1 February 1966: the first radio broadcast featuring works exclusively by Wuorinen (WBAI, New York City radio broadcast, repeated 1 March of the same year).

Various individuals have offered financial support and patronage to Wuorinen over the years. While a young composer he received patronage from Peter I.B. Levan, Mrs. Lyman A. Beeman, Mr. and Mrs. Joseph Revson, and Coburn Britton. The latter, in particular, has commissioned works from Wuorinen for many years. Many other individuals, corporate bodies, performers and ensembles have also commissioned Wuorinen to compose works for them or for special occasions. Wuorinen is unquestionably one of the very few contemporary American composers who has *consistently* received commissions for new concert music.

Otto Luening, Ussachevsky, and Beeson were Wuorinen's composition teachers at Columbia. (Today, Wuorinen believes their influence was negligible.) His scholarships and financial awards at the undergraduate level included the Alice M. Ditson and Arthur Rose fellowships. He won the Bearns Prize, the BMI (Broadcast Music Inc.) student composers award, and the Lili Boulanger Award. He was a fellow at the Bennington Composers Conference and the MacDowell Colony. He completed his Bachelor of Arts degree in 1961 and his Master of Arts degree in 1963. He was awarded an honorary doctorate by Jersey City State

College in 1971. Wuorinen's professional life at Columbia University continued after his studies were completed. He taught there as a lecturer (1964-1965), an instructor (1965-1969), and as an assistant professor (1969-1971). He also performed and composed a great deal. He was a co-founder of the Group for Contemporary Music.

Wuorinen's life at Columbia ended in 1971. In 1970 he won the Pulitzer Prize for Music (the prize is administered by Columbia University); this was the first time the prize had been awarded for a work of electronic music. One year later, he was denied tenure as a member of the teaching faculty. A controversy arose in the New York press and in music circles; charges and counter-charges appeared in many articles, including some in The *New York Times*. (These writings are chronicled in this book and may be accessed under the index entries "Tenure," and "Wuorinen, Charles Peter, tenure controversy of.")

By that time, however, Wuorinen had established himself as a prominent, young American composer. In particular, the Pulitzer Prize had given him the recognition that it typically brings its winners: national exposure, invitations to join the teaching faculties of prominent universities and colleges, and, most importantly, commissions to compose musical works for major symphony orchestras and ensembles. The tenure controversy resulted in his appointment to the composition faculty at the Manhattan School of Music, the nation's largest conservatory, which, ironically, was located across the street and a few blocks from Columbia University. (Wuorinen chose to leave Columbia immediately.)

Much of Wuorinen's musical and personal life has taken place on the upper west side of Manhattan. His brownstone is located on the east side of West End Avenue between 101 and 102 Streets (870 West End Avenue, New York, NY 10025). The building had been a tenement. Wuorinen acquired it in the 1960s and has been refurbishing parts of it ever since. Over the past two decades, an urban renewal process known as *gentrification* has been underway on the west side of Manhattan. This process, resulting largely from the creation of Lincoln Center for the Performing Arts, has involved the renovation, refurbishing, and in some cases, demolition of buildings on the upper west side of Manhattan; the activity has crept up toward Columbia University. Wuorinen's brownstone, however, might be considered atypical for its neighborhood in that most of the buildings lining West End Avenue (between 72nd Street and 104th Street, where West End Avenue merges with Broadway) are what New Yorkers call pre-war (World War I) apartment buildings — old, solid apartment buildings, almost every one rising to the same height, and now with doormen and high rents (those that have not gone condo or co-op). Wuorinen's brownstone is close to many of the up-town institutions and concert halls in which his works have been performed (Columbia University, Manhattan School of Music, Symphony Space, Lincoln Center, Merkin Concert Hall, the Juilliard School, Alice Tully Hall, etc.) St. Ignatius of Antioch Episcopal Church, where Wuorinen is an active parishioner, is located at West End Avenue and 87th Street. Several of his works have been performed there under the direction of Dr. Harold Chaney, the parish music director. His immediate neighborhood is loaded with restaurants of all ethnic varieties, people of many ethnic backgrounds, and the constant, abrasive, and frantic sounds and traffic of the upper west side: it is the live-wire environment of New York City.

The brownstone itself has a Gothic atmosphere. Visitors climb steep steps up the front stoop to approach the main entrance. The outer door opens to a tiny vestibule where there is a large bell hanging on the side of the door. Visitors clang the bell to announce their arrival. (I often found that this routine made me think I was beginning an Edgar Allen Poe story.) The parlor floor consists of the large front room (with a large bay window looking out on West End Avenue), where Wuorinen often has students sit to discuss their work. His composing studio is in the center of that level of the house, and contains two baby grand pianos, a desk, a bookcase or two, a computer, a telephone, a chair with the Columbia University insignia, and a few other items. The *Wall Street Journal*, a few books on various aspects of mathematics, astronomy or another science, and a magazine, such as *Scientific American*, can usually be found on one or both of the pianos. (Wuorinen's musical works often bear some relation to the subjects he reads. For example, his interest in fractal geometry is reflected in his compositions *Bamboula Squared* and *New York Notes*; the latter was given a performance with the mathematician Benoit Mandelbrot present for discussion). Further back on the first level of the brownstone are an abandoned kitchen and bathroom. Living quarters are on the lower level (dining and kitchen areas, guest room, bath, and laundry area). There is a garden that has been revitalized and made attractive. The second floor of the house contains the composer's bedroom and private living area. The top floor is an apartment occupied by the violinist Benjamin Hudson. Wuorinen's manager, Howard Stokar, also lives and works in the building.

In the early to middle 1980s the lower level of the house was refurbished. Modern kitchen appliances and new cabinets were installed, and some new furniture was added. A wine rack and Italian espresso machine became prominent features. The frenetic activity in the house and the state of some of its quarters are an indication of how precious time is considered by the composer. (One of my earliest recollections of visiting 870 West End was a winter afternoon in 1978, when I arrived six minutes early for a lesson. As I struck the large bell, I could hear Wuorinen playing the piano in his studio. He continued to play as I tolled the bell a second, and, then, a third time. Finally, I took a coin from my pocket and tapped very loudly three times on the glass panel of the door. Charles came running to see who was there, opened the door, told me I was early and asked me to go away and come back in five minutes!)

Wuorinen has a summer residence in Middle Valley, New Jersey. The building is a stone and wood country house with what the composer calls "The Great Room" at its center — a spacious living area with cathedral ceilings and beams crossing various spaces. On one side is the kitchen and a staircase leading to an upstairs bedroom. The other side has an entrance to a large room the composer uses as his studio, and a staircase to both the lower level and another upstairs bedroom. There is an outdoor porch off the first floor living area. This home is virtually inaccessible in the winter. Wuorinen uses it as much as he can during the other seasons, especially in the summer. It is well situated, close to Manhattan and the Rutgers University New Brunswick campus.

Wuorinen's compositional process might be termed *frugal* in that he wastes nothing. According to Howard Stokar, his manager, the composer often uses or reworks music materials from one work in a succeeding work. The materials may include pitch or rhythm content that Wuorinen felt could be used in a generative way in another work. For example, *Bamboula Beach* uses materials from the third movement of *Piano Sonata No. 3*; *Genesis* includes materials from *Five* and *String Quartet No. 3*; *Crossfire* includes materials from *Canzona* and *Six Pieces for Violin and Piano*; *Movers and Shakers* incorporates materials from *Mass*. Wuorinen transforms his music materials as part of his creative process.

Charles Wuorinen has taught at many institutions. Most of his teaching activities have taken place at the following educational schools: Princeton University (visiting lecturer, 1967-1968); New England Conservatory (visiting lecturer, 1968-1971); University of South Florida (adjunct lecturer, 1971-1972); Manhattan School of Music (1972-1979); University of Southern California (1981); and Rutgers University, where he is now a tenured professor. He has been composer-in-residence at Chamber Music Northwest (1978), the Grand Teton Music Festival (1979), the Cabrillo Music Festival in Aptos, California (1985), the Louisville Symphony Orchestra (1984) and the San Francisco Symphony (appointed 29 January 1985; the appointment was renewed and lasted for a total of four years). He has served on the boards of the American Composers Alliance, the American Music Center, Composers Recordings, Inc., and the American Composers Orchestra. He was a founder of the American Society of University Composers.

He has lectured extensively. His talks have concerned various aspects of contemporary music as well as his own music. Some lectures have consisted of performances and concerts attached to follow-up discussions at which students and audience members exchange ideas. Some of his lectures have been "Descriptions of a Compositional Method," "The Federal Government and Composers," "The Composer and University Performance," "The New Milieu of Composition," "Analysis as Relevant to Performance," and "Music Education in the 1970s." These lectures have been given usually at academic institutions: State University of New York (Buffalo, Fredonia, Troy, Morrisville, Oswego, Stony Brook); University of California (Los Angeles, San Diego); University of Colorado; University of Connecticut; University of Houston; University of Illinois at Urbana-Champaign; University of Iowa; University of Massachusetts; University of Michigan; University of South Florida; Washington and Lee University; Wesleyan University; Jersey City State College; William Paterson State College; C.W. Post College; Smith College; Eastman School of Music (University of Rochester); University of Rhode Island; University of Utah, Louisiana State University, and others.

The composer has also established himself as a pianist and conductor. From the beginning, his interest in performing was an intense one that complemented his compositional activity. He has said time and again, in his writings and lectures, that for him, composing is directly related to the problems and possibilities of performance. In addition to performing in some of his own works as a pianist, he has advanced the works of some younger contemporary composers by performing as a pianist and conductor at concerts of the Group for Contemporary Music, mostly in New York City. He has also performed as a pianist with the University of Iowa Orchestra, the Buffalo Philharmonic, the Royal Philharmonic (London), the New York Philharmonic, and the Chicago Symphony Orchestra. He was a co-founder, with Arthur Weisberg, of The New Orchestra,

New York City, and has conducted major orchestras in the United States and abroad (especially in Finland). He was a co-founder of the Group for Contemporary Music and was influential in creating the ensemble Speculum Musicae. He has appeared on radio and television, mostly in the northeastern part of the United States. (On 17 February 1986 he participated in a seven-hour tenth anniversary celebration of the American Composers Orchestra, broadcast on WNYC-FM radio, New York City.) Despite all this activity, relatively little has been written about Wuorinen as a performer. Probably less than ten percent of all concert reviews written about Wuorinen concern his work as a pianist or conductor, regardless of whether the review concerns his music or that of another composer in which Wuorinen is a performer. Articles or reviews mentioning his performing activities are described in this book; they can be accessed under the index entries "Wuorinen, Charles Peter, as pianist," "...as conductor," etc.

As mentioned earlier, Wuorinen was a co-founder (with Harvey Sollberger and Nicolas Roussakis) of the Group for Contemporary Music, probably the first ensemble in the United States created to perform contemporary music exclusively. The ensemble's high standards have been reflected in both its concert programs and the instrumental and vocal virtuosity of its players. A controversy arose in the late 1980s, when the New York State Council on the Arts insisted that the ensemble program more works by African-American composers and women composers if it was to continue receiving funds from the council. Wuorinen's position was that the ensemble's programming standards had only to do with the quality of a musical composition, *not* with the ethnic background or gender of any composer. He responded by disbanding the ensemble. (See the interview for a fuller discussion of this event.) Although the Group for Contemporary Music is still in existence, its concert activities have declined. The ensemble was revived at Rutgers University and has performed a few concerts there. Given the demise of grant monies in general, Wuorinen and others concerned feel it is more important, at this time, to spend what money is available on recordings, so that there is a documented legacy to leave behind. Susan Deaver, a graduate student at the Manhattan School of Music, is researching her doctoral dissertation on the history of the Group for Contemporary Music. (Bibliographical entries on this ensemble may be accessed via the index; these entries are also grouped together in the body of the annotated bibliography under the heading *Ensembles — Group for Contemporary Music.*)

Wuorinen has received virtually every award an American composer can win, except for the Grawemeyer Award, administered by the Louisville Symphony Orchestra. (He has submitted works to the Grawemeyer Award committee every year since the award's inception.) Wuorinen was composer-in-residence with that orchestra in 1984; the orchestra went on strike almost immediately after his arrival, and he was quickly invited to become composer-in-residence with the San Francisco Symphony, an offer he accepted. His prizes include the following: New York Philharmonic Young Composers Award (1954); Bennington Composers Conference Scholarships (1956-1960); Bearns Prize (1958, 1959, 1961); Alice M. Ditson Fellowship (1959); MacDowell Colony Fellowship (1960); Arthur Rose Teaching Fellowship (1960); Broadcast Music Inc., Student Composer Awards (1959, 1961, 1962, 1963); Phi Beta Kappa (1960); Lili Boulanger Memorial Award (1961, 1962); Regents College Teaching Fellowships (1961, 1962); Evans

Travelling Fellowship (1961); Festival Fellow, Santa Fe Opera (1962); World's Fair of Music and Sound (1962); American Academy of Arts and Letters (1967); Guggenheim Fellowship (1968, 1972); Ingram Merrill Fellowship (1969); Pulitzer Prize for Music (1970); Brandeis University Creative Arts Awards Citation in Music (1970); Special Citation, Koussevitzky International Recording Award (1970); Phoebe Ketchum Thorne Honorary Award (1973); National Endowment for the Arts Fellowships (1974, 1976); Creative Artists Public Service Award (1976); Arts and Letters Award, Finlandia Foundation (1976). In 1985 he won a MacArthur Foundation Award of more than $230,000. A more recent, highly prestigious award has been the invitation to be composer-in-residence at the American Academy in Rome. His commissions are too numerous to mention here (see the *Works and Performances* section for that information). He began to be paid for his works early in his career. I once asked him if he had ever turned down a commission. He replied: "Someone wanted a cello piece for $250 — I said no."

Charles Wuorinen's political philosophy has evolved from a rather liberal one in his student days to an extremely conservative one at present. *Current Biography 1972* includes an entry on him referring to a *New York Times* article in which Donal Henahan wrote Wuorinen confessed to "all the usual left-wing sympathies" but that he had become a kind of anarchist. Since I have known Charles Wuorinen (the fall of 1977), he has offered his opinions on political matters often without hesitation and frequently with disarming candor.

On 23 July 1970 President Richard M. Nixon held a state dinner at the White House for President Uhro Kekkonen of Finland. Wuorinen was an invited guest and was seated at a table for three; his dinner companions were the conservative columnist William Rusher (former publisher of the *National Review*) and the physicist Edward Teller, father of the hydrogen bomb. While preparing this book, I asked Charles if he could recall much about that evening, especially the principal topics he and the other two eminent gentlemen discussed over dinner. Unfortunately, he was not able to do so, or he preferred not to.

In the early 1980s there was a major disarmament demonstration in New York City's Central Park. Thousands of people came to New York to participate in the protest. It was around that time that the pianist Ursula Oppens had a set of calling cards made up for Charles. The cards were a spoof on his conservative viewpoint on many issues, and had been intended as an amusement. They were of the standard business card size. The information in the center of the card consisted of the composer's name, under which was the term "Composer" identifying the service. Then followed the slogan "Socialist Realism — With a Difference." In one of the lower corners of the card, over his telephone number, was the image of a tiny tractor. Wuorinen found the cards hilarious and distributed them to friends, some colleagues, and other selected individuals.

Wuorinen has been represented by several music publishers over the years, but has tried as much as possible to have everything he considers to be an important work published by C.F. Peters. During the course of my research for this book I came upon various pieces of juvenilia and many of his early works, some which had handwritten comments on them such as "transferred to McGinnis & Marx" or "returned to ACA." The oboist Josef Marx was an early fan of Wuorinen's. Marx performed some of Wuorinen's works and even provided an early commission. Most of the works published by McGinnis & Marx have been transferred to C.F. Peters. In response to one of my questionnaires, Wuorinen, remarked that Josef Marx had done virtually nothing to promote or sell the contemporary works he published. Wuorinen grew impatient. Many of those works were transferred to Peters in a swift contractual move on 20 January 1970. The *Piano Variations* is the only seminal work still with McGinnis & Marx. (Some other early works remain with McGinnis & Marx, the American Composers Alliance, Music for Percussion, or Theodore Presser.) Original manuscripts and all sketch materials are in the possession of the composer, except for a few original manuscripts, one of which is at the Library of Congress.

More biographical details and some brief discussions of specific works can be found in articles in the standard music biographical dictionaries. Entries for these reference tools can be accessed via the index heading "Biographical dictionaries," and "Chronologies." The entries are found in the *References — Scholarly Citations* part of the annotated bibliography.

As of this writing, Wuorinen has completed or is working on a number of compositions. One work is *Microsymphony*, for orchestra (premiere scheduled for 19, 20 and 23 March 1993, Zdenek Macal conducting the Philadelphia Orchestra in Philadelphia). *Concerto for Saxophone Quartet* (a working title) is being composed for the Rascher Saxophone Quartet and is scheduled for a March 1994 premiere, with Dennis Russell Davies conducting. The commission for this quartet is from the Orchester der Beethovenhalle Bonn. Wuorinen is also composing another saxophone quartet for the same group to be premiered prior to the concerto. It will be performed at the Mönchengladbach Festival and the Ludwig Forum in Aachen. Another new work, *Missa Renovata*, was scheduled for premiere in September 1992, in Rome. It is an alternate version of the 1982 *Mass* (without the motet), and designed for concert use. The vocal parts remain unchanged but the instrumentation has been expanded.

New recordings in preparation include an all-Wuorinen compact disk (Koch label). The works recorded will be *Five: Concerto for Amplified Violin and Orchestra*, *Archangel*, *Archæopteryx*, and *Hyperion*. Wuorinen conducts the Orchestra of St. Luke's, with David Taylor on bass trombone, and Fred Sherry, violoncello soloist. Another Koch label compact disk will feature Wuorinen's *String Quartet No. 2*, performed by the Group for Contemporary Music. The *Missa Brevis* has been recorded by Dr. Harold Chaney at St. Ignatius Episcopal Church, New York City, and is expected to be released commercially sometime in 1993. A recent noteworthy radio event was a 75-minute BBC Radio 3 program, broadcast on 18 October 1992. The program was a BBC Contemporary Music Program produced by Alan Hall, with Peter Paul Nash interviewing Wuorinen. Recordings of *Genesis*, and *Piano Concerto No. 3* were broadcast. The composer's textbook, *Simple Composition*, has been republished by C.F. Peters, and has also been published in Chinese.

There are at least two more books about Charles Wuorinen which need to be written. One would be a definitive biography; since the composer is only in his mid-fifties it is too soon for such a book to appear. The other book would be a detailed catalog of Wuorinen's musical sketches, papers, correspondence, and photographs that would provide future scholars with the primary source materials of his life and work.

Perhaps the best way to close this biographical sketch is with a letter I came across in Charles Wuorinen's files. The letter of recommendation had been written in support of a Guggenheim fellowship application:

> I have the profoundest admiration for the work of Charles Wuorinen and complete confidence in his judgement. His project exploratory of new resources in electronic music, as well as of his own sensibility as a composer, strikes me as one worth supporting, even though I am not able to gauge the details of what he proposes. Indeed, if he is breaking new ground, no one is able to make a judgment *now*.
>
> On the more general principle that Charles Wuorinen should be enabled to compose in relative freedom after his strenuous last years as teacher, performer, conductor, and musical director, I strongly urge the award of a fellowship to him.
>
> Jacques Barzun
> January 2, 1968

On a piece of stationary accompanying the letter was the following note: "Dear Charles — It's not usual to import 'fellowship opinions' to those recommended, but after writing to Guggenheim, it occurred to me that you might have other applications in later days and that I might not be around to say my say. So for *all* reasonable purposes this is yours to use in the good fight for support. A Happy New Year to you. Keep original, send Xerox! JB" In raised ink on the stationary was the message "With the compliments of Jacques Barzun."

Interview

Note: This interview is actually a composite of several interviews that took place (in person and by telephone) between October of 1987 and October of 1992. Two of the interview sessions took place at Charles Wuorinen's Manhattan residence. The composer was given the opportunity to examine a transcript of the final version prior to its publication.

BURBANK: The late pianist Paul Jacobs once told me that talent for musical composition manifests itself no later than age five. How old were you when you began composing?

WUORINEN: About five.

BURBANK: It would seem you got in just under the wire. What made you decide to start composing?

WUORINEN: I don't know. It was before I took piano lessons which I started, I believe, when I was six. My brother had been taking lessons around that time (he's seven years older than I), so perhaps it was sibling rivalry.

BURBANK: This is the scientist?

WUORINEN: He's an electrical engineer. He didn't particularly want to continue with piano, but I was interested, so I went instead. But before that I had already fiddled around at the piano and imitated singing commercials heard on the radio.

BURBANK: Were your parents musical people?

WUORINEN: No.

BURBANK: They didn't sing, they didn't play instruments?

WUORINEN: My mother played the piano a little.

BURBANK: Were both of your parents born and raised in Finland?

WUORINEN: No. My father was born in Finland and left there in 1916 running away from the Russians, when they began to conscript Finns into the Russian Army. He escaped in a very dramatic way and ultimately made his way here, to Massachusetts. My mother was born in Gardner, Massachusetts, of Finnish immigrant parents. (I found out late in her life that her family had in fact been Swedish, and had emigrated to Finland around 1600.) They were peasant landowners. My father's side may have had some Swedish blood in it as well, but we don't know. My mother was a first generation native.

BURBANK: Then English was a second language for your father?

WUORINEN: Yes, but not for my mother.

BURBANK: What was it like growing up with your brother? Was he interested in music; were the two of you competing?

WUORINEN: No, he was not interested in music.

BURBANK: Not at all?

WUORINEN: No. I was the only one in the family who was.

BURBANK: Were you also interested in science?

WUORINEN: Oh yes, I was very interested in astronomy, which I still am. Astrophysics, and such.

BURBANK: Did you consider any other vocations in your childhood or adolescence?

WUORINEN: Well, when I was very young I didn't know really whether I wanted to be an astronomer or a composer. But quite soon I decided on being a composer. Probably by the time I was 10 or a little older.

BURBANK: Did you consider a vocation to the priesthood at all?

WUORINEN: Doesn't everyone who has a religious impulse? From time to time I still do. It's a silly fantasy because I'm sure I'm completely unfit. But I did contemplate it when I was in high school.

BURBANK: Did you ever experiment with any of the other arts, especially the visual arts? Did you ever paint?

WUORINEN: No. My brother did but he gave it up in childhood and I think it was because of discouragement from my family. I've never been terribly responsive to visual arts although I think I've been brainwashed into believing that I have less response than I really do. Be that as it may, the one thing that I did try, never in any serious way but only as a vocation, was Chinese calligraphy. I was very struck by it when I first came across really excellent instances — struck by the fact that for the first time, with the visual, I could see or sense the flow of time. I could follow the brush strokes and their speed. This is an interest of mine which has been dormant for many years now, but I did practice it a little bit in a desultory way. I probably would have done more if I'd had more time, if I hadn't been too busy with music.

BURBANK: Did you save your art works?

WUORINEN: Oh, they're nothing but practice sheets. There are some lying around somewhere but they're no good. To learn how to do well requires years of sustained effort and I don't know whether I could ever have gotten good or even "average." But it would have required more devotion and time than I had for it.

BURBANK: Did your parents oppose or support your interest in becoming a composer?

WUORINEN: They opposed it, especially in the beginning; and, in fact, I don't think they ever really were comfortable with the notion.

My father died before I won the Pulitzer Prize but I remember that although I had already achieved a certain professional standing, nothing — no professional accomplishment, no musical accomplishment — that I ever achieved would elicit a stronger response from my parents than the news that I had been offered some university appointment or other. This always made them feel good. As is so often the case with parents, there never comes any real acceptance of the child, even when the child gets to be fifty.

In my childhood, my parents tried to discourage me from composing on the grounds that it was an insecure profession. (Of course, they were completely incapable of understanding what it was that impelled me.) On one particularly ludicrous occasion they sent me (I forget how old I was; early teens, I suppose) to a friend of theirs who was an ethnomusicologist in the Columbia University music department, saying that I should show him my little pieces, and that his advice was going to be the answer to everything, and that everything he said was to be taken with the utmost seriousness. I went to show him my pieces and he said, "Music is your dish." And so I came tripping back to my parents delighted that I had been given the seal of approval and expecting them to say "okay, now go right ahead," only to be told by my father (who was not infrequently given to policy reversals of an inexplicable and arbitrary sort) that this is just one person's opinion and counted for nothing. Late in her life my mother claimed that they really were terribly proud of me and were always supporting what I did but they just didn't want me to get spoiled by being praised too much. I responded that it would have been nice if they had praised me somewhat or even too little rather than not at all, instead of just opposing and worrying about every move that I wanted to make.

BURBANK: What about your brother? Did he have an opinion about your career in music?

WUORINEN: No.

BURBANK: There were no other siblings?

WUORINEN: No.

BURBANK: What is your view of aleatoric music, of compositions that involve elements of chance? You gave an interview some years ago in which you talked about a few of your works that had involved elements of aleatory.

WUORINEN: Oh, years ago I wrote a semi-indeterminate trio for flute, cello and piano. It's one of those *box pieces*, where there are fragments in boxes and each person plays in his own sandbox for a while, and then all move to the next sandbox. That was my one semi-aleatoric piece; it's from 1961, perhaps.

BURBANK: And that was the only one?

WUORINEN: That was the only one. But two other pieces — a 1962 cello and piano piece called *Duuiensela*, and an *Invention for Percussion Quartet* — use proportionate notation (if that can be considered chance-like).

BURBANK: In your basement, I came across a piece titled *Improvisation for Eleven Players* dated 1955, Gardner, Massachusetts and with the performance instruction "The performing artist is as much responsible for the creation of the piece as the composer."

WUORINEN: I said that?

BURBANK: That is what I found.

WUORINEN: I'm glad I got that out of my system before puberty. You know, I realize after the fact that a lot of things that became fashionable later I did and discarded as an adolescent.

BURBANK: "Players determine pitch by filling glasses with water."

WUORINEN: How hydraulic! I don't actually remember such a thing. But if you say it's there I suppose it must be. You see, that was just around the time that the electronic medium was beginning. I had heard a couple of things that interested me, not so much in themselves, but on the romantic notion of "expanding possibilities." So I began to look around. And I fairly quickly discovered not the galaxies of new possibilities that were advertised but just the limitations of the medium as we know them now.

BURBANK: Which of your works do you consider to be your best? Which please you the most?

WUORINEN: I can't really offer an answer that means anything because my opinion changes and since I'm usually at work on something new, I'm concerned with that more than anything else. There are certain pieces that, for a period of a few years, I am likely to think of as more favorite than others. But I don't have a favorite, really.

BURBANK: The 1986 *New York Times* article that announced your MacArthur Foundation award mentioned that you were doing something concerning musical structure at Bell Labs and/or at UCSD [University of California at San Diego], and I recall you said you had a couple of inquiries about that work. Can you tell me something about it?

WUORINEN: Unfortunately, the way it appeared in that article made it seem as if I had launched some great program of research. That, of course, was not the case. What I was doing was trying to find a kind of musical expression for some of the ideas originally put forward by Benoit Mandelbrot, the mathematician, who coined the term *fractals*. Since I became interested in fractal geometry (which was in the late 1970s), and then worked at Bell Labs, the subject has become very fashionable. It had been ignored before, put in a corner, not considered respectable. Now it has become a very faddish thing. And it's quite fascinating, actually.

Mandelbrot's study was based on the work of a number of rather obscure figures who dealt with turbulence, disorder, fragmentation, irregularity in natural objects and natural processes. For these he developed descriptive tools. They take too long to describe but they involve, among other things, the ideas of non-integral dimensionality and self-similarity of parts — mathematical notions which involve the replication of shapes or modes of behavior or different scales of size: These can be space or time. It occurred to me (certainly other people have considered it in more detail than I have) that this is a basic characteristic of music and that it is, in fact, proved that in well-composed music the same kinds of things tend to happen in the large as in the small. Scientists who have investigated this character of music have tended to deal with the actual acoustic signal that music makes. But I'm not concerned with that so much as with the structural, metaphorics question. What I did at Bell Labs (with Mark Liberman) was to try various experiments in which strings of pseudo-random material, usually pitches but sometimes other things, were generated and then subjected to traditional types of compositional organization, including twelve-tone procedures. What I wanted to do was to see whether or not these things sounded "composed," sounded purposively chosen. They did, at least by my lights. The random sequences were not just any old random sequences but were that of a kind called *1/f randomness*. That's essentially what was involved. In fact, this is the way the pitches and other aspects of *Bamboula Squared*'s tape part are made. It is the sort of thing that certainly could be the subject of a reflective monograph or even a book (that nobody would want to read). But it would involve much work and much serious scholarly activity to justify something of that scope.

BURBANK: Your only book, *Simple Composition*, the textbook on musical composition (which may now very well be the only such book by a contemporary American composer to be published in China) was first published in 1978. Do you have any plans to write another book, after *Simple Composition*?

WUORINEN: No, but I'd like to see an intelligent monograph on "fractal music" become available.

BURBANK: What is your opinion of IRCAM [Institut de Recherche et de Coordination Acoustique Musique], established in 1976 in Paris under the direction of Pierre Boulez?

WUORINEN: Well, I wait for something substantial to come out of it. It's true that there have been a few worthwhile pieces. Boulez's *Repons*, though I don't think it's the answer to everything or the culmination of all human aspiration as has been suggested. And there are a couple of other composers, like York Holler who have done reasonably well. But I have yet to see any sign that IRCAM is in any significant respect different or richer in facilities or in achievements than Stanford, than UCSD [University of California at San Diego], than MIT [Massachusetts Institute of Technology] or a host of other places. In other words, it's mainly another installation which, because it has the prestige of the French government behind it and oodles of money, is able to command great attention. It also commands attention from an American point of view because it's European and snotty. And let's not forget that the technology *all* came from Bell Labs, Stanford, M.I.T., and a little from UCSD. The institute contains very little indigenous technical work, as far as I know.

BURBANK: What are your projections for the future of electronic music?

WUORINEN: There is no question that the medium is all going to be based on digital synthesis: both with real-time control and, secondarily, computer-generated — not necessarily composed algorithmically.

As an artistic manifestation it's very difficult to predict quality. It seems to me that until there is some degree of standardization of instruments — and now I'm speaking of live performance and the use of computer and other electronic means of live performance — things will remain pretty chaotic; not much really worthwhile work is going to be done.

In this connection I once had an interesting visit at Stanford [University] during which John Chowning said that the present electronic instruments will never amount to anything unless they are somehow able to encompass satisfactorily the already existing repertory. I'd never heard that said before.

If that happens (if instruments are developed which can do, over certain broad categories, what is required to play a Beethoven piano sonata, for example, or the Schoenberg piano concerto, or other works for acoustical instruments, plus other things as well), then, I think, we're going to have a very rich development. And I assume it will happen sooner or later.

BURBANK: Do you believe that contemporary music in America has surpassed that of Europe?

WUORINEN: Of course, no question of it.

BURBANK: Why?

WUORINEN: First of all, the rational process of change. As we know, even from the history of European music, there have been times at which the center of compositional activity shifted, as it did, for example, from the Burgundians and Flemings to the Italians in the second quarter of the sixteenth century. So it would be only natural in the course of events (especially on the larger geographic canvas that is characteristic of our time) that the center would shift away from Europe where it has been for so long.

But beyond that is the fact that you do not have two world wars and totalitarian regimes in your backyard and maintain a healthy, continuing cultural life. I have heard it said that Europe really ceased to matter in a cultural sense after World War I: the war had already smashed it. Whether that is true or not, *after* Hitler and, *after* the Second World War, it seems Europe has had its creative impulse devastated.

So many people were driven out of Europe as a result of the Nazi activities — Jews and many others — that I don't think Europe has ever recovered. The natural tendency of all people to admire foreign things and the American tendency to denigrate its own cultural activity and elevate that of Europe, combined with the European system of public support all create the impression of a vitality over there, which, I think, is not real.

BURBANK: In terms of contemporary music in America, where do you think it is headed and why? Where will it go in the post-Cage, post-Carter, post-Babbitt era?

WUORINEN: You know, these predictions are always very risky. I don't know exactly, but I think it is easier to say what has happened recently and what is bad about it.

Recently, we've had the elevation of what is essentially pop music. Just as every moron in the late sixties was given an "A" in school because we had to define everybody as a genius, now, in the last few years, we have taken easy pop music — music which happens to be either immediately appealing to the unwashed or simply and easily assimilable in some other sense (familiar sounds, repetitive patterns, etcetera) and declared this to be high art so that we could then say, "Look, we have high art which appeals to a broad mass public." We are unable to give up the fantasy that somehow if we just did it right, if art music were somehow the right kind of art music, it would retain its position on Parnassus but at the same time be available to the lowest gutter-snipe.

This notion (which has been aggressively promoted by many critics for many years) now has been seized upon. It has been used to elevate those composers who write pop music but want to be regarded as serious. It has also been seized upon by some of the more opportunistic young who, with a sigh of relief, turn away from actually learning something about music and spend their time now courting a kind of public favor which, while strong, is nevertheless brief. What will happen next, I don't know. But I do make a prediction: Things normally get worse rather than get better. The question (and simply in terms of style changes — this has been the case over the years that I've observed the scene) one needs to ask is "What could possibly be worse than what we are enjoying at the moment?" That is a difficult question. But I think I have the answer: Concert Rap. That will be the next thing!

BURBANK: Do you still feel that New York City is the capital of the music world?

WUORINEN: Yes, but much less so than it was twenty-five years ago. It is still the center, but it is now the case that musical life in the United States is far less centralized than it used to be. Certainly the orchestras of Chicago and Cleveland, Pittsburgh, Boston and Philadelphia, and perhaps Los Angeles as well and almost San Francisco, are at least at the level at which the [New York] Philharmonic here plays.

In terms of new music, it's still true that most of the significant composers are in New York and its environs (more so than anywhere else, I think, in the world at the moment). That probably will not stay the same forever. The fact that The *New York Times* — the *one* organ that covers these things on a regular basis and that is read widely — is so hostile to serious new music and does so much to promote the pop wing of new music does not help the new music scene here at all.

There's one other point which is not musical but very significant: the fiscal and economic center of gravity is shifting to Asia. The Western style musical life of Japan and now, increasingly, places like Taiwan, Singapore, Hong Kong and Korea is becoming much more important than ever before. How that will affect matters in the long run, I really don't know. But it certainly is a big change that has come up in the last twenty to twenty-five years.

BURBANK: On your book-jacket blurb for Joan Peyser's biography of Leonard Bernstein you commented that her book goes into Bernstein's "dark side." What did you mean and what is your opinion of Bernstein's music?

WUORINEN: I didn't know the man personally so this is not from personal experience. But he seems to have used people up, let us say. A lot of people who have been associated with him have ended up in a very bad way and, like any megalomaniac, he's likely to have a very negative effect on people around him. Some have survived. And there are other unsubstantiated things one hears which are not very pleasant.

Bernstein the composer does not impress me. I think he's an excellent show composer and, if one likes that genre — the Broadway musical (and a lot of people do) — then he's made very strong contributions to that genre.

His serious music does not fly. It's regurgitive. Not that a piece of music has to break new ground all of the time, far from it. But simply, it doesn't speak with a voice which is particularly individual. It seems to me that Bernstein's problem as a composer is that he appears (and again I don't know this from anything but inference) to have a view of composing which is very much like the old Hollywood idea of nineteenth century composers. Anyone who really knows how to compose knows that this is not possible. And it's especially not possible in a time like ours where there are so many different kinds of music — past, present, foreign and domestic — available to everybody and in which, therefore, the notion that there are heaven-sent norms has to be treated with great skepticism.

Besides that, we have Stravinsky, we have Mahler, we have Copland, if we want, we really don't need music which recombines these elements in ways that are not always as interesting as they might be. We also have Hindemith, by the way. I once heard a performance of the *Violin Serenade* of Bernstein. I was amazed at how much is taken from Hindemith.

BURBANK: In a conversation we had some time ago you referred to Lincoln Center for the Performing Arts as the "Lincoln Shopping Center." What did you mean and how do you feel about such cultural institutions now that we are in the 1990s?

WUORINEN: Well, when I talked about Lincoln Center as "Lincoln Shopping Center" I was not saying that the institutions within it are all like K-Mart. What I'm saying is that the impulse to centralize everything and to package everything in ugly buildings covered with thirty-second-of-an-inch-thick slices of marble (which are now falling off after twenty-five years) is a very bad idea.

The Lincoln Center, the "arts center," notion (which has been imitated all over the country by now as well as in many other parts of the world), is one which is based on a very well meaning purpose but, I think, one which is very destructive to the arts. That is: In a democracy we should make it possible for everyone to "enjoy," or to be involved with or connected to, or have access to the arts. No one can be more in favor of having everyone have access to the arts, either as practitioners or public, than I. But there's a profound difference between having access — being able to hear an orchestral concert or a chamber music concert or see a play — and being on the receiving end (as a member of the lay public) of a lot of marketing, "outreach" and hype.

The Lincoln Center impulse, for all of its nobility of purpose, is basically one of enlarging the audience — the number of bodies. And so one has, in the case, say, of the orchestra, the unhealthy spectacle of nineteenth century warhorses (Beethoven symphonies, for example) played in halls which are four times as big as the rooms that those pieces were made to be played in to begin with. A 900-seat hall, which is what those pieces were typically performed in, has become a 3,500-seat hall. And those seats have to be filled. If there aren't 3,500 people who want to hear the Beethoven symphony you turn around and sell it like toothpaste.

This is the commercialization of serious art. It's not a new complaint, but the process has now reached a stage where there cannot be any more Beethoven played. But there is! Loren Maazel, for example, performed all nine Beethoven symphonies in a single day in Pittsburgh. What a hideous new idea! Lincoln Center embarks upon a cycle of performances in which every single note that Mozart ever wrote will be played. This is *their* answer! This is *their* program for cultural significance. Now that cannot possibly be taken seriously. And the point is that if the *attitude* were different, I wouldn't care if they put every concert in New York in Lincoln Center, or if they scattered it so that no hall was within five miles of another hall. What I'm concerned about is the attitude behind the thing: the notion that music and the other arts are commodities that should be sold. This is wrong.

BURBANK: Well, how did you feel about the cellist and contemporary music specialist Fred Sherry having been director of the Chamber Music Society of Lincoln Center? Did you think it was a positive appointment, given his strong commitment to contemporary music?

WUORINEN: I had hoped that it would be the beginning of a trend to appoint people with vision. The great fault of all these institutions (not just the ones at Lincoln Center but everywhere — the symphony orchestras, the opera houses), is that there is very, very little leadership exercised by the executive or the artistic direction of any of them.

The music directors and the soloists are constantly on the run, never at home, in the business of "not rocking the boat" for these huge institutions with their very large budgets. And the people who manage them are also maintaining an operation in which they want to protect very good salaries, in which many people are employed, and in which there are many other pressures than the artistic ones. From nowhere does there come significant, progressive artistic leadership.

Now with the appointment of Fred Sherry at Chamber Music Society, I think the Board recognized the need for a boldness of approach, which we had already seen in what he had accomplished prior to the appointment. Of course, he was attacked because change is uncomfortable. But I think that if these institutions are to survive and not go under within a generation (which is about the time I'd give them to last), there has got to be some really bold leadership.

The business of doing every piece Mozart ever wrote or doing all nine Beethoven symphonies in one day — these *desperate* ploys — these are like nothing more than the alcoholic who takes another drink to feel better. It works for the moment but kills him in the end.

BURBANK: Concerning government funding of the arts, would you like to see increased spending on new music by American composers and, for example, would you like to see an American composer featured on one of the *In Performance at the White House* concerts that have been broadcast nationally on public television?

WUORINEN: Well, that's a complex question. First of all, government support in the United States, I think, is a bad idea. I think it has had a destructive effect. It was originally promoted on the grounds that it would lessen commercial pressures on artistic institutions. As we have seen, it has increased them instead, because there is no one in government who has an appreciation of the arts as intrinsically meritorious.

The arts are vaguely thought to be a "good thing," but they are always justified, when government support is sought, on the grounds that they increase property values near the site of performances, they make jobs, they sell restaurant meals, they sell gasoline, book hotel rooms, parking spaces, they encourage tourism, and so on. The arts in our country are used also as avenues for affirmative action, for other forms of social engineering, for employment in the construction trade (as when arts centers are run up), for therapy, but never for themselves. That is because we remain — at least in our political life — a profoundly uncultured nation in which art is merely another thing to have, to buy. As a result, when the government — whether it's state, local or federal — supports the arts, the arts become another special interest constituency crowding up to the public feeding trough along with oil interests, farmers, and God knows what. And again, people in the arts learn all to quickly how to behave in order to get public money. They dilute their programs, they follow the dictates of the government about what they should perform, etc.

A few years ago, the State Council of New York attempted to tell me what I should program with the Group for Contemporary Music. That's why the Group for Contemporary Music doesn't exist anymore, except on paper. The Arts Council wanted affirmative action.

BURBANK: This is the New York State Council on the Arts?

WUORINEN: Yes. We've played plenty of music that "qualifies" but only because we thought it artistically deserving.

BURBANK: Did the Council mean the programming for performance of music by minority composers?

WUORINEN: Minorities and women.

BURBANK: Did they want you to incorporate minority and women performers as well?

WUORINEN: No, composers. They kept insisting that there was a repertoire that we were ignoring. So they were taking artistic control from us and I wouldn't have it. Anyway, the main problem with government support is that it *increases* commercial pressures because one must show that the citizenry is being served in large numbers and that there is a public need for the support. And whatever may be said about private "giving to the arts" in general, in the case of new music, government funding has caused almost a complete drying up of private funds: So that those organizations who are least able to withstand pressure from government about what they should perform and who should perform it, are the ones that are most susceptible.   There's nothing *they* can do, whereas the big symphony orchestras, when the National Endowment tentatively suggests they should play an American work say "Oh, we can't, you know" or they play the overture to *Candide*. That is the situation with government support. More of it is only going to make matters worse.

I think what needs to happen is that the private patron needs to be revived. There's been a tendency for foundations and other private philanthropic sources, including individuals, to start imitating the habits of the government in their patterns of support. It is a very unfavorable time.

BURBANK: What about *In Performance at the White House*?

WUORINEN: That's a different matter. When a public figure — political, financial, whatever — does something that is publicly visible to support some aspect of excellence in the arts, this is very good. Having a distinguished figure have some notice paid to him in the White House would be a good thing. That's quite different from establishing an arts-control bureaucracy.

But there is always a danger with official recognition of *culture*. That's true worldwide. With us it's particularly bad because given the cultural scene as it is now, it's likely that whoever happens to be most famous this week is assumed to be the best. It's quite likely that really undeserving people will be singled out for attention.

BURBANK: Over the years, you have commented unfavorably on music critics. While gathering and excerpting the many critical reviews of your works for my forthcoming book, it became apparent early on that your music seems to inspire critics to write something very strong and pungent, either pro or con. How do you account for this?

WUORINEN: I don't know. Not being a critic myself I cannot say what animates them. Of course, although practically all musicians would speak about practically all critics in very negative terms, we must remember that there are a few very fine music critics whose discourse about music is interesting, instructive to the layman, and who can take what I regard is the critic's proper role. That is, as a mediator between the professional musician, the professional composer and the lay public.

Many critics nowadays — and I think it was Harold Schonberg of The *New York Times* who really formulated and promoted this point of view — have a very different point of view, which, I think, is truly contemptible. They act as if they were representatives of the public and their responses are deliberately no more enlightened than those of the most casual, indifferent, untrained, and unconcerned member of the public. And yet they pretend to an authority at the same time which certainly the casual, indifferent, uninterested member of the lay public would never claim. There's a deep hypocrisy here.

I can't really answer your question of why my work provokes strong responses, one way or the other. I suppose that it has something to do either with the nature of the music or with the nature of the critics who respond to it. Or perhaps both.

BURBANK: Do you think that music criticism, in general, has improved over the part ten to fifteen years?

WUORINEN: Absolutely not. It's gotten much worse. (Again, with notable exceptions. There are always worthwhile people writing. One could name a few of them, after all — the name that always comes first to mind is the very civilized Andrew Porter. Or Robert Commanday of the San Francisco *Chronicle*. There are others as well.) But certainly the most influential critics writing in the most famous newspapers that print only what fits are not only unqualified as far as I can judge (I'm not sure they can read music), but unprepared when they hear a new work. (In thirty years on the New York musical scene I have seen a *New York Times* critic at rehearsal for a new piece of music exactly once, and he didn't stay.) I would like to give some of them a score-reading test, or an ear test.

BURBANK: What should the qualifications be for a music critic and would you also say a bit more about what you mean by their function as mediator?

WUORINEN: First of all, no one should presume to write about music who has not got basic musical skills. By that I mean the ability to play an instrument or sing to a passable degree (not necessarily to prevail in the professional arena), to read a score at a professional level, to be well-informed about all aspects of music history. And I mean not just the big show-time nineteenth century stuff but all music: ancient music, non-Western music, and, above all, the music of our own time. Furthermore, a critic should know something about the workings of the music world, not in a gossipy sense, but in a realistic practical sense: what it is to rehearse a piece, for example, if one is a performer; to learn to play it, or to write it, if one is a composer. These are basic qualifications.

Then I think it would also be nice for someone who is going to write about music to know how to write English. The graceless vulgar prose that characterizes so much of music criticism is completely unnecessary. It is the product of people who are untrained as writers; their language is repellent.

Finally, then, I think that the role of the critic should be as mediator between the profession of music and the public. The critic should not be an arbiter of the profession.

Some critics seem to regard any public musical activity as an attempt to defraud and take an approach of reflexive hostility. This is, I think, profoundly destructive. It creates contempt for the profession, for the making of music and for the art of music, in the minds of the public. The critic ought to be one who knows enough and is detached enough, yet involved enough, to care about the true values of the art, not about who's on top or who isn't, what's in this week and what is out.

Above all, the critic should be someone who is not *promoting* a particular point of view. All the time we find critics who want to kill one style of composition and promote another kind. Often they have a very strong effect, temporarily, of course. In the long run, they don't. But we have to live in the short run and they can make our lives extremely unpleasant for no good reason.

Their mission should be to lead the public away from its laziest responses and to encourage its higher impulses. Even the most indifferent, the most casual, the most uninvolved are capable of higher responses. What the critic should be doing (and what the profession itself should be doing as well) is exercising leadership which encourages these higher responses.

But instead, critics tend to regard the public as sheep to whom they must talk down or whom they can manipulate to promote their own agendas. It is that commitment to something above the gossip of the moment and the trend of the day that I would like to see in the critics. But of course, they are mostly superficial, and they must be in the business of making-and-breaking because so many of them are so insecure. Their promoting of agendas and fondness of gossip compensates for a well deserved feeling of inadequacy that many of them seem to possess.

BURBANK: In your opinion, what is the state of music education in the United States today?

WUORINEN: I think it's pretty bleak. Of course, I don't know the details of the training of music educators. But I do know that we have a nation of musical illiterates and cultural barbarians. What little I see of the training of music educators appalls me. There seems to be the notion that the field is education and the specialty is music rather than that the subject is music and the duty is teaching.

I remember reading an account of an advanced new scheme, which was put into effect in some of the public schools in New Jersey. Bright graduate students in history, mathematics, and other fields were allowed into the classrooms to teach children. Everybody expressed amazement that these people were able to teach even though they hadn't had any certification as teachers and hadn't been through the education mill.

Well, this demonstrates the sickness of the whole thing. The notion that one should master one's subject first and then find a way to convey it to students seems foreign to the minds of educators. That's point number one. Point number two is that, however that may be, the result of education in the public schools is to produce, as I said, a nation of musical illiterates — people for whom the great tradition of Western music doesn't exist. Later, when performing institutions, symphonies, chamber groups and the like, want to find an audience, they discover that they must either deal with a small band of devoted "specialists" (specialist listeners who have independently developed an interest in serious music) or oblige themselves to engage in *outreach* programs which inevitably result in the dilution and compromise of the thing that they're trying to convey.

The answer to all of this is not gimmicks, not music appreciation, but, rather, to teach simple, basic musical skills and literacy. That is, to read simple musical notation and to perform modestly on an instrument, or to sing. That should be a part of the basic requirements of universal education. It's as simple as that. When you teach children these skills you create a situation in which some contact on an active, *real*, level (as opposed to a passive level) has been made with music, without fun-and-games and foolishness, and some experience is had in the making of music. Of course, though simple, the music taught can't be junk; it has to be half-way decent. Those who sing have got to sing simple madrigals, for example, and not Broadway show tunes or rock songs. Those who play have got to play little pieces by Bach or little pieces that are equally easy by Schoenberg, and not junk from some piano method book. That goes without saying. If that simple, gimmick-free approach were taken, our musical life, our cultural life would be transformed.

BURBANK: What about music education at the college and university level?

WUORINEN: The colleges and universities spend most of their time (as they do increasingly in so many other fields) making up for the deficiencies of earlier education. After all, students today come into college who cannot write a complete sentence (they don't even know what a sentence is), who do not know where Australia is, who, as I saw recently, think that the country to the north of the United States is Maryland.

The state of music, not a required subject, is even worse. For college students, music means pop junk and nothing else. Except for those few who come with a self-motivated interest in serious things, they know nothing.

But what we're concerned with here is elevating the level, the sensibility of the public at large. I think that the present mess is yet one more failure of a huge bureaucratized public education system. I think public education should be abolished and replaced with open competition among private schools, perhaps with certification by some kind of independent body to ensure that everybody's getting certain basic skills; and, if need be, appropriate public assistance for those who can't afford tuition at private schools.

I don't know that there's any area of music teaching where anybody's doing a halfway decent job except, perhaps, in isolated instances. Interestingly enough, in those rare cases where one knows someone good who is teaching music in the public schools (I'm thinking of a woman I know who teaches string-playing in a small town in Kansas), or there is a music program with somebody who is halfway qualified, the children respond to it overwhelmingly. In the case that I just referred to, everybody in the school plays, or wants to play stringed instruments. The band man can't find people to blow his trumpets!

BURBANK: Do you think that the more serious kind of study, particularly with composition and musicology, is now taking place at the universities as opposed to the conservatories?

WUORINEN: It's hard to say.

BURBANK: Or does it depend upon who is on the faculty?

WUORINEN: It depends very much on who's on the faculty. You have to distinguish between the *high-falutin*, Ivy League universities that think they're great (and usually aren't), who have primarily theoretical and historical music departments without much performance and those great, midwestern universities, for example, that have schools of music, that is to say, conservatories attached to them and which often manage to combine the best of university and conservatory environments.

The problem with conservatories is that students can play but they can't think; the problem with universities is that they can talk but they can't play. In the case of university-trained composers there tends to be an unhealthy separation from the real world of performance in the public arena, and in the case of conservatory-trained composers there tends to be a brainless, following-along with the "music business."

The fact is, I think, that in our time it's almost impossible to find any particular *type* of venue that is *a priori* better for the training of musicians, especially composers, than any other. It depends very much on the contact one makes with the personality of the teacher and the kind of music one is interested in. I know in my own case at Columbia [University] that although I valued very much the counsel of Otto Luening, the other teachers I had were absolutely worthless (or nearly so), and that what I learned, I learned from professional life in the City of New York and from study on my own, not from anything in school.

This brings me to a final point. The way in which one should teach composition nowadays is very unclear to me. The way I, and everyone else, does it, I am convinced, is wrong because in the fragmented aesthetic/compositional time in which we live, there is not general agreement on what music should be or how one should write it. On the one hand, the instructor cannot present a shopping cart full of every conceivable approach to, every bit of momentary foolishness in the field of composition nor, on the other, can he put forward a particular way as the only to do it. All he can do is take what the student does and attempt to draw out of it, as well as he can, what the student intends.

But this is definitely not the best way to teach. The only real way to teach an art to another person is through apprenticeship, which means imitation. It means that the student works with the master either because he wants to produce the master's kind of work or because he has been apprenticed, perhaps involuntarily. (Of course, I'm referring to older times.) But however that may be, what he does is to follow the master. Under those conditions, he develops his own personality and eventually breaks off and establishes his own life. But we don't do things that way.

Therefore, I think we produce too many inadequate composers and often also, fail to give the truly gifted ones what they need to develop as rapidly as possible.

BURBANK: What is your assessment of the quality of musicianship — both that of composers and performers — of musicians employed by religious institutions?

WUORINEN: Well, some of them are perfectly professional. Generally, they're not. Of course, in the bigger places and the bigger centers you get a higher level and there are certainly some places that do very interesting things. After all, considering the financial limitations of many churches and synagogues, some do pretty well. It's just that the general atmosphere is one which is completely indifferent to all of this and which regards the liturgy and the music that goes with it essentially as marketing tools to get people to come in, to spend their money, and to believe in something *rather* than as an expression of a Faith which is already there. There's an enormous difference between those two things, one which is not well understood by the Church herself.

BURBANK: Finally, and in tandem with that response, what is your assessment of the state of sacred music (music composed for worship services) today?

WUORINEN: It's terrible, absolutely terrible. I think one of the very saddest things about our whole period is the complete failure of the Church — any sect thereof — to be a patron of art in the way it used to be. I think the essential point is that in the years when the Church was a true patron of what was worthwhile in the arts (sometimes it's true that what was produced was in the aggrandizement of the Princes of the Church), the greater part of it was an expression of Faith.

Today, on the other hand, the arts tend to be used as marketing devices by the churches. Hence, the unspeakable music which has come into the Roman [Catholic] Church after Vatican II (not that it was that good before), and the complete abdication of any sense that the Church ought to be in the business of allying itself with the *new* in art.

I think that the situation is doubly deplorable in view of the fact that the central failure of contemporary art is that art, for the most part, is completely absent of any religious impulse.

In the case of music, it is interesting to me that the most significant composers of our time — Stravinsky and Schoenberg — were men for whom religious issues were extremely important and in whose work the religious impulse is very pronounced. For the rest, most art in the post-religious era consists simply of the manifestation of the ego of the artist and, as such, it's very quick to lose its interest.

Now, what this means is that the Church has a responsibility (that it has absolutely ignored and completely shirked) to help in the survival of serious art of all sorts. Art as a manifestation of mere ego cannot go on forever, and we've already seen, in the flatulent productions of Socialist Realism, that art with a political message is even more contemptible than art which is merely the manifestation of a personal ego. But it seems to me that art and music which do not serve a transcendent purpose and are not, either directly or indirectly, involved in the expression of man's acknowledgement of a power higher than himself, very quickly degenerate into mere entertainment. One of the reasons why we confuse art and entertainment so readily and willingly today is precisely that the spiritual impulse that should be behind serious art is usually absent.

My point in saying these things here is that not just is it too bad for the Church that it doesn't support (or know about, or have the taste to recognize and discriminate) the worthwhile in serious contemporary music, but, more important, and from the point of view of the world of music, that the Church is not encouraging the production of spiritually significant work by composers who really have something to say in music. That is very sad.

Works and Performances

ORCHESTRA

W1 *Another Happy Birthday.* Instrumentation: 3(Picc)23(Bcl)3(Cbsn) 4331 T, P(1), Pf, Str. Duration: 1:30. Composed 15 April - 15 May 1988. Peters P67247*. Premiered 14-17 September 1988, Davies Symphony Hall, San Francisco. San Francisco Symphony; Herbert Blomstedt, conductor. Composed for the San Francisco Symphony, season opening, September 1988. Dedicated to Herbert Blomstedt. *See:* B6

W2 *Astra.* Instrumentation: 3(Picc)333(Cbsn) 4331 T, P(4), Pf, Hp, Str. Duration: 11:00. Composed 20 December 1989 - 12 February 1990. Peters P67334*. Premiered 11 August 1990, Tivoli Gardens, Copenhagen, Denmark *(Schleswig-Holstein Festival)*; Leonard Slatkin, conductor. Commissioned by James H. Ottaway, Jr., for the American Soviet Youth Orchestra 1990 tour.

> **Historical note:** This work was to have had at least nine additional performances (all by the American Soviet Youth Orchestra but with the conductors specified below). All of the performances were cancelled. The original performance schedule was as follows: 25 July 1990, Dzintary Hall, Riga, Latvia, Catherine Comet, conductor (the originally scheduled world premiere); 26 July 1990, Talinn, Estonia, Catherine Comet, conductor; 6 August 1990, Matze Hall, Sion, Switzerland *(Tibor Varga Festival)*, Catherine Comet, conductor; 12 August 1990, Concertgebouw, Amsterdam, Catherine Comet, conductor; 15 August 1990, Hollywood Bowl, Los Angeles, Alexander Lazarev, conductor; 21 August 1990, Chicago *(Ravinia Festival)*, Leonard Slatkin, conductor; 26 August 1990, Finney Chapel, Oberlin, Ohio, Leonard Slatkin, conductor; 28 August 1990, West lawn of the Capitol, Washington, D.C., Leonard Slatkin, conductor; 30 August 1990, Mann Music Center, Philadelphia, Leonard Slatkin, conductor. Howard Stokar, Wuorinen's manager, informed Richard Burbank that these performances were cancelled due to massive confusion in the administration of and logistical arrangements for the concerts. *See:* D75

W2a 4 October 1991, Finney Chapel, Oberlin College Conservatory of Music, Oberlin, Ohio. Oberlin Orchestra, Robert Spano, conductor. *See:* D75

W3 *Bamboula Beach*. Instrumentation: 3(Picc)33(Bcl)3(Cbsn) 4331 T, P(2), Pf, Str. Duration: 6:00. Composed 1 September - 13 October 1987. Peters P67205*. Premiered 4 February 1988, Gusman Center for the Performing Arts, Miami, Florida. New World Symphony; Michael Tilson Thomas, conductor. (Inaugural concert of the New World Symphony). Commissioned by Michael Tilson Thomas and the New World Symphony for their opening concert. Dedicated to Michael Tilson Thomas.

> **Historical note:** Wuorinen's contract for this commission stated that the piece must reflect the cultural diversity of Miami. While Wuorinen was composer-in-residence with the San Francisco Symphony he telephoned Michael Tilson Thomas in Miami and asked exactly what the term meant. Tilson Thomas replied that the music should in some way reflect the Cuban and Jewish influences of the city. While they were on the phone, a janitor in the hallway happened to be whistling a Cuban tune. Tilson Thomas ran out into the hallway, listened to the tune and immediately dictated it to Wuorinen over the phone. Later, Wuorinen used the tune in this piece and added certain pitch inflections to add a Jewish sound. At the end of the premiere performance, both Cubans and Jews in the audience approached Wuorinen praising his use of their musical tunes and sounds. *See:* B22 - B29

W3a 2 December 1988, Gusman Center for the Performing Arts, Miami, Florida. New World Symphony; Michael Tilson Thomas, conductor. *See:* B25

W3b 13 July 1989, Operà-Bastille, Paris. New World Symphony; Michael Tilson Thomas, conductor. European premiere. *See:* B26, B27

W3c 5 August 1989, Teatro Colon, Buenos Aires. New World Symphony; Michael Tilson Thomas, conductor. Latin American premiere. *See:* B28

W3d 10 August 1989, Sao Paulo, Brazil. New World Symphony; Michael Tilson Thomas, conductor.

W3e 13 August 1989, Washington, D.C. New World Symphony; Michael Tilson Thomas, conductor.

W3f 14 December 1989, Carnegie Hall, New York City. New World Symphony; Michael Tilson Thomas, conductor. *See:* B29

W4 *Bamboula Squared*. Instrumentation: 3(Picc)23(Bcl)2 4231 T, P(2), Pf, Str, Computer generated tape. Duration: 16:30. Composed 30 December 1983 - 21 January 1984, mostly in La Jolla, California (computer generated tape realized at the Computer Audio Research Laboratory, University of California, San Diego, January - March, 1984). Peters P67013*. Premiered 4 June 1984, Avery Fisher Hall, Lincoln Center for the Performing Arts, New York City; American Composers Orchestra, Wuorinen, conductor (New York Philharmonic's festival of contemporary music titled *Horizons '84: The New Romanticism — a Broader View*). Dedicated to Lee G. Ray and Mark B. Dolson.

> **Historical note:** The American Composers Orchestra was hired by the New York Philharmonic because the New York Philharmonic itself did not have adequate

service during the days allotted for the work's rehearsal and performance. In the published score Wuorinen writes: "Grateful acknowledgement is made to F. Richard Moore, Director [CARL]; and for the indispensable assistance of Lee G. Ray and Mark B. Dolson, to whom the work is dedicated." According to a brief description of the project in a subsequent annual report from CARL "Both the score and the sounds in the tape part of this piece were entirely computer-generated. The note-list was produced via a C program written by Lee Ray which used a controlled random process to generate times, durations, and pitches for notes. The actual sounds were produced through a plucked-string algorithm written in C by Mark Dolson." *See:* B30 - B45, B737, B857, B1044

W4a 15-18 November 1984, Pikes Peak Center, Colorado Springs, Colorado. Colorado Springs Symphony: Wuorinen, conductor. *See:* B37 - B39

W4b 26 September 1987, North Recital Hall, School of Music, University of Louisville, Louisville, Kentucky. Louisville Orchestra; Wuorinen, conductor. *See:* B42

W4c 11 January 1990, Mandeville Center Auditorium, University of California at San Diego, La Jolla, California. San Diego Symphony; Wuorinen, conductor. *See:* B44, B45, B1044

W5 *Concerto for Amplified Violin and Orchestra.* Instrumentation: Amplified violin solo, 3334 4331 P(6), Pf, Hp, Str. Duration: 20:30. Composed 25 June 1971 - 2 April 1972, in Aspen (CO), Chicago, Denver, Hanover (NH), Iowa City (IA), Lenox (MA), Milwaukee, New York City, North Platte (NE), and Tampa (FL). Peters P66511*. Premiered 4 August 1972, Tanglewood Shed, Tanglewood, Massachusetts. Boston Symphony Orchestra, Michael Tilson Thomas, conductor; Paul Zukofsky, violin soloist. Commissioned by the Fromm Music Foundation for Michael Tilson Thomas and Paul Zukofsky, and for the Boston Symphony Orchestra's observance of the twentieth anniversary of the Foundation, at the Berkshire Music Center. Dedicated to Paul Fromm. *See:* D30, D80, B152 - B182, B891

W5a 1 April 1973, Kleinhans Music Hall, Buffalo, New York. Buffalo Philharmonic Orchestra, Michael Tilson Thomas, conductor; Paul Zukofsky, violin soloist. *See:* D30, D80, B168, B169, B172

W5b 24 October 1973, Carnegie Hall, New York City. Buffalo Philharmonic Orchestra, Michael Tilson Thomas, conductor; Paul Zukofsky, violin soloist. New York City premiere. *See:* B170, B171

W5c 1 June 1974, *Ojai Festival*, Ojai, California. Los Angeles Philharmonic; Michael Tilson Thomas, conductor; Paul Zukofsky, violin soloist. West coast premiere. *See:* B173 - B177

W6 *Concerto for Violin and Orchestra.* Instrumentation: 2222 4231 T, P, Hp, Str. Duration: 13:53. Composed 2 June - 1 July 1958, and 23 July 1958. Written for Max Pollikoff. Unpublished. Never performed. *See:* B183, B891

W7   *Concertone for Brass Quintet and Orchestra.* Instrumentation: Brass quintet, 2(Picc)222 422(BTr)1 T, P(2), Str. Duration: 13:52. Composed 26 April 1960, and 13 June - 10 July 1960, in New York City. McGinnis & Marx. Premiered 19 February 1964, Iowa City, Iowa. University of Iowa Symphony Orchestra and Iowa Brass Quintet; James Dixon, conductor. Dedicated to The New York Brass Quintet, Robert Nagel, director.

W7a   18 April 1967, Carnegie Hall, New York City. American Brass Quintet and the National Orchestral Association; John Barnett, conductor.

W8   *Contrafactum.* Instrumentation: 3333 4332 T(2), P(4), 2 Pfs, Str. Duration: 20:00. Composed 28 January - 21 June 1969, in Gardner (MA), Lisbon, London, New York City. Peters P66386*. Premiered 19 November 1969, The Auditorium (Main lounge of the Iowa Memorial Union), University of Iowa, Iowa City, Iowa. University of Iowa Symphony Orchestra, James Dixon, conductor. Dedicated to James Dixon. *See:* B188 - B196, B891, B1090

W8a   16 September 1975, Carnegie Hall, New York City. The New Orchestra, Wuorinen, conductor. New York premiere. Inaugural concert of this orchestra. *See:* B189 - B194

W9   *Crossfire.* Instrumentation: 3(Picc)23(E♭, Bcl)2 4331 T, P(2), Pf, Str. Duration: 11:00. Composed 7 October - 16 December 1984. Peters P67066*. Premiered 9-10 May 1985, Meyerhoff Hall, Baltimore. Baltimore Symphony Orchestra; David Zinman, conductor. Commissioned by the Baltimore Symphony Orchestra. Dedicated to Randolph S. Rothschild and Joseph Meyerhoff. *See:* B197 - B200, B857

W9a   12 May 1985, Carnegie Hall, New York City. Baltimore Symphony Orchestra; David Zinman, conductor. New York premiere.

W9b   6 October 1990, State University of New York at Stony Brook, N.Y. Brad Lubman, conductor.

W10   *Delight of the Muses.* Instrumentation: 222(A)2 42(C)31 T, Vibr, Pf, Hp, Str. Duration: 30:00. Composed 1991. Peters P67394*. Premiered 29 January 1992 (first staged performance), New York State Theater, Lincoln Center for the Performing Arts, New York City. New York City Ballet; Peter Martins, choreographer; New York City Ballet Orchestra, Wuorinen conductor. Principal dancers: Nilas Martins, Jock Soto, Darci Kistler. Other dancers: Stacey Calvert, Jennifer Ringer, Kathleen Tracey, Arch Higgins, Richard Marsden, Robert Lyon, Monique Meunier, Tom Gold, Elizabeth Walker. Costumes by Barbara Matera and Steven Rubin. Wuorinen incorporated in the score excerpts of two Mozart piano sonatas (K.281, K.283) and stage music from Mozart's *Don Giovanni.*

   Historical Note: The work contains puns on ballet and choreography with dance steps such as "pas de chat volé" and "gargouillade." A piano reduction of the score was also prepared for ballet rehearsals. In addition, Peter Martins had been given a tape of the score prior to the creation of his choreography. *See:* W10b, B201 - B205

W10a 26 July 1991, Saratoga Performing Arts Center, Saratoga Springs, New York. Wuorinen, conductor. A reading, not a performance.

W10b 9 November 1991, State University of New York at Stony Brook. SUNY Stony Brook Orchestra, Brad Lubman, conductor.
Historical note: This performance was actually the world premiere of the unchoreographed music, and was arranged so that Peter Martins could have a tape of the work from which he would choreograph the music.

W10c 23 July 1992, Saratoga Performing Arts Center, Saratoga Springs, New York. New York City Ballet. Principal dancers included Darci Kistler.
Historical note: This performance followed the controversy surrounding the arrest of Peter Martins on charges of wife-beating brought against him by his wife, Darci Kistler. *See:* B205

W11 *Ecclesiastical Symphonies.* Instrumentation: 3(3 Picc)33 in A (Bcl)3 4331 T, P(4), Hp, Pf, Str, Tape. Duration: 12:30. Composed 2 January - 9 September 1980. Peters P66851a*. Premiered 21 February 1981, Centennial Hall, Augustana College, Rock Island, Illinois. Augustana Symphony Orchestra; Daniel Culver, conductor. Commissioned by Augustana College in observance of the 100th anniversary of the Handel Oratorio Society. Originally titled *Sacred Symphonies*; Wuorinen later decided he preferred a different title. The work consists of four orchestral movements that are also part of Wuorinen's larger work for chorus and orchestra, *The Celestial Sphere.* *Ecclesiastical Symphonies* may be performed separately or as part of the larger work. *See:* W162, B224 - B226

W11a 15 October 1981, Finlandia House, Helsinki. Helsinki Philharmonic Orchestra; Wuorinen, conductor. *See:* B224 - B226

W11b 23 October 1981, Tampere, Finland. Tampere Philharmonic Orchestra; Wuorinen, conductor.

W12 *Fanfare for the Houston Symphony.* 3(Picc)333 4331 T, Xyl, P(1), Str. Duration: 1:04. Composed 19-23 February 1986, in San Francisco. Peters P67116*. Premiered 15-16 March 1986, Jones Hall, Houston, Texas. Houston Symphony; Wuorinen, conductor. Commissioned by the Houston Symphony in observance of the sesquicentennial year of the State of Texas.

W12a 24 June 1989, First Congregational Church, San Francisco. San Francisco Symphony Youth Orchestra; Leif Bjaland, conductor. New & Unusual Music series concert.

W12b 22 August 1990, Grant Park, Chicago. Zdenek Macal, conductor.

W13 *Five: Concerto for Amplified Cello and Orchestra.* Instrumentation: Vc solo, 2(Picc)22(Bcl)2(Cbsn) 4231 T, P(2), Hp, Str. Duration: 21:00. Composed 1 April - 9 September 1987. Peters P67203*. Premiered 28 April 1988 (first staged performance), New York State Theater, Lincoln Center for the Performing Arts, New York City. New York City Ballet; Jean-Pierre Bonnefoux, choreographer; New York City Ballet Orchestra; Wuorinen, conductor; Fred Sherry, violoncello soloist. Principal dancers: Maria Calegari, Jock Soto, Michael Byars, Damian Woetzel, and soloists. Other dancers: Barbara Britton, Allison Brown, Alexia Hess, Heather Jurgensen, Romy Karz, Kathleen Tracey, Wendy Whelan, Paul Boos, Ben Huys, Russell Kaiser, Robert Lyon, Philip Neal, Alexandre Proia and Brian Reeder. Scenery by Gary Stephan; scenery supervised by Mark Stanley. Costumes by Barbara Matera. Lighting by Mark Stanley. This ballet was made possible by grants from The Evelyn Sharp Foundation and The Sharp Foundation. Orchestral preparation of *American Music Festival* music commissions was aided by a grant from the National Endowment for the Arts. *See:* B245 - B252

W13a 24 April 1988, Guggenheim Museum, New York City. Jean-Pierre Bonnefoux, choreographer. New York City Ballet dancers Jock Soto, Maria Calegari, Michael Byars, Damian Woetzel, and Allison Brown. A preview of the world premiere staged performance consisting of excerpts from a tape recording of the work. Included a panel discussion with Wuorinen, Jean-Pierre Bonnefoux, Annalyn Swann (Editor-in-Chief, *Savvy* magazine), Fred Sherry (cellist), David Oei (pianist) and Gary Stephan (set design). This event was produced by Mary Cronson.

W13b 1 May 1988, New York State Theater, Lincoln Center for the Performing Arts, New York City. All details same as for **W13**. *See:* B245 - B252

W13c 20-21 July 1988, Saratoga Performing Arts Center, Saratoga, New York. New York City Ballet; New York City Ballet Orchestra, Wuorinen, conductor; Fred Sherry, violoncello soloist.

W13d 6 November 1989, Carnegie Hall, New York City. Orchestra of St. Luke's; Wuorinen, conductor; Fred Sherry, violoncello soloist. This performance constituted the concert form premiere of the work.
  Historical note: The performance was ruined by a loud 120 Hz hum distortion in the amplification equipment. *See:* B247 - B249

W13e 31 March 1990, Herbst Theatre, San Francisco. San Francisco Symphony; Alasdair Neale, conductor; Fred Sherry, violoncello soloist. West coast premiere. *New & Unusual Music* series final concert of the 1989-1990 season. *See:* B250 - B252

W14 *The Golden Dance.* Instrumentation: 3(Picc)3(EH)3(Bcl)3(Cbsn) 4331 T(2), P(4), Pf/Cel, Str. Duration: 21:00. Composed 23 July 1985 - 16 May 1986, in New York City and San Francisco. Peters P67143*. Premiered 10-14 September 1986, Davies Symphony Hall, San Francisco.

San Francisco Symphony; Herbert Blomstedt, conductor. Composed for the San Francisco Symphony's 75th anniversary, as part of the Meet the Composer residency.

Historical note: Wuorinen made the following stand-up remarks at this performance: "The problem that you have as an audience frequenting concerts of this sort, of course, is that most of the music you hear is music you've already heard, and what you have already heard — even when you haven't heard it before — is in fact something that you have, indeed, heard. You may find, in the case of my work, however, that certain aspects of it you have *not* heard before. These are the parts which I contributed. With these parts, and with the entire work, I would like to suggest that the correct way of hearing the piece is to avoid trying to find a correct way of hearing it — simply to remain calm, under all circumstances. There is nothing to fear." *See:* D36, B277 - B299, B857

W14a   13 February 1987, Carnegie Hall, New York City.   San Francisco Symphony; Herbert Blomstedt, conductor. New York premiere. *See:* B279, B287, B288

W14b 16 February 1987, Royal Festival Hall, London. San Francisco Symphony; Herbert Blomstedt, conductor. London premiere. *See:* B280, B281, B292

W14c 22 February 1987, Brucknerhaus, Linz, Austria. San Francisco Symphony; Herbert Blomstedt, conductor. This concert was billed as the European premiere although the work was performed in London on 16 February 1987. *See:* W14b, B282

W14d   24 February 1987, Philharmonie, Berlin.   San Francisco Symphony; Herbert Blomstedt, conductor. First performance in Germany. *See:* B283 - B285

W14e 3 March 1987, Teatro Communale, Florence, Italy.   San Francisco Symphony; Herbert Blomstedt, conductor. First performance in Italy. *See:* B289, B290

W15 *Machault Mon Chou.* Instrumentation: 22(EH)3(Bcl)(Cbsn) 4231 T, P, Hp, Str. Duration: 11:00. Composed 1 July - 21 August 1988, in New York City. Peters P67254*. Premiered 24-27 May 1989, Davies Symphony Hall, San Francisco. San Francisco Symphony; Herbert Blomstedt, conductor. Dedicated to Herbert Blomstedt.

Historical note: The material for this work is drawn from the *Messe de Notre Dame* by Guillaume de Machault. *See:* B344 - B348

W15a 11 January 1990, Mandeville Center Auditorium, University of California, San Diego, La Jolla, California.   San Diego Symphony; Wuorinen, conductor.

Historical note: This was the first concert of a concert series celebrating twentieth century music and Pulitzer Prize winners; Wuorinen also conducted works by Igor Stravinsky. *See:* B345, B346

W15b   15-17 November 1990, Symphony Hall, Boston.   Boston Symphony Orchestra; Catherine Comet, conductor.

W15c 3-5 January 1991, Symphony Hall, Atlanta, Georgia. Atlanta Symphony Orchestra; Catherine Comet, conductor.
    Historical note: This performance was both the Atlanta premiere of the work and Comet's debut with the Atlanta Symphony Orchestra. *See:* B347

W15d 18 & 22 January 1991, Philadelphia Academy of Music, Philadelphia, Pennsylvania. Philadelphia Orchestra; Riccardo Muti, conductor. *See:* B348

W15e 26 January 1991, Providence, Rhode Island. Rhode Island Philharmonic; Catherine Comet, conductor.

W16 *Movers and Shakers.* Instrumentation: 3(Picc)3(EH)33 4331 T, P, Pf, Str. Duration: 26:40. Composed 24 July 1983 - 31 July 1984. Peters P67016*. Premiered 13-15 December 1984, Severance Hall, Cleveland, Ohio. Cleveland Orchestra; Christoph von Dohnanyi, conductor. Commissioned by the Cleveland Orchestra, the Musical Arts Association, Mr. and Mrs. Robert G. Klein, the Ohio Arts Council, and the Cleveland Foundation. Dedicated to Christoph von Dohnanyi. *See:* D60, B376 - B390, B857

W16a 5 February 1985, E.J. Thomas Hall, Cleveland, Ohio. Cleveland Orchestra; Christoph von Dohnanyi, conductor. *Tuesday Musical Club Series* concert.

W16b 6 February 1986, Los Angeles. Los Angeles Philharmonic; Herbert Blomstedt, conductor. West coast premiere. *See:* B383

W16c 8 March 1986, College Avenue Gymnasium, Rutgers University, New Brunswick, New Jersey. San Francisco Symphony; Herbert Blomstedt, conductor. New York premiere. *See:* B384

W16d 9 March 1986, Carnegie Hall, New York City. San Francisco Symphony; Herbert Blomstedt, conductor. *See:* B387 - B389

W17 *Music for Orchestra.* Instrumentation: 2222 4220 T, P, Str. Duration: 6:24. Composed October 1956, in New York City. Peters P67335*. Premiered 1 December 1956, Columbia University, New York City; Howard Shanet, conductor. Commissioned by the Columbia University Orchestra. *See:* B391

W18 *Orchestral and Electronic Exchanges.* Instrumentation: 3333 4331 T, P(3), Hp, Pf, Str, Tape. Duration: 14:45. Composed 10 May 1964 - 1 March 1965, in Lenox (MA) and New York City. Peters P66388*. Premiered 30-31 July 1965, Philharmonic Hall, Lincoln Center for the Performing Arts, New York City. New York Philharmonic *(French-American Festival)*; Lukas Foss, conductor.
    Historical note: Wuorinen intended to compose additional parts to this work but never did. The tape part was realized at the Columbia-Princeton Electronic Music Center. *See:* B405 - B416

W18a 11 May 1967, Tilson Music Hall, Indiana State University, Terre Haute, Indiana. Indianapolis Symphony Orchestra; Igor Buketoff, conductor. *Fine Arts Festival* at Indiana State University. *See:* B413, B414

W18b 21 April 1969, Lisbon, Portugal. Emissora Nacional Orchestra; Igor Buketoff, conductor.

W19 *Piano Concerto No. 1.* Instrumentation: Pf Solo, 3(Picc Alto)333 4331 T, P(3), Hp, Str. Duration: 17:40. Composed 30 July 1965 - 13 January 1966, in New York City. Peters P66387*. Premiered 4 May 1966, University of Iowa, Iowa City, Iowa. University of Iowa Symphony Orchestra; James Dixon, conductor; Wuorinen, piano soloist. *See:* D7, D13, D58, B447 - B455, B891

W19a 1 October 1967, Kleinhans Music Hall, Buffalo, New York. Buffalo Philharmonic Orchestra; Lukas Foss, conductor; Wuorinen, piano soloist. *American Music in the University* project. *See:* B448, B449

W19b 8-10 October 1967, Troy, New York. Buffalo Philharmonic Orchestra; Lukas Foss, conductor; Wuorinen, piano soloist. *See:* D58

W20 *Piano Concerto No. 2.* Instrumentation: Amplified Piano, 3333 4331 T, P(6), Str, Pf. Duration: 25:20. Composed 7 October 1973 - 23 May 1974, in Gardner (MA), Nashville, New York City, Oberlin (OH), and Salt Lake City (UT). Peters P66604*. Premiered 6 December 1974, Avery Fisher Hall, Lincoln Center for the Performing Arts, New York City. New York Philharmonic; Erich Leinsdorf, conductor; Wuorinen, piano soloist. Composed under a grant from the National Endowment for the Arts, for the New York Philharmonic.
　　Historical note: The solo piano is amplified, preferably the Baldwin ED-1. The music is conceived for antiphonal projection involving external sets of speakers in the hall and on stage (separate from the piano). Amplification of the soloist is essential; the antiphonal deployment of the soloist's music, however, is ornamental and may be omitted. *See:* B456 - B469

W20a 17 October 1975, Orchestra Hall, Chicago. Chicago Symphony Orchestra; Erich Leinsdorf, conductor; Wuorinen, piano soloist. Chicago premiere. *See:* B468

W20b 17 May 1988, Bergamo, Italy. Jeffrey Swan, piano soloist.

W21 *Piano Concerto No. 3.* Instrumentation: Pf Solo, 323(Bcl)2 4231 T, P(3), Hp, Str. Duration: 26:30. Composed 14 August 1982 - 27 May 1983. Peters P66978*. Premiered 4-5 May 1984, Troy Savings Bank Music Hall, Troy, New York. Albany Symphony Orchestra, Julius Hegyi, conductor; Garrick Ohlsson, piano soloist. Commissioned by the Albany Symphony Orchestra for Julius Hegyi and Garrick Ohlsson; paid for by the New Music Program of the National Endowment for the Arts; the Northeast Orchestral Consortium, the Rustam K. Kermani Foundation; and the New York State

Council on the Arts. Dedicated to Peter R. Kermani. *See:* D36, B470 - B494, B857

W21a 29 October 1985, Woolsey Hall, New Haven, Connecticut. New Haven Symphony Orchestra; Murry Sidlin, conductor; Garrick Ohlsson, piano soloist. *See:* W21

W21b 18 May 1986, Bardavon 1869 Opera House, Ulster Performing Arts Center, Poughkeepsie, New York. Hudson Valley Philharmonic; Imre Pallo, conductor; Garrick Ohlsson, piano soloist.

> **Historical note:** Imre Pallo created a controversy at the beginning of the second half of the program by thanking the audience for "putting up with modern music." **See:** B482 - B484, B486

W22 *Prelude to Kullervo.* Instrumentation: Tuba Solo, 3232 4330 T, P, Pf, Str. Duration: 5:45. Composed 13 August - 6 September 1985. Peters P67089*. Premiered 21 November 1985, St. Peter's Church (E. 54th Street and Lexington Avenue), New York City. Columbia University Orchestra; Howard Shanet, conductor; David O. Brainard, tuba. Commissioned by Howard Shanet and the Columbia University Orchestra, with the support of Citicorp/Citibank and Frank O. Brainard, in honor of the 150th anniversary of the publication of the Finnish epic *Kalevala.* Composed for David Brainard. Dedicated to Howard Shanet. *See:* B562

W23 *A Reliquary for Igor Stravinsky.* Instrumentation: 4(Picc)22(Bcl)3 4231 T, P(3), Hp, Pf, Str. Duration: 16:30. Composed 17 December 1974 - 28 January 1975, in Middle Valley (NJ) and New York City. Peters P66631*. Premiered 1 June 1975, Ojai, California. Michael Tilson Thomas, conductor. Commissioned jointly by the *Ojai Festival* and the Buffalo Philharmonic Orchestra, for Michael Tilson Thomas. Dedicated to Vera Stravinsky and Robert Craft.

> **Historical note:** The work is based on Igor Stravinsky's last fragments; it was performed twice on this program. Stravinsky's *Symphony in C* was scheduled to be performed on the program. Due to insufficient rehearsal time Stravinsky's *Symphonies of Wind Instruments* was performed instead. (The official reason given for the program change was that the program would be too long, given the audience's desire to hear Wuorinen's piece twice.) *See:* B566 - B576

W23a 28 January 1977, Manhattan School of Music, New York City. Students of Manhattan School of Music; Wuorinen, conductor. Concert presented by the Group for Contemporary Music. New York premiere. *See:* B570

W23b 8 February 1979, Finlandia Hall, Helsinki. Helsinki Philharmonic Orchestra; Wuorinen, conductor. First performance in Finland. *See:* B571

W23c 15 June 1983, Avery Fisher Hall, Lincoln Center for the Performing Arts, New York City. New York Philharmonic (*Horizons '83*, Program VI); Gunther Schuller, conductor. This concert was billed as the New York premiere but was not. *See:* W23a, B573, B574

W24 *Rhapsody for Violin and Orchestra*. Instrumentation: Vn Solo, 3332 4331 T, P(2), Pf, Hp, Str. Duration: 19:31. Composed 19 June - 5 December 1983, in Cleveland and other places. Peters P67018*. Premiered 16-18 January 1985, Davies Symphony Hall, San Francisco. San Francisco Symphony; Edo de Waart, conductor; David Kobialka, violin soloist. Commissioned by the San Francisco Symphony for the 1984-85 season. Composed for Daniel Kobialka. Dedicated to Edo de Waart.

> **Historical note:** Wuorinen originally titled the work *Rhapsody in Black*. **See:** B577 - B581, B857

W25 *Short Suite*. Instrumentation: 2(Picc)222 4221 T, Xyl, Str. Duration: 15:00. Composed 22 May - 2 October 1981, in New York City. Peters P66927*. Premiered 13-14 February 1983, State University of New York at Purchase, Purchase, New York. American Composers Orchestra; Wuorinen, conductor. Commissioned for the Milwaukee Symphony Orchestra by a consortium supported in part by the National Endowment for the Arts, and consisting of the American Composers Orchestra (New York), the Milwaukee Symphony Orchestra, the Oakland Symphony Orchestra, and the Tri-City Symphony. Dedicated to James Roy.

> **Historical note:** This work had originally been commissioned by the New Hampshire Symphony Orchestra. According to Wuorinen, that orchestra defaulted on the commission in December of 1981; the commission was then transferred to the consortium listed above. The work also had title history in that the following titles preceded *Short Suite: It Don't Mean a Thing; Easy Smalls; Easy Suite*. **See:** B593 - B599, B857

W25a 13 April 1985, Ohio Theater, Play House Square, Cleveland, Ohio. Footpath Dance Company; Alice Rubenstein, choreographer. Dancers: Loren Balogh, Karen Tradler, Catherine Hoggs, Judith Peck, William Wade, Deaner Young. Costumes by Raymond J. Zandler II.Lighting by George Kinney. Set by Thomas Dunn.

> **Historical note:** This was a choreographed ballet performance danced to a tape recording of the music. The work was retitled *Discovery* for this performance. Synopsis: A loving tribe of primitive people is released from its cocoon-like environment and begins to explore unknown space. **See:** B593 - B595

W25b 27 September 1985, Uihlein Hall, Milwaukee Performing Arts Center, Milwaukee. Milwaukee Symphony Orchestra; Wuorinen, conductor. **See:** B596, B597

W26 *Symphony No. 1 [Symphony In One Movement]*. Instrumentation: 2222 4321 T, P, Pf, Str. Duration: 10:14. Composed 26 December - 3 January 1958. American Composers Alliance/Composer Facsimile Edition. Premiered 7 March 1958, Great Hall, Cooper Union, New York City (*Music in the Making* series); Howard Shanet, conductor.

> **Historical note:** According to Wuorinen's *Register of Works*, Leopold Stokowski studied the score and returned it as did Nadia Boulanger, who found that it "struck her very deeply."

W27 *Symphony No. 2 [Symphony II]*. Instrumentation: 2222 4231 T, P(2), Pf, Str. Duration: 15:03. Composed 28 November - 24 December 1958 and 5 - 15 January 1959. American Composers Alliance/Composer Facsimile Edition. Premiered 27 February 1959, Great Hall, Cooper Union, New York City (*Music in the Making* series); Howard Shanet, conductor. Written for Howard Shanet. *See:* B672, B673

W28 *Symphony No. 3*. Instrumentation: 3333 4331, T, P(3), Pf, Str. Duration: 17:00. Composed 1 - 22 September 1959, in New York City. American Composers Alliance/Composers Facsimile Edition*.   Premiered 11 November 1959, Carnegie Hall, New York City. Orchestra of America; Richard Korn, conductor. Composed for and dedicated to the Orchestra of America.

> **Historical note:** Like Wuorinen's *Musica Duarum Partia Ecclesiastica*, this work contains a section near the end described: *La deploration de Johannes Okeghem, of Josquin des Prez. See:* D2, D56, W53, B674 - B687

W28a 20 January 1961, Tampere, Finland. Tampere Philharmonic Orchestra; Eero Kosonen, conductor. European premiere.

W29 *Tashi*. Instrumentation: Cl, Vn, Vc, Pf, Soli, 3233, 4331 T, P(5), Hp, Str. Duration: 30:20. Composed 8 April 1975 - 10 January 1976, in Middle Valley (NJ). Peters P66697*. Premiered 13 October 1976, Severance Hall, Cleveland, Ohio. Cleveland Orchestra (*Music of Today* program) and Tashi Quartet (Peter Serkin, piano; Richard Stoltzman, clarinet; Ida Kavafian, violin; Fred Sherry, violoncello) as soloists; Wuorinen, conductor. Dedicated to Tashi.

> **Historical note:** This orchestral version and the chamber version of *Tashi* were both part of the same commission. *See:* B692 - B694

W30 *Two-Part Symphony*. Instrumentation: 3222 4221 T, P(4), Hp, Pf, Str. Duration: 21:00. Composed 28 November 1977 - 1 August 1978, in New York City. Peters P66779*. Premiered 11 December 1978, Alice Tully Hall, Lincoln Center for the Performing Arts, New York City. American Composers Orchestra; Dennis Russell Davies, conductor. Composed under a grant from the National Endowment for the Arts for the American Composers Orchestra. Dedicated to Dennis Russell Davies. *See:* D22, B776 - B793

W30a November 1979, Berlin. Radio Symphonie Orchester Berlin; Arthur Weisberg, conductor.

W30b 18 November 1981, Davies Symphony Hall, San Francisco.   San Francisco Symphony; Dennis Russell Davies, conductor. *See:* B793

CHAMBER ORCHESTRA

W31 *Alternating Currents*. Instrumentation: Fl, Ob, Bb Cl, Bsn, Hrn, Pf (4 Hands), T, 4221. Duration: 5:33. Composed July - 1 August 1957, in

New York City. Unpublished. Premiered August 1957, Bennington, Vermont. Bennington Composers Conference; Henry Brant, conductor.
Historical note: A reading, not a performance.

W32 *Ancestors.* Instrumentation: Ob, Bsn, Hrn, P(2), Str. Duration: 9:00. Composed 28 May - 16 June 1978, in Buffalo (NY), Middle Valley (NJ), and New York City. Peters P66778*. Premiered 10 August 1978, Reed College, Portland, Oregon. Chamber Music Northwest; Wuorinen, conductor. Commissioned by Chamber Music Northwest; dedicated to Sergia Luca. *See:* D71, D79

W33 *Archæopteryx.* Instrumentation: Bass Trb Solo, 3 Fls (Picc), 2 Cls(Bcl), 2 Hrns, Tuba, Marimba, Pf. Duration: 15:00. Composed 7 July - 12 November 1978, in Middle Valley (NJ), and New York City. Peters P66810*. Premiered 1 July 1982, *Caramoor Festival*, Caramoor, New York (outdoor concert). St. Luke's Chamber Ensemble; Wuorinen, conductor; David Taylor, trombone soloist. *See:* B15

W33a 16 April 1983, Merkin Concert Hall, Abraham Goodman House, New York City. St. Luke's Chamber Ensemble; Wuorinen, conductor; David Taylor, trombone soloist. *See:* B16

W34 *Canzona.* Instrumentation: Fl, Ob(EH), Cl(Bcl), Bsn, Trp, Vibr, Pf, Hp, Vn, Va, Vc, Cb. Duration: 14:20. Composed 22 January - 9 June 1971, in Lexington (MA), Madison (WI), and New York City. Peters P66451*. Premiered 31 January 1972, Town Hall, New York City. Speculum Musicae; Wuorinen, conductor. Composed for Speculum Musicae; dedicated to the memory of Igor Stravinsky. *See:* B63 - B66, B891

W34a 25 April 1975, Baird Auditorium, Smithsonian Institution, Washington, D.C. The American Camerata for New Music; John Stephens, music director. Smithsonian Resident Associate Program concert. Washington, D.C. premiere. *See:* B65

W35 *Chamber Concerto for Flute and Ten Instruments.* Instrumentation: Fl Solo, P(4), Hp, Gtr, Pf, Cemb, Cel, Cb. Duration: 13:20. Composed 11 March - 4 May 1964, in New York City. Peters P66393*. Premiered 9 August 1964, Theatre-Concert Hall, Tanglewood, Lenox, Massachusetts *(Festival of Contemporary American Music).* Fromm Players; Melvin Strauss, conductor; Harvey Sollberger, flute soloist. Commissioned by the Berkshire Music Center under a grant from the Fromm Music Foundation. Composed for Harvey Sollberger; dedicated to Paul Fromm. *See:* D5, B91 - B109, B891

W35a 22 January 1965, Coolidge Auditorium, Library of Congress, Washington, D.C. Melvin Strauss, conductor; Harvey Sollberger, flute soloist. *See:* B96, B97

W35b 23 January 1965, Town Hall, New York City. Melvin Strauss, conductor; Harvey Sollberger, flute soloist. New York City premiere.

W35c 24 January 1966, Leo S. Bing Center, Los Angeles. Chamber ensemble selected by Lawrence Morton; Wuorinen, conductor; Harvey Sollberger, flute soloist. *Monday Evening Concerts. See:* B98

W35d 9 September 1968, Grace Rainey Rogers Auditorium, Metropolitan Museum of Art, New York City. Performers consisted of Tanglewood musicians; Paul Zukofsky, conductor; Harvey Sollberger, flute soloist. *See:* B99

W35e 21 May 1969, Jordan Hall, New England Conservatory, Boston. Paul Zukofsky, conductor; Harvey Sollberger, flute soloist. Boston premiere.

W36 *Chamber Concerto for Oboe and Ten Instruments.* Instrumentation: Ob Solo, Tba, T, P(5), Hp, Pf, Cb. Duration: 17:00. Composed 15 May - 26 July 1965, in New York City. Peters P66392*. Premiered 8 November 1965, McMillin Theatre, Columbia University, New York City. Group for Contemporary Music; Wuorinen, conductor; Josef Marx, oboe soloist. Commissioned by the Koussevitzky Music Foundation, Library of Congress. Composed for Josef Marx; dedicated to the memory of Serge and Natalie Koussevitzky.
   Historical note: The holograph of the manuscript is located in the Music Division, Library of Congress. *See:* B110, B111

W36a 27 February 71, Great Hall, Krannert Center for the Performing Arts, University of Illinois at Urbana-Champaign. University of Illinois Contemporary Chamber Players (Wilma Zonn, oboe soloist; Howard Bolin, tuba; Frederick Fairchild, Thomas Siwe, James Theobald, Michael Udow, Mark Johnson, James Baird, percussion; Joyce Rosenfeld, harp; Thomas Baker, piano; Chris Byrne, double-bass); Paul Zonn, conductor. This concert was part of the *Saturday Smörgåsbord*, a multi-theater event, and the gala opening of the 1971 *Festival of Contemporary Arts*.

W36b 25 March 1984, Jordan Hall, New England Conservatory, Boston. Boston Musica Viva (Dean Anderson, Neil Grover, Patrick Hollenbeck, John Grimes, Gary Di Perna, Myron Romanul, percussion; Robert Carriker, tuba; Timothy Pitts, double-bass; Caitron Yeats, harp; Randall Hodgkinson, piano; Richard Pittman, conductor. Boston premiere and the only performance of this work by this ensemble.

W37 *Chamber Concerto for Tuba.* Instrumentation: Tba Solo, 4(Picc), Alto)2(EH)02 (Cbsn) 4000 P(12 Drums; 1 player). Duration: 17:00. Composed 22 September 1969 - 6 August 1970, in Boston, Gardner (MA), Houston, Iowa City (IA), Lenox (MA), New York City, Northampton (MA), and Washington, D.C. Peters P66383*. Premiered 7 March 1971, Kaufmann Concert Hall, 92 St. YM-YWHA. Wuorinen, conductor;

Donald Butterfield, tuba. A *Music In Our Time* series concert. Written for Donald Butterfield. *See:* D29, B112 - B119

W37a 5 August 1971, Aspen, Colorado. Richard Dufallo, conductor; Donald Butterfield, tuba soloist. *Aspen Music Festival,* 1971 conference on contemporary music.

W37b 23 September 1971, Carnegie Recital Hall, New York City. Various players including the American Brass Quintet; Wuorinen, conductor; Donald Butterfield, tuba soloist. Performed twice at this concert. *See:* B114, B115

W37c 8 December 1971, Great Hall, Krannert Center for the Performing Arts, University of Illinois at Urbana-Champaign. University of Illinois Contemporary Chamber Players: Kathi Tessin, Mary Leathers, Chris Wargo, Jeff Sarver, flute; Wilma Zonn, oboe; Paul Chilcote, English horn; Charles Lipp, bassoon; Craig Chambers, contrabassoon; David Whaley, Sue Whaley, David Barford, Alfred Blatter, horn; Daniel Perantoni, tuba soloist. *New Music Series concert.*

W37d 18 December 1972, Manhattan School of Music, New York City. Group for Contemporary Music. *See:* B116

W37e 20 February 1983, Main Classroom Building Auditorium, Cleveland State University, Cleveland, Ohio. Cleveland Chamber Orchestra; Edwin London, conductor. Ronald Bishop, tuba soloist. *See:* B118

W37f 22 April 1991, Ijsbreker, Amsterdam. Jim Gordon, conductor; Helfred V.D. Veen, tuba soloist.

W38 *Chamber Concerto for Violoncello and Ten Players.* Instrumentation: Vc Solo, Fl, Ob(EH), Cl(Bcl), Bsn, P(2), Pf, Vn, Va, Cb. Duration: 16:25. Composed 18 January - 14 June 1963, in New York City. Peters P66391*. Premiered 17 February 1964, New York City. Group for Contemporary Music: Arthur Bloom, conductor; Robert Martin, violoncello soloist. Composed for Joel Krosnick.
    Historical note: Wuorinen's *Register of Works* has the dedication crossed out for this composition. *See:* D10, B120 - B131, B857, B891

W38a 16 November 1964, McMillin Theatre, Columbia University, New York City. Group for Contemporary Music; Gunther Schuller, conductor; Robert Martin, violoncello soloist. *See:* B120

W38b 18 May 1966, Maison de l'O.R.T.F., l'office de radiodiffusion-télévision française, Paris. Orchestre Ars Nova de l'O.R.T.F.; Gunther Schuller, conductor. European premiere. *See:* B121

W38c 6 November 1966, Knox-Albright Gallery, Buffalo, New York. Wuorinen, conductor; Robert Martin, violoncello soloist.

W38d 6 July 1970, Honolulu, Hawaii. Juilliard Ensemble; Dennis Russell Davies; Fred Sherry, violoncello soloist.

W38e 29 November 1970, Alice Tully Hall, Lincoln Center for the Performing Arts, New York City. Juilliard Ensemble; Dennis Russell Davies, conductor; Fred Sherry, violoncello soloist. First concert of The Juilliard School's *New and Newer Music* series. *See:* B122

W38f 2 November 1981, Kaufmann Concert Hall, 92nd St. Y, New York City. Group for Contemporary Music; Fred Sherry, violoncello. *See:* B128

W38g 16 February 1988, St. John's, Smith Square, London. Lontano Ensemble; Odaline de la Martinez, conductor; Timothy Hugh, violoncello soloist. *USA Uptown/Downtown* concert. United Kingdom premiere. *See:* B131

W39 *Composition for Violin and Ten Instruments*. Instrumentation: Vn Solo, 2 Obs, Bcl, 2 Hrns, 2 Trbs, P, Pf, Cb. Duration: 11:08. Composed 8 November 1963 -24 February 1964, in New York City. Peters P66390*. Premiered 26 April 1964, New York City (*Music In Our Time* concert). Arthur Bloom, conductor; Max Pollikoff, violin soloist. Dedicated to Max Pollikoff. *See:* B137, B138

W39a 22 August 1964, Bennington, Vermont. Bennington Composers Conference orchestra; Arthur Bloom, conductor; Max Pollikoff, violin soloist.

W39b 26 September 1964, Town Hall, New York City. Efrain Guigui, conductor; Max Pollikoff, violin soloist.

W39c 24 February 1965, Kaufmann Concert Hall, 92nd St. Y, New York City. Wuorinen, conductor; Max Pollikoff, violin soloist.

W40 *Concert-Piece for Piano and String Orchestra*. Instrumentation: Pn Solo, Str. Duration: 13:43. American Composers Alliance/Composer Facsimile Edition. Composed June- July 1956, in Gardner (MA), and New York City. Premiered 18 August 1956 in Bennington, Vermont. Bennington Composers Orchestra string players; Henry Brant, conductor; Lionel Nowak, piano soloist.

W41 *Concertante I*. Instrumentation: Vn Solo, Str(5231). Duration: 10:14. Composed 1 - 27 June 1957, in New York City. Unpublished. Premiered 7 July 1957, Middlebury, Vermont. Vermont Chamber Orchestra; Alan Carter, conductor; Max Pollikoff, violin soloist.
      Historical note: The first movement of this work is a revised version of *Summer Music*. This composition won the 1958 Columbia University Bearns Prize, then $600. *See:* W56

W41a 24 August 1957, Bennington, Vermont. Bennington Composers Conference string players; Alan Carter, conductor; Max Pollikoff, violin soloist.

W42 *Concertante II.* Instrumentation: Solo Vn, Pn, Str(6221). Duration: 10:55. Composed 20 - 23 June 1958. American Composers Alliance/Composer Facsimile Edition. Premiered 6 July 1958, Middlebury, Vermont. Vermont Chamber Orchestra; Alan Carter, conductor; Max Pollikoff, conductor. Written for and dedicated to Max Pollikoff.

    Historical note: This composition is a reorchestrated version of the first two movements of Wuorinen's *Violin Concerto. See:* W6, B140, B141, B183, B891

W42a 6 August 1958, Bennington, Vermont. Bennington Composers Conference; Alan Carter, conductor; Max Pollikoff, violin soloist.

W42b 24 January 1959, Kaufmann Concert Hall, 92nd St. Y, New York City. Alan Carter, conductor; Max Pollikoff, violin soloist. *Music In Our Time* concert. New York premiere. *See:* B140, B141

W42c 15 August 1959, Stowe, Vermont. Vermont Symphony Orchestra; Alan Carter, conductor; Max Pollikoff, violin soloist.

W42d 30 January 1962, Brooklyn Academy of Music, Brooklyn, New York. American Scandinavian Chamber Orchestra; Douglas Isaacson, conductor; Kenneth Goldsmith, violin soloist.

W43 *Concertante III.* Instrumentation: Solo Harpsichord, Ob, Vn, Va, Vc. Duration: 16:33. Composed 19 April - 4 May 1959, in New York City. McGinnis & Marx. Premiered 2 August 1961, School of Sacred Music, Union Theological Seminary, New York City. Leonard Raver, harpsichord; Josef Marx, oboe; Paul Wolfe, violin; George Grossman, viola; Joan Brockway, violoncello.

    Historical note: This work had originally been composed for the New York Chamber Soloists (Mel Kaplan, director; Albert Fuller, harpsichord), for their Spring 1959 European tour. The work was never performed in Europe. There is also a version of this work for solo piano with oboe and string orchestra. Wuorinen does not consider that version to be a separate work. *See:* B142 - B144

W43a August 1959, Bennington, Vermont. Bennington Composers Conference: Douglas Nordli, piano; Robert Bloom, oboe; George Grossman, viola; Alexander Kougell, violoncello.

    Historical note: This event was a reading and preceded the premiere performance.

W43b 30 September 1961, C.V. Whitney Estate, Old Westbury, Long Island, New York. *Long Island Little Orchestra Society Music Festival*; Clara Roesch, conductor.

    Historical note: This performance was of the version for piano with oboe and string orchestra.

W43c 8 December 1961, Carnegie Recital Hall, New York City. Leonard Raver, harpsichord; Josef Marx, oboe; Alan Ohmes, violin; George Grossman, viola; Joan Brockway, violoncello. *See:* B142, B143

W43d 12 January 1962, San Francisco Museum of Art, San Francisco. Gerhard Samuel, conductor.
> **Historical note:** This concert was the result of the Pacifica Foundation's national composition contest. *See:* B144

W44 *Concertante IV.* Instrumentation: Vn Solo, Pf Solo, Fl, Ob, Cl, Bsn, Hrn, Trp, Str(4221). Duration: 19:52. Composed 28 June and 13 July - 6 August 1959, in New York City. American Composers Alliance/Composer Facsimile Edition. Premiered 29 August 1959, Bennington, Vermont. Bennington Composers Conference staff orchestra; Roger Goeb, conductor; Max Pollikoff, violin soloist; Douglas Nordli, piano soloist. Composed for Max Pollikoff and Douglas Nordli. *See:* B145, B146

W44a 26 December 1959, Kaufmann Concert Hall, 92nd St. Y, New York City. Howard Shanet, conductor; Max Pollikoff, violin soloist; Douglas Nordli, piano soloist. *See:* B145, B146

W45 *Concertino.* Instrumentation: 2(2Piccs)24(E♭, Bcl, Cbcl)2(Cbsn) 4000 Str(with Cb Solo). Duration: 16:00. Composed 13 July - 6 October 1984. Peters P67017* (Peters 67017a - version for 15 solo instruments). Premiered 5 February 1985, Alice Tully Hall, Lincoln Center for the Performing Arts, New York City. Winds of Parnassus; Anthony Korf, conductor. Commissioned by the Koussevitzky Music Foundation. Dedicated to the memory of Serge and Natalie Koussevitzky.
> **Historical note:** This work may be played in two ways: 1) as orchestra piece with a large solo group (the solo double-bass should be played with the winds); 2) as a chamber work, either a) omitting the *Ripieno* Strings (retaining the solo double-bass), or b) replacing the *Ripieno* String sections with solo string. The version premiered above was the one for 15 solo instruments. The Winds of Parnassus is a subset ensemble of Parnassus. *See:* B147 - B151, B857

W46 *An Educator's "Wachet Auf".* Instrumentation: Fl, Ob, 2 Cls, Bsn, 2 Hrns, Trp, Trb, T, 5 Vlns, Vla, Vc, Cb. Duration: 7:60. Composed September - 7 October 1961; 17-19 October 1961. Unpublished. Never performed. Part of J.S. Bach's cantata *Wachet auf, ruft uns eie Stimme* (BWV 140); a transcription of the chorale and the opening chorus.

W47 *Evolutio Transcripta.* Instrumentation: 111(A)1 1110 Pf, Str(4221). Duration: 8:46. Composed 12 - 25 July 1961, in New York City. Peters P67363*. Premiered 19 August 1961, Carriage Barn, Bennington College, Bennington, Vermont. Bennington Composers Conference staff orchestra; Paul Wolfe, conductor. Dedicated to the memory of Lili Boulanger.
> **Historical note:** This work is a transcription of *Evolutio: Organ. See:* W147, B231 - B236

W47a 24 January 1962, Kaufmann Concert Hall, 92nd St. Y, New York City. Hartt Chamber Players; Wuorinen, conductor. A *Music In Our Time* concert. New York premiere. *See:* B234

W48 *Galliard*. Instrumentation: 2(Picc)222 2210 Pf, Str. Duration: 13:30. Composed 15 January - 17 April 1987, in New York City and San Francisco. Peters P67179*. Premiered 27-28 September 1987, Cleveland State University, Cleveland, Ohio. Cleveland Chamber Orchestra; Edwin London, conductor. Commissioned by Edwin London for the Cleveland Chamber Orchestra. Dedicated to Edwin London.

W48a 19-20 March 1988, St. Ann's Church, Brooklyn, New York City. St. Luke's Orchestra; Fred Sherry, conductor. *Arts at St. Ann's* concert.

W49 *Grand Bamboula*. Instrumentation: String Orchestra (at least 66442). Duration: 5:45. Composed 12 June - 8 August 1971, in Aspen (CO), Denver, Gardner (MA), Hanover (NH), Iowa City (IA), New York City, and North Platte (CO). Peters P66453*. Premiered 30 September and 2 October 1972, Hancher Auditorium, University of Iowa, Iowa City, Iowa. University of Iowa Symphony Orchestra; James Dixon, conductor. Written for and dedicated to Howard Shanet.

　　Historical note: These premiere performances celebrated the opening of the Hancher Auditorium concert hall. *See:* D16, D82, B300 - B307

W49a 19 March 1975, Town Hall, New York City. The Light Fantastic Players; Daniel Shulman, conductor.

W49b 13 May 1985, Legion of Honor's Little Theater, San Francisco. Parlante Orchestra; Steven Andre Dibner, conductor. *See:* B303

W49c 12 February 1988, Eastman School of Music, University of Rochester, Rochester, New York. Vanguard Ensemble.

W49d 15 October 1988, Queen Elizabeth Hall, London. Matrix Ensemble; Robert Ziegle, conductor.

W49e 8 May 1989, Herbst Theatre, San Francisco. Sinfonia San Francisco.

W49f 6 November 1989, Festaal des Neuen Rathauses, Linz, Austria. American Music Ensemble Wien; Hobart Earle, conductor. Austrian premiere.
　　Historical note: This concert was broadcast live on Austrian radio.

W49g 7 November 1989, Minoritensaal, Graz, Austria. American Music Ensemble Wien; Hobart Earle, conductor. *See:* B306, B307
　　Historical note: This concert was broadcast live on Austrian radio.

W49h 8 November 1989, Konzerthaus (Mozartsaal), Vienna. American Music Ensemble Wien; Hobart Earle, conductor. *See:* B305
　　Historical note: This concert was broadcast live on Austrian radio.

W49i 30 October 1990, New Haven, Connecticut. New Haven Symphony Orchestra; Michael Palmer, conductor.

W50 *Hyperion.* Instrumentation: 1111 1110 Pf, Vn, Va, Vc, Cb. Duration: 16:00. Composed 17 August - 22 November 1975. Peters P66657*. Premiered 21 March 1976, Town Hall, Adelaide, Australia *(Adelaide Festival of Arts).* Contemporary Chamber Ensemble; Arthur Weisberg, conductor. Commissioned by Mr. & Mrs. Gus Hines of Adelaide. Dedicated to Arthur Weisberg. *See:* D64, D65, B314 - B319

W50a 20 October 1976, Helsinki, Crypt of Helsinki Cathedral. Contemporary Music Ensemble of the Finnish Broadcasting Company; Ulf Söderblom, conductor. *See:* B317

W50b 7 March 1977, Eisner and Lubin Auditorium, New York University, New York City. Contemporary Chamber Ensemble; Arthur Weisberg, conductor. New York premiere. *See:* B318

W50c 29 March 1989, McMillin Theatre, Columbia University, New York City. Parnassus; Anthony Korf, conductor.

W51 *Into the Organ Pipes and Steeples.* Instrumentation: Picc, Cl, Sax, Pf(2), T, Str(2 Vla, 2 Vc, Cb). Duration: 3:41. Composed August 1956. Published in *New Music (A Quarterly Publishing Modern Compositions),* Volume 30, Number 2 (January 1957). Premiered 22 August 1956, Bennington, Vermont. Bennington Composers Conference staff musicians; Henry Brant, conductor.

> **Historical note:** The above performance was a reading. The work had originally been titled *The Descent With Music.* Wuorinen's instructions in the score state the most effective placement of instruments in this antiphonal piece is: strings behind and above the audience, 1st piano in front, 2nd piano behind the audience, winds and timpani on either side of the audience.

W52 *The Magic Art: An Instrumental Masque Drawn From the Works of Henry Purcell.* Instrumentation: 1(Picc)2(EH)1(Bcl)2 2210 T, Hp, Pf, Str. Duration: 80:00. Composed 20 November 1977 - 20 June 1979. Peters P66809*. Premiered 26 September 1979, St. Paul, Minnesota. St. Paul Chamber Orchestra; Wuorinen, conductor. Commissioned by the St. Paul Chamber Orchestra. Dedicated to Dennis Russell Davies.

> **Historical note:** Any number of movements may be excerpted from the complete score to form suites. In particular, Scenes 1, 5 and 6 from Act I, and Numbers 2 and 4 from Scene 2, Act II, have alternate, reduced instrumentation (without trumpets, trombone, harp, and timpani.); this particular reduction has been performed as *Suite from the Magic Art. See:* D34, D72, B349 - B358

W52a 15 October 1981, Finlandia House, Helsinki. Helsinki Philharmonic Orchestra; Wuorinen, conductor.

> **Historical note:** Three movements of the work were performed: *Games, Renewal,* and *Celebration. See:* B350 - B353

W52b 23 October 1981, Tampere University Auditorium, Tampere, Finland. Tampere Philharmonic Orchestra; Wuorinen, conductor. *See:* B354

W52c 29 October 1981, Oulu, Finland. Oulu City Orchestra; Wuorinen, conductor.

W52d 13 December 1981, Brooklyn Academy of Music, New York City. Brooklyn Philharmonia; Lukas Foss, conductor. *See:* B355

W52e 12 February 1982, Uihlein Hall, Milwaukee. Milwaukee Symphony Orchestra; Lukas Foss, conductor.
> **Historical note:** Three movements of the work were performed: *Fanfare, Chaconne,* and *Finale. See:* B356

W52f 4-6 October 1984, Kentucky Center for the Arts, Louisville, Kentucky. Louisville Ballet; Jean-Pierre Bonnefoux, choreography; Louisville Orchestra; Wuorinen, conductor. Dancers: Clark Reid, Dale Brannon, Helen Starr, Diane Downes. Sets by John Walker.
> **Historical note:** A ballet performance titled *Courtly Dances,* by Bonnefoux. Described as a kind of medieval party, with the participants enacting a series of celebrations and encounters. Only one section of the work was choreographed/performed. *See:* B357

W52g 4 February 1985, Guggenheim Museum, New York City. Jean-Pierre Bonnefoux, choreography. Dancers: Patricia McBride, Alexandre Proia (from the New York City Ballet), Jeffrey Gribler (from the Pennsylvania Ballet) and ten students from the School of American Ballet.
> **Historical note:** A showcase performance danced to a tape recording of the music. *See:* B358

W52h 22 May 1988, Davies Symphony Hall, San Francisco. San Francisco Symphony Youth Orchestra; Leif Bjaland, conductor.

W52i 1 & 3 May 1989, Columbus, Ohio. Columbus Symphony Orchestra; Michael Morgan, conductor.

W52j 16 & 18 November 1989, Gusman Center for the Performing Arts, Miami, Florida. New World Symphony; Leif Bjaland, conductor.

W52k 16 September 1990, London. London Symphony Orchestra; Michael Tilson Thomas, conductor.

W52l 21 November 1991, Yale School of Music, New Haven, Connecticut. Wuorinen, conductor.

W53 *Musica Duarum Partium Ecclesiastica.* Instrumentation: Solo Brass Quartet, 2 Trp, Hrn, Trb, Tuba, 3 T, Pf, Organ. Duration: 16:58. Composed 17 February - 13 April 1959, in New York City. American Composers Alliance/Composer Facsimile Edition. Never performed.
> **Historical note:** Like *Symphony No. 3* this work contains a section near the end titled *La deploration de Johannes Okeghem of Josquin des Prez. See:* W28

W54 *On Alligators*. Instrumentation: Fl, Ob, Cl, Bsn, 2 Vn, Va, Vc. Duration: 17:00. Composed 13 March - 27 July 1972, in Amagansett (MA?), Glens Falls (NY), Hancock (MA), and New York City. Peters P66533*. Commissioned by the University of South Florida.

> **Historical note:** First performance unknown. The premiere performance had been scheduled for 22 April 1973 at the University of South Florida, Tampa. Faculty artists were to perform. Wuorinen withdrew the work and cancelled the performance for a lack of rehearsal time.

W54a Week of 3 February 1975, Horace Mann Auditorium, Columbia University, New York City. The Light Fantastic Players; Daniel Shulman, conductor. *See:* B404

W55 *Salve Regina: John Bull*. Instrumentation: 2 Fls, Ob, EH, Bcl, Hrn, Trp, 2 Trbs, T, Pf, Vn, Va, Vc. Duration: 7:58. Composed 23 September - 4 October 1966, in New York City. Peters P66450*. Premiered 31 October 1966, McMillin Theatre, Columbia University, New York City. Group for Contemporary Music; Wuorinen, conductor.

W56 *Summer Music*. Instrumentation: Vn Solo, Fl, Ob, B♭ Cl, Hrn, Bsn, String Quintet. Duration: 6:30. Composed June 1957. American Composers Alliance. Never performed. Composed for Max Pollikoff.

> **Historical note:** This work was slightly altered to become the first movement of *Concertante I* for violin solo and strings. The rescored version is for strings alone. *See:* W41

W57 *The Winds*. Instrumentation: Fl, Ob, Cl, Bcl, Bsn, Trp, Trb, Tba, Pf. Duration: 14:30. Composed 8 November 1976 - 16 February 1977, in New York City. Peters P66707*. Premiered 19 May 1977, Carnegie Recital Hall, New York City. Parnassus; Anthony Korf, conductor. Commissioned by Mr. & Mrs. Frank Brainard for Parnassus. Dedicated to Anthony Korf. *See:* D24, B815 - B817

W57a December 1978, Carnegie Recital Hall, New York City. Parnassus; Anthony Korf, conductor. *See:* B816

INSTRUMENTAL AND CHAMBER MUSIC

W58 *Adapting to the Times*. Instrumentation: Violoncello and piano. Duration: 15:55. Composed 6 August 1968 - 16 February 1969, in Ann Arbor (MI), London, New York City, and Yellow Springs (OH). Peters P66373 (2 scores needed for performance). Premiered 25 February 1970, Bowker Auditorium, University of Massachusetts, Amherst, Massachusetts. *Faculty Recital Series*: Joel Krosnick, violoncello; Wuorinen, piano. Written for and dedicated to Joel Krosnick. *See:* B1 - B4, B891

W58a 21-22 January 1970, Cyprus Hilton, Nicosia, Cyprus. Fred Sherry, violoncello; Wuorinen, piano.

> **Historical note:** The 22 January performance was broadcast live on Cyprus television.

W58b 24 September 1970, Thessalonika, Greece. Fred Sherry, violoncello; Wuorinen, piano.

W58c 25 September 1970, Hellenic American Cultural Center, Athens, Greece. Fred Sherry, violoncello; Wuorinen, piano.

W58d 16 October 1970, Stanford University, Palo Alto, California. Joel Krosnick, violoncello; Wuorinen, piano.

W58e 23 January 1972, Baltimore Museum of Art, Baltimore, Maryland. Fred Sherry, violoncello; Wuorinen, piano. Group for Contemporary Music concert. *See:* B1

W59 *Album Leaf.* Instrumentation: Violin and Violoncello. Duration: 2:00. Composed 24 August - 17 September 1976, in Middle Valley (NJ) and New York City. Unpublished. No known public performances. Dedicated to Ayda and Fred Sherry.
  Historical note: This composition was a birthday present for Fred Sherry, who was given the manuscript as a gift. The work has been performed at private gatherings; the dates of these performances are not known.

W60 *Arabia Felix.* Instrumentation: Fl, Bsn, Vibr, Pf, Amplified Gtr, Vn. Duration: 10:50. Composed 22 May - 2 November 1973, in Hancock (MA), Lenox (MA), and New York City. Peters P66577 (Score); P66577a (Parts). Premiered 23 February 1974, Carnegie Recital Hall, New York City. New York Composer's Ensemble: Joe Spivak, flute; Bruce Taub, bassoon; Alison Nowak, violin; Stephen Dydo, electric guitar, Ken Hosley, vibraphone; Erik Lundborg, piano; Peter Lieberson, conductor. Written for and dedicated to the New York Composer's Ensemble.
  Historical note: In addition to the following selected performances, Brad Lubman has conducted many performances of this work in the United States. *See:* D27, B7 - B14, B857

W60a 27-28 July 1974, tent, Wheatleigh Estate, Lenox Arts Center, Lenox, Massachusetts. Wheatleigh Chamber Players: Harvey Sollberger, flute; Daniel Reed, violin; Joseph Passaro, vibraphone; electric guitar, bassoon and piano players unknown; Wuorinen, conductor. Concert titled *Charles Wuorinen: Profile of a Composer. See:* B8

W60b 3 March 1976, Borden Auditorium, Manhattan School of Music, New York City. Troupe for Contemporary Music and Dance. *See:* B9

W60c 11 December 1990, Manhattan School of Music, New York City. Manhattan School of Music Contemporary Ensemble; Claire Heldrich, conductor.

W61 *Archangel.* Instrumentation: Bass Trombone and String Quartet. Duration: 12:00. Composed 21 August - 26 October 1977, in Helsinki, Middle Valley (NJ) and New York City. Peters P66783 (5 scores needed for performance). Premiered 18 December 1978, Borden Auditorium, New York City. David Taylor, bass trombone; Columbia String Quartet. A Group for Contemporary Music concert. Commissioned by and dedicated to David Taylor. *See:* D31, B17, B18

W62 *Bassoon Variations.* Instrumentation: Bassoon, Harp and Timpani. Composed 23 November 1971 - 19 February 1972, in New York City. Peters P66454 (3 scores needed for performance). Premiered 28 October 1973, Sanders Theatre, Harvard University, Cambridge, Massachusetts. Boston Symphony Chamber Players: Sherman Walt, bassoon; Ann Hobson, harp; Everett Firth, timpani. Commissioned by and dedicated to Leonard Hindell. *See:* D19, B46 - B49

W63 *Bearbeitungen über das Glogauer Liederbuch.* Instrumentation: Flute (Piccolo), Clarinet (Bass Clarinet), Violin and Contrabass (Vc). Duration: 7:00. Composed 15-29 June 1962, in New York City. Peters P66396. Premiered 17 July 1962, University of Hartford *(University of Hartford Summer Concert Series)*, Hartford, Connecticut. Stanley Aronson, flute; Henry Larsen, clarinet; Bernard Lurie, violin; Bertram Turetzky, contrabass.
    Historical note: Wuorinen titled the six movements: *Pauli de Broda Carmen; De Ezels Crone; Der Notter Schwantcz; Der Entepris; Helas le Bon Temps (Tinctoris); Gross Szenen (Tertius). See:* D16, B50 - B54

W63a 17 December 1962, Columbia University, New York City. Group for Contemporary Music: Sophie Sollberger, flute; Stanley Walden, clarinet; Doris Allen, violin; Bertram Turetzky, contrabass. New York premiere.

W63b 27-28 July 1974, tent, Wheatleigh Estate, Lenox Arts Center, Lenox, Massachusetts. Wheatleigh Chamber Players: Harvey Sollberger, flute; Michael Sussman, clarinet; Daniel Reed, violin; Fred Sherry, violoncello. Concert titled *Charles Wuorinen: Profile of a Composer. See:* B50

W63c 10 March 1981, Helen M. Hosmer Hall, Crane School of Music, Potsdam College of Arts and Science, Potsdam, New York. Susan Deaver, flute; David Stanton, clarinet; Linda Quan, violin; Madeline Shapiro, violoncello.

W63d 8 May 1990, Innova Design Center, Houston. Houston Symphony New Music Ensemble: Aralee Dorough, violin; Thomas LeGrand, flute; Eric Halen, clarinet; David Malone, double-bass. An *Innova Concert. See:* B54

W64 *Bicinium.* Instrumentation: 2 Oboes. Duration: 4:00. Composed 22 January - 13 February 1966, in Los Angeles and New York City. Peters P66374. Premiered 10 May 1967, Greenwich House Music School, New York City. Josef Marx and Judith Martin, oboes. Composed for and dedicated to Josef Marx and Judith Martin.
    Historical note: Wuorinen's *Register of Works* notebook indicates that he gave the manuscript to John Cage. The manuscripts of John Cage's monograph *Notations* are

located at Northwestern University, Evanston, Illinois, as is the correspondence associated with that project. Specifically, the following letters from Wuorinen can be found in the *Notations Collection*, Northwestern University Music Library: Wuorinen to Cage, 27 September 1966, typed letter signed; Wuorinen to Cage, 21 November 1966, autograph letter signed; Wuorinen to Cage, 27 December 1966, typed letter signed; Wuorinen to Dick Higgins, 25 January 1967, typed letter signed; and Wuorinen to Miss [Alison] Knowles, 20 March 1967, autograph letter signed. Each letter is approximately one page long, although most are only one paragraph in length. *See:* B55 - B57, B891

W64a 29 April 1968, C.W. Post College, Long Island, New York. Josef Marx and Judith Martin, oboes.

W64b 17 April 1990, The Doma Gallery, New York City. Vanguard Ensemble.

W65 *Cello Variations I.* Instrumentation: Violoncello Solo. Duration: 9:00. Composed 10 April - 2 October 1970, in Athens (Greece), Gardner (MA), Iowa City (IA), Lenox (MA), London, New York City, Nicosia (Cyprus), and Thessalonika (Greece). Peters P66385. Premiered 8 December 1970, Blauvelt Theatre, Philadelphia. Written for and dedicated to Fred Sherry. *See:* B87 - B90

W65a 23 December 1970, New York Cultural Center, New York City. Fred Sherry, violoncello solo. New York premiere. *See:* B87

W65b 26 March 1971, Los Angeles. Joel Krosnick, violoncello solo. West coast premiere.

W65c 24 January 1972, Grace Rainey Rogers Auditorium, Metropolitan Museum of Art, New York City. Fred Sherry, violoncello solo. *See:* B88

W65d 27-28 July 1974, tent, Wheatleigh Estate, Lenox Arts Center, Lenox, Massachusetts. Wheatleigh Chamber Players: Fred Sherry, violoncello solo. Concert titled *Charles Wuorinen: Profile of a Composer*. *See:* B89, B90

W66 *Cello Variations II.* Instrumentation: Violoncello Solo. Duration: 7:00. Composed 20 August - 20 October 1975, in Chicago, Middle Valley (NJ) and New York City. Peters P66669. Premiered December 1976 on a WQXR (The *New York Times* radio station, New York City) live broadcast. Fred Sherry, violoncello solo. Dedicated to Fred Sherry.

W67 *Composition for Oboe and Piano.* Instrumentation: Oboe and Piano. Duration: 14:43. Composed 21 November 1964 - 29 May 1965, in New York City. Peters P66375 (2 scores needed for performance). Premiered 3 April 1966, Gardner Museum, Boston, Massachusetts. Josef Marx, Oboe; Wuorinen, piano. Written for and dedicated to Josef Marx. *See:* D20, B132 - B138

W67a 18 February 1967, Carnegie Recital Hall, New York City. Josef Marx, oboe; Wuorinen, piano. New York premiere.

W67b 6 May 1967, Le Havre, France. Performers unknown. European premiere.

W67c 14 May 1967, University of Maryland, College Park, Maryland. Ivar Luade, oboe; Margit Lundstrom, piano.

W67d 6 August 1967, Town Hall, Provincetown, Massachusetts. Josef Marx, oboe; Wuorinen, piano.

W67e 12 May 1969, C.W. Post College, Long Island, New York. Josef Marx, oboe; Wuorinen, piano.

W68 *Concert for Doublebass Alone.* Instrumentation: Solo Contrabass. Duration: 5:30. Composed 12 - 28 October 1961, in New York City. McGinnis & Marx. Premiered 11 May 1962, Southport, Connecticut. Bertram Turetzky, solo contrabass. Written for and dedicated to Bertram Turetzky. *See:* D57, B139

W68a 8 March 1963, Smith Music Hall, University of Illinois at Urbana-Champaign. *University of Illinois School of Music Festival of Contemporary Arts.* Bertram Turetzky, solo contrabass.

W68b 11 March 1969, University of Connecticut, Storrs, Connecticut. Alvin Brehm, solo contrabass.

W68c 19 November 1969, Composers Theatre, New York City. Alvin Brehm, solo contrabass.

W68d 1 August 1979, *Grand Teton Music Festival*, Jackson Hole, Wyoming. Roger Ruggieri, contrabass. *Music In the Present Tense* series.

W69 *Consort of Four Trombones.* Instrumentation: Four Trombones. Duration: 5:33. Composed 1-9 March 1960, in New York City. Peters P67361. Premiered 4 April 1960, Carnegie Recital Hall, New York City. New Music Chamber Ensemble: Bill Wall, Don Dougherty, Bill Motzing, James Schmit, trombones; Jerome C. Keller, conductor. Concert titled *An Evening of Contemporary Music.* *See:* B186, B187

W69a 25 March 1963, Hartt College of Music, Hartford, Connecticut. Joseph Sintau, Donald Mactavish, Eric Nisula, Edward Laster, trombones.

W70 *Cycle of Elaborations.* Instrumentation: Oboe and Piano. Duration: 11:13. Composed 8 November - 10 March 1964. Unpublished. Never performed. Composed for and dedicated to Josef Marx.
> **Historical note:** This work had the subtitle *The First Piece Plain.* Wuorinen's *Register of Works* notebook states it is the first piece in the cycle. Wuorinen decided to withdraw the work before it was ever performed.

W71 *Divertimento for Alto Saxophone and Piano.* Instrumentation: Alto Saxophone and Piano. Duration: 11:10. Composed 16 July - 22 August 1982, in Middle Valley (NJ), New York City, and San Francisco. Peters P66929. Premiered 6 March 1983, Carnegie Recital Hall, New York City. Christopher Ford, alto saxophone; Wuorinen, piano. Commissioned by the Peggy and Yale Gordon Charitable Trust. Dedicated to Christopher Ford. *See:* D40, B206 - B208

W71a 10 April 1983, Renwick Gallery, Washington, D.C. Christopher Ford, alto saxophone; pianist unknown. *See:* B207

W71b 18 March 1986, University of Texas at Austin. Daniel Goble, alto saxophone; Eduard Laurel, piano.

W71c 12 November 1987, Smith Music Hall, University of Illinois at Urbana-Champaign. Daniel Goble, alto saxophone; Celso Chavez, piano.

W72 *Divertimento for String Quartet.* Instrumentation: String Quartet. Duration: 11:10. Composed 29 August - 25 September 1982, in Middle Valley (NJ). Peters P66928 (Score); P66928a (Parts). Premiered 9 May 1983, Glens Falls, New York. Atlantic String Quartet. Dedicated to Giovannina and Virginia de Blasiis.
    Historical note: Wuorinen's *Register of Works* notebook states this piece is a reworking of his *Divertimento for Alto Saxophone and Piano. See:* W71

W72a 13 November 1989, Glens Falls, New York. Atlantic String Quartet.

W72b 18 March 1990, Blackman Auditorium, Boston. Atlantic String Quartet.

W73 *Doctor Faustus Lights the Lights.* Instrumentation: Narrator, Cl, Sax(Cl), Bsn, Vc, P(1), T, Pf. Duration: 30:12. Composed December 1956 - 18 January 1957, in New York City. American Composes Alliance. Premiered 8 April 1957, Rooftop Theatre, New York City. Charles Russo, saxophone and clarinet; Morris Newman, bassoon; Martha Blackman, violoncello; Howard V. Hyning, percussion; timpani player unknown; Douglas Nordli, piano; Leon Hyman, conductor. Dancers: Paul Sanasardo, Donya Feuer, Ellen Green. This performance was a dance adaptation by Paul Sanasardo based on Gertrude Stein's work of the same title. *See:* B209

W73a 18 January 1958, Carnegie Recital Hall, New York City. Larry Diegel, conductor.

W74 *A Doleful Dompe On Deborah's Departure As Well As Borda's Bawdy Badinage.* Instrumentation: English Horn, Violin and Violoncello. Duration: 3:40. Composed 13-20 September 1986. Peters P67141. Premiered at a private party, 13 November 1986, San Francisco.
    Historical note: This work was composed at the request of Peter Pastreich for Deborah Borda's departure from the San Francisco Symphony. Borda had been general

manager of the orchestra. The manuscript was presented to her at the private performance.

W75 *Double Solo for Horn Trio*. Instrumentation: Horn, Violin and Piano. Duration: 14:00. Composed 21 September - 27 December 1985; revised 30 December 1985, in New York City, San Francisco, and other locations. Peters P67126. Premiered 16 March 1986, Alice Tully Hall, Lincoln Center for the Performing Arts, New York City. Speculum Musicae: William Purvis, horn; Benjamin Hudson, violin; Aleck Karis, piano. Commissioned by Speculum Musicae for their 15th anniversary concert. Dedicated to Benjamin Hudson and William Purvis.

W75a 8 February 1988, Longy School of Music, Boston. Collage New Music Ensemble.

W76 *Duo for Violin and Piano*. Instrumentation: Violin and Piano. Duration: 14:48. Composed 4 October 1966 - 26 January 1967, in Buffalo (NY) and New York City. Peters P66376 (2 scores needed for performance). Premiered 17 April 1968, Greenwich House Music School, New York City. Paul Zukofsky, violin; Wuorinen, piano. Composed for and dedicated to Paul Zukofsky. *See:* D9, B210 - B216, B891

W76a 6 November 1968, Town Hall, New York City. Paul Zukofsky, violin; Wuorinen, piano. *See:* B210

W76b 29 October 1968, New England Conservatory, Boston. Paul Zukofsky, violin; Wuorinen, piano.

W76c 11 March 1978, Francis Parker School Auditorium, Chicago. Benjamin Hudson, violin; Wuorinen, piano. Chicago premiere. *See:* B216

W76d 24 October 1984, Terrace Theatre, Kennedy Center for the Performing Arts, Washington, D.C. Benjamin Hudson, violin; Wuorinen, piano. A concert of the Kennedy Center's *American Composers* series.

W77 *Duuiensela*. Instrumentation: Violoncello and Piano. Duration: 8:58. Composed 28 February and 2-14 April 1962, in New York City. McGinnis and Marx. Premiered 30 April 1962, Jewish Community Centre, New Haven, Connecticut. Joel Krosnick, violoncello; Jens Nygaard, piano. Composed for and dedicated to Joel Krosnick. *See:* B217 - B223, B891

W77a 4 May 1962, McMillin Theatre, Columbia University, New York City. Joel Krosnick, violoncello; Jens Nygaard, piano. New York premiere.

W77b 8 August 1962, Bennington Composers Conference, Bennington, New York. Joel Krosnick, violoncello; Wuorinen, piano. *See:* B218, B219

W77c 29 October, 5 & 12 November 1962, New School for Social Research, New York City. *New School Rehearsal Seminars* (an open, public rehearsal). Joel Krosnick, violoncello; Wuorinen, piano.

W77d 11 March 1963, Columbia University, New York City. Joel Krosnick, violoncello; Wuorinen, piano. *See:* B220

W77e 31 March 1963, National Gallery of Art, Washington, D.C. Joel Krosnick; violoncello; Wuorinen, piano. Washington, D.C. premiere.

W77f 20 March 1964, Brandeis University, Waltham, Massachusetts. Madeline Foley, violoncello; Martin Boykan, piano.

W77g 30 November 1964, Los Angeles. Laurence Lesser, violoncello; Ellen Mack, piano. *Monday Evening Concerts.*

W77h 6 December 1964, Dunster House, Harvard University, Cambridge, Massachusetts. Joan Brockway, violoncello; Beverly Schuler, piano. This performance was broadcast on radio.

W77i 22 February 1966, San Francisco Tape Center, San Francisco. Eugene Wilson, violoncello; David Blodli, piano.

W78 *8 Variations.* Instrumentation: Violin and Harpsichord. Duration: 6:18. Composed 14 October - 6 November 1960, in New York City. American Composers Alliance. Premiered 21 June 1961, School of Sacred Music, Union Theological Seminary, New York City. Max Pollikoff, violin; Leonard Raver, harpsichord. Commissioned by Daniel Pinkham. Dedicated to Robert Brink and Daniel Pinkham. *See:* B227

W78a 31 July 1961, School of Sacred Music, Union Theological Seminary, New York City. Max Pollikoff, violin; Leonard Raver, harpsichord.

W78b 22 February 1964, Schwab Auditorium, Penn State University, State College, Pennsylvania. Joanne Zagst, violin; Leonard Raver, harpsichord.

W79 *Fanfare for Rutgers University.* Instrumentation: 2 Hrns, 2 Trps, 2 Trbs. Duration: 1:45. Composed 17 July - 19 September 1986. Peters P67142. Premiered 10 November 1986, Meadowlands, New Jersey *(Rutgers Capital Fund Dinner).* Wuorinen, conductor.

W80 *Fantasia.* Instrumentation: Violin and Piano. Duration: 15:00. Composed 17 March - 15 December 1974, in Middle Valley (NJ), Nashville (TN), and New York City. Peters P66605 (2 scores needed for performance). Premiered 14 December 1975, Baltimore Museum of Art, Baltimore. Paul Zukofsky, violin; Wuorinen, piano. Commissioned by the Chamber Music Society of Baltimore for its 25th anniversary. *See:* D35, B237 - B242

W80a 2 February 1977, Carnegie Recital Hall, New York City.   Benjamin Hudson, violin; Wuorinen, piano. *See:* B238

W80b 11 March 1978, Francis Parker School Auditorium, Chicago. Benjamin Hudson, violin; Wuorinen, piano. Chicago premiere. *See:* B239, B240

W80c 8 March 1981, Park School, Baltimore.   Benjamin Hudson, violin; Wuorinen, piano. A Group for Contemporary Music concert. *See:* B241

W81 *Fast Fantasy.* Instrumentation: Violoncello and Piano. Duration: 15:00. Composed 8 July - 8 August 1977, in Middle Valley (NJ), New York City and San Francisco. Peters P66785 (2 scores needed for performance). Premiered 13 February 1979 at a recording session for Finnish Radio, Helsinki. Dedicated to Fred Sherry.
    Historical note: This composition was a birthday present for Fred Sherry. *See:* D37, D69, B243, B244

W81a 10 December 1979, Borden Auditorium, Manhattan School of Music, New York City. Fred Sherry, violoncello; Wuorinen, piano. A Group for Contemporary Music concert. *See:* B243

W81b 25 November 1988, Library of Congress, Washington, D.C. Fred Sherry, violoncello; Wuorinen, piano.
    Historical note: This concert was subsequently broadcast on radio across throughout the United States. *See:* B244

W82 *Flute Variations I.*   Instrumentation: Flute Solo.   Duration: 5:44. Composed 3 September - 11 December 1963, in New York City. McGinnis & Marx. Premiered 18 December 1963, Donnell Library (New York Public Library), New York City. Harvey Sollberger, flute soloist. Dedicated to Harvey Sollberger.
    Historical note: Wuorinen originally subtitled this work *A Book of Interpolations: Composition B*, but dropped the subtitle when he decided that *A Book of Interpolations: Composition A (Piano Variations)* and *A Book of Interpolations: Composition C (Variations á 2)* were each independent works. *See:* D17, D76, B253 - B257, B891

W82a 23 March 1964, Washington & Lee University, Lexington, Virginia. Harvey Sollberger, flute soloist.

W82b 14 November 1964, Henry Street Settlement, New York City. Sophie Sollberger, flute soloist.

W82c 9 November 1964, Carnegie Recital Hall, New York City.   Sophie Sollberger, flute soloist. *See:* B255

W82d 13 February 1965, Greenwich House Music School, New York City. Harvey Sollberger, flute soloist. *American Music Festival* concert.

W82e 14 March 1965, Carnegie Recital Hall, New York City. Sophie Sollberger, flute soloist. *Fontainbleau Concert.*

W82f 31 July 1965, Illini Union Ballroom, University of Illinois at Urbana-Champaign. Patrick Purswell, flute soloist. A program of the University of Illinois School of Music *Summer Workshop in Analysis and Performance of Contemporary Music.*

W82g 14 February 1967, University of Colorado, Boulder, Colorado. Harvey Sollberger, flute soloist.

W82h 28 January 1971, New England Conservatory, Boston. Elizabeth Lawson, flute soloist.

W83 *Flute Variations II.* Instrumentation: Flute Solo. Duration: 6:30. Composed 6 October - 4 December 1968, in New York City. Peters P66377. Premiered 17 April 1969, Jersey City State College, Jersey City, New Jersey. Composed for and dedicated to Harvey Sollberger. *See:* D17, B258 - B266

W83a 12 May 1969, C.W. Post College, Long Island, New York. Harvey Sollberger, flute soloist.

W83b 14 March 1970, University of Houston, Houston, Texas. Byron Hester, flute soloist.

W83c 8 December 1970, Blauvelt Theatre, Philadelphia. Harvey Sollberger, flute soloist.

W83d 27-28 July 1974, tent, Wheatleigh Estate, Lenox Arts Center, Lenox, Massachusetts. Harvey Sollberger, flute soloist. A Wheatleigh Chamber Players concert. Concert titled *Charles Wuorinen: Profile of a Composer.* *See:* B258

W83e 8 May 1990, Innova Design Center, Houston, Texas. Lynette Mayfield, flute soloist. An *Innova Concert* (Houston Symphony New Music Ensemble). *See:* B266

W84 *Fortune.* Instrumentation: Cl in A, Vn, Vc, Pf. Duration: 16:45. Composed 12 February - 30 November 1979, in Helsinki, Middle Valley (NJ), New York City, San Francisco, and St. Paul (MN). Peters P66829 (Score); P66829a (Set of Parts). Premiered October 1980 in a basement in Bonn, Germany. David Singer, clarinet; Benjamin Hudson, violin; Fred Sherry, violoncello; Wuorinen, piano. Commissioned for Tashi by the City of Bonn for the 1980 *Beethoven Festival.* Dedicated to Tashi.

> **Historical note:** The two movements are titled *Before, After.* The premiere performance had been scheduled for 5 June 1980 in Bonn, with Tashi (Richard Stoltzman, clarinet; Ida Kavafian, violin; Fred Sherry, violoncello; and Peter Serkin, piano) the scheduled performers. According to Wuorinen, that performance was cancelled because

Peter Serkin felt depressed and decided not to play the concert, thereby cutting his three colleagues out of a paying engagement and cutting Wuorinen out of a first performance. The October 1980 performance was subsequently arranged but was under-publicized and relegated to taking place in the basement — accommodating about 60 people — of some building in Bonn. *See:* D77, B267

W84a 18 February 1981, Louisiana State University, Baton Rouge, Louisiana. David Singer, clarinet; Benjamin Hudson, violin; Fred Sherry, violoncello; Wuorinen, piano. *See:* B267

W85 *Grand Union.* Instrumentation: Violoncello and Drums. Duration: 13:15. Composed 3 July - 7 September 1973, in Gardner (MA), Hancock (NH), Lenox (MA), and New York City. Peters P66572 (2 scores needed for performance). Premiered 5 November 1973, Museum of Contemporary Art, Chicago. Speculum Musicae. Commissioned by the Thorne Music Fund for the Lenox Arts Center. Dedicated to Fred Sherry.
> **Historical note:** This composition was a birthday present for Fred Sherry, on his 25th birthday. *See:* B308 - B310

W85a 27-28 July 1974, tent, Wheatleigh Estate, Lenox Arts Center, Lenox, Massachusetts. Fred Sherry, violoncello; Joseph Passaro, drums. A Wheatleigh Chamber Players concert. Concert titled *Charles Wuorinen: Profile of a Composer. See:* B309, B310

W86 *Harp Variations.* Instrumentation: Harp, Violin, Viola, and Violoncello. Duration: 11:40. Composed 1 December 1971 - 16 February 1972, in New York City and Tampa (FL). Peters P66456 (4 scores needed for performance). Premiered 17 April 1973, Carnegie Recital Hall, New York City. Gloria Agostini, harp; Composers String Quartet. Commissioned by and dedicated to Gloria Agostini. *See:* B311

W87 *Horn Trio.* Instrumentation: Horn, Violin and Piano. Duration: 10:30. Composed 12 March - 3 May 1981, in Iowa City (IA), Middle Valley (NJ), New York City, and Rock Island (IL). Peters P66897 (Score); P66897a (Set of Parts). Premiered 18 April 1983, Kaufmann Concert Hall, 92nd St. Y, New York City. Julie Landsman, horn; Benjamin Hudson, violin; Wuorinen, piano. Commissioned by and dedicated to Julie Landsman. *See:* B313

W87a 24-25 & 29 May 1988, Los Angeles. Southwest Chamber Music Ensemble.

W87b 19 September 1988, Los Angeles. Southwest Chamber Music Ensemble.

W87c 21 March 1990, Weill Recital Hall, New York City. William Purvis, horn; Benjamin Hudson, violin; Alan Feinberg, piano.

W88 *Horn Trio Continued.* Instrumentation: Horn, Violin and Piano. Duration: 9:30. Composed 8 April - 31 May 1985, in Hartford (CT), and Middle

Valley (NJ). Peters P67088 (Score); P67088a (Set of Parts). Premiered 24 May 1988, Los Angeles. Southwest Chamber Music Ensemble. Commissioned by Speculum Musicae. *See:* W87

W88a 25 & 29 May 1988, Los Angeles. Southwest Chamber Music Ensemble.

W88b 19 September 1988, Schoenberg Institute, University of Southern California, Los Angeles. Southwest Chamber Music Ensemble.

W88c 21 March 1990, Weill Recital Hall, New York City. William Purvis, horn; Benjamin Hudson, violin; Alan Feinberg, piano.

W89 *Joan's.* Instrumentation: Fl, Cl in a, Vn, Vc, Pf. Duration: 5:45. Composed 1-23 December 1979, in Middle Valley (NJ), and New York City. Peters P66828 (5 scores needed for performance). Premiered 23 March 1980, Alice Tully Hall, Lincoln Center for the Performing Arts, New York City. Da Capo Chamber Players: Patricia Spencer, flute; Laura Flax, clarinet; Joel Lester, violin; Andre Emilianoff, violoncello; Joan Tower, piano. Commissioned by the Da Capo Chamber Players in observance of their 10th anniversary. Dedicated to Joan Tower. *See:* D25, D61, B332 - B337, B891

W90 *The Long and the Short.* Instrumentation: Violin Solo. Duration: 9:00. Composed 11 January - 18 June 1969, in Gardner (MA), and New York City. Peters P66379. Premiered 4 August 1969, Berkeley, California. Paul Zukofsky, violin soloist. Composed for and dedicated to Paul Zukofsky. *See:* D12, D35, B338 - B343

W90a 17 October 1969, University of Texas at Austin, Austin, Texas. Paul Zukofsky, violin soloist.

W90b 3 December 1969, BBC Studios, London. Paul Zukofsky, violin soloist.
    Historical note: Zukofsky performed the work twice on that day; the other performance was at the U.S. Embassy in London.

W90c 15 December 1969, Oberlin College Conservatory of Music, Oberlin, Ohio. Paul Zukofsky, violin soloist.

W90d 5 May 1971, New England Conservatory, Boston. Paul Zukofsky, violin soloist.

W90e 11 March 1978, Francis Parker School Auditorium, Chicago. Benjamin Hudson, violin soloist. Chicago premiere. *See:* B341

W90f 24 October 1984, Terrace Theatre, Kennedy Center for the Performing Arts, Washington, D.C. Benjamin Hudson, violin soloist. The Kennedy Center's *American Composers* series.

W90g 2 February 1989, The Juilliard School, New York City. Mark Steinberg, violin soloist. A concert of The Juilliard School's *Contemporary Music Festival*.

W90h 5 December 1989, Settlement Music School, Philadelphia. Benjamin Hudson, violin soloist.

W91 *Movement for Wind Quintet*. Instrumentation: Fl, Ob, B♭ Cl, Hrn, Bsn. Duration: 3:40. Composed 1958. Merion Music/Theodore Presser, Plate Number 144-40008-7, New Music Edition. No known performance as a single work.

> **Historical note:** This work is actually the first movement of Wuorinen's *Wind Quintet No. 2*. It is possible that this movement had been performed prior to the premiere performance of the entire quintet. *See:* W128

W92 *Nature's Concord*. Instrumentation: Trumpet and Piano. Duration: 11:00. Composed 14 January - 20 August 1969, in New York City. Peters P66380 (2 scores needed for performance). Premiered 29 October 1969, in a studio of the Irish State Radio, Ireland. Ronald Anderson, trumpet; pianist unknown. Commissioned by and dedicated to Ronald Anderson. *See:* B392, B393, B891

W92a 11 November 1969, Studio für Neue Musik, Munich, Germany. Ronald Anderson, trumpet; pianist unknown. First concert performance.

W92b 26 April 1970, Kaufmann Art Gallery, 92nd St. Y, New York City. Ronald Anderson, trumpet; Robert Miller, piano. A *Music In Our Time* series concert. The work was performed three times.

W92c 23 June 1970, Dutch Radio Hilversum, Holland. Ronald Anderson, trumpet; pianist unknown.

W92d 27 June 1970, Cologne WDR, Germany. Ronald Anderson, trumpet; pianist unknown.

W92e 11 November 1970, State University of New York at Stony Brook, Stony Brook, Long Island, New York. Ronald Anderson, trumpet; Robert Miller, piano.

W92f 4 March 1982, University Theatre, New York University, New York City. Ronald Anderson, trumpet, Louis Karchin, piano. Concert titled *Wolpe and His Influence*; the event was a tribute to Stefan Wolpe and was a part of the *Washington Square Contemporary Music Series*. *See:* B393

W93 *New York Notes*. Instrumentation: Fl, Cl, Vn, Vc, P, Pf. Duration: 20:00. Composed 3 May 1981 - 6 February 1982, in Lubbock, Texas. Peters P66926*. Premiered 8 November 1982, California State University, Sacramento, California. New York New Music Ensemble; Robert Black, conductor. Commissioned by and dedicated to the New York New Music Ensemble. *See:* D38, B394 - B399

W93a 16 November 1982, Carnegie Recital Hall, New York City. New York New Music Ensemble; Robert Black, conductor. New York premiere.

W93b 21 June 1988, Alice Tully Hall, Lincoln Center for the Performing Arts, New York City. Chamber Music Society of Lincoln Center; Fred Sherry, conductor.

> **Historical note:** This performance incorporated the tape part of *Bamboula Squared*, which had been specially added for this performance and had been recalculated using a NeXT computer. A concert of the *New York International Festival of the Arts*.

W93c 19-20 April 1990, Guggenheim Museum, New York City. Group for Contemporary Music; Wuorinen, conductor.

> **Historical note:** This concert featured the addition of computer synthesized sound and was filmed for national television broadcast on PBS. It was the first of two concerts of the *Works In Process* series, and was also accompanied by a slide show of images generated by fractal geometry. The mathematician Benoit Mandelbrot, Wuorinen, and moderator Joan Peyser held a public discussion both before and after the performance. *See:* W93e, B395, B855, B856, B858

W93d 8 May 1990, Innova Design Center, Houston, Texas. Houston Symphony New Music Ensemble. An *Innova Concert*. *See:* B396

W93e 8 & 10 March 1991, Alice Tully Hall, Lincoln Center for the Performing Arts, New York City. Chamber Music Society of Lincoln Center; Wuorinen, conductor.

> **Historical note:** This concert featured *The Fractal Cosmos*, a visual retrospective for computer controlled slide projectors by mathematician Benoit Mandelbrot and Richard Voss, shown simultaneously with the performance of the music. *See:* W93c

W94 *Octet.* Instrumentation: Ob, Cl, Hrn, Trb, Vn, Vc, Cb, Pf. Duration: 13:40. Composed 7 November 1961 - 11 February 1962, in New York City. McGinnis & Marx (Score available for purchase; parts available on rental). Premiered 27 September 1962, Carnegie Recital Hall, New York City. New York Chamber Society: Henry Schuman, oboe; Saul Kurz, clarinet; Boris Rybka, horn; Arnold Fromm, trombone; Herbert Sorkin, violin; Joel Krosnick, violoncello; Claude Feldman, contrabass; Lalan Parrott, piano; Alvin Brehm, conductor. Composed for and dedicated to the Hartt Chamber Players. *See:* B400 - B403

W94a 30 January 1963, Smith College, Northampton, Massachusetts. Hartt Chamber Players; Edwin London, conductor.

W94b 22 February 1963, Carnegie Recital Hall, New York City. Hartt Chamber Players; Ralph Shapey, conductor.

W94c 8 February 1966, Carnegie Recital Hall, New York City. Contemporary Chamber Ensemble; Arthur Weisberg, conductor.

W94d 11 March 1966, Coolidge Auditorium, Library of Congress, Washington, D.C. Contemporary Chamber Ensemble; Arthur Weisberg, conductor. *See:* B402

W95 *Piano Trio*. Instrumentation: Violin, Violoncello and Piano. Duration: 10:15. Composed 28 May - 2 August 1983, in Middle Valley (NJ), New York City, and Rome, Italy. Peters P66977 (3 scores needed for performance). Premiered 1 October 1983 (preview performance), Kean College, Union, New Jersey. Arden Trio: Suzanne Ornstein, violin; Clay Ruede, violoncello; Thomas Schmidt, piano. Commissioned by the Arden Trio under a grant from Chamber Music America with support from the Mary Flagler Cary Charitable Trust and the Jerome Foundation. Dedicated to the Arden Trio.
    Historical note: Wuorinen believes there was a performance of this work at the Abbey of Fossanova, Pontino, Italy. *See:* B512 - B515

W95a 5 October 1983, Kaufmann Concert Hall, 92nd St. Y, New York City. Arden Trio: Suzanne Ornstein, violin; Clay Ruede, violoncello; Thomas Schmidt, piano.
    Historical note: The *New York Times* billed this concert as the official world premiere. *See:* B513

W95b 30 October 1983, John Wesley Powell Auditorium, Cosmos Club, Washington, D.C. Arden Trio: Suzanne Ornstein, violin; Clay Ruede, violoncello; Thomas Schmidt, piano. *See:* B514

W95c 2 December 1983, Wayne State University, Detroit, Michigan. Arden Trio: Suzanne Ornstein; violin; Clay Ruede, Violoncello; Thomas Schmidt, piano. A *Pro Musica* concert. *See:* B515

W95d 15 & 17 April 1988, Brooklyn Conservatory, Brooklyn, New York. Omni Ensemble.

W96 *6 Pieces for Violin and Piano*. Instrumentation: Violin and Piano. Duration: 15:30. Composed 2 April - 10 May 1977, in Middle Valley (NJ). Peters P66744. Premiered 18 April 1978, Town Hall, New York City. Max Pollikoff, violin; Wuorinen, piano. Dedicated to Max Pollikoff.
    Historical note: This composition was adapted from *Six Songs for Two Voices* as a present for Pollikoff. *See:* W181, D23, D35, D63, D74, B600 - B609

W96a 24 October 1984, Terrace Theatre, Kennedy Center for the Performing Arts, Washington, D.C. Benjamin Hudson, violin; Wuorinen, piano. A concert of the Kennedy Center's *American Composers* series.

W96b 30 October 1984, Mandel Hall, Chicago. Chicago Ensemble: Delmar Pettys, violin; Gerald Rizzer, piano. *See:* B607

W96c 30 April 1989, Great Barrington, Vermont. Katherine Hannauer, violin; Anne Chamberlain, piano.

W97 *Sonata for Flute and Piano.* Instrumentation: Flute and Piano. Duration: 15:26. Composed 5 January - 5 February, 1960, in New York City. American Composers Alliance/Composer Facsimile Edition. Premiered 17 November 1962, WNYC radio broadcast (New York City). Sophie Schulz, flute; Howard Rovics, piano. *See:* D67

W97a August 1960, Bennington Composers Conference (reading), Bennington, Vermont. Jean Kershaw, violin; Douglas Nordli, piano.

W97b 25 November 1962, Museum of the City of New York, New York City. Sophie Schulz, flute; Howard Rovics, piano.

W97c 9 February 1963, Henry Street Settlement Music School, New York City. Sophie Schulz, flute; Howard Rovics, piano.

W98 *Sonata for Violin and Piano.* Instrumentation: Violin and Piano. Duration: 20:00. Composed 1 January 1988 - 19 June 1988. Peters P67255. Premiered 25 November 1988, Coolidge Auditorium, Library of Congress, Washington, D.C. Benjamin Hudson, violin; Garrick Ohlsson, piano. Commissioned by the Library of Congress (McKim Fund) for and dedicated to Benjamin Hudson and Garrick Ohlsson.
       Historical note: This concert was subsequently broadcast on radio throughout the United States and in Europe. *See:* D37, D69, B611 - B614

W98a 12 October 1989, Guggenheim Museum, New York City. Benjamin Hudson, violin; James Wynn, piano. New York premiere.
       Historical note: At this concert Hudson played a blue-stained violin made by Christophe Landon; the instrument had a rooster's head carved in the wood scroll. *See:* B612

W98b 5 April 1990, Salmon Recital Hall, Chapman College, Orange, California. Peter Marsh, violin; Gloria Cheng, piano. A concert of the Southwest Chamber Music Society. West Coast premiere. *See:* B613, B614

W98c 6 April 1990, Wright Auditorium, Pasadena Public Library, Pasadena, California. Peter Marsh, violin; Gloria Cheng, piano.

W98d 8 April 1992, Graduate Center, City University of New York, New York City. David Wolfe, violin; Caroline Esposito, piano.

W98e 11 April 1992, 28 East 20th Street (Theodore Roosevelt birthplace). David Wolfe, violin; Caroline Esposito, piano.

W99 *Sonatina for Woodwind Quartet.* Instrumentation: Fl, Ob, Cl, Bsn. Duration: 6:58. Composed July 1956, in Gardner, Massachusetts. New Music Edition Corp., (American Music Center), New York City (published 4 March 1957). Premiered 15 August 1956, Bennington, Vermont (reading). Lois Schaeffer, flute; Robert Bloom, oboe; Wally Shapiro, clarinet; Morris Newman, bassoon.

W100 *Spectrum.* Instrumentation: Solo Violin, Brass Quintet (2 Trps, Hrn, Trb, Tba), and Piano. Duration: 9:35. Composed 17-26 March 1958, in New York City. Unpublished. Premiered 10 April 1958, Barkley Hotel, Philadelphia. Max Pollikoff, violin soloist; University Brass Ensemble; Douglas Nordli, piano. A *Music In Our Time* series concert.

> **Historical note:** This work originally had a duration of 11:35; Wuorinen cut it down to 9:35.

W101 *Speculum Speculi.* Instrumentation: Fl, Ob, Bcl, Cb, P(1), Pf. Duration: 14:35. Composed 8 August - 15 October 1972, in Lenox (MA), Middle Valley (NJ), and New York City. Peters P66534 (Score); P66534a (Set of Parts). Premiered 14 January 1973, Chester Fritz Auditorium, University of North Dakota, Grand Forks, North Dakota. Speculum Musicae; Fred Sherry, conductor. Commissioned by the Walter W. Naumberg Foundation for Speculum Musicae. *See:* D15, B616 - B629, B891

W101a 21 February 1973, Carnegie Recital Hall, New York City. Speculum Musicae. New York premiere. *See:* B617

W101b 19 December 1985, St. John's, Smith Square, London. Lontano Ensemble. A concert of *The Americas* series presented by Odaline de la Martinez and the Lontano Ensemble. *See:* B629

W101c 8 January 1991, Merkin Concert Hall, Abraham Goodman House, New York City. Parnassus; Anthony Korf, conductor.

W102 *Spinoff.* Instrumentation: Violin, Contrabass and Congas. Duration: 6:10. Composed 8 March - 13 April 1983. Peters P66970 (3 scores needed for performance). Premiered 18 May 1983, Symphony Space, New York City. Speculum Musicae: Benjamin Hudson, violin; Donald Palma, contrabass; Joseph Passaro, congas. Composed for Speculum Musicae. Dedicated to Benjamin Hudson. *See:* D32, D35, B630 - B634

W102a 2 & 12 February 1988, Eastman School of Music, University of Rochester, Rochester, New York. Vanguard Ensemble.

W102b 20 September 1988, Arnold Schoenberg Institute, University of Southern California, Los Angeles. B. Socher, violin; Dennis Trembly, contrabass; R. Carroll, congas.

W102c 3 December 1989, Sanders Theatre, Harvard University, Cambridge, Massachusetts. Speculum Musicae: Benjamin Hudson, violin; Donald Palma, contrabass; Joseph Passaro, congas.

W103 *String Quartet.* Instrumentation: String quartet. Duration: 17:13. Composed February - April 1957. Unpublished. Premiered August 1957, Bennington Composers Conference; Henry Brant conductor.

W104 *String Quartet No. 1.* Instrumentation: String Quartet. Duration: 21:45. Composed 6 August 1970 - 21 January 1971, in Iowa City (IA), Lenox (MA), Los Angeles, New York City and Palo Alto (CA). Peters P66395 (4 scores needed for performance). Premiered 11 October 1971, Goodman Theater, Chicago. Fine Arts Quartet. Commissioned by Mr. & Mrs. Lee A. Freeman for the Fine Arts Musical Foundation of Chicago. Dedicated to the Fine Arts Quartet. *See:* D11, D41, B635 - B641, B891

W104a 12 May 1975, Hunter College of the City University of New York, New York City. Speculum Musicae: Rolf Schulte, Daniel Reed, violins; Daniel Phillips, viola; Fred Sherry, violoncello. *See:* B640

W105 *String Quartet No. 2.* Instrumentation: String Quartet. Duration: 19:00. Composed 31 December 1978 - 20 May 1979, in Buffalo (NY), Cologne (Germany), Helsinki, London, Middle Valley (NJ), and New York City. Peters P66808 (4 scores needed for performance). Premiered 1 August 1979, *Grand Teton Music Festival* stage, Jackson, Wyoming. A concert of the *Music In the Present Tense* series. Columbia String Quartet: Benjamin Hudson, Carol Zeavin, violins; Janet Lyman Hill, viola; André Emelianoff, violoncello. *See:* B642 - B646

W105a 8 March 1980, Valencia, California. *CalArts* annual contemporary music festival. West coast premiere. *See:* B644

W105b 10 April 1980, Lepercq Space, Brooklyn Academy of Music. A concert of the *Meet the Moderns* series. New York premiere. *See:* B645

W105c 21 April 1991, Ethical Culture Society, New York City. Group for Contemporary Music: Benjamin Hudson, Carol Zeavin, violins; Lois Martin, viola; Joshua Gordon, violoncello. *See:* B646

W106 *String Quartet No. 3.* Instrumentation: String Quartet. Duration: 25:32. Composed 24 October - 15 January, 1987, in Pittsburgh and New York City. Peters P67199 (Score); P67199a (Set of Parts). Premiered 6 November 1987, Hopkins Center, Dartmouth College, Hanover, New Hampshire. Franciscan String Quartet. Commissioned by Dartmouth College for the 25th anniversary of the Hopkins Center. *See:* D37, D39, B647, B648, B649

W106a 5 January 1988, Merkin Concert Hall, Abraham Goodman House, New York City. Columbia String Quartet: Benjamin Hudson, Carol Zeavin, violins; Lois Martin, viola; Fred Sherry, violoncello. A Group for Contemporary Music concert. *See:* B647

W106b 25 November 1988, Library of Congress, Washington, D.C. Benjamin Hudson, Carol Zeavin, violins; Lois Martin, viola; Fred Sherry, violoncello.
   Historical note: This concert was subsequently broadcast on radio throughout the United States and in Europe. *See:* B649

W106c 7 April 1989, Pasadena, California. Southwest Chamber Music Society. West coast premiere.

W106d 9 April 1989, Los Angeles. Southwest Chamber Music Society.

W106e 23 April 1989, Rutgers University, New Brunswick, New Jersey. Benjamin Hudson, Carol Zeavin, violins; Lois Martin, viola; Fred Sherry, violoncello. A Group for Contemporary Music concert.

W107 *String Sextet.* Instrumentation: 2 Vns, 2 Vas, 2 Vcs. Duration: 18:00. Composed 3 August 1988 - 20 April 1989. Peters P67306 (Score); P67306a (Set of Parts). Premiered 4 November 1989, Oliver Swan Porter Memorial Auditorium, Covington, Georgia. Chamber Music Society of Lincoln Center: Ani Kavafian, Ida Kavafian, violins; Paul Neubauer, Walter Trampler, violas; Fred Sherry, Leslie Parnas, violoncellos. A concert of the Concert Association of Newton County. Dedicated to Fred Sherry. *See:* B650 - B654

W107a 5 November 1989, Annie Russe Theater, Rollins College, Winter Park, Florida. Chamber Music Society of Lincoln Center: Ani Kavafian, Ida Kavafian, violins; Paul Neubauer, Walter Trampler, violas; Fred Sherry, Leslie Parnas, violoncellos. A concert of the Bach Society of Winter Park.

W107b 7 November 1989, Pabst Theatre, Milwaukee. Chamber Music Society of Lincoln Center: Ani Kavafian, Ida Kavafian, violins; Paul Neubauer, Walter Trampler, violas; Fred Sherry, Leslie Parnas, violoncellos.

W107c 9 November 1989, Clemson University, Clemson, South Carolina. Chamber Music Society of Lincoln Center: Ani Kavafian, Ida Kavafian, violins; Paul Neubauer, Walter Trampler, violas; Fred Sherry, Leslie Parnas, violoncellos.

W107d 10 November 1989, Langford Auditorium, Vanderbilt University, Nashville, Tennessee. Chamber Music Society of Lincoln Center: Ani Kavafian, Ida Kavafian, violins; Paul Neubauer, Walter Trampler, violas; Fred Sherry, Leslie Parnas, violoncellos.

W107e 11 November 1989, Ossining High School, Ossining, New York. Chamber Music Society of Lincoln Center: Ani Kavafian, Ida Kavafian, violins; Paul Neubauer, Walter Trampler, violas; Fred Sherry, Leslie Parnas, violoncellos.

W107f 12 November 1989, Folly Theater, Kansas City, Missouri. Chamber Music Society of Lincoln Center: Ani Kavafian, Ida Kavafian, violins; Paul Neubauer, Walter Trampler, violas; Fred Sherry, Leslie Parnas, violoncellos.

W107g   17-19 November 1989, Alice Tully Hall, Lincoln Center for the Performing Arts, New York City. Chamber Music Society of Lincoln Center: Ani Kavafian, Ida Kavafian, violins; Paul Neubauer, Walter Trampler, violas; Fred Sherry, Leslie Parnas, violoncellos. New York premiere performances.

> **Historical note:** The seven performances that preceded these New York premiere performances were considered preview performances. *See:* B651, B652

W107h   1 October 1992, Merkin Concert Hall, Abraham Goodman House, New York City. Speculum Musicae: Curtis Macomber, Carol Zeavin, violins; Sarah Adams, Lois Martin, violas; Eric Bartlett, Christopher Finckel, violoncellos. *See:* B653, B654

W108   *String Trio.* Instrumentation: Violin, Viola, and Violoncello. Duration: 15:00. Composed 27 September - 19 November, 1967, and 26 January 1968. Peters PP66382 (Score); P66382a (Set of Parts). Premiered 27 October 1968, National Gallery of Art, Washington, D.C. Potomac String Trio: Judith Shapiro, violin; Melissa Graybeal; viola; Thea Cooper, violoncello. Commissioned by and dedicated to the Potomac String Trio. *See:* D16, B655 - B664, B857, B891

W108a   3 April 1969, Greenwich House Music School, New York City. Potomac String Trio: Judith Shapiro, violin; Melissa Graybeal, viola; Thea Cooper, violoncello. New York premiere.

W108b   8 March 1971, New York Shakespeare Theatre, New York City. Speculum Musicae: Rolf Schulte, violin; Jeanne Graham, viola; Fred Sherry, violoncello. *See:* B656

W108c   27 April 1974, Carnegie Recital Hall, New York City. Speculum Musicae: Rolf Schulte, violin; Jeanne Graham, viola; Fred Sherry, violoncello. *See:* B658, B659

W108d   4 February 1985, Guggenheim Museum, New York City. Tashi: Ida Kavafian, violin; Ik Hwan, viola; Fred Sherry, violoncello. Choreography: Jean-Pierre Bonnefoux. Dancers: Roy Kaiser, Melissa Podcasy and Jeffrey Gribler (Pennsylvania Ballet).

> **Historical note:** This performance was the premiere of the work done as a ballet.
> *See:* B663

W109   *Subversion.* Instrumentation: String Septet (String Orchestra optional). Duration: 8:46. Composed August - September 1956, in Gardner (MA), and New York City. American Composers Alliance/Composer Facsimile Edition. Premiered August 1957, Bennington Composers Conference, Bennington, Vermont. Henry Brant, conductor.

W110   *Tashi.* Instrumentation: Clarinet, Violin, Violoncello, Piano (Chamber Version for 4 Instruments). Duration: 30:20. Composed 10 January 1975 and 8 April - 16 August 1975 in Middle Valley (NJ). Peters P66665.

Premiered 15 January 1976, Colorado State College, Colorado Springs, Colorado. Tashi: Richard Stoltzman, clarinet; Ida Kavafian, violin; Fred Sherry, violoncello; Peter Serkin, piano. Dedicated to Tashi.
Historical note: This version was composed first; the orchestral version came later. *See:* B688 - B691

W110a   18 January 1976, Walnut, California. Tashi: Richard Stoltzman, clarinet; Ida Kavafian, violin; Fred Sherry, violoncello; Peter Serkin, piano. West coast premiere.

W110b   18 February 1976, Kaufmann Concert Hall, 92nd Street Y, New York City.   Tashi: Richard Stoltzman, clarinet; Ida Kavafian, violin; Fred Sherry, violoncello; Peter Serkin, piano. New York premiere.
Historical note: The *New York Times* erroneously reported that this concert was the world premiere. *See:* B688, B689, B690

W111   *Three Cadenzas for the Mozart Concerto in C Major for Oboe and Piano.* Instrumentation: Solo Oboe. McGinnis & Marx.

W112   *3 Mass Movements.* Instrumentation: Solo Violin. Duration: 10:13. Composed July 1957, in New York City. Unpublished. Premiered 28 July 1957, East Hampton, New York. Max Pollikoff, violin soloist. A concert of the *Music In Our Time* series. Composed for Max Pollikoff.

W112a   11 August 1957, Bennington Composers Conference, Bennington, Vermont. Max Pollikoff, violin soloist.

W113   *Three Pieces for String Quartet.* Instrumentation: String Quartet. Duration: 1:42. Composed 3 August 1958. Unpublished. Premiered 9 August 1958, Bennington Composers Conference, Bennington, Vermont. Performed by amateur musicians at the conference.

W114   *Tiento Sobre Cabézón.* Instrumentation: Fl, Ob, Vn, Va, Vc, Harpsichord, Pf. Duration: 3:34. Composed 21-25 June 1961, in New York City. Peters P67336*. Premiered 2 August 1961, School of Sacred Music, Union Theological Seminary, New York City.   John Wion, flute; Josef Marx, oboe; Paul Wolfe, violin; George Grossman, viola; Joan Brockway, violoncello; Leonard Raver, harpsichord; Robert Stigall, piano; Thomas Dunn, conductor.
Historical note: Wuorinen's *Register of Works* notebook contains the following note about this piece: "*Tiento Sobre Cabézón*, being a transcription of Antonio de Cabézón's *Tiento del Primer Tono*, from the *Obras de musica para Tecla, Arpa, y Vihuela* (1578). Cabézón - 1510-66. Original medium: organ." *See:* B696, B697

W115   *Trio Concertante.* Instrumentation: Oboe, Violin, and Piano. Duration: 12:04. Composed 12-24 September and 2-10 October 1958. American Composers Alliance/Composer Facsimile Edition. Premiered 31 October 1958, Sloan Hall, Emma Willard School, Troy, New York. Robert Bloom, oboe; Max Pollikoff, violin; and Douglas Nordli, piano. Composed for Max Pollikoff.

W115a 9 December 1958, New York City. Mel Kaplan, oboe; Max Pollikoff, violin; Douglas Nordli, piano. Max Pollikoff's chamber music readings.

W115b 5 April 1959, University of Massachusetts at Amherst. Mel Kaplan, oboe; Max Pollikoff, violin; Douglas Nordli, piano. A concert of the *Music In Our Time* series.

W116 *Trio for Bass Instruments.* Instrumentation: Bass Trombone, Tuba and Contrabass. Duration: 8:30. Composed 3 October - 13 November 1981, in Corpus Christi (TX), Oulu (Finland), and Tampere (Finland). Peters P66917 (3 scores needed for performance). Premiered 14 April 1983, Carnegie Recital Hall, New York City. New Music Consort. Commissioned by and dedicated to David Brainard.
   Historical note: There were originally two versions of this work. Wuorinen combined them into one version, the only version that now exists. *See:* D66, B761 - B764

W116a 8 May 1990, Innova Design Center, Houston, Texas. Houston Symphony New Music Ensemble: David Waters, bass trombone; David Kirk, tuba; Mark Shapiro, double-bass. An *Innova Concert. See:* B763

W117 *Trio for Violin, Cello and Piano.* Instrumentation: Violin, Cello, Piano. Duration: 10:15. Composed 28 May - 2 August 1983. Unpublished. Premiered 1 October 1983, Kean College, Union, New Jersey. Arden Trio. Commissioned by the Arden Trio and Chamber Music America.

W118 *Trio [No. 1 for Flute, Cello and Piano].* Instrumentation: Flute, Violoncello, Piano. Duration: 4:16. Composed 2-5 December 1961, in New York City. McGinnis & Marx. Premiered 14 December 1961, Barnard College, New York City. Harvey Sollberger, flute; Joel Krosnick, violoncello; Wuorinen, piano; Charles Whittenberg, conductor. A *Columbia Composers Concert.*
   Historical note: This work is an improvised piece. The following note by Wuorinen appears on the score: "In this work, each performer moves (on signal) through a series of sections marked by letters. While he is in any one section, he may play the fragments there in any order. The 'conductor's' part involves only a general control of the ensemble, except at the very end, where traditional ensemble must be briefly observed. Finally, he is cautioned against prolonging any section, as improvisation quickly becomes a bore." *See:* W118c, W119, B748

W118a 22 February 1962, Greenwich House Music School. Harvey Sollberger, flute; Joel Krosnick, violoncello; Wuorinen, piano. A concert of the *WNYC American Music Festival* (broadcast on WNYC radio).

W118b 15 May 1962, McMillin Theatre, Columbia University, New York City. Harvey Sollberger, flute; Joel Krosnick, violoncello; Wuorinen, piano. A recital of new flute music arranged by Harvey Sollberger.

W118c   18 December 1962, Carnegie Recital Hall, New York City.   Harvey Sollberger, flute; Joel Krosnick, violoncello; Wuorinen, piano.   Concert titled *A Musical Offering for Stefan Wolpe.*

> **Historical note:** For this concert Wuorinen changed the title of the trio to *Piece for Stefan Wolpe.* In his *Register of Works* notebook, Wuorinen lists this as the sixth performance of this work. His *Trio No. 2*, however, is subtitled *Piece for Stefan Wolpe.* Wuorinen was unsure which trio was performed at this concert.   Given the dates of composition of the second trio it is possible that the first trio was substituted at this concert but billed as the second trio.   It is also possible that the second trio was performed and that Wuorinen listed the dates of composition of that work (through 26 December 1962) as such because he made changes to the work after this performance. A concert review published in *Aufbau*, however, refers to the title *Trio*, not *Trio No. 2* or *Second Trio*. *See:* W119, B748

W119   *Trio No. 2 for Flute, Cello and Piano.* Instrumentation: Flute, Violoncello and Piano. Duration 8:30. Composed 27 November - 26 December 1962, in New York City.   Peters P66381 (3 scores needed for performance). Premiered 6 May 1963, McMillin Theatre, Columbia University, New York City. Harvey Sollberger, flute; Joel Krosnick, violoncello; Wuorinen, piano.   One of three *Ditson Concerts* titled *Three Evenings of Music and Dance.* Composed in observance of Stefan Wolpe's sixtieth anniversary; subtitled *Piece for Stefan Wolpe.* Dedicated to Stefan Wolpe, Joel Krosnick and Harvey Sollberger. *See:* W118, W118c, B748 - B759

W119a   17 May 1963, C.W. Post College, Long Island, New York.   Harvey Sollberger, flute; Joel Krosnick, violoncello; Wuorinen, piano.

W119b   28 July 1963, North Rehearsal Hall, University of Iowa, Iowa City, Iowa.   Harvey Sollberger, flute; Joel Krosnick, violoncello; Wuorinen, piano.

W119c   21 May 1963, Carnegie Recital Hall, New York City.   Harvey Sollberger, flute; Joel Krosnick, violoncello; Wuorinen, piano.   Concert titled *New Solo and Chamber Works.* *See:* B751, B753

W119d   6 August 1963, University of Rhode Island, Kingston, Rhode Island. Harvey Sollberger, flute; Joel Krosnick, violoncello; Wuorinen, piano.

W119e   17 August 1963, Carriage Barn, Bennington College, Bennington, Vermont. Bennington Composers Conference. Harvey Sollberger, flute; Joel Krosnick, violoncello; Wuorinen, piano. *See:* B754

W119f   13 March 1964, New School for Social Research, New York City. Harvey Sollberger, flute; Robert Martin, violoncello; Wuorinen, piano. *See:* B755

W119g   17 February 1967, Music Hall, University of Colorado, Boulder, Colorado.   Joan Smith, flute; James Stroud, violoncello; David Burge, piano.   This concert was an event of the second *Festival of Contemporary Music* at the University of Colorado. *See:* B756

W119h 16 March 1968, Hellenic American Union, Athens, Greece. Performers unknown.

W119i 16 October 1970, Carnegie Recital Hall, New York City. Patricia Spencer, flute; Helen Harbison, violoncello; Joan Tower, piano.

W119j 30 August 1991, Bennett Hall, Chicago *(Ravinia Festival)*. New Music Consort: Judith Pearce, flute; Madeline Shapiro, violoncello; Martin Goldray, piano.
Historical note: During this concert Shapiro's E-string broke and briefly halted the performance of the trio. *See:* B759

W120 *Trio No. 3 for Flute, Cello and Piano*. Instrumentation: Flute, Violoncello and Piano. Duration: 16:30. Composed 20 May 1972 - 3 January 1973, in Glens Falls (NY), Lenox (MA), New York City, and Rochester, New York. Peters P66578 (3 scores needed for performance). Premiered 28 March 1973, New York Cultural Center, New York City. Harvey Sollberger, flute; Fred Sherry, violoncello; Wuorinen, piano. Commissioned by and dedicated to Stephen Fisher. *See:* B760

W121 *Triptych*. Instrumentation: Violin, Viola and Percussion(2). Duration: 12:04. Composed 1-8 November 1957. American Composers Alliance/Composer Facsimile Edition. Premiered 19 January 1958, Kaufmann Concert Hall, 92nd St. Y, New York City. The inaugural concert of the *Music In Our Time* series. Max Pollikoff, violin; Walter Trampler, viola; Mo Goldenberg, percussion; William Goldenberg, piano.
Historical note: This work was composed specifically for the inaugural concert of Pollikoff's concert series. The percussionist on piano uses mallets on the piano strings. *See:* B765, B766

W121a August 1958, Bennington Composers Conference, Bennington, Vermont.
Historical note: This performance was actually a reading and was recorded; the recording was never commercially released. As far as Wuorinen knows, the recording no longer exists.

W121b 22 April 1961, Donnell Library Auditorium (New York Public Library), New York City. Max Pollikoff, violin; Ralph Hersch, viola; Larry Jacobs, percussion; Douglas Nordli, (inside) piano. *See:* B766

W122 *Trombone Trio*. Instrumentation: Tenor Trombone, Mallet Instruments and Piano. Duration: 8:00. Composed 1 June - 22 July 1985. Peters P67149 (Score); P67149a (Set of Parts). Premiered 6 November 1986, Merkin Concert Hall, Abraham Goodman House, New York City. Parnassus: Ronald Borror, trombone; James Preiss, percussion; Edmund Niemann, piano.

W122a 12 July 1988, Rutgers Summerfest, New Brunswick, New Jersey. 20th Century Music Group.

W123   *Turetzky Pieces.* Instrumentation: Flute, Clarinet and Contrabass. Duration: 12:50. Composed 18-27 May 1960, in New York City. Peters P67365. Premiered 7 August 1960, Westbrook, Connecticut. *Westbrook Chamber Music Festival.* Stanley Aronson, flute; Henry Larsen, clarinet; Bertram Turetzky, contrabass. Composed for and dedicated to Bertram Turetzky. *See:* B767 - B771

W123a 14 August 1960, Guilford, Connecticut. Stanley Aronson, flute; Henry Larsen, clarinet; Bertram Turetzky, contrabass. An *Olsen Foundation Concert.*

W123b 7 October 1960, Living Theater, New York City. Stanley Aronson, flute; Henry Larsen, clarinet; Bertram Turetzky, contrabass. New York premiere. *See:* B767, B768

W123c 16 April 1961, Jessup Gallery (Westport Public Library), Westport, Connecticut. Stanley Aronson, flute; Henry Larsen, clarinet; Bertram Turetzky, contrabass. A Hartt Chamber Players concert.

W123d 10 July 1961, Hartford, Connecticut. Stanley Aronson, flute; Henry Larsen, clarinet; Bertram Turetzky, contrabass. *University of Hartford Summer Concert.* Hartford premiere.

W123e 28 March 1965, both Hofstra University and C.W. Post College, Long Island, New York. Nancy Turetzky, flute; Henry Larsen, clarinet; Bertram Turetzky, contrabass.
     Historical note: There were two performances, one at each academic institution.

W123f 31 May 1972, University of California at Davis, Davis, California. Nancy Turetzky, flute; Jerome Rosen, clarinet; Bertram Turetzky, double bass. *See:* B769

W124   *Variations à 2.* Instrumentation: Flute and Piano. Duration: 11:03. Composed 20 September 1963 - 17 January 1964. McGinnis & Marx. Never performed. Dedicated to Harvey Sollberger.
     Historical note: Wuorinen originally subtitled this work *A Book of Interpolations: Composition C*, but dropped the subtitle when he decided *A Book of Interpolations: Composition A (Piano Variations)* and *A Book of Interpolations: Composition B (Flute Variations I)* were each independent works. It is also the last work Wuorinen copied himself on a regular basis. *See:* W82, W138

W125   *Violin Variations.* Instrumentation: Solo Violin. Duration: 11:00. Composed 26 February - 20 April 1972. Peters P66510. Premiered 14 May 1972, Kaufmann Concert Hall, 92nd St. Y, New York City. Max Pollikoff, violin soloist. A concert of the *Music In Our Time* series. Commissioned by Max Pollikoff, with funds from Ellen Loeb. *See:* B794 - B797

W125a 7 December 1977, Carnegie Recital Hall, New York City. Linda Quan, violin soloist. A New Music Consort concert. *See:* B795

W125b 11 March 1978, Francis Parker School Auditorium, Chicago. Benjamin Hudson, violin soloist. Chicago premiere. *See:* B796

W125c 18 April 1980, Great Hall, Cooper Union, New York City. Benjamin Hudson, violin soloist.

W125d 18 February 1981, Louisiana State University, Baton Rouge, Louisiana. Benjamin Hudson, violin soloist. A concert of the 36th annual *LSU Festival of Contemporary Music*. *See:* B797

W125e 24 October 1984, Terrace Theatre, Kennedy Center for the Performing Arts, Washington, D.C. Benjamin Hudson, violin solist. A concert of the Kennedy Center's *American Composers* series.

W125f 12 July 1988, Rutgers Summerfest, Rutgers University, New Brunswick, New Jersey. Todd Reynolds, violin soloist.

W125g 7 November 1988, St. Ignatius of Antioch Episcopal Church, New York City. Todd Reynolds, violin soloist. Concert titled *ZACCHO presents An Evening of Contemporary Choral Music In Celebration of Charles Wuorinen's 50th Birthday.*

W126 *Wind Quintet.* Instrumentation: Fl, Ob, Cl, Bsn, Hrn. Duration: 15:00. Composed 11 May - 10 September 1977 in Middle Valley (NJ), and New York City. Peters P66784. Premiered 24 February 1978, Great Hall, Cooper Union, New York City. Boehm Quintette: Laura Conwesser, flute; Phyllis Bohl, oboe; Don Stewart, clarinet; Joseph Anderer, horn; Matthew Shubin, bassoon. Commissioned by and dedicated to the Boehm Quintette. *See:* B810 - B814

W126a 18 June 1980, Cleveland Museum of Art, Cleveland, Ohio. Boehm Quintette: Laura Conwesser, flute; Phyllis Bohl, oboe; Don Stewart, clarinet; Joseph Anderer, horn; Matthew Shubin, bassoon. *See:* B812, B813

W126b 7 July 1980, Amphitheater, Chautauqua, New York. Boehm Quintette: Laura Conwesser, flute; Phyllis Bohl, oboe; Don Stewart, clarinet; Joseph Anderer, horn; Matthew Shubin, bassoon. *See:* B814

W127 *Wind Quintet No. 1.* Instrumentation: Fl, Ob, Cl, Bsn, Hrn. Duration: 9:13. Composed September - October 1956. Unpublished. Premiered 16 January 1957, New York City(?) Performers unknown.

W127a August 1957, Bennington Composers Conference, Bennington, Vermont. Roger Goeb, conductor.

W128 *Wind Quintet No. 2.* Instrumentation: Fl, Ob, Cl, Bsn, Hrn. Duration: 6:25. Composed 1-9 February 1958. Unpublished. Premiered 11 February 1958, Barnard Parlor, Barnard College, New York City. Roger Goeb, conductor. Written for Max Pollikoff's chamber music readings.

> **Historical note:** This concert was a reading, not a public performance. Wuorinen's *Movement for Wind Quintet,* although considered by Wuorinen to be a separate work, is the first movement of this composition. *See:* W91

W128a August 1958, Bennington Composers Conference, Bennington, Vermont. New Art Woodwind Quintet.

> **Historical note:** This concert was a reading, not a public performance.

PIANO

W129 *Album Leaf.* Instrumentation: Piano Solo. Duration: 1:33. Composed 21-24 May 1984, in New York City. Unpublished. Premiered 30 May 1984, Waldorf Astoria Hotel, New York City. Wuorinen, piano. Dedicated to Howard Klein.

> **Historical note:** This event was part of an Arts & Business Council luncheon held in honor of Howard Klein, as a gesture of thanks for his philanthropic support of the arts while he was at the Rockefeller Foundation. Wuorinen presented the original manuscript to Klein. *See:* B5

W130 *Bagatelle.* Instrumentation: Piano Solo. Duration: 7:45. Composed 8 December 1987 - 5 January 1988, in New York City. Peters P67232. Premiered 12 June 1989, Albright-Knox Gallery, Buffalo, New York. Elissa Stutz, piano. Commissioned by and dedicated to Elissa Stutz. *See:* B19 - B21

W130a 6 May 1989, Old First Church, San Francisco. Wuorinen, piano.

> **Historical note:** This event was the final concert with Wuorinen as the advisor to the *New and Unusual Music Series.* The concert was broadcast live on radio station KPFA. *See:* B19

W130b 3 November 1989, Merkin Concert Hall, Abraham Goodman House, New York City. Elissa Stutz, piano. New York premiere.

W130c 8 May 1990, Innova Design Center, Houston, Texas. Houston Symphony New Music Ensemble; Wuorinen, piano. An *Innova Concert. See:* B20

W131 *The Blue Bamboula.* Instrumentation: Piano Solo. Duration: 10:40. Composed 10 September - 16 December 1980, in Bonn (Germany), Middle Valley (NJ), New York City, and Washington, D.C. Peters P66532. Premiered 29 May 1981, in Tokyo. Ursula Oppens, piano. Commissioned by and dedicated to Ursula Oppens. *See:* D35, D39, D68, B58 - B62

W131a 6 January 1983, Kaufmann Concert Hall, 92nd St. Y, New York City. Ursula Oppens, piano. *See:* B58

W131b 1 December 1986, Town Hall, New York City. Ursula Oppens, piano. *See:* B60

W131c 24 April 1988, Armor Hall, Wave Hill, New York. Martin Goldray, piano. A New Music Consort concert.

W131d 12 July 1988, Rutgers University, New Brunswick, New Jersey. Jacob Smullyan, piano. Rutgers Summerfest.

W131e 3 November 1988, Merkin Concert Hall, Abraham Goodman House, New York City. Elissa Stutz, piano.

W131f 4 June 1989, Baird Recital Hall, Buffalo, New York. Martin Goldray, piano.

W131g 18 January 1990, Princeton University, Princeton, New Jersey. Garrick Ohlsson, piano.

W131h 3 March 1991, Theatre des Champs-Elysees, Paris. Ursula Oppens, piano.

W132 *Capriccio.* Instrumentation: Piano Solo. Duration: 12:40. Composed 29 December 1980 - 2 March 1981, in Baton Rouge, (LA), Iowa City (IA), Los Angeles, and New York City. Peters P66428. Premiered 14 April 1982, Symphony Space, New York City. Alan Feinberg, piano. Commissioned by and dedicated to Robert Miller.
   Historical note: Robert Miller commissioned this work to celebrate his 50th birthday concert. He died before he could perform it. The *New York Times* stated the work was the last that Miller commissioned from any composer. *See:* B67, B68

W132a 12 April 1985, Northwest Church, Fresno, California. Alan Feinberg, piano. A concert of the *Keyboard Concerts 85* series. *See:* B68

W132b 12 July 1988, Rutgers University, New Brunswick, New Jersey. Alan Feinberg, piano. Rutgers Summerfest.

W133 *Josquin: Ave Christe.* Instrumentation: Piano Solo. Duration 5:00. Composed 10-22 January 1988. Peters P67253. Premiered 16 February 1988 at a private performance in New York City. Dedicated to Stephen Fisher.
   Historical note: Fisher was given the original manuscript at this private, premiere performance. This work is a transcription for piano of a motet by Josquin des Prez.

W134 *Making Ends Meet.* Instrumentation: Piano 4 Hands. Duration: 14:53. Composed 24 June - 21 September 1966, in Gardner (MA), Lenox (MA), and New York City. Peters P66372. Premiered 19 May 1968, East Garden Court, National Gallery of Art, Washington, D.C. Jean and Kenneth Wentworth, pianists. Composed for and dedicated to Jean and Kenneth Wentworth. *See:* D18, B359 - B370, B891

W134a 5 February 1969, Brussels, Belgium. Jean and Kenneth Wentworth, pianists.
> **Historical note:** This performance was broadcast on Brussels Radio.

W134b 14 February 1969, Purcell Room, London. Jean and Kenneth Wentworth, pianists.

W134c 13 April 1969, Carnegie Recital Hall, New York City. Robert Miller and Wuorinen, pianists. New York premiere. *See:* B361

W134d 21 May 1969, Jordan Hall, New England Conservatory, Boston. Robert Miller and Wuorinen, pianists.

W134e 30 October 1969, Alice Tully Hall, Lincoln Center for the Performing Arts, New York City. Jean and Kenneth Wentworth, pianists. *See:* B362 - B365

W134f 2 February 1970, Sandors Music Studio, Liverpool, England. Jean and Kenneth Wentworth, pianists.

W134g 19 November 1970, Alice Tully Hall, Lincoln Center for the Performing Arts, New York City. Jean and Kenneth Wentworth, pianists. *See:* B366, B367

W135 *Piano Sonata No. 1.* Instrumentation: Piano Solo. Duration: 20:00. Composed 1 July - 13 December 1969, in Gardner (MA), Iowa City (IA), and New York City. Peters P66371. Premiered 14 December 1970, Kay Spiritual Life Center, Washington, D.C. Alan Mandel, piano. Dedicated to Robert Miller.
> **Historical note:** The above title is the one used by C.F. Peters in their catalog. Wuorinen titled the work *Piano Sonata.* This work is different and distinct from Wuorinen's *Sonata for Piano* (1958). *See:* D14, B495 - B506, B891

W135a 23 December 1970, New York Cultural Center, New York City. Robert Miller, piano. New York premiere. *See:* B497

W135b 2 February 1971, Munich. Ursula Oppens, piano. European premiere.

W135c 5 February 1971, West Berlin. Ursula Oppens, piano.

W135d 10 February 1971, London. Ursula Oppens, piano.

W135e 1 March 1971, Grace Rainey Rogers Auditorium, Metropolitan Museum of Art, New York City. Ursula Oppens, piano.

W135f 3 May 1971, National Theatre, Brasilia, Brazil. Thomas MacIntosh, piano. Latin American premiere.

W135g 18 July 1972, Greenwich Mews Theater, New York City. Ursula Oppens, piano. A concert of the *Hear America First* series. *See:* B498, B499

W136 *Piano Sonata No. 2.* Instrumentation: Piano Solo. Duration: 28:00. Composed 11 January - 13 April 1976, in New York City. Peters P66668. Premiered 2 October 1976, Kennedy Center for the Performing Arts, Washington, D.C. Jeffrey Swann, piano. Commissioned by Jeffrey Swan on a grant from the Edyth Bush Charitable Foundation, Inc., for the *Bicentennial Piano Series* of the Washington Performing Arts Society. Dedicated to the memory of Edyth Bush.

    Historical note: The above title is the one used by C.F. Peters in their catalog. Wuorinen titled the work *Second Sonata/for piano/that is/A Triple Discourse Containing/A Prelude/Three Movements Intermixed/a pause;/The Same Resumed; and/the Whole Completed/with/A Postlude.* *See:* B507, B834, B839

W137 *Piano Sonata No. 3.* Instrumentation: Piano Solo. Duration: 21:00. Composed 3 June - 21 October 1986. Peters P67167. Premiered 29 March 1989, Town Hall, New York City. Alan Feinberg, piano. Composed under a National Endowment for the Arts Consortium Commission for Alan Feinberg (with Ursula Oppens, Robert Shannon). Dedicated to Alan Feinberg.

    Historical note: The above title is the one used by C.F. Peters in their catalog. Wuorinen titled the work *Third Piano Sonata.* An earlier performance may have been given in Honolulu but not billed as the world premiere. A London performance scheduled for 27 November 1987 (Alan Feinberg performing) was cancelled. *See:* B508, B509

W137a 31 March 1989, Gerald R. Daniel Recital Hall, California State University, Long Beach, California. Alan Feinberg, piano. West coast premiere. *See:* B510

W137b 11 April 1990, Arnold Schoenberg Institute, University of Southern California, Los Angeles, California. Alan Feinberg, piano.

W137c 31 May 1992, Institute of Contemporary Arts, London. Alan Feinberg, piano. European premiere. A concert of the *New MusICA* series. *See:* B511

W138 *Piano Variations.* Instrumentation: Piano Solo. Duration: 7:08. Composed 15 June - 26 November 1963, in New York City. McGinnis & Marx. Premiered 13 January 1964, Columbia University, New York City. Wuorinen, piano. A Group for Contemporary Music concert.

    Historical note: Wuorinen originally subtitled the work *A Book of Interpolations: Composition A,* but later dropped the subtitle when he decided that *A Book of Interpolations: Composition B (Flute Variations I)* and *A Book of Interpolations: Composition C (Variations á 2)* were each independent works. The work is on the repertory list for the *International American Music Competition for Pianists* sponsored by Carnegie Hall and The Rockefeller Foundation. *See:* D4, B516 - B540

W138a 17 January 1964, Mandel Hall, University of Chicago, Chicago. Wuorinen, piano. A *Fromm Foundation Concert.*

W138b 13 May 1964, Adams House, Harvard University, Cambridge, Massachusetts. Wuorinen, piano.

W138c 13 August 1964, Theatre-Concert Hall, Tanglewood, Lenox, Massachusetts. Wuorinen, piano. *Festival of Contemporary American Music. See:* B517 - B519

W138d 26 January 1965, Carnegie Recital Hall, New York City. Wuorinen, piano. *See:* B520

W138e 9 March 1965, University of Colorado, Boulder, Colorado. David Burge, piano.

W138f 26 August 1965, Instituto Torcuato di Tella, Buenos Aires. Carla Hübner, piano. The fourth *Festival de Musica Contemporanea,* celebrating the fifth anniversary of the creation of the institute (Latin American Center for High Musical Studies), held under the auspices of the Argentine section of the ISCM (International Society for Contemporary Music) and the National Foundation for the Arts, Argentina. Latin American premiere. *See:* B521 - B523

W138g 23 November 1965, Sala de Experimentacion, Audiovisual dell Instituto Torcuato di Tella, Buenos Aires. *See:* B524 - B528

W138h 20 October 1966, Carnegie Recital Hall, New York City. David Burge, piano.

W138i 15 April 1968, Roosevelt University, Chicago. Easley Blackwood, piano.

W138j 12 March 1969, Purcell Room, London. Easley Blackwood, piano. European premiere. *See:* B533

W138k 24 November 1969, Los Angeles. Charles Fierro, piano. *Monday Evening Concerts.*

W138l 5 November 1973, Carnegie Recital Hall, New York City. David Burge, piano. *See:* B535, B536

W138m 6 November 1973, University Museum, University of Pennsylvania, Philadelphia, Pennsylvania. David Burge, piano. *See:* B537

W138n 19 May 1989, Weill Recital Hall, New York City. Robert Thomas, piano.

W139 *Scherzo.* Instrumentation: Piano Solo. Duration: 3:00. Composed August 1953, in New York City. Unpublished. Premiered 13 May 1956, Town Hall, New York City. Wuorinen, piano.
    Historical note: Wuorinen's *Register of Works* notebooks states this composition won the 1954 New York Philharmonic Young Composer's award. *See:* B591

W140 *Self-Similar Waltz.* Instrumentation: Piano Solo. Duration: 1:66. Composed 23 October - 3 November 1977. Peters P66735 (In C.F. Peters collection titled *Waltzes by 25 Contemporary Composers*). Dedicated to Robert Helps. Premiered 11 May 1978, School of Music, Northwestern University, Evanston, Illinois. Mark Phelps, piano. Concert organized by Robert Moran. *See:* B592

W140a 5 February 1979, The Kitchen, New York City. Pianist unknown. *See:* B592

W140b 29 July 1991, *Summerfest*, Minneapolis, Minnesota. Garrick Ohlsson, piano.

W141 *Sonata for Piano.* Instrumentation: Piano Solo. Duration: 13:02. Composed 14 April - 26 May 1958. American Composers Alliance/Composer Facsimile Edition. Premiered 16 December 1958, Salon de Musique, Barbizon Plaza, Barbizon Hotel, New York City. Douglas Nordli, piano. Composed for Douglas Nordli.
> **Historical note:** This piano sonata preceded those numbered 1, 2, and 3.

W141a 9 August 1958, Bennington Composers Conference, Bennington, Vermont. Lionel Nowak, piano. This event was a reading that preceded the world premiere.

W141b 29 December 1958, Paine Hall, Harvard University, Cambridge, Massachusetts. Douglas Nordli, piano. A concert presented by the College Music Association.

W141c 15 May 1959, McMillin Theatre, Columbia University, New York City. Douglas Nordli, piano.

W141d 22 April 1961, Donnell Library Auditorium (New York Public Library), New York City. Douglas Nordli, piano. *See:* B610

W142 *Song and Dance.* Instrumentation: Piano Solo. Duration: 6:35. Composed August and December 1955, in New York City. Unpublished. Premiered 13 May 1956, Town Hall, New York City. Wuorinen, piano. *See:* B615

W143 *Three Prepositions for Piano.* Instrumentation: Piano Solo. Duration: unknown. Composed 3-5 a.m., 9 December 1958. Unpublished. Composed for Vladimir Ussachevsky for publication in *New Music Edition*. Never performed.
> **Historical note:** The work was never published in *New Music Edition*.

W144 *Twelve Short Pieces.* Instrumentation: Piano Solo. Duration: 4:30. Composed 9-17 December 1973, in New York City. Peters P66579. Premiere not documented. Dedicated to Stephen Fisher.

Historical note: According to Howard Stokar, Wuorinen's manager, this work has been performed many times, though records of the performances were not kept. In addition, C.F. Peters was unable to provide details of any performances. *See:* B773 - B775

W145   *Two Tranquil Pieces (I. Song. II. Pastorale.).* Instrumentation: Piano Solo. Duration: 5:27. Composed Summer 1956. Unpublished. Never performed.

HARPSICHORD

W146   *Harpsichord Divisions.* Instrumentation: Harpsichord Solo. Duration: 12:56. Composed 10 April - 2 July 1966, in Iowa City (IA), New York City, and Paris. Peters P66370. Never performed. Commissioned by and dedicated to Paul Jacobs. *See:* B312

ORGAN

W147   *Evolutio: Organ.* Instrumentation: Organ Solo. Duration: 8:46. Composed 30 May - 19 June 1961, in New York City. Peters P67362. Premiered 8 April 1962, Church of the Advent, Boston, Massachusetts. Leonard Raver, organ. A concert of the 1962 Boston Chapter *Festival of the American Guild of Organists.* Composed for Leonard Raver. Dedicated to the memory of Lili Boulanger.
   Historical note: Wuorinen received the Lili Boulanger Award on 13 March 1961. Nadia Boulanger subsequently suggested to him that he dedicate this work to the memory of her deceased sister. Nadia Boulanger attended the premiere performance. *See:* W47

W147a   1 August 1962, St. Paul's Chapel, Columbia University, New York City. Leonard Raver, harpsichord. *See:* B228

W147b   28 November 1967, Church of the Ascension, New York City. Leonard Raver, harpsichord. *See:* B229

W147c   19 April 1985, Church of the Ascension, New York City. Organist unknown. A concert of the American New Music Consortium's fourth annual festival. *See:* B230

W148   *Homage à Bach.* Instrumentation: Organ Solo. Duration: 7:10. Composed August(?) 1955, in Gardner, Massachusetts. Unpublished. Premiered 30 June 1956, First Congregational Church, Gardner, Massachusetts. Theodore Pierce, organ. Dedicated to John Wuorinen.
   Historical note: The dedicatee is Wuorinen's brother. The work was composed for John Wuorinen's wedding. The composer subtitled this work *Organ Toccata.*

W149   *Natural Fantasy.* Instrumentation: Organ Solo. Duration: 11:30. Composed 25 August - 7 April 1985. Peters P67148. Premiered 31 January 1988, Park Avenue Christian Church, New York City. David Shuler, organ. Commissioned by David Shuler under a National Endowment for the Arts Consortium grant.

PERCUSSION

W150 *The Bells.* Instrumentation: Carillon. Duration 9:00. Composed 2 June 1965 - 21 January 1966, in Los Angeles and New York City. American Composers Alliance. Never performed. Commissioned by Daniel Robins.

W151 *Invention for Percussion Quintet.* Instrumentation: P(5): Player 1 - Celesta; Player 2 - Xylophone and Glockenspiel; Player 3 - Vibraphone and Chimes; Player 4 - Timpani and Bass Drum; Player 5 - Piano. Duration: 5:43. Composed 2-12 January 1962, in New York City. Music for Percussion, Inc. Publisher's Number E-25-22, Ensemble Series, Paul Price, editor. Premiered 6 March 1962, Manhattan School of Music, New York City. Ben Lanzarone, celesta; John Bergamo, xylophone, glockenspiel; Max Neuhaus, vibraphone, chimes; Wuorinen, Raymond DesRoches, timpani, bass drum; Ernest Ulmer, piano. Dedicated to Paul Price.

> **Historical note:** Max Neuhaus also played timpani with Wuorinen and DesRoches at this performance. The following is a preferatory note from the score: "The celesta functions as a background to the main music of this composition. Therefore, it must always (except for certain rare places) play *p*, and maintain a calm detachment from the rest of the piece. It must not play inaccurately even where the noise of the foreground swallows it altogether, for even the loudest portions of the foreground may suddenly clear, revealing the celesta-background."

W152 *Janissary Music.* Instrumentation: Percussion Solo. Duration: 12:28. Composed 14 February - 9 April 1966, in New York City. Peters P66378. Premiered 26 October 1966 (Part I only), Swarthmore, Pennsylvania; 12 March 1967 (Part II), Carnegie Recital Hall, New York City. Raymond DesRoches performed both performances. Composed for and dedicated to Raymond DesRoches. *See:* D6, B320 - B331

W152a 18 January 1967, MacBride Auditorium, Center for New Music, University of Iowa, Iowa City, Iowa. William Parsons, percussion. Part I only. *See:* B320

W152b 29 January 1967, Hope Martin Theatre, Waterloo, Iowa. William Parsons, percussion. Part I only. *See:* B321

W152c 1 May 1967, McMillin Theatre, Columbia University, New York City. Raymond DesRoches, percussion. A Group for Contemporary Music concert. First complete performance (Part I and Part II).

W152d 15 August 1967, Tanglewood, Lenox, Massachusetts. Raymond DesRoches, percussion. A Group for Contemporary Music concert held at the *Tanglewood Festival of Contemporary American Music*.

W152e 27 November 1967, Bing Center of the County Museum of Art, Los Angeles. Kenneth Watson, percussion. *Monday Evening Concerts. See:* B322

W152f 24 November 1968, Town Hall, New York City. Raymond DesRoches, percussion. *See:* B323

W152g 6 October 1985, Old First Church, San Francisco. Steven Schick, percussion.
> **Historical note:** The program notes for this concert erroneously stated this was the world premiere. Wuorinen happened to be in attendance and told the audience there have been more than 250 performances of the work. In addition to this performance, Schick performed the work in Sao Paulo, Brazil; at the Sadler's Wells, London; in Paris; and in Sydney, Australia (all of these performances were in 1990). *See:* B330

W153 *Percussion Duo.* Instrumentation: Mallet Instruments (1 Player) and Piano. Duration: 14:00. Composed 10 February - 11 July 1979, in Helsinki, Middle Valley (NJ), and New York City. Peters P66820 (2 scores needed for performance). Premiered 29 October 1979, Center for New Music, University of Iowa, Iowa City, Iowa. Steven Schick, percussion; James Avery, piano. Commissioned by Steven Schick. Dedicated to Steven Schick and James Avery. Commission funded in part by the Hancher Circle for the Performing Arts.
> **Historical note:** Wuorinen originally titled the work *Sounds Resound* but later decided he did not like that title. *See:* D28, B417 - B422

W153a 6 May 1980, Merkin Concert Hall, Abraham Goodman House, New York City. Parnassus. New York premiere.

W153b 7 August 1988, East Brunswick, New Jersey. New Jersey Percussion Ensemble: Peter Jarvis, percussion; Robert Dowling, piano.

W153c 28 November 1988, Los Angeles County Museum, Los Angeles. Daniel Druckman, percussion; Alan Feinberg, piano.

W153d 20 October 1990, Smithsonian Institution, Washington, D.C. 20th Century Consort.

W154 *Percussion Symphony.* Instrumentation: Percussion Ensemble of 24 Players. Duration: 38:00. Composed 14 February - 13 September 1976, in Middle Valley (NJ). Peters P66706.* Premiered 19 May 1977, William Paterson State College, Wayne, New Jersey. New Jersey Percussion Ensemble; Wuorinen, conductor. Composed under a grant from the National Endowment for the Arts for the New Jersey Percussion Ensemble. Dedicated to Raymond DesRoches.
> **Historical note:** Only the first movement was performed at this event. *See:* D21, D33, B423 - B446

W154a 26 January 1978, Somerset County College, Somerville, New Jersey. New Jersey Percussion Ensemble; Wuorinen, conductor. First complete performance.

W154b 2 October 1984, Kaufmann Concert Hall, 92nd St. Y, New York City. The New Jersey Percussion Ensemble; Peter Jarvis, conductor. A Group for Contemporary Music concert. *See:* B442, B443

W154c 21 March 1988, Symphony Space, New York City. New Music Consort; Claire Heldrich, conductor.

W155 *Prelude and Fugue for 4 Percussionists.* Instrumentation: P(4): Player 1 - Temple Blocks; Player 2 - Cymbals, Gong; Player 3 - Snare Drums, Gong; Player 4 - Timpani. Duration: 6:15. Composed March(?) 1955, in New York City. Music for Percussion, Inc. Ensemble Series, Paul Price, editor. Plate number E-16-22. Premiered 1 March 1956, Recital Hall, School of Music, University of Illinois at Urbana-Champaign. University of Illinois Percussion Ensemble: George Boberg, temple blocks; Robert Swanson, 2 suspended cymbals, gong; Richard Paschke, 2 snare drums, gong; Jeanette Rucker, timpani; Paul Price, conductor. *See:* D1, D62, D70, D73, B559 - B561

W155a 19 April 1960, Smith Music Hall, School of Music, University of Illinois at Urbana-Champaign, Urbana, Illinois. University of Illinois Percussion Ensemble: Dannee Newton, temple blocks; Thomas Siwe, suspended cymbals, gong; Juanita Randall, snare drums, gong; Lloyd Jones, timpani.

W155b 11 May 1962, Manhattan School of Music, New York City. Manhattan Percussion Ensemble; Paul Price, conductor. New York premiere.

W156 *Ringing Changes.* Instrumentation: Percussion Ensemble of 12 Players: Almglocken, Cymbals, Tam-tams, Timpani, String Drums, Chimes, Vibraphones (2), Piano 4-hands, Drums, Anvils (or Breakdrums). Duration: 17:00. Composed 23 March 1969 - 10 January 1970. Peters P66394*. Premiered 28 April 1970, William Paterson State College, Wayne, New Jersey. New Jersey Percussion Ensemble; Wuorinen, conductor. Composed for the New Jersey Percussion Ensemble. Dedicated to Raymond DesRoches.
> **Historical note:** This premiere was interrupted by a disturbance. The concert was a noon program. *Ringing Changes* was the last work to be performed and made the concert run over a full hour. A Professor of Communications who was scheduled to have a large class the next hour in the same hall grew impatient (the performance simply continuing) and routed Wuorinen and the ensemble by applying a power-saw to a handy microphone. *See:* D10, B582 - B590, B857

W156a 29 April 1970, Jersey City State College, Jersey City, New Jersey. New Jersey Percussion Ensemble; Wuorinen, conductor.
> **Historical note:** This performance was a follow-up performance to the premiere which had been interrupted by a disturbance.

W156b 4 May 1970, McMillin Theatre, Columbia University, New York City. New Jersey Percussion Ensemble; Wuorinen, conductor. A Group for Contemporary Music concert. New York premiere.

W156c 31 March 1975, Manhattan School of Music, New York City. New Jersey Percussion Ensemble; Raymond DesRoches, conductor. A Group for Contemporary Music concert. *See:* B586

W156d 9 June 1990, Rutgers University Theatre, Camden, New Jersey. New Jersey Percussion Ensemble; Raymond DesRoches, conductor.

ELECTRONIC TAPE

W157 *Beast 708.* Instrumentation: Computer Generated Tape; Alternate version for Fl, Cl in A, 2 Hrns, 2 Trbs, Vibr, Pf, Vn, Cb. Duration: 2:00 plus 1:42 for each repetition (number of repetitions ad lib). Composed 12-24 December 1980, in New York City. Peters P66857*. Premiered 12 January 1981, Arnold Schoenberg Institute, University of Southern California, Los Angeles. Student musicians of the University of Southern California; Wuorinen, conductor. Dedicated to Lukas Foss.

> **Historical note:** The music librarians at the University of Southern California could not find any record that this premiere performance actually took place, though Wuorinen insists that he did indeed conduct the premiere there on the above date but that the performance was not reviewed. Wuorinen's full title for the work is *Beast 708/(for Humans)/Being a Transcription of the Output/of the Computer Program/called/Beast 708.*

W157a 15-16 January 1981, Brooklyn Academy of Music, New York City. Brooklyn Philharmonia; Lukas Foss, conductor.

W158 *Consort from Instruments and Voices.* Instrumentation: Electronic Tape. Duration: 8:42. Composed 17 September 1960 - 11 January 1961. American Composers Alliance. Premiered 15 January 1961, Kaufmann Concert Hall, 92nd St. Y, New York City. A concert of the *Music In Our Time* series. Realized at the Columbia-Princeton Electronic Music Center, December 1960 - January 1961. R.A. Heaton, technical supervision.

> **Historical note:** The dates of composition include preparation of the score through execution on tape. *See:* B184 - B185

W158a 12 July 1961, International House, New York City. Wuorinen, technical supervision. A concert of the *Columbia Composers Concert* summer series.

W159 *Time's Encomium.* Instrumentation: For Synthesized and Processed Synthesized Sound. Duration: 31:35. Composed 28 January 1968 - 20 January 1969, in Ann Arbor (MI), Belgrade (Yugoslavia), Chapel Hill (NC), Colorado Springs (CO), London (England), New York City, and Sveti Stefan (Yugoslavia). Peters P66455*. Premiered 2 March 1969, Newark, New Jersey. Part II only. Commissioned by Nonesuch Records. Realized at the Columbia-Princeton Electronic Music Center.

> **Historical note:** This work has been written about more than any other composition by Wuorinen. Awarded the Pulitzer Prize for music, 1970. *Time's Encomium* is also the only work Wuorinen created (in part or whole) at the Columbia-Princeton Electronic Music Center that was commercially recorded. *See:* D8, B698 - B747, B840, B841, B845, B846, B891, B1090

W159a 16 August 1969, Tanglewood, Lenox, Massachusetts. Part II only.

W159b 15-18 September 1969, Electric Circus, New York City. Part II only. Eight performances; two per day.

W159c 14 March 1970, University of Houston, Houston, Texas. Part II only.

W159d 8-9 May 1970, State University of New York at Albany, Albany, New York. First complete performance.

W159e 20 August 1970, Tanglewood, Lenox, Massachusetts. Both parts performed.

W159f 30 November 1970, McMillin Theatre, Columbia University, New York City. Part II only. Group for Contemporary Music 10th anniversary concert. *See:* B717

W159g 1 June 1989, Rutgers University, New Brunswick, New Jersey. A *New Jersey Composers Guild* concert.

STAGE WORKS

W160 *The Politics of Harmony.* Instrumentation: ATB Soli, 2 Fls(2 Alto, Picc), 2 Tbas, P(3), Pf, 2 Hps, 2 Vns, 2 Cbs. Duration: 35:00. Composed 27 September 1966 - 17 November 1967, in Albany (NY), Buffalo (NY), Boulder (CO), Fredonia (NY), Gardner (MA), Iowa City (IA), Lenox (MA), New York City, St. Louis, Syracuse (NY), and Terre Haute (IN). Peters P66389*. Premiered 28 October 1968, McMillin Theatre, Columbia University, New York City. Text by Richard Monaco. Valarie Lamoree, alto; Jack Litten, tenor; F. Summers or Harris Poor, bass; players from the New York Philharmonic; Wuorinen, conductor. A Group for Contemporary Music concert.

Historical note: Wuorinen's full title for this work is *The Politics of Harmony/A Masque/Stolen Out of Ancient Authors/by Richard Monaco/and set for voices and instruments by Charles Wuorinen.* The work consists of thirty-five parts, some of which have the same title but not necessarily the same music: 1. Preluding Drums; 2. Prologue; Bass Aria: The Yellow Emperor Creates Music in Pure Chüeh' Mode; 3. First Narration; 4. First Ch'in Tune; 5. Second Narration; 6. First Dialogue; 7. Second Ch'in Tune; 8. First Dialogue Continued; 9. Third Narration; Grand Pause: Travelling to Ch'in; 10. Symphony: Banquet; 11. Second Dialogue; 12. Third Ch'in Tune; 13. Second Dialogue, Continued; 14. Third Ch'in Tune Concluded; 15. Third Dialogue; 16. Fourth Narration; 17. Fourth Ch'in Tune; 18. Fourth Narration Concluded; 17. Fourth Ch'in Tune; 18. Fourth Narration Concluded; 19. Second Symphony: Appearance of Sixteen Dark Cranes; 20. Fifth Ch'in Tune; 21. Fourth Narration Concluded; 22. Third Symphony: Dark Cranes: a. Crying of Sixteen Dark Cranes. b. Dancing of the Same; 23. Fourth Narration Concluded; Grand Pause: Drinking to Master K'uang's Health; 24. Alto Aria. Trope: Another Description of the Sixteen Dark Cranes. Interlude 1. Verse 2. Interlude 2. Verse 3; 25. Fourth Dialogue. Fourth Symphony: Music to Assemble Ghosts and Spirits; 26. Fifth Narration; 27. Sixth Ch'in Tune; 28. Fifth Narration Concluded; 29. Fifth Symphony: Black Clouds Arise in the Northwest; 30. Seventh Ch'in Tune; 31. Fifth Narration Continued; 32. Sixth Symphony: Storm Wind and Torrent. Disorder is Brought

About by Natural Calamities. Ice; 33. Sixth Narration; 34. Seventh Symphony: Drought; 35. Postlude. *See:* D59, B541 - B556, B857, B891

W160a 1 October 1971, Martinson Hall, Shakespeare Festival Public Theater, New York City. Players from the New York Philharmonic; Pierre Boulez, conductor. A concert of the *New York Philharmonic Prospective Encounter Series.*

> **Historical note:** This event was noteworthy because it was probably the only one at which Boulez conducted a work by Wuorinen and because of the critical reaction to the performance. *See:* B543 - B548, B552, B554, B555

W161 *The W. of Babylon.* Instrumentation: 8 Soloists, Narrator, 2(Picc)2(EH)-2(Bcl)2(Cbsn) 2221 P(3), Hp, Pf, Str. Duration: 2 hours. Composition dates unknown except for Act I which was completed 14 March 1975. Peters P66656*. Text by Renaud Charles Bruce. Premiered 15 December 1975, Borden Auditorium, Manhattan School of Music, New York City. Catherine Rowe, Merja Sargon, Judith Bettina, sopranos; Douglas Perry, tenor; Richard Frisch, baritone; Kenneth Bell, bass; David Holtzman, piano; Coburn Britton, narrator; Daniel Shulman, conductor. Commissioned by the National Opera Institute and for the Light Fantastic Players by the New York State Council on the Arts. Dedicated to Daniel Shulman.

> **Historical note:** This premiere was of preview excerpts, not a full concert premiere or a staged performance, and was supported by the Manhattan School of Music, the Alice M. Ditson Fund of Columbia University and private individuals (in addition to the sources of funding listed above). Wuorinen's full title for the work is *The W. of Babylon/or/The Triumph of Love Over Moral Depravity/A Baroque Burlesque/in Two Acts/by/Renaud Charles Bruce/Set to Music by/Charles Wuorinen.* The work is Wuorinen's only opera. The libretto contains puns on and/or references to titles of other Wuorinen compositions: "Are you, then, time's encomium? Is your whole life become another sorry contrafactum? ... Are they adapting to the times, an analysis of variable canonical correlations, or — counter-revolutionary — ringing changes? What are, exactly, the politics of harmony?" The *Prolegomenon* to Bruce's text includes the following statement: "If, then, in this — the only intention of this pasticcio [the lives of the 17th century characters speaking directly to contemporary life] — I have succeeded, my readers will rightly apprehend it as a cry of rage against the racist, tyrannical exploitation in America of the majority by ethnic minorities, the economic and political imperialist aggression by the peoples of the Third World against the United States, and the present Federal system of confiscatory taxation of the rich." The *Prolegomenon* is dated 27 June 1971, St. Benets Abbey, Norfolk. The entire text of the work is dedicated to Coburn Britton, described by Bruce as "Beloved Applist." *See:* B798 - B809

W161a 27-28 July 1974, tent, Wheatleigh Estate, Lenox, Massachusetts. Catherine Rowe, soprano; Wuorinen, tenor.

> **Historical note:** This performance consisted only of one vocal duet from the work. The concert was titled *Charles Wuorinen: Profile of a Composer. See:* B798, B799

W161b 20 January 1989, Herbst Theatre, San Francisco. Miriam Abramowitsch, Thomas Manguem, Judy Hubbell, John Duykers. First full concert performance.

> **Historical note:** This concert performance had originally been schedule for 18 December 1987, but was cancelled due to the pregnancy of one of the singers. Wuorinen

described the libretto, at this event, as "a somewhat racy set of amatory permutations set in one of the lustier moments of the 17th century." This concert was a joint commission of the National Opera Institute and the New York State Council on the Arts. *See:* B805 - B809

CHORUS AND ORCHESTRA

W162 *The Celestial Sphere.* Instrumentation: SATB, 3(3 Picc)33 in A (Bcl)3 4331 T, P(4), Hp, Pf, Str, Tape. Duration: 57:00 (Tape duration 1:00 in Part II). Composed 2 January - 9 September 1980, in Baltimore, Binghamton (NY), Buffalo (NY), Gardner (MA), Iowa City (IA), Jackson Hole (WY), Los Angeles, Middle Valley (NJ), New York City, Rock Island (IL), and San Francisco. Peters P66851* (2 volume set). Text from William Fuller's *Lord, What Is Man?* (1693), *The Acts.* Premiered 25 April 1981, Centennial Hall, Augustana College, Rock Island, Illinois. Handel Oratorio Society and Augustana Symphony Orchestra; Donald Morrison, conductor. Commissioned by Augustana College in observance of the 100th anniversary of the Handel Oratorio Society. Dedicated to the Handel Oratorio Society in gratitude for one hundred years of faithful song of God. The four orchestral movements may be excerpted and played (in order) as an instrumental work entitled *Ecclesiastical Symphonies.*

> **Historical note:** Wuorinen's full title and subtitle is: *The Celestial Sphere/An Oratorio/For Mixed Chorus/And Orchestra/Containing: I. Symphony About the Empyrean/Lord, What Is Man? (William Fuller, 1693) (Solemn Setting)/II. Symphony About the Ascension/The Ascension (Acts)/III. Symphony About the Holy Ghost/The Pentecost (Acts)/IV. Second Symphony About the Empyrean/Lord, What is Man? (Joyous Setting).* The tape part of the work consists of a two-channel tape which may be used at one point (Pentecost) where there is a provision for a two-minute interlude. The tape part can be replaced by silence if desired. The tape was something Wuorinen created at Bell Labs, and is only tangentially related to the piece. *See:* W11, B69 - B86

W162a Summer 1981. National Public Radio (NPR) broadcast of the premiere performance, which had been taped.

> **Historical note:** This was a nation-wide broadcast (including New York City, Chicago, Boston, Philadelphia, Cleveland, Pittsburgh, Cincinnati, and Augustana) at various times throughout the summer of 1981 by special arrangement with the Seattle Development Fund of NPR.

W163 *Genesis. (Invocation. Interlude I: Meditation. Creation History. Interlude II: Cosmology. Doxology.)* Instrumentation: SATB, 3(Picc)33(Bcl)3(Cbsn) 4331 T, P(3), Pf, Hp, Str. Duration: 35:00. Composed 27 April - 1 December 1989. Peters P67352*. Sources of text: *The Bible, Liber Usualis*, missal, breviary, gradual, antiphonal. Premiered 26-28 September 1991, Davies Symphony Hall, San Francisco. San Francisco Symphony; San Francisco Symphony Chorus; Vance George, director. Commissioned by the Orchestras of Honolulu, Minnesota and San Francisco.

> **Historical note:** The work contains two instrumental interludes. The Honolulu Symphony Orchestra never performed the work due to problems with its chorus. Howard Stokar, Wuorinen's manager, informed Richard Burbank that the Honolulu Symphony Orchestra's name has been removed from the score. *See:* B268 - B276

W163a   20-21 November 1992, Orchestra Hall, Minneapolis.   Minnesota Orchestra; Edo de Waart, conductor.   *See:* B276

CHORAL

W164   *An Anthem for Epiphany*.   Instrumentation: SATB, Trp, (C), Org. Duration: 4:00.   Composed 17 May - 3 June 1974, in Fresno (CA), Los Angeles, New York City, and Ojai (C).   Peters P66606.   Text from the books of Matthew, Mark, Luke and John, New Testament, The Bible. Never performed.   Commissioned by Trinity Parish, New York City. Dedicated to Larry King.

> **Historical note:** Wuorinen's full title is *An Anthem for Epiphany, on Fragments of the Gospels*.

W165   *A Solis Ortu*.   Instrumentation: SATB a cappella.   Duration: 2:00. Composed 1988, completed 7 February 1989.   Peters P67252.   Premiered 30 December 1990, St. Ignatius of Antioch Episcopal Church, New York City.   St. Ignatius Choir: Nancy Barnes, Nancy Temple, sopranos; Holly Durniak, Anna Spolina, Catalina Vasquez, altos; Daniel Schreibman, L. Dean Todd, tenors; David Caldwell, Richard Porterfield, basses; Dr. Harold Chaney, organist and conductor.   Dedicated to Stephen Fisher.

> **Historical note:** This premiere was performed as part of the Solemn Mass.

W166   *Be Merry All That Be Present*.   Instrumentation: SATB, Organ (or Fl, 2 Vns, Vc).   Duration: 4:00.   Composed November 1957, in New York City. Peters P67360*.   Text: Anon. (16th century).   Premiered 26 January 1958, Church of the Transfiguration, New York City.   Vocalists unknown; Stuart Gardner, conductor.

W166a   15 November 1959, King's Chapel, Boston, Massachusetts.   King's Chapel Choir; Daniel Pinkham, conductor.

W167   *Faire, If You Expect Admiring, and Turne Backe, You Wanton Flyer*. Instrumentation: TTBB a cappella.   Duration not specified.   Composed Winter 1956.   Lawson-Gould Music Publishers, Inc. (G. Schirmer Inc., sole representative.)   Octavo Edition, No. 684.   *Lawson-Gould Choral Series*.   Plate number L.G.Co.684.   Text: two lute songs by Thomas Campion.   Premiered 13 May 1956, Town Hall, New York City.   Trinity School Glee Club; John Harms, conductor.

W168   *Madrigale Spirituale Sopra Salmo Secundo*.   Instrumentation: TB, 2 Obs, 2 Vns, Vc, Pf.   Duration: 4:28.   Composed 6-18 August 1960, in Bennington (VT) and New York City.   Peters P67364*.   Text: Psalmus II, Vulgate 1-4.   Premiered 27 August 1960, Bennington Composers Conference, Bennington College, Bennington, Vermont.   Earl Rogers, tenor; Robert Miller, baritone; Mel Kaplan and Robert Bloom, oboes; Max Pollikoff, Alan Ohmes, violins: Alexander Kougell, violoncello; Ezra Sims, piano.   Composed for Daniel Pinkham and the King's Chapel Choir, Boston.   Dedicated to Daniel Pinkham.

W168a 13 November 1960, King's Chapel, Boston. King's Chapel Choir: vocalists unknown; Richard Summers, oboe; Robert Brink, Jerre Gibson, violins; Eleftherios Eleftherakis, viola; Judith Davidoff, violoncello; Ronald Steelman, contrabass; Edward Low, organ. First public performance.
Historical note: The work was performed twice on this occasion.

W168b 27 March 1961, St. Thomas Church, New York City. James Mitchell, baritone; Richard Christopher, bass; Josef Marx and Judith Martin, oboes; Bernard Lurie, Marie Blewet, violins; Bertram Turetzky and Leonard Raver, continuo. New York premiere.
Historical note: For this performance a baritone and bass were used instead of a tenor and baritone.

W169 *Mannheim 87.87.87.* Instrumentation: Unison Chorus and Organ. Duration: 2:00. Composed 5-13 April 1973, in New York City and Tampa (FL). Peters P66550. Premiered 1 May 1973, Cathedral of St. John the Divine (Episcopal), New York City. Performers unknown. Commissioned by Trinity Parish for the Liturgical Music Conference at the Cathedral of St. John the Divine (30 April - 2 May 1973). *See:* B371, B903

W170 *Mass. (Symphonia. Kyrie. Gloria. Sanctus. Agnus Dei. Motet* [verses from the 12th chapter of the *Gospel According to St. John*].*)* Instrumentation: SATB (with Sopr Solo), Vn, 3 Trbs, Org. Duration: 30:00. Composed 8 February - 9 July 1982, in New York City. Peters P66930*. Premiered 20 November 1983, St. Ignatius of Antioch Episcopal Church, New York City. St. Ignatius Choir: Nancy Barnes, Mary Magestro, Nancy Temple (soloist), sopranos; Joan Epro, Sally Fenley, altos; Martin Gonzalez, countertenor; Greg Carder, Robert Craig, L. Dean Todd, tenors; Bruce Detrick, Richard Frisch, Thomas Lester, Stuart Price, basses; Dr. Harold Chaney, choirmaster; Ronald Borror, Hugh Eddy, trombones; David Taylor, bass trombone; Benjamin Hudson, violin; Harold Chaney, organ; Wuorinen, conductor. Commissioned by St. Luke-in-the-Fields Church (Episcopal), New York City, and Coburn Britton. Dedicated to Coburn Britton.
Historical note: Wuorinen's full title for the work is *Mass/for the Restoration of St. Luke-in-the-Fields/for/Mixed Chorus (with Soprano Solo)/and/Violin, Three Trombones, and Organ/Containing Also/A Symphonia/for use as a Processional and Recessional/and/A Communion Motet*. The Motet was not performed. This work was commissioned to celebrate the rededication of St. Luke's, destroyed by fire on the night of 6 March 1981. This premiere performance had at first been scheduled to take place at St. Luke's at the rededication, but for reasons of poor musicianship of some performers and administrative confusion, took place at St. Ignatius instead. The premiere was financed by a grant from the Liturgical Music Foundation with the assistance of a grant from Meet the Composer. Wuorinen offered the following note at the premiere: "The performing forces have symbolic roles. The violin, in association with the occasional soprano solo, is the individual soul. The chorus is the congregation of the Faithful. The organ encompasses the natural world. The trombones are the voices of angels, and there are three, to harmonize with the Trinity. The instrumental music used for entrance and exit celebrates the glory of God in the world He has made. This music thus encloses the smaller, human world of the Mass itself. The composition is my act of worship." **See:** B372, B857

W170a   20 April 1986, St. Luke-in-the-Fields Church, New York City. Performers unknown; David Shuler, conductor. First performance at St. Luke-in-the-Fields Church.

> **Historical note:** Due to this performance taking place during Eastertide and because of Episcopal Rite II rubrics, only the Motet, Kyrie and Anthem were performed. The clergy did not enter the church using the Processional.

W170b   7 November 1988, St. Ignatius of Antioch Episcopal Church, New York City. Naomi Itami, Eileen Reisner, sopranos; Susan Altabet, Linda Indian, altos; Robert Allen, David Smith, tenors; Joseph Neal, Joseph Ness, basses; Ronald Borror, Hugh Eddy, trombones; David Taylor, bass trombone; Todd Reynolds, violin.

> **Historical note:** This concert was presented by the ensemble Zaccho, and was titled *An Evening of Contemporary Choral Music In Celebration of Charles Wuorinen's 50th Birthday.*

W170c   18 November 1990, St. Luke-in-the-Fields Church, New York City. Performers unknown; David Shuler, conductor.

> **Historical note:** This performance marked the first time the motet was performed.

W171   *Missa Brevis.* Instrumentation: SATB, Organ. Duration: 8:00. Composed 1991. Peters P67425. Premiered 23 February 1992, St. Ignatius of Antioch Episcopal Church, New York City. St. Ignatius Choir: Nancy Barnes, Jan Bishop, Nancy Temple, sopranos; Anna Spolina, Catalina Vasquez, altos; Stephen Lee, countertenor; Ethan Fran, L. Dean Todd, tenors; Richard Boukas, Richard Porterfield, Raymond Willingham, basses; Dr. Harold Chaney, organist and conductor. Dedicated to Dr. Harold Chaney.

> **Historical note:** Wuorinen composed this work to celebrate the 20th anniversary of Harold Chaney's music ministry at St. Ignatius Church. Wuorinen intended the music to be liturgically usable. The work was recorded the same evening for a disc release, supervised and issued by Harold Chaney. *See:* B374

W172   *O Filii et Filiae.* Instrumentation: Mixed Chorus. Duration: not listed. Composed 1953, in New York City. Unpublished. Text: 15th century French plainsong, in English and Latin. Premiered 2 May 1954, Town Hall, New York City. John Harms Chorus; John Harms, conductor. *See:* D55

W173   *The Prayer of Jonah.* Instrumentation: SATB, Vns, Vla, Vc, Cb. Duration: 11:02. Composed 1-28 October 1962, in New York City. Unpublished. Text from Book of Jonah, second chapter. Premiered 21 March, 1963, Museum of Modern Art, New York City. Kings Chapel Choir (of Boston); Kohon String Quartet, Stewart Sankey, contrabass; Daniel Pinkham, conductor. Commissioned by Daniel Pinkham under a grant from the Ford Foundation. Dedicated to Daniel Pinkham. *See:* D3, B557, B558

W173a 24 March 1963, Kings Chapel, Boston. Kings Chapel Choir; Cambridge Festival Orchestra String Quartet; Daniel Pinkham, conductor. Boston premiere.
Historical note: This concert was part of a series titled *Experiments in Choral Music, 1963.*

W174 *Super Salutem.* Instrumentation: TTBB, 2 Hrns, 3 Trps, 3 Trbs, Tba, P, Pf. Duration: 7:00. Composed 1 August - 30 September 1964, in Bennington (VT), Lenox (MA), and New York City. Peters P66397*. Never performed. Commissioned by Robert Stewart for the Glee Club of Washington and the University.

W175 *Symphonia Sacra.* Instrumentation: Tenor, Baritone, Bass Soli, 2 Vns, 2 Obs, Cb, Organ. Duration: 12:49. Composed 6-19 February 1961, in New York City. American Composers Alliance/Composer Facsimile Edition. Text: Vulgate: Psalms 17: 9-13; 54: 4-8; 17: 14-17; 77: 67-70. Premiered 27 March 1961, St. Thomas Church, New York City. The Hartt Chamber Players: James Mitchell, tenor; Richard Christopher, baritone; Edward Watts, bass; Bernard Lurie, Marie Blewet, violins; Josef Marx, Judith Martin, oboes; Bertram Turetzky, bass; Leonard Raver, organ. *See:* B665 - B671

W175a 9-10 May 1961, McMillin Theatre, Columbia University, New York City. Hartt Chamber Players: James Mitchell, tenor; Richard Christopher, baritone; Edward Watts, bass; P. Ruder, B. Budinszki, violins; Josef Marx, Judith Martin, oboes; Bertram Turetzky, contrabass; Wuorinen, conductor.
Historical note: These were the first two historic concerts given by the Columbia-Princeton Electronic Music Center. In April 1961 Wuorinen made an electronic (4-channel) tape under the technical supervision of R.A. Heaton, which was a realization of the organ part and specifically created for this concert. *Symphonia Sacra* was performed on the concert of 9 May. *See:* B665 - B667, B669, B671

W175b 5 March 1962, St. Thomas Church, New York City. Hartt Chamber Players: Richard Donahue, tenor; Richard Christopher, baritone; Marvin Hayes, bass; P. Ruder, B. Budinszki, violins; Josef Marx, Judith Martin, oboes; Bertram Turetzky, contrabass; Leonard Raver, organ; Wuorinen, conductor.
Historical note: This concert was in honor of Nadia Boulanger.

W175c 14 March 1962, Schwab Auditorium, Penn State University, State College, Pennsylvania. Hartt Chamber Players: Richard Donahue, tenor; Richard Christopher, baritone; Marvin Hayes, bass; P. Ruder, B. Budinszki, violins; Josef Marx, Judith Martin, oboes; Bertram Turetzky, contrabass; Leonard Raver, organ; Wuorinen, conductor.
Historical note: This concert was in honor of Nadia Boulanger.

W176 *Te Decet Hymnus.* Instrumentation: SATB, Soli, T, Organ, Pf. Duration: 25:00. Composed June - July 1954, in Gardner (MA). Unpublished. Premiered 13 May 1956, New York City. Trinity School Glee Club; Wuorinen, piano; John Harms, conductor.

Historical note: There was no organist at this performance; the organ part was played on a second piano. *See:* B695

VOCAL

W177 *The Door In the Wall.* Instrumentation: 2 Mezzo-sopranos (or 1 Mezzo and 1 Soprano), Piano. Duration: 2:01. Composed 14-20 February 1960, in New York City. American Composers Alliance/Composer Facsimile Edition. Text by Wesley Strombeck. Premiered 22 April 1960, Barnard Parlor, Barnard College, New York City. Janet Baxter, soprano; Susan Thiemann (Suki Sommer), mezzo-soprano; Wuorinen, piano.

   Historical note: This song was conceived as part of a pair, with *On the Raft* being the other part. Both songs were premiered at this concert.

W177a 9 May 1960, Carnegie Recital Hall, New York City. Janet Baxter, soprano; Susan Thiemann (Suki Sommer), mezzo-soprano. A concert of the *Composers' Laboratory Program of American Vocal Music.*

W178 *A Message to Denmark Hill.* Instrumentation: Baritone, Flute, Violoncello and Piano. Duration: 26:00. Composed 20 May - 8 September 1970, in Gardner (MA), Lenox (MA), and New York City. Peters P66384* (4 scores needed for performance). Text by Richard Howard. Premiered 20 October 1970, 6 St. Luke's Place, New York City. Richard Frisch, baritone; Harvey Sollberger, flute; Fred Sherry, violoncello; Wuorinen, piano. Commissioned by and dedicated to Renaud Bruce.

   Historical note: This premiere was a private performance at the home of Coburn Britton; no critics were in attendance. Wuorinen's full title for the work is *A Message to Denmark Hill/from/Untitled Subjects/by/Richard Howard/and Made into a Cantata/for/Baritone, with Flute, Cello, and Piano.*

W178a 23 December 1970, New York Cultural Center, New York City. Richard Frisch, baritone; Harvey Sollberger, flute; Fred Sherry, violoncello; Wuorinen, piano. First public performance. *See:* B373

W178b 11 January 1971, Columbia University, New York City. Richard Frisch, baritone; Harvey Sollberger, flute; Fred Sherry, violoncello; Wuorinen, piano.

W178c 26 February 1971, State University of New York at Stony Brook, Stony Brook, Long Island, New York. Richard Frisch, baritone; Harvey Sollberger, flute; Fred Sherry, violoncello; Wuorinen, piano.

W179 *On the Raft.* Instrumentation: 2 Mezzo-sopranos (or 1 Mezzo and 1 Soprano) and Piano. Duration: 1:49. Composed 28 March 1960. American Composers Alliance/Composer Facsimile Edition. Text by Wesley Strombeck. Premiered 22 April 1960, Barnard Parlor, Barnard College, New York City. Janet Baxter, soprano; Susan Thiemann (Suki Sommer), soprano; Wuorinen, piano.

   Historical note: This song was conceived as being part of a pair, with *The Door In the Wall* being the other part. Both songs were premiered at this concert.

W179a 9 May 1960, Carnegie Recital Hall, New York City. Janet Baxter, soprano; Susan Thiemann (Suki Sommer), mezzo-soprano. A concert of the *Composers' Laboratory Program of American Vocal Music.*

W180 *Psalm 39.* Instrumentation: Baritone and Guitar. Duration: 11:00. Composed 24 May - 18 August 1979, in Jackson Hole (WY), Middle Valley (NJ), New York City, and San Francisco. Peters P66819. Text: Biblical. Premiered 11-12 November 1979, Terrace Theatre, Kennedy Center for the Performing Arts, Washington, D.C. Richard Frisch, baritone; David Starobin, guitar. Commissioned by and dedicated to Richard Frisch and David Starobin. *See:* D26, B563 - B565

W181 *Six Songs for Two Voices. (Start. To Astarte. Twelve Lines In Two Seasons. Villanelle for Joy. Evensong. The Polish Rider.)* Instrumentation: Countertenor (or Alto) and Tenor, Ob, Bsn, 2 Hrns, Vn, Vc. Duration: 15:30. Composed 5 February - 10 May 1977. Peters P66743*. Text by Coburn Britton. Premiered 26 January 1978, Somerset County College, Wayne, New Jersey. Paul Sperry, Keith Romano, vocal soloists; New York Baroque Ensemble; Wuorinen, conductor. Commissioned by Somerset County College. Dedicated to Coburn Britton. *See:* W96

W182 *A Song to the Lute in Musicke.* Instrumentation: Soprano and Piano. Duration: 3:00. Composed 25 September 1969 - 29 January 1970, in Iowa City (IA), London, and New York City. Peters P66452. Text attributed to Richard Edwards, 16th century. Premiered 11 January 1971, McMillin Theatre, Columbia University, New York City. Valarie Lamoree, soprano; Wuorinen, piano. Dedicated to Valarie Lamoree.

    Historical note: This work was originally composed for the *Lawson-Gould Song Collection* but was withdrawn from Lawson-Gould and assigned to C.F. Peters on 6 December 1971.

W183 *3 Songs for Tenor and Piano.* Instrumentation: Tenor and Piano. Duration: 9:00. Composed 16 December 1978 - 13 January 1979, in Middle Valley (NJ), and New York City. Peters P66811. Text by Coburn Britton. Premiered 11 April 1979, Studio of WFMT radio, New York City. Paul Sperry, tenor; Wuorinen, piano.

    Historical note: This premiere was without an audience, and was created as a recording for subsequent broadcast on WFMT radio.

W184 *Twang.* Instrumentation: Mezzo-soprano (or Soprano) and Piano. Duration: 2:00. Composed 26 March 1988 - 24 April 1989. Peters P67312. Text by Wallace Stevens. Composed for Howard Stokar's 30th birthday. Dedicated to Howard Stokar. (Private premiere — Wuorinen had no record of the date.)

    Historical note: This work has been performed a number of times, though no records of the performances have been kept since the performances have taken place mostly at private gatherings. The New York New Music Ensemble has also performed the work in Germany.

W184a 14 October 1992, Kathryn Bache Miller Theatre, Columbia University, New York City. New York New Music Ensemble; Lisa Pierce, soprano; James Winn, piano.

> **Historical note:** This concert was titled *Opening Night of Sonic Boom* and was presented by the New York Consortium for New Music, as part of its 1992 *Fall Festival of New Music. See:* B772

W185 *Wandering In This Place.* Instrumentation: Mezzo-soprano. Duration: 1:27. Composed March 1957. Unpublished. Never performed. Composed for Betty Tiedemann.

W186 *A Winter's Tale.* Instrumentation: Soprano, Cl, Hrn, Vn, Va, Vc, Pf; or Soprano, Pf. Duration: 25:00. Composed 1992. Peters P67422. Text: Dylan Thomas. Commissioned by the Brown Foundation for seven ensembles: Chamber Music Society of Lincoln Center; Chamber Music Society of Baltimore; Thamyris (Atlanta); Chamber Music Northwest; Southwest Chamber Music Ensemble; Da Camera (Houston). Dedicated to Howard Stokar. Premiered 12 October 1992, Spivey Hall, Clayton State College, Atlanta, Georgia. Thamyris: Cheryl Boyd-Waddell, soprano; Laura Gordy, piano.

Discography

1957

D1 *Prelude & Fugue for Percussion.* Phil Kraus, musical direction; performers unnamed. Huntington Station, N.Y., Golden Crest Records, Inc., 1957. Label No.: CR4004. Duration: 2:40. LP, 33⅓ rpm, 12 inches, microgroove. Series: *Golden Crest Laboratory Series.*
   Container notes unsigned. Cover art by Ludwig Lund. High fidelity Golden Sound. Title on container: *Phil Kraus presents CONFLICT: A High Fidelity Study in Percussion.* With works by Douglas R. Allan, Michael Colgrass, Jack H. McKenzie and Phil Kraus. **Historical note:** Wuorinen's personal log states this recording was made in November, 1957. *See:* W155, D62, D63, D74, B559, B561

1962

D2 *Symphony No. 3.* Japan Philharmonic Orchestra, Akeo Watanabe, conductor. New York City: Composers Recordings, Inc., 1962? Label No.: CRI 149. Duration 17:30. LP, 33⅓ rpm, 12 inches, stereo.
   Container notes by Don Jennings. Cover art by Joseph del Gaudio; calligraphy by Yasuhide Kobashi. Re-issued at least once with different cover art on container. With a work by Elias Tanenbaum. *See:* W28, B678, B679

1964

D3 *The Prayer of Jonah.* King's Chapel Choir of Boston with the Cambridge Festival Strings, Daniel Pinkham, conductor; Jean Lunn, soprano; Jeanekke Barton, mezzo-soprano; Richard Conrad, tenor; Irving Pearson, bass. Wellesley, Mass.: Cambridge Records, 1964. Label No.: CRS 1416. Duration: 10:40. LP, 33⅓ rpm, 12 inches, stereo. Recorded in Jordan Hall, Boston, 1963.

Container notes unsigned. Edition recorded: McGinnis and Marx. Title on container: *4 Contemporary Choral Works*. Includes portrait of Wuorinen. With works by Ulysses Kay, Ned Rorem, and William Flanagan. *See:* W173, B557, B558

1966

D4   *Piano Variations.* David Burge, piano. Advance Records, 1966. Label No.: FGR-3. Duration: 8:02. LP, 33⅓ rpm, 12 inches, mono.

Container notes unsigned. Cover art by Helen Strong. Production engineer: Philip F. Dering II. Title on container: *David Burge Plays New Piano Music*. With works by Salvatore Martirano, George Crumb and George Rochberg. *See:* W138, B529, B530, B539

1969

D5   *Chamber Concerto for Flute and Ten Players.* The Group for Contemporary Music; Wuorinen, conductor; Harvey Sollberger, flute soloist. New York City: Composers Recordings, Inc., 1969? Label No.: CRI SD 230. Duration: 14:50. LP, 33⅓ rpm, 12 inches, stereo.

Container notes by Carter Harman. Cover design by Judith Lerner. Cover picture courtesy of *STEELWAYS*, a publication of the American Iron and Steel Institute. Recording processed in Universal Stereo. With a work by Donald Martino. *See:* W35, B101, B102, B104, B107

D6   *Janissary Music.* Raymond DesRoches, percussion. New York City; Composers Recordings, Inc., 1969? Label No.: CRI SD 231. Duration: 12:30. LP, 33⅓ rpm, 12 inches, stereo.

Container notes unsigned. Edition recorded: ACA. Cover art by Don Kingman, Jr. With works by George Rochberg and Robert Parris. **Historical note:** DesRoches required thirteen hours to record this work to his satisfaction. *See:* W152, B324, B325, B328

D7   *Piano Concerto (Piano Concerto No. 1).* The Royal Philharmonic Orchestra; James Dixon, conductor; Wuorinen, piano soloist. New York City; Composers Recordings, Inc., 1969? Label No.: CRI SD 239. Duration: 20 minutes. LP, 33⅓ rpm, 12 inches, stereo.

Container notes unsigned. Cover art by Judith Lerner. Title on container: *Piano Concertos By Ben Weber and Charles Wuorinen*. Recorded by Robert Auger; produced by Carter Harman. With a work by Ben Weber. *See:* W19, B451 - B453, B455

D8   *Time's Encomium.* New York City: Nonesuch Records, 1969? Label No.: H-71225. Duration: Side 1, 14:53; Side 2, 16:47. LP, 33⅓ rpm, 12 inches, stereo.

Container notes by Wuorinen. Cover art by Hess and/or Antupit. Coordinator: Teresa Sterne; Art Director: William S. Harvey. Title on container: *Time's Encomium for Synthesized Sound and Processed Synthesized Sound Realized at the Columbia-Princeton Electronic Music Center, New York*. A Nonesuch Records Commission. *See:* W159, B698 - B704, B713, B715, B720 - B726, B731, B732, B734, B736, B739

1971

D9 *Duo for Violin and Piano.* Paul Zukofsky, violin; Wuorinen, piano.
Hamburg, Germany: AR in collaboration with Deutsche Grammophon,
1971 Label No.: 0654 086. Duration: 14:56. LP, 33⅓ rpm, stereo.
Series: *Acoustic Research Contemporary Music Project*, no. 4.
Container notes by John David Boros, in English, German and French. Cover
art by Dietmar Winkler. Recording engineer: Marc Aubort; container printed in
Germany by Gebrüder Jänecke, Hannover; manufactured by Deutsche Grammophon
Gesellschaft, Hamburg. With another work by Roger Sessions. *See:* W76, B211 - B213

D10 *Chamber Concerto for Violoncello and Ten Players.* The Group for
Contemporary Music. Wuorinen, conductor; Fred Sherry, cello soloist.
Other players: Harvey Sollberger, flute; Josef Marx, oboe and English
horn; Jack Kreiselman, clarinet and bass clarinet; Donald MacCourt,
bassoon; Jeanne Benjamin, violin; John Graham, viola; Alvin Brehm,
double-bass; Robert Miller, piano; Raymond DesRoches, Richard Fitz,
Claire Heldrich, percussion. New York City: Nonesuch records, p1971.
Label No.: H-71263. Duration: 18:22. LP, 33⅓ rpm, 12 inches, stereo.
See: W38, B123, B126
Ringing Changes. The New Jersey Percussion Ensemble; Raymond
DesRoches, director. Players: Joseph Passaro, vibraphone and timpani;
Marty Martini, Louis Oddo, vibraphone; Dean Poulsen, Eugene McBride,
piano; Ken Hosley, Donald Mari, drums; Matthew Patuto, brakedrums;
Doreen Holmes, almglocken; Michael Moscariello, cymbals; Vincent
Potuto, Jr., tamtams; James Pugliese, string drum and chimes. *See:* W156,
B582, B584, B585, B587
Container notes by Wuorinen. Cover art by Herb Tauss. Engineering: Marc J.
Aubort, Joanna Nickrenz (Elite Recordings, Inc.); mastering: Robert C. Ludwig (Sterling
Sound, Inc.), a Dolby-system recording. Coordinator: Teresa Sterne; art direction:
Robert L. Heimall; Cover design: Paula Bisacca.

1972

D11 *String Quartet (Sting Quartet No. 1).* The Fine Arts Quartet; Leonard
Sorkin, Abram Loft, violins; Bernard Zaslav, viola; George Sopkin,
violoncello. Turnabout, p1972. Label No.: TV-S 34515. Duration:
23:55. LP, 33⅓ rpm, 12 inches, stereo.
Container notes partially by Wuorinen and feature concert review quotes. Title
on container: *The Contemporary Composer in the U.S.A.* Recorded with Dolby S/N
Stretcher. Reissued as a compact disk in 1992 by Music & Art Programs of America,
Inc. *See:* W104, D41

1973

D12 *The Long and the Short.* Paul Zukofsky, violin; Gilbert Kalish, piano.
New York City: Mainstream, p1973. Label No.: MS 5016. Duration:
9:05. LP, 33⅓ rpm, 12 inches, stereo.
Container notes by Elliot W. Galkin. Artists and repertoire: Earle Brown;
photography: Earle Brown; recording engineer: Elliot Scheiner. Title on container:

New Music for Violin and Piano. With works by George Crumb, Isang Yun, and John Cage. Includes portrait of Wuorinen. *See:* W90, B339, B342

1974

D13 *Piano Concerto (Piano Concerto No. 1).* New York City: International Contemporary Music Exchange, p1974. Label No.: ICME-1. Duration not listed. 2 sound discs (set), 33⅓ rpm, 12 inches, stereo.

Container notes on the ICME by Igor Buketoff, discography, and "Contemporary American Music for Orchestra: An Historian's Perspective" by John Vinton. Title on container: *The International Contemporary Music Exchange, Inc., Presents the Outstanding Contemporary Orchestral Compositions of the United States.* With works by Earle Brown, Elliott Carter, Aaron Copland, George Crumb, Lukas Foss, Roy Harris, Charles Ives, Carl Ruggles, William Schuman, Samuel Barber, Henry Cowell, Jacob Druckman, Lou Harrison, Alan Hovhaness, Wallingford Riegger, George Rochberg, Gunther Schuller, Virgil Thomson, and Edgard Varèse. *See:* W19

D14 *Piano Sonata (Piano Sonata No. 1).* Robert Miller, piano. New York City: Composers Recordings, Inc., p1974. Label No.: CRI SD 306. Duration: 19:00. LP, 33⅓ rpm, 12 inches, stereo.

Container notes partially by Wuorinen. Produced by Carter Harman. This recording was made possible by a grant from the Alice M. Ditson Fund of Columbia University. With works by Stefan Wolpe, Yehudi Wyner, and George Perle. *See:* W135, B500, B501, B503, B506

D15 *Speculum Speculi.* Speculum Musicae; Fred Sherry, conductor. Players: Paul Dunkel, flute; Steve Taylor, oboe; Virgil Blackwell, bass clarinet; Donald Palma, contrabass; Ursula Oppens, piano; Richard Fitz, percussion. New York City: Nonesuch Records, p1974. Label No.: H-71300. Duration: 14:48. LP, 33⅓ rpm, 12 inches, stereo. Recorded February 1974 at Rutgers Presbyterian Church, New York City.

Container notes by Wuorinen. Cover art by Don Brautigam. Coordinator: Teresa Sterne; design and art direction: Paula Bisacca. Engineering and musical supervision: Marc J. Aubort, Joanna Nickrenz (Elite Recordings, Inc.); mastering: Robert C. Ludwig (Sterling Sound, Inc.). A Dolby-system recording. Piano/Baldwin SD-10. With a work by Donald Martino. *See:* W101, B618, B619, B621, B623, B624, B626

1975

D16 *Bearbeitungen über das Glogauer Liederbuch.* Speculum Musicae; Fred Sherry, conductor. Players: Paul Dunkel, flute; Virgil Blackwell, clarinet, bass clarinet; Daniel Reed, violin. New York City: Nonesuch Records, p1975. Label No.: H-71319. Duration: 7:08. LP, 33⅓ rpm, 12 inches, stereo. *See:* W63, B51, B52

Grand Bamboula for String Orchestra. The Light Fantastic Players; Daniel Shulman, conductor. Players: Linda Quan, Curt Macomber, Joel Lester, Kathy Seplow, Rolf Schulte, Susan Long (Violin I); Daniel Reed, Nancy Elan, Sandy Strenger, Sin-tung Chiu, Joanna Jenner (Violin II); Lois Martin, Christie Shepherd, Jake Kella, Judson Griffin (Viola); Mark Shuman, Chris Finckel, Helen Harbison, Lisa Lancaster (Violoncello);

Andrée Brière, Michael Willens (Double-bass). Duration: 5:56. *See:* W49, B302

String Trio. Speculum Musicae. Players: Rolf Schulte, violin; John Graham, viola; Fred Sherry, violoncello. Duration: 16:28. *See:* W108, B661
Container notes by Wuorinen. Cover art by Don Brautigam. Coordinator: Teresa Sterne; design and art direction: Paula Bisacca; engineering and musical supervision: Marc J. Aubort, Joanna Nickrenz (Elite Recordings, Inc.); mastering: Robert C. Ludwig (Sterling Sound, Inc.). A Dolby-system recording.

D17 *Flute Variations I.* Harvey Sollberger, flute. New York City: Nonesuch Records, p1975. Label No.: HB-73028. Duration: 6:53 2 LPs, 33⅓ rpm, 12 inches, stereo. *See:* W81, B257
Flute Variations II. Harvey Sollberger, flute. Duration: 7:24 *See:* W83, B260, B263
Container notes by Harvey Sollberger. Cover art by Robert Monroe. Coordinator: Teresa Sterne; design and art direction: Paula Bisacca. Musical supervision and engineering: Marc J. Aubort, Joanna Nickrenz (Elite Recordings, Inc.); mastering: Robert C. Ludwig (Sterling Sound, Inc.). A Dolby-system recording. Title on container: *Twentieth Century Flute Music.* With works by Luciano Berio, Mario Davidovsky, Kazuo Fukushima, Burt Levy, Roger Reynolds, Nicolas Roussakis, Preston Trombly, Edgard Varèse, and Peter Westergaard. Wuorinen performs as pianist in the Westergaard work *(Divertimento on Discobobbolic Fragments)* and the Fukushima work *(Three Pieces from Chū-u).*

D18 *Making Ends Meet.* Jean Wentworth, Kenneth Wentworth, pianists. New York City: Desto, 1975? Label No.: DC-7131. Duration not listed. LP, 33⅓ rpm, 12 inches, stereo.
Container notes by Jean Wentworth. Recorded by Marc Aubort. Manufactured in the U.S.A. for home use only. With works by William Sydeman, Joel Spiegelman, and Lawrence Moss. *See:* W134, B369, B370

1977

D19 *Bassoon Variations.* Donald MacCourt, bassoon; Susan Jolles, harp; Gordon Gottlieb, timpani. New York City: New World Records, p1977. Label No.: NW 209. Duration: 12:05. LP, 33⅓ rpm, 12 inches, stereo. Series: *Recorded Anthology of American Music.* Recorded at Columbia Studios, 30th Street, New York City.
Container notes by Eric Salzman. Edition recorded: C.F. Peters. Cover design by Elaine Sherer Cox. Cover art; David Smith's *Untitled II* (India ink, egg yolk and water color); collection of Whitney Museum of American Art, New York City. Producer: Sam Parkins; Associate Producer: Elizabeth Ostrow; Recording Engineer: Stan Tonkel; Tape Editors: Noel Harrington, Randy Payne; Mastering: Lee Halko (Sterling Sound, Inc.). Title on container: *New Music for Virtuosos.* This recording was made possible through a grant from the Rockefeller Foundation. *See:* W62, B47 - B49

D20 *Composition for Oboe and Piano.* James Ostryniec, oboe; Wuorinen, piano. Malibu, California: Orion, 1977? Label No.: ORS 78288. Duration: 16:00. Recorded June 17, 1977 at RCA Recording Studios, New York City. LP, 33⅓ rpm, 12 inches, stereo.
Container notes unsigned. Edition recorded: C.F. Peters. Cover art by Amalie Rothschild. Edited by Lawrence Moss; produced by Giveon Cornfield; recording

engineer: Patrick Martin. Dolby process. With works by Ernst Krenek and Lawrence Moss. *See:* W67, B134, B136

1978

D21   *Percussion Symphony*. The New Jersey Percussion Ensemble; Raymond DesRoches, director; Wuorinen, conductor. Players: James Hurst, glockenspiel; Doreen Holmes, chimes; Bruce Tatti, xylophone; Edmund Fay, vibraphone; Richard Sacks, marimba; Dean Poulsen, celesta; Aleck Karis, piano I; Diane Battersby, piano II; Dale Diesel, inside piano; Ernest Buongiorno, antique cymbals; Vincent Varcadipane, triangles, bell plates; James Pugliese, brake drums, almglocken; James di Palma, high cymbals; Jeffrey Pinnas, low cymbals; Robert Paddock, gongs; Ted Sturm, gongs; Michael Holmes, gong; Peter Jarvis, gongs, woodblock; Peter Alexander, temple blocks, tambourine. New York City: Elektra/Asylum/Nonesuch, p1978. Label No.: H-71353. Duration: 41:53. LP, 33⅓ rpm, 12 inches, stereo. Recorded March, 1978, at the John Harms Englewood Plaza for the Performing Arts, Englewood, New Jersey.

   Container notes by Wuorinen; Wuorinen biography unsigned. Edition recorded: C.F. Peters. Cover art by Ron Walotsky. Coordinator: Teresa Sterne. Design and art direction: Paula Bisacca; engineering and musical supervision: Marc J. Aubort; Joanna Nickrenz (Elite Recordings, Inc.); mastering: Robert C. Ludwig (Masterdisk Corp.). A Dolby-system recording. Manufactured by Elektra/Asylum/Nonesuch Records, a Division of Warner Communications, Inc. Awarded an Audio Excellence Record Award for 1979. *See:* W154, D33, B423 - B441

1979

D22   *Two-Part Symphony*. American Composers Orchestra; Dennis Russell Davies, conductor. New York City: Composers Recordings, Inc., p1979. Label No.: CRI SD 410. Duration: 23:30. LP, 33⅓ rpm, 12 inches, stereo. Series: *American Contemporary*. Recorded live in Alice Tully Hall, New York City, 11 December 1978.

   Container notes by H. Wiley Hitchcock. Edition recorded: C.F. Peters. Cover art by Judith Lerner. Produced by Carter Harman; recorded by David Hancock; electronic transformations by Michael Riesman. Titles on container: *American Composers Orchestra*. With a work by John Cage. *See:* W30, B779 - B792

1980

D23   *Six Pieces for Violin and Piano*. John Ferrell, violin; James Avery, piano. Malibu, California: Orion, 1980? Label No.: ORS 80381. Durations: 1:30; 2:35; 1:33; 3:39; 4:38; 4:18. LP, 33⅓ rpm, 12 inches, stereo.

   Container notes by John Boe. Produced by Giveon Cornfield. With a work by Guillaume Lekeu. *See:* W96, D35, D63, D74, B605, B606

D24   *The Winds*. Parnassus; Anthony Korf, conductor. New York City: New World Records, p1980. Label No.: NW 306. Duration: 14:53. LP, 33⅓ rpm, 12 inches, stereo. Series: *Recorded Anthology of American Music*. Recorded at RCA Recording Studios, New York City.

Container notes: "A New York School: Three Generations of Composers" by Jeffrey Kresky. Edition recorded: C.F. Peters. Cover design: Michael Sonino. Cover art: Morris Louis's *Point of Tranquility* (acrylic on canvas; the Hirshhorn Museum and Sculpture Garden, Washington, D.C.). Producer: Elizabeth Ostrow. Recording and mixing engineer: Paul Goodman; assisting engineers: Tom Brown, John Cue; Tape editing: Don Van Gordon (Soundwave Recording Studios); mastering: Robert Ludwig (Masterdisk). Photographs: Jane Hamborsky. Includes portrait of Wuorinen. Title on container: *Parnassus Plays Works By Stefan Wolpe, Mario Davidovsky, Charles Wuorinen, Erik Lundborg, David Olan*. With works by Stefan Wolpe, Mario Davidovsky, Erik Lundborg, and David Olan. *See:* W57, B817

1981

D25 *Joan's*. Da Capo Chamber Players. Players: Patricia Spencer, flute; Laura Flax, clarinet; Joel Lester, violin; André Emelianoff, violoncello; Joan Tower, piano. New York City: Composers Recordings, Inc., p1981. Label No.: CRI SD 441. Duration: 6:27. LP, 33⅓ rpm, 12 inches, stereo. Series: American Contemporary. Recorded by David Hancock, New York City, February and March 1981.

Container notes by Gregory Sandow. Cover art by Judith Lerner. Produced by Carter Harman and Carolyn Sachs. Title on container: *The Da Capo Chamber Players Celebrate Their Tenth Anniversary*. A composer supervised recording. With works by Joseph Schwantner, Shalumit Ran, Joan Tower, George Perle, and Philip Glass. **Historical note:** "This recording employed hand-made ribbon microphones in pairs, spaced six feet apart, in the best available acoustical environment. Their output was fed to a 30 IPS Studer A-80 tape recorder, slightly modified for constant velocity record-playback characteristics. In this way the need for conventional (and troublesome) noise reduction devices was eliminated. Lacquer masters were cut from the original tapes, employing an Ortofon transducer system with motional feedback. To minimize groove echo, the lacquer masters were processed within twelve hours using the latest European equipment and techniques. Strict quality control pressings were made of the purest available vinyl." — Container. *See:* W89, B335 - B337

D26 *Psalm 39*. Richard Frisch, baritone; David Starobin, guitar. New York City: Bridge, p1981. Label No.: BDG 2001. Duration: 11:33. LP, 33⅓ rpm, 12 inches, stereo.

Container notes by William Bland. Cover art by Ronald Roxbury. Production: David Starobin; recorded and mastered by David Hancock. Title on container: *New Music With Guitar, Volume 1*. With works by Hans Werner Henze, Barbara Kolb, and William Bland. *See:* W180, B565

1982

D27 *Arabia Felix*. Harvey Sollberger, flute; Donald MacCourt, bassoon; David Starobin, guitar; Benjamin Hudson, violin; Raymond DesRoches, vibraphone; Robert Miller, piano; Wuorinen, conductor. New York City: Composers Recordings, Inc., p1982. Label No.: CRI SD 463. Duration: 11:05. LP, 33⅓ rpm, 12 inches, stereo. Series: *American Contemporary*. Recorded May 1981, New York City.

Container notes unsigned. Edition recorded: C.F. Peters. Cover art by Judith Lerner. Produced by Carter Harman; associate producer: Carolyn Sachs. A composer-supervised recording. Includes portrait of Wuorinen with Nicolas Roussakis and Harvey Sollberger. **Historical note:** This recording is dedicated to the memory of Robert Miller

(1930-1981). The recording session for *Arabia Felix* was Miller's last performance. *See:* W60, B11

D28   *Percussion Duo.* James Avery, pianist; Steven Schick, percussionist. New York City: Composers Recordings, Inc., p1982. Label No.: CRI SD 459. Duration: 13:59. LP, 33⅓ rpm, 12 inches, stereo. Series: *American Contemporary.* Recorded by Stephen Julstrom, Iowa City, Iowa, June 1981.

   Container notes unsigned. Cover art by Judith Lerner. Produced by Carter Harman; associate producer: Carolyn Sachs. A composer-supervised recording. This recording received an American Composers Alliance Recording Award. With works by John Lennon, Eleanor Cory, and Chester Biscardi. *See:* W153, B417, B418, B420

1983

D29   *Chamber Concerto for Tuba.* The Group for Contemporary Music; Wuorinen, conductor; David Brainard, tuba soloist. New York City: Composers Recordings, Inc., p1983. Label No.: CRI 491. Duration: 18:58. LP, 33⅓ rpm, 12 inches, stereo. Series: *American Contemporary.* Recorded December 1972 in New York City.

   Container notes unsigned. Edition recorded: C.F. Peters. Cover art by Judith Lerner. Recorded by David Hancock, December 1972, New York City, and Michael Riesman, December 1981, New York City. Remixed by Riesman, March 1983. Produced by Carter Harman. This recording was made possible, in part, with public funds from the New York State Council on the Arts. Additional funding was provided by the Martha Baird Rockefeller Fund for Music, Inc., and private donors. A composer-supervised recording. With a work by Glen Lieberman. **Historical note**: Initially, this recording of the concerto consisted only of the ensemble without the tuba soloist. (According to Wuorinen, the tuba part was too difficult for the tuba player.) Some ten years later, Michael Riesman remixed (dubbed in) the solo tuba part on top of a tape that had been made of the orchestra part. That remixing comprises this recording of the concerto. *See:* W37, B119

D30   *Concerto for Amplified Violin and Orchestra.* The University of Iowa Symphony Orchestra; James Dixon, conductor; Paul Zukofsky, violin. Iowa City, Iowa: University of Iowa Press, p1983. Label No.: 8319. Duration: 21:32. 33⅓ rpm, 12 inches, stereo.

   Container includes a brief biography of Wuorinen. Recorded by the Recording Studios, School of Music, the University of Iowa. Recording engineers: Lowell Cross, William Heinrichs, James March, and Thomas Mintner. Title on container: *New Music From The University Of Iowa.* Also contains works by Peter Todd Lewis and Richard Hervig. Cover photo on jacket consists of an image produced by the Laser Deflection System, designed by Lowell Cross, director of The University of Iowa School of Music Recording Studios. *See:* W5, B181, B182

1985

D31   *Archangel.* David Taylor, bass trombone; Benjamin Hudson, violin; Carol Zeavin, violin; Louise Schulman, viola; Fred Sherry, violoncello. Tenafly, N.J.: Triple Letter Brand Records, p1985. Label No.: TR520695; TLB 1409. Duration not listed. LP, 33⅓ rpm, 12 inches, stereo. Recorded 31 March 1981, Church of the Holy Trinity, New York City.

Container notes by David Taylor, edited by David Wright. Cover photo by Theo Bergstrom. Album cover concept: Ronnie Taylor. Back container photography by Marianne Barcellona. Producers: Ronnie and David Taylor; mastered at Trutone Records by Phil Austin; manufactured at Trutone Records, Haworth, N.J.; graphics: Mike Rufino. With works by Eric Ewazen, David Liebman, and Frederic Rzewski. *See:* W61, B18

D32 *Spinoff.* Benjamin Hudson, violin; Donald Palma, double-bass; Joseph Passaro, conga drums. New York City: Bridge, p1985. Label No.: BDG 2005. Duration: 6:36. LP, 33⅓ rpm, 12 inches. Recorded November 12, 1984, Vanguard Studios.

Container notes by Peter Lieberson. Edition recorded: C.F. Peters. Cover art by P. Craig Russell. Producer: David Starobin; engineer: Fred Miller; associate engineers: Tom Lazarus, Paul Zinman, David Hancock; album coordinators: Victoria Roth, Rebecca Starobin; design: Brighton Typography, Ltd. Title on container: *Speculum Musicae: A Fifteenth Anniversary Album*. Includes portrait of Wuorinen. With works by Peter Lieberson and Seymour Schifrin. **Historical note:** Wuorinen wrote the following commentary for the container: "The fifteenth anniversary of the founding of *Speculum Musicae* affords an opportunity to reflect on the achievements of this distinguished ensemble. If certain slightly older new music performing groups were the result of composers asserting their own rights in the performance of their own music, one can say that Speculum represented in its founding the first flowering of a remarkable group of young musicians for whom — finally! — the music of their own time had become their own musical mother tongue. They brought to contemporary music the flair of virtuosi, and a love of what they played that has gone far beyond the requirements of the merely professional. Over the years, Speculum Musicae has kept these commitments and characteristics, and still (at fifteen) possesses the excellent enthusiasm which gave it birth." *See:* W102, D32, B631 - B633

1987

D33 *Percussion Symphony.* The New Jersey Percussion Ensemble; Raymond DesRoches, director; Charles Wuorinen, conductor. New York City: Elektra/Asylum/Nonesuch, p1987. Label No.: 79150-2. Duration: 40:40. CD, 4¾ inches, digital audio.

Container notes by Wuorinen. A reissue of the 1978 LP recording. Cover art by Don Brautigam. Title on container: *Percussion Music*. With works by Edgard Varèse, Michael Colgrass, David Saperstein and Henry Cowell. *See:* W154, D21, B423 - B441

D34 *Suite from "The Magic Art".* The Louisville Orchestra; Lawrence Leighton Smith, conductor. Louisville, Kentucky: First Edition Records, 1987. Label No.: KM 15474; LS#792. Duration: 25:25. LP, 33⅓ rpm, 12 inches. Series: *The Louisville Orchestra First Edition Records* — The 167th Release. Recorded 10 April 1985 in the Robert Whitney Hall, Kentucky Center for the Arts.

Container notes by Wuorinen. Cover art by Julius Friedman. Wayne S. Brown, Executive Director; Andrew Kazdin, Producer. Production of this recording was supported by a grant from the National Endowment for the Arts. *See:* W52, D72

1988

D35   *The Blue Bamboula.* Garrick Ohlsson, piano. New York City: Bridge, p1988. Label No.: BCD 9008. Duration: 11:20. CD, 4¾ inches, digital stereo. *See:* W131, D39, D68, B61, B62
>   Container notes by Michael Steinberg. Cover photo by Frederic Petters. Producer: David Starobin; engineer: Paul Goodman; mastering: Paul Zinman (N.Y. Digital); administrative supervision: Michael Leavitt; managing director: Rebecca Starobin; design: Brighton Typography, Ltd. Piano: Bösendorfer; violin (make): Sergio Peressone.

>   *Fantasia.* Benjamin Hudson, piano; Garrick Ohlsson, piano. Duration: 17:16. *See:* W80, B242

>   *The Long and the Short.* Benjamin Hudson, violin. Duration: 9:29. *See:* W90, B343

>   *Six Pieces for Violin and Piano.* Benjamin Hudson, violin; Garrick Ohlsson, piano. Duration: 19:44. *See:* W96, D23, D63, D74, B608, B609

>   *Spinoff.* Benjamin Hudson, violin; Donald Palma, double-bass; Joseph Passaro, conga drums. Duration: 6:30. *See:* W102, D32, B631 - B633
>   Engineer: Fred Miller.

D36   *The Golden Dance.* San Francisco Symphony; Herbert Blomstedt, conductor; Jack Von Geem, percussion soloist. New York City: Elektra/-Asylum/Nonesuch, p1988. Label No.: 9 79185-2. Duration: 22:59. CD, digital audio (LP or Cassette also available). Recorded 16 September 1986 at Davies Symphony Hall, San Francisco. *See:* W14, B294 - B299

>   *Piano Concerto No. 3.* San Francisco Symphony; Herbert Blomstedt, conductor; Garrick Ohlsson, piano soloist. Duration: 30:03. CD, 4¾ in., digital audio. Recorded 22 September 1986 at Davies Symphony Hall. Series: *Meet the Composer Orchestra Residency Series. See:* W21, B489, B491, B491 - B494
>   Container notes by Michael Steinberg. Edition recorded: C.F. Peters. Cover art by Morris Louis *(Beth Chaf, 1959-60).* Photo courtesy of Andre Emmerich Gallery. Produced by Marc Aubort and Joanna Nickrenz; engineered by Elite Recordings, Inc. Art Direction and Design: Ink-a-Dinka, Inc.

1990

D37   *Fast Fantasy.* Group for Contemporary Music. Fred Sherry, violoncello; Wuorinen, piano. New York City: New World Records, p1990. Label No.: NW 385-2. Duration: 15:47. CD, 4¾ inches, digital. Series: Recorded Anthology of American Music. Recorded 25 November 1988 at the Coolidge Auditorium, Library of Congress, Washington, D.C. *See:* W81

>   *Third String Quartet.* Benjamin Hudson, violin; Carol Zeavin, violin; Lois Martin, viola; Fred Sherry, violoncello. Duration: 29:12. *See:* W106, D69

>   *Sonata for Violin and Piano.* Benjamin Hudson, violin; Garrick Ohlsson, piano (guest artist). *See:* W98, D69
>   Container notes by Tim Page. Cover art: Random Fractal Subdivision © Richard F. Voss/IBM Research (Fractal art based on computer analysis of Picasso's Les Demoiselles d'Avignon; cover design: Bob Defrin. Produced by Marc J. Aubort and Joanna Nickrenz (Elite Recordings, Inc.). Recording made possible with grants from the

Andrew W. Mellon Foundation, and the McKim Fund, Music Division, Library of Congress.
Also available on LP.

D38 *New York Notes.* New York New Music Ensemble; Robert Black, conductor. Players: Jayn Rosenfeld, flute; Jean Kopperud, clarinet; Linda Quan, violin; Chris Finckel, violoncello; Daniel Druckman, percussion; Elizabeth DiFelice, piano. Newton Centre, Mass.: GM Recordings/Harmonia Mundi USA, p1990. Label No.: GM 2028CD. Duration: ca. 22 minutes. CD, 4¾ inches, digital, stereo. Recorded 24 January 1989 at Rutgers Presbyterian Church, N.Y.
    Container notes unsigned. Edition recorded: C.F. Peters. Engineer: Marc J. Aubort; digital editing and producer: Joanna Nickrenz; design: Jerry Newton; project director: A G Merrill Hurlbut; executive producer: Gunther Schuller. With works by Joseph Schwantner and Susan Blaustein. *See:* W93, B399

1992

D39 *The Blue Bamboula.* Ursula Oppens, piano. Berkeley: Music & Arts Programs of America, p1992. Label No.: CD699. Duration: 11:02. CD, 4¾ inches, digital stereo. Recorded 1991 at the American Academy and Institute of Arts and Letters, New York City.
    Container note by Wuorinen. Title on container: *American Piano Music of Our Time. Vol. II.* Cover photo by Christian Steiner. Producer/Engineer/Editor: Judith Sherman; Piano: Steinway; Piano maintenance: Ed Wedberg; Project director: Frederick J. Maroth. With works by Conlon Nancarrow, Frederic Rzewski, Tobias Picker, John Harbison, and Anthony Davis. *See:* W131, D35, D68

D40 *Divertimento for Alto Saxophone and Piano.* John Sampen, saxophone; Marilyn Shrude, piano. Label No.: Neuma 450-80. Duration: 9:27.
    Cover art by Mark Rothko *(Untitled, 1960),* Toledo Museum of Art. Designed by Susan Calkins; produced by Shirish Korde. Recording engineers: Mark Bunce, Harry Norrins. Edited by Mark Bunce. Digital mastering by Northeastern Digital Recording, Southborough, Massachusetts. *See:* W71

D41 *String Quartet (String Quartet No. 1).* The Fine Arts Quartet; Leonard Sorkin, Abram Loft, violins; Bernard Zaslav, viola; George Sopkin, violoncello. Berkeley, CA: Music & Art Programs of America, Inc. Label No.: CD-707. Duration: 24:00. CD, 4¾ inches, digital, stereo.
    A reissue of the 1972 Turnabout LP recording. Container notes by Wuorinen. Recording engineer: Raymond Weisling. Issued under license from the Moss Music Group, a division of Essex Entertainment, Inc. Contains a photograph of Wuorinen. On this compact disk the Wuorinen work is on side one instead of side two. *See:* W104, D11

COMMERCIAL RELEASES — WUORINEN AS PERFORMER

1964

D42   *Echoi*, by Lukas Foss. Wuorinen, piano; Raymond DesRoches, percussion; Arthur Bloom, clarinet; Robert Martin, violoncello (Group for Contemporary Music). Epic, 1964. Label No.: BC 1286; LC 3886. Duration: 27:46. LP, 33⅓ rpm, 12 inches, stereo.

> Container notes unsigned. Produced by Paul Myers and Lukas Foss. Also available on monaural (Epic LC 3886). *See:* B1057

1970

D43   *Cursive*, by Chou Wên-chung. Harvey Sollberger, flute; Wuorinen, piano. New York City: Composers Recordings, Inc., p1970. Label No.: CRI SD 251. Duration: not listed. 2 LPs, 33⅓ rpm, 12 inches, stereo.

> Container notes unsigned. Cover art by Judith Lerner. Edition recorded: C.F. Peters. Produced by Carter Harman. Recorded by Jerry Newman and Jerry Bruck. This recording was made possible by a grant from the American Institute and the National Academy of Arts & Letters; the Martha Baird Rockefeller Fund for Music; and the Alice Ditson Fund of Columbia University. Historical note: This   was   the   first recording devoted exclusively to the music of Chou Wên-chung. *See:* B1041

1971

D44   *Pierrot Lunaire*, by Arnold Schoenberg.   Contemporary Chamber Ensemble; Arthur Weisberg, conductor; Jan DeGaetani, voice. (Wuorinen does not perform on this recording, but wrote the program notes.) New York City: Nonesuch Records, p1971. Label No.: Nonesuch H-71251. Duration: 34:27. LP, 33⅓ rpm, 12 inches, stereo.

> Container notes by Wuorinen.

1972

D45   *Nonet*, by David Diamond. Wuorinen conducting the string nonet. New York City: Composers Recordings, Inc., p1972. Label No.: CRI SD 294. Duration: 16:05. LP, 33⅓ rpm, 12 inches, stereo.

> Container notes unsigned. With another work by Diamond and works by David Del Tredici.

D46   *Three Movements for Quintet*, by Raoul Pleskow. Rolf Schulte, violin; Allen Blustine, clarinet; Sophie Sollberger, flute; Fred Sherry, violoncello; Robert Miller, piano; Wuorinen, conductor. New York City: Composers Recordings, Inc., p1972. Label No.: CRI SD 302. Duration: 7:30. LP, 33⅓ rpm, 12 inches. stereo.

> Container notes unsigned. Cover art by Judith Lerner. Produced by Carter Harman. A composer-supervised recording. With works by Edward Miller, Joan Tower and Elie Yarden.

1973

D47 *Trio (1962)*, by Otto Luening. Harvey Sollberger, flute; Fred Sherry, violoncello; Wuorinen, piano. New York City: Composers Recordings Inc., p1973. Label No.: CRI SD 303. Duration: 10:00. LP, 33⅓ rpm, 12 inches, stereo.
　　Container notes mostly by Luening. Cover art by Judith Lerner. Produced by Carter Harman; recorded by David Hancock. A composer-supervised recording.

1974

D48 *Divertimento for Flute, Cello and Piano*, by Harvey Sollberger. Harvey Sollberger, flute; Fred Sherry, violoncello; Wuorinen, piano. New York City: Composers Recordings, Inc., p1974. Label No.: CRI SD 319. Duration: 12:35. LP, 33⅓ rpm, 12 inches, stereo.
Impromptu for Piano, by Harvey Sollberger. Wuorinen, piano. Duration: 10:20.
　　Container notes partially by Sollberger. Cover art by Judith Lerner. Produced by Carter Harman; recorded by David Hancock. Title on container: *Modern Instrumental Music*. A composer-supervised recording. This recording was made possible by grants from the American Composers Alliance, the Martha Baird Rockefeller Fund for Music, Inc., and the National Institute-American Academy of Arts and Letters. With a work by Fred Lehrdahl.

1975

D49 *Motet and Madrigal*, by Raoul Pleskow. Wuorinen, conductor; Judith Allen, soprano; Paul J. Sperry, tenor. New York City: Composers Recordings, Inc., p1975. Label No.: CRI SD 342. Duration: 6:30. LP, 33⅓ rpm, 12 inches, stereo. Series: *American Contemporary*. Recorded 18 November 1974.
　　Container notes partially by Raoul Pleskow. Edition recorded: ACA. Title on container: *American Contemporary: New Trends*. With works by Irwin Bazelon, Paul Lansky, M. Zuckerman, and L. Cross.

1977

D50 *Déserts*, by Edgard Varèse. Group for Contemporary Music; Wuorinen, conductor. New York City: Composers Recordings, Inc., p1977? Label No.: CRI SD 268. Duration: 23:30. 2 LPs, 33⅓ rpm, 12 inches, stereo. Recorded at the Columbia-Princeton Electronic Music Center.
　　Container notes unsigned. Cover art by Stephen Allen Whealton (separations provided by the Polaroid Company). Produced by Carter Harman. Title on container: *Columbia-Princeton Electronic Music Center Tenth Anniversary Celebration*. With works by Otto Luening, Milton Babbitt, Vladimir Ussachevsky, Pril Smiley, Alice Shields, Bülent Arel, and Mario Davidovsky. Includes a booklet on the history of the Columbia-Princeton Electronic Music Center. *See:* D52, B1049

1980

D51 *La bocca della verità*, by George Rochberg; *Rhapsodie*, by Ralph Shapey. James Ostryniec, oboe; Wuorinen, piano. New York City: Composers Recordings, Inc., p1980. Label No.: CRI SD 423. Durations: 11:45 (Rochberg); 6:15 (Shapey). LP, 33⅓ rpm, 12 inches, stereo. Series: *American Contemporary*. Recorded April through July, 1979, New York City.

> Container notes unsigned. Title on container: *Music for Oboe*. With works by R. C. Seeger, Gunther Schuller, J. Julian, and L. Singer. Subsequently released by CRI in 1985 on a cassette tape consisting of works only by George Rochberg. *See:* D53

1985

D52 *Déserts*, by Edgard Varèse. Group for Contemporary Music; Wuorinen, conductor. New York: Composers Recordings, Inc., p1985. Label No.: ACS 6010. Duration: 23:30. 1 sound cassette, 1⅞ ips, stereo. Dolby processed. Series: *Anthology Series*.

> Container notes by various people. Edition recorded: Colfranc. Title on container: *Electronic Music: The Pioneers*. With works by Vladimir Ussachevsky, Milton Babbitt, and Otto Luening. Previously released as an LP. *See:* D50

D53 *La boca della verità*, by George Rochberg. James Ostryniec, oboe; Wuorinen, piano. New York City: Composers Recordings, Inc., p1985. Label No.: ACS 6013. Duration: 11:45. Cassette tape, analog, 1⅞ ips, 3⅞ × 2½ in., Dolby processed, stereo. Series: *Anthology series*. Recorded 1979, New York City. Previously released on LP as CRI SD 423.

> With other works by Rochberg. *See:* D51

1987

D54 *Concerto for Piano and Orchestra*, by Milton Babbitt. American Composers Orchestra; Wuorinen, conductor; Alan Feinberg, piano. New York City: New World Records, p1987. Label No.: NW 346-2. Duration: 25:44. CD, 4¾ inches, digital, stereo. Recorded 20 January 1986, at Lehman Center for the Performing Arts, Lehman College, Bronx, N.Y. Series: *Recorded Anthology of American Music*.

> Container notes by Andrew Mead. Editions recorded: C.F. Peters. Cover design: Bob Defrin; cover photograph: David Michael Kennedy. Digital editing: Paul Zinman (New York Digital Recording, Inc.); Direct metal mastering: Robert C. Ludwig (Masterdisk). This recording was made possible with grants from the National Endowment for the Arts, the New York State Council on the Arts, and Francis Goelet. With another work by Milton Babbitt. Also available as an LP. *See:* B1047

NON-COMMERCIAL SOUND RECORDINGS

1954

D55 *O Filii et Filiae*. The John Harms Chorus. Paramus, N.J.: Presto Recording Corp., 1954. LP, 33⅓ rpm, 12 inches. Recorded at Town Hall, New York City, 2 May 1954.

Historical note: Wuorinen believes this recording is probably that of his first professional performance as a composer. *See:* W172

1959

D56 *Symphony No. 3*. Orchestra of America; Richard Korn, conductor. Recording Guarantee Project (American International Music Fund, Koussevitzky Music Foundation), 1959. Duration: 17:00. 1 sound tape reel, 7½ ips, 1 track, 7 inches, mono. Recorded live in Carnegie Hall, New York City, 11 November 1959. Limited edition.

Container note specifies restrictions for use of this recording. The OCLC (Online Computer Library Center, Dublin, Ohio) national shared-cataloging bibliographic database indicates that the New York Public Library is the only institution to own this tape (OCLC Bibliographic Record #16972153). *See:* W28

1963

D57 *Concert for Double Bass Alone*. The Hartt Chamber Players. Duration: 5:05 plus 30 seconds of applause. 1 tape reel, 7½ ips.

Festival of 8 March 1963, University of Illinois at Urbana-Champaign. *See:* W68

1967

D58 *Concerto for Piano and Orchestra (Piano Concerto No. 1)*. Buffalo Philharmonic Orchestra; Lukas Foss, conductor; Wuorinen, piano soloist. Recording Guarantee Project (American International Music Fund, Koussevitzky Music Foundation), 1967. Duration: 19:30. 1 sound tape reel, 7½ ips., 2 track, 7 inches, mono. Recorded live 1 October 1967 at Kleinhans Music Hall, Buffalo, New York. Limited edition.

Container note specifies restrictions for use of this recording. The OCLC (Online Computer Library Center, Dublin, Ohio) national shared-cataloging bibliographic database indicates that the New York Public Library is the only institution to own this tape (OCLC Bibliographic Record #16972113). *See:* W19, W19b

1971

D59 *The Politics of Harmony*. Place and date of recording unknown, but probably not earlier than 1971. 1 tape reel, 3¾ ips., 4-track, 7 inches, mono. Recorded on one side only.

At Indiana University, Bloomington, Indiana. Donated by Robert Orchard. *See:* W160

1977

D60 *[Charles Wuorinen Interview, April 1, 1977]*. Recorded for use by the Voice of America, 1977. 1 sound tape reel, analog, 7½ ips, double track, 10 inches, mono. Series: *Voice of America Library Collection* (Library of Congress).

At the Library of Congress, copied from a Voice of America 7 inch tape. Interviewed in Cleveland, Ohio, on his work being performed by the Cleveland Orchestra *(Movers and Shakers)*. *See:* W16

1980

D61 *Joan's*. Da Capo Chamber Players. Bowling Green, Ohio: College of Musical Arts, p1980. 2 sound cassettes, analog, Dolby processed, stereo. Recorded at Bowling Green State University College of Musical Arts, Bryan Recital Hall, April 23, 1980. *See:* W89, D25

1981

D62 *Prelude and Fugue for Percussion*. Indiana University Percussion Ensemble; William Roberts, director; William Roberts and Norman Weinberg, directors. Duration: 7:04. 1 sound tape reel, 7½ ips., 2 track, 7 inches, stereo. Recorded 3 August 1981.

Also exists as a sound recording (3 tape reels, 7½ ips., 2 track, 7 inches, stereo) recorded on 1 March 1986. Indiana University, Bloomington, Ind.; School of Music; Program No. 118, 1981-1982. *See:* W155, D1, D70, D73

1983

D63 *Hyperion*. Indiana University New Music Ensemble; Harvey Sollberger, director; Steve Rosen, conductor. Duration: 17:27. On reel 3 of 3 sound tape reels, 7½ ips., 2 track, 7 inches, stereo. Recorded 18 October 1983.

Indiana University, Bloomington, Ind.; School of Music; Program No. 184, 1983-1984. *See:* W50

D64 *Six Pieces for Violin and Piano*. Gregory Fulkerson, violin; Robert Shannon, piano. Duration: 17:37. On reels 2 and 3 of 3 sound tape reels, 7½ ips., 2 track, 7 inches, stereo. Recorded 3 October 1983.

Indiana University, Bloomington, Ind.; School of Music; Program No. 143, 1983-1984. *See:* W96, D23, D35, D74

1985

D65 *Hyperion*. Indiana University New Music Ensemble; Harvey Sollberger, director; David Bowden, conductor. Duration: 17:12. On reel 2 of 3 sound tape reels, 7½ ips., 2 track, 7 inches, stereo. Recorded 19 March 1985.

Indiana University, Bloomington, Ind.; School of Music; Program No. 679, 1984-1985. *See:* W50

D66 *Trio for Bass Instruments.* University of Illinois Contemporary Chamber Players. Duration: 9:07. On reel 2 of 3 sound tape reels, 7½ ips., 2 track, 7 inches, stereo. Recorded 25 February 1985.

    Indiana University, Bloomington, Ind.; School of Music; Program No. 601, 1984-1985. *See:* W116

1986

D67 *Sonata for Flute and Piano.* Indiana University New Music Ensemble; Harvey Sollberger, flute. Duration: 16:35. On reel 1 of 3 sound tape reels, 7½ ips., 2 track, 7 inches, stereo. Recorded 22 April 1986.

    Indiana University, Bloomington, Ind.; School of Music; Program No. 739, 1985-1986. *See:* W97

1987

D68 *The Blue Bamboula.* Indiana University New Music Ensemble; Harvey Sollberger, director. (Pianist not specified.) Duration: 10:29. On reel 1 of 3 sound tape reels, analog, 7½ ips., 2 track, 7 inches, stereo. Recorded 3 December 1987.

    Program titled: *New Music and the Computer: The Cutting Edge.* Indiana University, Bloomington, Ind.; School of Music; Program No. 342, 1987-1988. *See:* W131, D35, D39

1988

D69 *Fast Fantasy.* Group for Contemporary Music. Fred Sherry, violoncello; Wuorinen, piano. Library of Congress Music Division Concert, 25 November 1988. Duration not listed. 2 sound tape reels, 7½ ips., 2 track, 10 inches, stereo. Recorded 25 November 1988 in the Coolidge Auditorium of the Library of Congress, Washington, D.C. *See:* W81
Sonata for Violin and Piano. Benjamin Hudson, violin; Garrick Ohlsson, piano (guest artist). *See:* W98, D37
Third String Quartet. Benjamin Hudson, Carol Zeavin, violins; Lois Martin, viola; Fred Sherry, violoncello. *See:* W106, D37

    First performance of the sonata, commissioned by the McKim Fund. Program titled: *The Music of Charles Wuorinen.* Rich Kleinfeldt functioned as announcer. Concert given under the auspices of the McKim Fund; produced by the Music Division and the Recording Laboratory of the Library of Congress. Library of Congress also holds version edited for broadcast (RWB 8609-8610). Subsequently released as a compact disc by New World Records.

1989

D70 *Prelude and Fugue for Percussion.* Eastman Percussion Ensemble; John Beck, Director. Duration: 6:52. On 1 of 3 sound tape reels, analog, 15 ips., 2 track, 10 inches, Dolby-A, stereo. Recorded 21 November 1989 in the Eastman Theatre.

    Eastman School of Music, University of Rochester, Rochester, N. Y.; Program, 1989-1990. *See:* W155, D1, D62, D70, D73

1990

D71 *Ancestors*. Graduate Chamber Orchestra, Eastman School of Music; Sydney Hodkinson, conductor. Duration: 10:05. On 1 of 3 sound tape reels, analog, 15 ips., 2 track, 10 inches, Dolby-A, stereo. Recorded 4 March 1990 in Kilbourn Hall, Eastman School of Music.

Eastman School of Music, University of Rochester, Rochester, N.Y.; Program, 1989-1990. *See:* W32

D72 *Prelude and Fugue for Percussion*. Indiana University Percussion Ensemble; William Roberts, conductor. Duration: 7:10. On reel 1 of 2 sound tape reels, analog, 7½ ips., 2 track, 7 inches, stereo. Recorded 26 February 1990.

Indiana University, Bloomington, Ind.; School of Music; Program No. 586, 1989-1990. *See:* W155, D1, D62, D70

D73 *Six Pieces for Violin and Piano*. Nina Lutz, violin; Marilyn Monken, piano. Duration: 19:06. On 1 of 2 sound tape reels, digital, 2 track, 10 inches, stereo. Recorded 11 November 1990 in Kilbourn Hall, Eastman School of Music.

Eastman School of Music, University of Rochester, Rochester, N.Y.; Program 1990-1991. *See:* W96, D23, D35, D63

D74 *Suite from "The Magic Art"*. Indiana University Chamber Orchestra; Harvey Sollberger, conductor. Duration: 25:27. On reel 3 of 3 sound tape reels, analog, 7½ ips., 2 track, 7 inches, stereo. Recorded 16 September 1990.

Indiana University, Bloomington, Ind.; School of Music; Program No. 128, 1990-1991. *See:* W52, D34

1991

D75 *Astra*. Oberlin Orchestra; Robert Spano, conductor. Duration not listed. On reel 1 of 2 sound tape reels, analog, 7½ ips., 7 inches. Recorded 4 October 1991, Finney Chapel, Oberlin College, Oberlin, Ohio.

Recording of the American premiere performance. Oberlin College Conservatory of Music, Oberlin, Ohio; Program No. 11, 1991-1992. *See:* W2, W2a

D76 *Flute Variations I*. Indiana University School of Music Student Recital; Harvey Sollberger, director. (Flute player unidentified.) Duration: 6:32. On reel 2 of 3 sound tape reels, analog, 7½ ips., 2 track, 7 inches, stereo. Recorded 6 August 1991.

Program titled: *Students of Harvey Sollberger*. Indiana University, Bloomington, Ind.; School of Music; Program No. 91, 1991-1992. *See:* W81, D17

D77 *Fortune*. New Music Consort; Claire Heldrich, conductor. Duration not listed. 1 sound cassette, analog, stereo. Dolby processed. Recorded 20 April 1992 in the John C. Borden Auditorium, Manhattan School of Music, New York City. With works by Anne LeBaron, Krzysztof Penderecki, and Oliver Lake. *See:* W84

NON-COMMERCIAL SOUND RECORDINGS — WUORINEN AS PERFORMER

1979

D78 *Ancestors.* The Finnish Radio Symphony Orchestra; Wuorinen, conductor. Studio recording made 9 February 1979. *See:* W32

D79 *Neither,* by Morton Feldman. Manhattan School of Music Repertory Orchestra; Wuorinen, conductor; Lynne Webber, soprano. 1 sound cassette, 4 track, stereo. Recorded at the Manhattan School of Music, Recording Center 20 February 1979; originally recorded 21 November 1978. *See:* B1054

1981

D80 *Concerto for Amplified Violin and Orchestra.* The Finnish Radio Symphony Orchestra; Wuorinen, conductor. Studio recording made 9 October 1981. *See:* W5

NON-COMMERCIAL SOUND RECORDINGS — VIDEO RECORDINGS

1986

D81 *Spring Ballet — American Composers: A Celebration in Music and Dance Featuring the Music of Copland, Wuorinen, Barber, Ives, Heiden, and Sousa.* Indiana University Ballet Theater. Choreography: Jean-Pierre Bonnefoux; Indiana University Orchestra; George Calder, conductor; artistic supervisor: Harold F. Mack; costume designer: Nancy Steele; lighting designer: Allen R. White. 1 videocassette (VHS), color, ½ inch. Dress rehearsal, recorded 27 February 1986. The second work choreographed is Wuorinen's *Grand Bamboula.*
　　Features music of Wuorinen, Aaron Copland, Samuel Barber, Charles Ives, Bernhard Heiden, and John Philip Sousa. Indiana University, Bloomington, Ind.; School of Music; Program No. 479, 1985-1986. *See:* W49

1988

D82 *Charles Wuorinen, Lourdes Lopez & William Forsythe.* Produced by Celia Ipiotis and Jeff Bush. New York City: ARC Videodance, c1988. 1 videocassette, sd., color, ½ inch. Duration: 29:00. Series: *Eye On Dance,* no. 255. Celia Ipiotis interviews Wuorinen, who discusses new perspectives gained by dancers and choreographers.

Writings About Wuorinen

INDIVIDUAL WORKS

Adapting to the Times

B1   Galkin, Elliott. "Music Notes: Contemporary Ensemble in Concert at the Museum of Art." The *Sun* [Baltimore], 24 January 1972, p. B4.
>Galkin writes that of all the works on the program this was the most "ambitious and dissonant in its linear projection." *See:* W58e

B2   Powell, Verna. "Reviews: Strings." The *American Music Teacher* 24, no. 6 (June/July 1974), p. 45.
>A review of the C.F. Peters edition of the work. "This piece will extend the limitations, stretch the imagination, and boggle the mind of all but a few." *See:* W58

B3   *Music of the Last Forty Years Not Yet Established In the Repertoire: A Survey Conducted By the Fromm Music Foundation at Harvard 1974-1975.* Cambridge, Massachusetts: The Foundation, 1975.
>The study lists *Adapting to the Times* as one of twenty-four works by Wuorinen considered by the Fromm Foundation to be among "important but neglected or infrequently performed musical works dating from the last forty years." (l. 1) *See:* W58, B891

B4   "Wuorinen." *International Music Guide 1981.* London: Tantivy Press, 1981.
>A review of the C.F. Peters edition. The reviewer writes Wuorinen's "heavy slashing solo line and rather barren use of repeated note patterns overmuch smack of midnight oil." (p. 290) *See:* W58

Album Leaf for Howard Klein

B5   "Music People: Payment in Kind." *Ovation Magazine* [New York City], January 1985.
>Includes a brief mention that three members of the Board and Advisory Council of Meet the Composer, including Wuorinen, had presented pianist Howard Klein with a piano composition. [P] *See:* W129

Another Happy Birthday

B6   Kosman, Joshua. "It's Blomstedts Orchestra Now." *San Francisco Sunday Examiner and Chronicle*, 4 September 1988, *Datebook (Fall Arts Special: Music)*.
The very brief article mentions *Another Happy Birthday* is one of two Wuorinen works to be premiered by the San Francisco Symphony that season but expresses disappointment that the work is "all of one minute in length." *See:* W3

Arabia Felix

B7   Rockwell, John. "St. Paul Chamber Ensemble is Heard; University Composers Offer Program Here." The *New York Times*, 25 February 1974, p. 21.
Rockwell writes the piece had "a surprisingly accessible, exciting finale, full of stuttering syncopations." *See:* W60

B8   Rosenfeld, Jay C. "Music Review: Musical High Jinks at Wheatleigh." The *Berkshire Eagle* [Berkshire, Massachusetts], 28 July 1974.
The critic says the performers were dispersed throughout the tent and that Wuorinen maintained control by means of "imperious gestures." *See:* W60a

B9   Porter, Andrew. "Musical Events: Music to Attending Ears." The *New Yorker*, 29 March 1976, p. 100.
Porter calls the work "glittering" and says "it can be counted as a hit among the works of this prolific, hit-or-miss composer." *See:* W60b

B10   Smith, Patrick J. "Reports: New York." The *Musical Times*, June 1976, p. 511.
Smith briefly comments that the work was among the more interesting and well-played pieces at the *Celebration of Contemporary Music* at the Juilliard School during the winter of 1976.

B11   "Records." *Keynote* [New York City], November 1983.
This record review says Wuorinen "seems as fascinated as ever by hard-to-hear intellectual processes, but also willing to write music of attractive surface." *See:* D27

B12   Commanday, Robert. "Hard Listening and No Letup." *San Francisco Chronicle*, 7 October 1986, p. 44.
Commanday writes the piece resembles "an extensive and subtle rhythmic flux." He also says the performance was not the best. *See:* W60

B13   Tawa, Nicholas. *A Most Wondrous Babble: American Art Composers, Their Music, and the American Scene, 1950-1985.* Westport, Connecticut: Greenwood Press, 1987.
"Around the mid-seventies, Wuorinen's style began to show modifications in the total serialism he had usually favored. *Arabia Felix*, for example, indicates a different direction. The severe dissonances of the earlier works are less obvious. A greater rhythmic drive, owing much to [Igor] Stravinsky, appears." (p. 99) *See:* W60

B14 Kresky, Jeffrey. "The Recent Music of Charles Wuorinen." *Perspectives of New Music* 25, nos. 1-2 (1987), pp. 410-417.
  Arabia Felix is discussed in this important article. *See:* W60, B857

Archæopteryx

B15 Kerner, Leighton. "Two Meaningful Pieces." *Village Voice* [New York City], 17 August 1982, p. 68.
  Kerner says the work is a good example of Wuorinen's "fastidiousness in designing and balancing intricately related figures in a musical carpet." *See:* W33

B16 Page, Tim. "St. Lukes Chamber Ensemble Plays Archæopteryx." The *New York Times*, 19 April 1983.
  Page writes the work "possesses a snarling beauty, and a near-theatrical sense of drama." *See:* W33a

Archangel

B17 Porter, Andrew. "Musical Events: Intuitions." The *New Yorker*, 15 January 1979, pp. 94-96.
  Porter calls it "a severe, concentrated work" and praises David Taylor's performance. *See:* W61

B18 Bourne, Michael. "Dave Taylor." *Downbeat* 55 (August 1988), pp. 52-53.
  A profile of the bass trombonist David Taylor. The article mentions that Taylor's first recording as a recitalist includes a recording of *Archangel*. *See:* D31

Bagatelle

B19 Commanday, Robert. "S.F. Finale For Wuorinen In New Music." *San Francisco Chronicle*, 8 May 1989, Section F, p. 2.
  This is a review of the final concert featuring Wuorinen as advisor to the San Francisco Symphony's *New and Unusual Music Series*. Commanday notes Wuorinen chose to make this piece the last he would give on the series and that it is Wuorinen's "least energetic rhythmically, least intense and dissonant" musical composition. *See:* W130a

B20 Ward, Charles. "Composer Prefers to Let Music Speak for Itself." *Houston Chronicle*, 11 May 1990.
  Ward writes the work's mood and style "suggested a dissonant New Age music." *See:* W130c

B21 Burge, David. "Music Reviews: Keyboard Music." *Notes* 48, no. 1 (September 1991), pp. 300-301.
  A review of the C.F. Peters edition. "It appears that the composer has sought here to scale down his usually formidable technical requirements, both compositionally and pianistically, especially with regard to rhythm." (p. 300) *See:* W130

Bamboula Beach

B22   Roos, James. "Bamboula Beach Is Musical Gumbo." The *Miami Herald*,
3 February 1988, p. 5D.
    Pre-concert publicity for the premiere performance. Roos describes the amusing
process by which the "musical materials loosely related to South Florida" were gathered
for the composer to use. *See:* W3

B23   "New World Symphony Debuts." *Miami Today*, 4 February 1988.
    Pre-concert publicity for the premiere performance. The writer says the piece
includes snippets of "UM's [University of Miami] fight song and a popular Cuban folk
tune." *See:* W3

B24   Eldridge, John. "New World Symphony Is Impressive." The *Miami Herald*,
5 February 1988, p. 7C.
    The reviewer writes the music sounds like Miami, with "moments of violence,
rounded by edges of steady, playful rhythm and a jazzy, jungly undercurrent." *See:* W3

B25   Ruhlmann, William. "Miami Proves a Warm Host to the Annual New
Music." *New York City Tribune*, 12 December 1988.
    This review reports the work's title is "Samboila Beach" and says its themes and
tempi were "tossed around the orchestra like a hot potato." *See:* W3a

B26   Macia, Jean-Luc. "Le New World Symphony et Tilson Thomas a L'Opera:
La Bastille des Jeunes." *La Croix l'Evenment* [Paris] 25 July 1989, p. 17.
    A review of the European premiere (Paris). Macia writes the work is curious and
is a melange of aggressive dodecaphonia and afro-Cuban percussion. *See:* W3b

B27   Roos, James. "Storming the Bastille." The *Miami Herald*, 30 July 1989.
    A review of the European premiere (Paris). Roos calls the work a "12-tone
fiesta." The New World Symphony, conducted by Michael Tilson Thomas, also
performed the Prelude to the third act of Richard Wagner's *Lohengrin*. Roos reports that
Eva Wagner Pasquier, great-granddaughter of Richard Wagner, said of the orchestra
(made up specifically of young American musicians): "I don't think any of us expected
playing on such a virtuoso level." *See:* W3b

B28   Do Pico, Mauricio. "Entertainment: A New World of Youthful Music."
Buenos Aires Herald, 10 August 1989, p. 12.
    In this review of the South American premiere, Do Pico praises the orchestration.
He also states Michael Tilson Thomas "warned in Italianized Spanish 'ajústense los
cinturones (fasten your seat-belts)'" and that a member of the audience was heard to say
"at least it was short." *See:* W3c

B29   Porter, Andrew. "Musical Events: Harmonious." The *New Yorker*, 15
January 1990, pp. 76-79.
    Porter's review of the New York premiere calls the work important and
substantial, and notes it serves its function well as a concert opening piece. *See:* W3f

Bamboula Squared

B30   Rockwell, John. "Music: Third in Series of Computer Works." The *New York Times*, 6 June 1984, p. C24.

Rockwell says the piece "made an enormous, exuberant racket" and that "it left this listener cold." *See:* W4

B31   Davis, Peter G. "Hazy Horizons." *New York*, 25 June 1984, pp. 60-61.

The critic says the piece is "an exhilarating needle shower of plucked electronic effects." (p. 60) *See:* W4

B32   Porter, Andrew. "Musical Events: Sound-Houses." The *New Yorker*, 9 July 1984, pp. 80, 82-83.

This concert review contains historical information about IRCAM (Institute de Recherche et de Coordination Acoustique /Musique), headed by Pierre Boulez in Paris, the Center for Music Experiment and the Computer Audio Research Laboratory at the University of California, San Diego, headed by F. Richard Moore, and other aspects of electronic and computer music. The New York Philharmonic *Horizons '84* contemporary music festival is described in detail. Porter writes *Bamboula Squared* features "uncommon eventfulness." (p. 83) He sums up his assessment of the work with the following sentence: "There's something sunlike about Wuorinen's best works: he cometh forth as a bridegroom out of his chamber, and rejoiceth as a giant to run his course." (p. 83) Porter also mentions Wuorinen conducted the American Composers Orchestra at this third concert of the festival, which included a performance of Milton Babbitt's *Correspondences*. (The New York Philharmonic did not have service available during the all of the days allotted for the festival; the American Composers Orchestra was hired for this concert.) *See:* W4

B33   Kerner, Leighton. "Music as Will and Idea." *Village Voice* [New York City], 10 July 1984, p. 67.

Kerner terms the work a "clangorous, orchestra-tape party piece." *See:* W4

B34   Smith, Patrick J. "Horizons '84 — 'A Broader View of Romanticism is Very Broad Indeed." *High Fidelity/Musical America* 34, no. 10 (October 1984), pp. MA24-MA25.

Smith writes: "I found the tape interpolations far tamer in inspiration than the orchestral ones." (p. MA25) *See:* W4

B35   Swan, Annalyn. "Music: Romantic Longings." *Atlantic* 254, no. 5 (November 1984), pp. 134-136.

Swan says "one walks away exhilarated from a work that is neatly squared yet bursting with fun." (p. 136) She also discusses trends in contemporary music since the 1960s. *See:* W4

B36   "Research Projects: Bamboula Squared." *Annual Report 1983-1984*. The Center for Music Experiment. Ed. John D. Lauer. San Diego: The University of California, 1984.

This brief article describes Wuorinen's residence at The Center for Music Experiment and mentions *Bamboula Squared* was the result of his work there: "During Wuorinen's residency, he was to investigate computer techniques for controlled random processes relevant to musical composition and, in the course of that investigation, produce a major composition involving computer processing together with an article for publication which would report on his developments at CARL [Computer Audio Research Laboratory]." (p. 6) *See:* W4

B37 Cramer, Owen. "Review: Guest Artists, Symphony Makes Beautiful Music." *Colorado Sun,* 16 November 1984.

The critic says the taped sounds resembled "a super Jewsharp going on a steel drum, creating rhythms and clusters of sound that pleased in combination with the orchestral instruments." *See:* W4a

B38 Johns, Gilbert R. "Harrell's 'ethereal' Cello Brightens Symphony Stage." *Gazette Telegraph* [Colorado Springs, Colorado], 17 November 1984.

The reviewer noted the performance was a fine one but wondered whether the musicians were attentive to Wuorinen out of respect or "possibly out of terror instilled by such a work." *See:* W4a

B39 Griffin, Glen. "Mathematics Aside, Bamboula Adds Up to Exciting Music." *The Denver Post,* 19 November 1984.

"Big and splashy, rhythmically exciting and, mirabile dictu, using an orchestra effectively *[Bamboula Squared]* packs a punch quite independent of its large component of instrumentalists." *See:* W4a

B40 Kresky, Jeffrey. "The Recent Music of Charles Wuorinen." *Perspectives of New Music* 25, nos. 1-2 (1987), pp. 410-417.

Bamboula Squared is discussed in this important article. *See:* W4, B857

B41 Ray, Lee. *An Application of Computer-Aided Composition Within An Independent Musical Context.* (M.A. thesis.) La Jolla: University of California at San Diego, 1987.

"Using the CARL software distribution and a suite of programs written by this author, an orchestra and tape piece, *Bamboula Squared*, was created which exemplifies the music described herein." (Abstract, pp. v-vi) Ray's second chapter, "The Evolution of a Production Project," includes background information on his collaboration with Wuorinen for the computer music part of the piece. Ray states the collaboration began when he received four sketches from Wuorinen that were examples of what might be done with the program *cmusic* and that the collaboration was at first technical. Ray goes on to say the process was an iterative one: "The piece which eventually emerged came very much from our collaboration and discussions, my generating sounds and our evaluating them, and my ability to create CAC [Computer-aided composition] software for the CARL system." (p. 3) *See:* W4

B42 Grant, Nancy S. "Louisville Celebrates Sounds of Our Time." *Symphony Magazine* 38, no. 6 (December 1987), pp. 17-20, 62.

This article discusses the *SoundCelebration* held by the Louisville Orchestra in September 1987. *Bamboula Squared* is described as "a marriage of quadraphonic tape and orchestra." *See:* W4b

B43 Moore, F. Richard. *Elements of Computer Music.* Englewood Cliffs, New Jersey: Prentice Hall, 1990.

The chapter "Instruments" has a section called "Subtractive Synthesis and Physical Models" which includes a discussion of what Moore terms the "Karplus-Strong plucked string algorithm" and a reference to *Bamboula Squared*. Moore mistakenly writes that the piece was composed for "chamber orchestra and computer-generated sounds." (p. 291) The work is scored for full orchestra and tape. *See:* W4

B44 Dierks, Donald. "First Pulitzer Concert at UCSD Is a Prize-Winner." *San Diego Union*, 12 January 1990.

Dierks writes the electronic sounds contributed "entirely new and intriguing tone colors to instrumental sounds that were already bright and energetic." *See:* W4c

B45 Herman, Kenneth. "Visceral Offerings by Wuorinen Redeems Avant-Garde Concert." *Los Angeles Times* [San Diego County Edition], 13 January 1990.

The critic says the piece "seemed to fuse Alban Berg's declamatory operatic style with Stravinsky's motivic development." Herman also comments on Igor Stravinsky's *Dumbarton Oaks Concerto* and *L'Histoire de Soldat*, performed on the same program: "There was a time, during Wuorinen's student years, when even Stravinsky's scribbled grocery lists were hailed as monumental art. How foolish that uncritical hero worship seems now. But don't tell that to our distinguished guest composer [Wuorinen]." *See:* W4c

Bassoon Variations

B46 Snyder, Louis. "Premiere and a Celebration at BSO's Chamber Concert." *Christian Science Monitor*, 30 October 1973.

The reviewer says that "while not instantly lovable, [the piece] sustains interest and even invites repetition." *See:* W62

B47 Smoley, Lewis M. "Music In the Modern Manner." *American Record Guide* 41, no. 2 (December 1977), pp. 49-51.

A review of the New World recording. He writes the variations are "intended more to present the compositional style than technical virtuosity of the soloist," and that the tone colors produced by the three instruments (bassoon, harp, timpani) constitutes the most successful aspect of the composition. *See:* D19

B48 Terry, Kenneth. "Record Reviews: Babbitt, Bassett, Smith, Wuorinen." *Downbeat*, 12 January 1978, p. 28.

A review of the New World recording. Terry states the "synthesis of serial and non-serial techniques produces an original hybrid, unified by rhythm as much as by the 12-tone set." *See:* D19

B49 Cohn, Arthur. *Recorded Classical Music. A Guide to Compositions and Performances*. New York: Schirmer Books, 1981.

A review of the New World recording: "Serial fermentation is the modus operandi, and, as usual with Wuorinen, there is superb instrumental workmanship and top professional technical skill." (p. 2109) *See:* D19

Bearbeitungen über das Glogauer Liederbuch

B50 Rosenfeld, Jay C. "Music Review: Musical High Jinks at Wheatleigh." The *Berkshire Eagle* [Berkshire, Massachusetts], 28 July 1974.

Rosenfeld writes the work was "probably composed by Orlando de Wuorinen in style antique." He also says the page-turner was hilarious as he tried to accommodate all four players. *See:* D63b

B51   Kenngott, Louise. "A Little Bit Of All 'Rite'." The *Milwaukee Journal*, 18 April 1976.
A review of the Nonesuch recording. "Young New Yorkers all [Speculum Musicae, The Light Fantastic Players] they make contemporary music their specialty, and perform it with distinction." *See:* D16

B52   Cohn, Arthur. *Recorded Classical Music. A Critical Guide to Compositions and Performances*. New York: Schirmer Books, 1981.
A review of the Nonesuch recording. Cohn calls the music "enchanting" and says the players of Speculum Musicae (Paul Dunkel, Virgil Blackwell, Daniel Reed, and Fred Sherry) "uphold the outstanding reputation of that organization in their playing." (p. 2111) *See:* D16

B53   Watkins, Glen. *Soundings: Music In the Twentieth Century*. New York: Schirmer Books, 1988.
The chapter "Uses of the Past" includes this sentence: "His [Wuorinen's] 1962 setting for modern instruments of pieces from the Glogauer Liederbuch (c. 1480) is not unlike [Peter Maxwell] Davies *Renaissance Scottish Dances (1973).* (p. 642) *See:* W63

B54   Ward, Charles. "Composer Prefers to Let Music Speak for Itself." *Houston Chronicle*, 11 May 1990.
The reviewer says the music showed a "dextrous handling of the instrumentation." *See:* W63d

Bicinium

B55   Moore, Carmen. "Music: Greenwich House Finale." *Village Voice* [New York City], 18 May 1967, p. 16.
Moore writes Wuorinen "employed a two-part writing of contrary motions at times reminiscent of [Igor] Stravinsky's choral work of the last two decades." *See:* W64

B56   Cage, John. *Notations*. New York: Something Else Press, 1969.
This monograph is a collection of music manuscripts assembled to benefit the Foundation for Contemporary Performance Arts. Cage writes in his preface: "The collection was determined by circumstances rather than any process of selection." Wuorinen's *Bicinium* is a work in the collection. Alison Knowles helped edit this book; her husband at the time, Dick Higgins, published it under the name "Something Else Press." Original correspondence associated with this project is located at Northwestern University. *See:* W64

B57   *Music of the Last Forty Years Not Yet Established In the Repertoire: A Survey Conducted By the Fromm Music Foundation at Harvard 1974-1975*. Cambridge, Massachusetts: The Foundation, 1975.
This survey lists *Bicinium* as one of the twenty-four works by Wuorinen considered by the Fromm Music Foundation to be among "important but neglected or infrequently performed works dating from the last forty years." (l. 1) *See:* W64, B891

The Blue Bamboula

B58   Holland, Bernard. "Recital: Ursula Oppens." The *New York Times*, 9 January 1983, p. 47.

Holland calls the piece "an extended kind of scherzo, full of unexpected flashes of color and movement, sudden outbursts and veering changes of direction." *See:* W131a

B59 "New Music Corner: Charles Wuorinen." *Keyboard Classics* 4, no. 1 (January-February 1984), pp. 34-36.

A brief article containing an overview of Wuorinen's music and ideas. It includes the final section from *The Blue Bamboula*, published by C.F. Peters. [P] *See:* W131

B60 Page, Tim. "Music: Oppens at the Piano." The *New York Times*, 3 December 1986, p. C22.

Page says it was a "wonderfully clever, fiendishly difficult romp, reckless and carefully controlled at the same time, dispatched with aplomb by Ms. Oppens." *See:* W131b

B61 Rooney, Dennis D. "Record Reviews." The *Strad* 100, no. 1195 (November 1989), p. 985.

A review of the Bridge recording. "[Garrick] Ohlsson serves it *[Blue Bamboula]* up as a dazzling tour de force." *See:* D35

B62 Berrett, Joshua. "Record Reviews." *American Music* 8 (1990), pp. 121-123.

A review of the Bridge recording. "Garrick Ohlsson plays the work to the hilt of the Bösendorfer, reveling in the work's rhythmic energy." (p. 121) *See:* D35

Canzona

B63 DeRehn, Andrew. "Debuts & Reappearances." *High Fidelity/Musical America* 22, no. 5 (May 1972), pp. MA20-MA21.

"I might have been more alert but was preoccupied in a futile effort to make sense of Wuorinen's spasmodic note-spinning." (p. MA21) *See:* W34

B64 Ericson, Raymond. "Accent on Music of 20th Century." The *New York Times*, 2 February 1972, p. 32.

Ericson says the work has more "drive" than most of Wuorinen's music and that the "instrumental interplay is always attractive and even witty." *See:* W34

B65 McLellan, Joseph. "American Camerata for New Music." The *Washington Post*, 26 April 1975, p. D7.

A review of the Washington, D.C. premiere. The critic states the work "showed a brilliant capacity for manipulating the resources of a small ensemble." *See:* W34a

B66 *Music of the Last Forty Years Not Yet Established In the Repertoire: A Survey Conducted By the Fromm Music Foundation at Harvard 1974-1975.* Cambridge, Massachusetts: The Foundation, 1975.

The survey lists *Canzona* as one of the twenty-four works by Wuorinen considered by the Fromm Music Foundation to be among the "important but neglected or infrequently performed musical works dating from the last forty years." (l. 1) *See:* W34, B891

Capriccio

B67 Libbey, Theodore W., Jr. "Contemporary Music." The *New York Times*, 12 April 1982.
Pre-concert publicity about the four-hour concert honoring the deceased pianist Robert Miller. The concert featured the premiere of *Capriccio*, the last work Miller had commissioned. *See:* W132

B68 Skei, Allen B. "Feinberg, Good Taste, Solid Music." The *Fresno Bee*, 14 April 1985.
"The work overall makes an exceptionally strong impression." *See:* W132a

The Celestial Sphere

B69 "Augie Commissions New Work." The *Argus* [Rock Island, Illinois], 30 March 1980.
An article announcing the commissioning of the work. [P] *See:* W162

B70 "Pulitzer Prize Winner Will Compose: Handel Oratorio Society Commissions Major Work." The *Observer* [Augustana College], 16 April 1980, p. 1.
An article announcing the commissioning of the work. [P] *See:* W162

B71 "After One Hundred Years, A New 'Hallelujah'." *Augustana College Magazine*, November 1980, pp. 3, 17.
An article announcing the commissioning of the work as well as a historical overview of the Handel Oratorio Society. "A major new work by Charles Wuorinen, regardless of occasion, is enough to draw music critics from their east and west-coast fastness even to the Mississippi Valley." (p. 3) *See:* W162

B72 "Handel Society to Premiere Oratorio." The *Argus* [Rock Island, Illinois], 5 April 1981, p. 11.
Pre-concert publicity about the premiere. [P] *See:* W162

B73 "100th Anniversary Season Concludes With 'The Celestial Sphere'." The *Observer* [Augustana College], 8 April 1981, p. 3.
Pre-concert publicity about the premiere. *See:* W162

B74 "World Premiere for Handel's Hundred." *Quad-City Times* [Davenport, Iowa], 10 April 1981.
Pre-concert publicity about the premiere. [P] *See:* W162

B75 "Composer to Spend Week at Augie." The *Argus* [Rock Island, Illinois], 12 April 1981.
Pre-concert publicity about the premiere. [P] *See:* W162

B76 Arloff, Bill. "Celestial Sphere Composer Climax's 100th Season." The *Observer* [Augustana College], 12 April 1981.
Pre-concert publicity about the premiere. [P] *See:* W162

B77 "Field Day For Percussionists." The *Argus* [Rock Island], 19 April 1981.
Pre-concert publicity about the premiere. "The extensive use of percussion isn't just embroidery. It is essential in creating the driving rhythms that define Wuorinen's music." *See:* W162

B78 Baldwin, Nick. "Oratorio Premiere at Augustana." *Des Moines Register*, 19 April 1981.
Pre-concert publicity about the premiere. *See:* W162

B79 Lane, Marilyn. "Poem Inspires Handel Society Commemorative." *Quad-City Times* [Davenport, Iowa], 25 April 1981, p. 3.
Pre-concert publicity about the premiere. Wuorinen is interviewed in this article and makes the following comment: "An entertainer reproduces something that is a hit. A serious composer tries to express an idea as seriously and honestly as he can." [P] *See:* W162

B80 Sanders, Charles H. "World Premiere Rocks Centennial." The *Argus* [Rock Island, Illinois], 26 April 1981.
The first of several reviews of the premiere performance. Sanders claims the work shows the influences of a number of composers, including Olivier Messiaen and Leonard Bernstein. He also writes: "Perhaps, a more apt appellation might be 'Concerto for Percussion With Encounters of a Vocal Kind'." *See:* W162

B81 McElwain, Bill. "Exciting Premiere of New Oratorio." The *Daily Dispatch* [Moline, Illinois], 27 April 1981.
McElwain writes "it very possibly will be classified as a major musical work of the 20th century." He also comments "perhaps only a Divine presence could have created such a sunburst of sound." [P] *See:* W162

B82 "'Celestial Sphere' Is Complex, Effective." *Quad-City Times* [Davenport, Iowa], 28 April 1981.
"The composer did achieve his objective, however, because the effect was as though one were listening to other-worldly sounds, clashing and bouncing as they were against each other." [P] *See:* W162

B83 Heath, Ross. "Celestial Sphere Shines." The *Observer* [Augustana College], 29 April 1981, p. 3.
Heath describes how Wuorinen used a mathematical function of randomness and comments: "When asked why he used this particularly mathematical music for the Holy Spirit, he said nothing is more mathematical than anything else." [P] *See:* W162

B84 "World Premiere!" *Augustana College Magazine* [Rock Island, Illinois], July 1981, pp. 7-9.
"It was a visual as well as an auditory experience. Exotic instruments dangled and glittered." (p. 8) *See:* W162

B85 Hiemenz, Jack. "Augustana College's Major Premiere: Wuorinen's 'Celestial Sphere' Stirs and Fascinates." *High Fidelity/Musical America* 3, no. 10 (October 1981), pp. MA20-MA25.
"In this majestic choral/orchestral tapestry, Wuorinen has made a powerful statement and added to a repertory badly in need of replenishing. That I was the only visiting critic in attendance — what happened to you, oh Chicago, Des Moines, St.

Louis? — is an indication that provincialism isn't always confined to the provinces." (p. MA25) *See:* W162

B86   McElwain, Bill. "If You Don't Like Wuorinen's Music, Eat Your Words." *Daily Dispatch* [Moline, Illinois], 31 August 1986.

This article is about Wuorinen having won a MacArthur Foundation award and contains comments on Wuorinen's earlier appearances in the midwest. Recalling *The Celestial Sphere*, McElwain writes: "It was an eerie and yet beautiful sound — the sound of shimmering, quivering, unfathomable mysteries." *See:* W162

Cello Variations I

B87   Hughes, Allen. "Poet and Composer Join in a Recital." The *New York Times*, 25 December 1970, p. 34.

Hughes praises Fred Sherry's performance and says Wuorinen's exploitation of the instrumental colors was "sturdy and interesting." *See:* W65a

B88   Henahan, Donal. "Fred Sherry's Cello Program Marked by Fierce Enthusiasm." The *New York Times*, 26 January 1972, p. 33.

"It threw Mr. [Fred] Sherry problems of technique that put one in mind of the Kodály sonata." *See:* W65c

B89   Rosenfeld, Jay C. "Music Review: Musical High Jinks at Wheatleigh." The *Berkshire Eagle* [Berkshire, Massachusetts], 28 July 1974.

The critic mentions that Fred Sherry performed "wearing a mask of Satan or Lucifer." Nothing is said of the music. *See:* W65d

B90   Salisbury, Wilma. "A New Turn for Music Theater." The *Plain Dealer* [Cleveland], 25 August 1974, p. 4-F.

Salisbury merely describes the work as "fiendishly difficult." *See:* W65d

Chamber Concerto for Flute and Ten Instruments

B91   Hammerich, R.C. "Lenox Quartet in Program at Tanglewood." The *Springfield Union* [Springfield, Massachusetts], 10 August 1964.

"The piece produced so many deafening crashes and total silences it made the preceding works seem like lullabies." *See:* W35

B92   Klein, Howard. "Contemporary Music Fete Opens at Tanglewood." The *New York Times*, 10 August 1964, p. 22.

"Single ideas were spread out among several instruments, Bach contributing one fragment." *See:* W35

B93   Salzman, Eric. "Tanglewood's Youth Week." *New York Herald Tribune*, 12 August 1964.

Salzman calls Wuorinen an enormously gifted young man who tackles composition in large forms, but says "his forms are too incoherent to bear the weight of the fat content." *See:* W35

B94   Steinberg, Michael. "Festival Within Festival: Contemporary American Music at Tanglewood." The *Boston Globe*, 16 August 1964.

This review devotes considerable space to the work and terms it "an extraordinary virtuoso vehicle for the newly extended flute technique." Steinberg praises flutist Harvey Sollberger by calling him "incomparable." *See:* W35

B95 Steinberg, Michael. "Young Talent at Tanglewood." *New York Herald Tribune*, 23 August 1964, *(The Sunday Herald Tribune Magazine)*, p. 31.

Steinberg describes some of the flute effects and says "timbres, textures and intensities function virtually as the themes of the piece." *See:* W35

B96 McCorkle, Donald M. "Aural Horizons and Cacaphony." *Evening Star* [Washington, D.C.], 23 January 1965.

McCorkle briefly describes the work as being "both dense and sparse." *See:* W35a

B97 Porter, Cecilia. "At Coolidge Auditorium: Avant-Garde Set Attends 'In' Concert." The *Washington Post*, 23 January 1965, p. E15.

Porter mistakenly uses the term variations to describe this concerto. She writes: "These continuous variations were the most exciting ideas on the program." *See:* W35a

B98 Bernheimer, Martin. "Composers Talented But Lack Flair." The *Los Angeles Times*, 26 January 1966, *(Part V)*, p. 7.

Bernheimer says the work is called a concerto because the flute dominates the music, "seemingly by dint of lung power and determination alone." *See:* W35c

B99 Ericson, Raymond. "Young Man With a Violin." The *New York Times*, 3 November 1968, *(Arts & Leisure)*, p. D19.

In this article about violinist Paul Zukofsky, Ericson mentions that the violinist had conducted a chamber concerto by Wuorinen. The event referred to was the 9 September 1968 New York City concert at which Zukofsky conducted the *Chamber Concerto for Flute and Ten Players. See:* W35d

B100 Brozen, Michael. "Debuts & Reappearances: Fromm Commissions." *High Fidelity/Musical America* 18, no. 12 (December 1968), p. MA14-MA15.

Brozen states "the implications of all those drum rolls, trills, tremolos, and expectant pauses are unfulfilled." *See:* W35d

B101 Hamilton, David. "Records 1968." The *Nation*, 23 December 1968, pp. 701-702.

A review of the best recordings of the year; *Chamber Concerto for Flute and Ten Players* is listed. *See:* W35, D5

B102 Klein, Howard. "Recordings: A New Look for An Old Label." The *New York Times*, 25 March 1969, *(Arts & Leisure)*, p. 32D.

An article about the history of Composers Recordings, Inc., (CRI), containing a discography that includes the CRI recording of this work. *See:* W35, D5D

B103 Boretz, Benjamin. "Conversation With Charles Wuorinen." *Contemporary Music Newsletter* 3, nos. 7-8 (November-December 1969), pp. 4-8.

Boretz begins by writing: "Of all the composers in our midst, Charles Wuorinen is probably the most responsible for the activity on which we have come to depend to hear new pieces, and to hear them adequately performed." The interview features an extensive discussion of the *Chamber Concerto for Flute and Ten Players. See:* W35

B104 Shupp, Enos E. "Miscellaneous." The *New Records* 40, no. 1 (March 1972), p. 15.

> A review of the Nonesuch recording: "It is good construction but boring music."
> *See:* W35, D5

B105 *Music of the Last Forty Years Not Yet Established In the Repertoire: A Survey Conducted By the Fromm Music Foundation at Harvard 1974-1975.* Cambridge, Massachusetts: The Foundation, 1975.

> The survey lists *Chamber Concerto for Flute and Ten Players* as one of the twenty-four works by Wuorinen considered by the Fromm Music Foundation to be among the "important but neglected or infrequently performed musical works dating from the last forty years." (l. 1) *See:* W35, B891

B106 Bedford, Frances. "A Survey of Twentieth-Century Music for Percussion and Harpsichord." *Woodwind World-Brass & Percussion* 17, no. 6 (November-December 1978), pp. 40-43.

> Bedford lists this work and writes: "Percussion holds a dominant part of the ensemble interacting with the flute." (p. 41) *See:* W35

B107 Cohn, Arthur. *Recorded Classical Music. A Critical Guide to Compositions and Performances.* New York: Schirmer Books, 1981.

> A review of the CRI recording. Cohn praises Harvey Sollberger's flute technique. Of the concerto, Cohn writes: "He [Wuorinen] fully proves his creative brief." (p. 2108) *See:* W35, D5

B108 Tawa, Nicholas. *A Most Wondrous Babble: American Art Composers, Their Music, and the American Scene, 1950-1985.* Westport, Connecticut: Greenwood Press, 1987.

> "Although the [instrumental] treatment guarantees clarity, it also results in a certain hardness of sound." (p. 99) *See:* W35

B109 *A Life For New Music. Selected Papers of Paul Fromm.* Ed. David Gable and Christoph Wolff. Cambridge, Massachusetts: Department of Music, Harvard University (Distributed by Harvard University Press), 1988.

> The appendix "Works Commissioned by the Fromm Music Foundation, 1952-1987" lists the *Chamber Concerto for Flute and Ten Players. See:* W35

Chamber Concerto for Oboe and Ten Instruments

B110 Strongin, Theodore. "Varese Tribute Paid at Concert." The *New York Times*, 9 November 1965, p. 51.

> Strongin writes that his review was based on having heard the work at a rehearsal since the premiere performance came too late for press deadline. He says the concerto is Wuorinen's most successful work and possesses a "don't-take-me-for-granted quality." *See:* W36

B111 Waters, Edward N. "Harvest of the Year: Selected Acquisitions of the Music Division." The *Quarterly Journal of the Library of Congress* 24, no. 1 (January 1967), pp. 46-82.

Includes a brief mention that the holograph of this work has been acquired by the Music Division of the Library of Congress. Wuorinen is described as being "prominent among the American avant-garde." (p. 63) *See:* W36

Chamber Concerto for Tuba

B112 Cox, Ainslee. "The Journal Reviews: YMHA, New York." *Music Journal* 29, no. 5 (May 1971), p. 67.

"The piece works, mainly due to the composer's organizational skills, though the tuba often seemed an orphan." *See:* W37

B113 Brooks, John Benson. "Caught in the Act: Don Butterfield — Charles Wuorinen." *Downbeat* 38, no. 2 (June 1971), pp. 27-28.

Brooks focuses on Don Butterfield's tuba technique by saying "he has the man-shot-out-of-a-canon, paratrooper, and ant-into-the-cracks acts down to a fine art." (p. 27) *See:* W37

B114 Hiemenz, Jack. "Debuts & Reappearances: Don Butterfield, Bass Tuba." *High Fidelity/Musical America* 22, no. 1 (January 1972), p. MA19.

"The tuba's lines continually sounded like mere background or underpinning." *See:* W37

B115 Hughes, Allen. "Butterfield Gives Concert for Tubas." The *New York Times*, 25 September 1971, p. 17.

Hughes says nothing specifically about the concerto except to call the performance "admirable" and note that it was performed twice. *See:* W37b

B116 Rockwell, John. "Debuts & Reappearances: Group for Contemporary Music." *High Fidelity/Musical America* 23, no. 3 (March 1973), p. MA23.

Rockwell writes the music sounded "a bit dry, for all its ingenuity of detail." *See:* W37d

B117 *Music of the Last Forty Years Not Yet Established In the Repertoire: A Survey Conducted By the Fromm Music Foundation at Harvard 1974-1975.* Cambridge, Massachusetts: The Foundation, 1975.

The survey lists *Chamber Concerto for Tuba* as one of the twenty-four works by Wuorinen considered by the Fromm Music Foundation to be among the "important but neglected or infrequently performed musical works dating from the last forty years." (l. 1) *See:* W37, B891

B118 Tartaglia, Leonard. "Chamber Concerto Effective Adventure." *Plain Dealer* [Cleveland], 22 February 1983.

Tartaglia writes the "composer's music could well benefit from a Leonard Bernstein-like spoken and played analysis beforehand." *See:* W37e

B119 Schwarz, K. Robert. "Classical Reviews." *High Fidelity* 34, no. 4 (April 1984), pp. 64-76.

A review of the CRI recording: "The end result is that, while admirable, the Concerto seems almost a period piece, a product of another era." (p. 76) *See:* D29

Chamber Concerto for Violoncello and Ten Players

B120   Taruskin, Richard. "Modern Music." *Columbia Daily Spectator* [New York City] 59, no. 37 (19 November 1964), pp. 2-3.
Taruskin writes that although Wuorinen has a great ear for sound, the music was exasperating: "Also exasperating was Wuorinen's habit of projecting the many ideas with which the piece is brimming all at the same time, with the result that he really projects nothing at all but an undigested and much too complicated total texture." *See:* W38a

B121   Maguire, Jan. "Paris Heard 20th-Century U.S. Music." *New York Herald Tribune*, 27 May 1966.
A review of the European premiere. Maguire writes that the music "is worked out in intricate detail, the relationship of every note to every other note having been examined." *See:* W138b

B122   DeRehn, Andrew. "Debuts & Reappearances: Juilliard: 'New and Newer Music'." *High Fidelity/Musical America* 21, no. 23 (March 1971), pp. MA23.
"The valiant cellist Fred Sherry fought a losing battle trying to force his music into the limelight." *See:* W38e

B123   Harrison, Max. "Records: American Composers." *The Times* [London], 20 January 1973, p. 9.
A review of the Nonesuch recording. Harrison says the concerto may have been an example of "furious intensity, frantic activity." *See:* D10

B124   Fennelly, Brian. "Music Reviews." *Notes* 30, no. 2 (December 1973), pp. 346-369.
A review of the C.F. Peters edition. "The published score is an attractive reproduction of the composer's manuscript and a welcome arrival in the documentation of his development." *See:* W38

B125   *Music of the Last Forty Years Not Yet Established In the Repertoire: A Survey Conducted By the Fromm Music Foundation at Harvard 1974-1975.* Cambridge, Massachusetts: The Foundation, 1975.
The survey lists *Chamber Concerto for Violin and Ten Players* as one of the twenty-four works by Wuorinen considered by the Fromm Music Foundation to be among the "important but neglected or infrequently performed musical works dating from the last forty years." (l. 1) *See:* W38, B891

B126   Cohn, Arthur. *Recorded Classical Music. A Critical Guide to Compositions and Performances.* New York: Schirmer Books, 1981.
A review of the Nonesuch recording. Cohn calls the performance "magnificently detailed." He says the concerto possesses a "rich urgency but cuts away from any past lineage." (p. 2108) *See:* D10

B127   "Wuorinen." *International Music Guide. 1981.* London: Tantivy Press, 1981.
The reviewer calls the piece "a pungent little frise" with "plenty of brash pugillism but fewer deeper qualities." (p. 290) *See:* W38

B128 Sanders, Linda. "The Old Frontiers." The *Soho News* [New York City], 1 December 1981, p. 58.

"Fred Sherry is a marvelous player, yet for this piece it sounded like he got his cello at Sears." *See:* W38f

B129 Tawa, Nicholas. *A Most Wondrous Babble: American Art Composers, Their Music, and the American Scene, 1950-1985.* Westport, Connecticut: Greenwood Press, 1987.

"Extremely difficult to play, the music is as idiomatic to the instruments as serialism would allow." (p. 98) *See:* W38

B130 Kresky, Jeffrey. "The Recent Music of Charles Wuorinen." *Perspectives of New Music* 25, nos. 1-2 (1987), pp. 410-417.

Chamber Concerto for Cello and Ten Players is discussed in this important article. *See:* W38, B857

B131 Marks, Anthony. "Concerts: Lontano." The *Musical Times* 129, no. 1742 (April 1988), p. 200.

A review of the London premiere. "It was logical and understandable but lacked mystery." *See:* W38g

Composition for Oboe and Piano

B132 Fennelly, Brian. "Music Reviews." *Notes* 30, no. 2 (December 1973), pp. 346-369.

A review of the C.F. Peters edition. Fennelly states that only "the most proficient players" are able to perform the piece and that the music contains "some striking instances of canonic writing." (p. 357) *See:* W67

B133 Jerome, Wilbert D. "Reviews: Woodwinds." The *American Music Teacher* 23, no. 5 (April/May 1974), p. 47.

A review of the C.F. Peters edition. The reviewer writes that Wuorinen's intentions are "sonic rather than structural" and that the piece is useful for "oboists of extremely sophisticated ability." *See:* W67

B134 Morgan, Robert P. "Classical." *High Fidelity* 29, no. 1 (January 1979), pp. 73-94.

A review of the Orion recording. The reviewer briefly talks about the rhythmic element of the work and calls the piece "strong and substantial." (p. 81) *See:* D20

B135 ["Reviews."] *Neue Musikzeitung* [Regensburg], July 1980, p. 25.

"The serial compositional style with its very spread out ambitus in both instruments presents high technical demands on both players." *See:* W67

B136 Cohn, Arthur. *Recorded Classical Music. A Critical Guide to Compositions and Performances.* New York: Schirmer Books, 1981.

A review of the Orion recording: "Straightforward serialism, nonacademic in its procedures, strongly contrasted in the presentation of the total material." (p. 2110-2111) *See:* D20

Composition for Violin and Ten Instruments

B137 Ericson, Raymond. "Music In Our Time Winds Up Season." The *New York Times*, 27 April 1964, p. 26.

A review of the premiere. Ericson says the piece is "often arresting in its undulation of dynamics." *See:* W39

B138 Sigmon, Carl P. "Chamber Music: Music In Our Time." *Musical America* 84, no. 6 (July 1964), p. 46.

"Although Wuorinen is one of the noisier and more dissonant composers (so was Haydn), this work offers surprises." The critic also says the piece contains "a new ingredient, humor, which seems more an afterthought than an integral source of the music." *See:* W39

Concert for Doublebass Alone

B139 Neubert, Bernard David. *Contemporary Double-Bass Works: An Analysis of Style, Performance Techniques and Notational Practices.* (D.M.A. dissertation) Austin, Texas: University of Texas at Austin, 1982.

The chapter titled "A General Survey of Technical and Notational Developments in Unaccompanied Double Bass Works Since 1959" includes a one-page discussion of this piece. The author writes, in part: "This work introduces two new sound resources which involve pizzicato techniques, pizz quasi guitarra and pizz tremolo, both of which are used quite effectively. Pizzicato glissandos are another interesting device used. However, the pitch parameter is the primary focus here, and this requires wide registral shifts and difficult double, triple, and even quadruple stops." (p. 74) *See:* W68

Concertante II

B140 "Music In Our Time Opens Fourth Season." The *New York Times*, 26 January 1959, p. 16.

The reviewer says Wuorinen's piece was "quite interesting" and notes that the performance was excellent. *See:* W42b

B141 Salzman, Eric. "Pollikoff Series Begins 'Y' Season." The *New York Times*, 26 January 1959, p. 24.

Salzman praises Max Pollikoff's solo performance. He also writes Wuorinen's piece is too long but calls it "a lean work with few sonority tricks." *See:* W42b

Concertante III

B142 Robison, Judith. "Chamber Music Program Offers Baroque Pieces." *New York Herald Tribune*, 9 December 1961.

Robison says the music involved "medievalisms as well as twelve-tone technique." *See:* W43c

B143 Salzman, Eric. "6 Players Offer Chamber Works." The *New York Times*, 9 December 1961, p. 21.

Salzman describes the piece as being "completely inconsistent." *See:* W43c

B144 Bloomfield, Arthur. "A Star Is Born." *Musical America* 82, no. 3 (March 1962), p. 14.
    The critic writes that the music is "piquant" with "plaintive melody and an agreeably neo-classic spirit." Bloomfield also says Gerhard Samuel's conducting was excellent. The title of the article refers to the sudden conducting debut of Seiji Ozawa at another concert, also reviewed in this article. *See:* W43d

Concertante IV

B145 "New Edition of Music In Our Time Offered." *New York Herald Tribune*, 28 December 1959.
    "It sounds at moments like 'severe' Copland, neo-Stravinskian neo-classicism — name it, it was probably there! One wondered on occasion if he was kidding all of us." *See:* W44a

B146 Baruch, David J. "Music In Our Time." *Musical America* 80, no. 2 (15 January 1960), p. 17.
    The critic claims Wuorinen demonstrated that he has an extremely sensitive ear, but that "it seemed in the main a torrent of undeveloped material." *See:* W44a

Concertino

B147 Page, Tim. "The Winds of Parnassus Come to Tully Hall." The *New York Times*, 3 February 1985, *(Arts & Leisure)*, p. 21.
    Pre-concert publicity about the premiere of *Concertino*. A photograph of the ensemble is featured. The founder and music director, Anthony Korf, is quoted as saying: "The Wuorinen is a stunning dramatic work [that] fits into the continuum of Western music." *See:* W45

B148 Crutchfield, Will. "Music: Parnassus Winds." The *New York Times*, 10 February 1985, p. 56.
    Crutchfield writes that on a first hearing "the most damaging weakness was a lack of continuity." *See:* W45

B149 Porter, Andrew. "Musical Events: Melodious Winds Have Birth." The *New Yorker*, 18 February 1985, pp. 112, 115-117.
    "Inspiration seemed to have flagged. But it ended with a memorable, Berliozian sound — a B blown out across seven octaves." *See:* W45

B150 Schwarz, Robert. "Debuts & Reappearances: New York." *High Fidelity/Musical America* 35, no. 6 (June 1985), pp. MA28-MA29.
    The reviewer writes that although the music was expressive, he felt there was a lack of direction. "This lack of direction ultimately made the work appear as no more than a compendium of clever modernist devices." (p. MA29) *See:* W45

B151 Kresky, Jeffrey. "The Recent Music of Charles Wuorinen." *Perspectives of New Music* 25, nos. 1-2 (1987), pp. 410-417.
    Concertino is discussed in this important article. *See:* W45, B857

Concerto for Amplified Violin and Orchestra

B152 Henahan, Donal. "Music: A New Way of Looking at the New — And the Old." The *New York Times*, 16 July 1972, p. D11.

In this article about the Fromm Music Foundation Henahan mentions that Wuorinen's *Concerto for Amplified Violin and Orchestra* was the most recent work to be commissioned by the foundation. *See:* W5

B153 Conway, Richard. "Concert Series Hits Flat Note." *News* [Springfield, Massachusetts], 5 August 1972.

A local review and one of the many reviews of the premiere performance. The critic calls it "well constructed and solid in musical terms." Later in the review, however, Conway writes: "The reader will undoubtedly infer that I did not like it. The reader is right." *See:* W5

B154 Hammerich, R.C. "Modern Composers Served Valiantly." The *Springfield Union* [Springfield, Massachusetts], 5 August 1972.

The critic says the composition was "apparently very carefully organized to sound frequently screechy and occasionally painful." He misspells the composer's name: "Wjorinen." *See:* W5

B155 Henahan, Donal. "Electric-Violin Shocks Some." The *New York Times*, 6 August 1972, p. 48.

Henahan raises questions about the use of amplification but concludes: "Wuorinen's concerto asks the right questions, even if he may not have found all the right answers." *See:* W5

B156 Rosenfeld, Jay C. "Music Review: Ceccato Debuts at Tanglewood." The *Berkshire Eagle* [Berkshire, Massachusetts], 7 August 1972.

"The final straw was the ascending and descending glissandi for the solo instrument which in magnification became nauseating." *See:* W5

B157 Snyder, Louis. "BSO — Amplified Wuorinen." The *Christian Science Monitor*, 7 August 1972, p. 5.

Sndyer states that the concerto is "a massive architectural structure joined and beamed with the most solid of musical materials." *See:* W5

B158 Steinberg, Michael. "Tanglewood: Some Dissonance." The *Boston Globe*, 8 August 1972.

Steinberg devotes a considerable portion of his review to Wuorinen but says very little of the music. He recounts the controversy surrounding the rehearsals and how the players of the Boston Symphony felt about Wuorinen. He also describes how Wuorinen did not hesitate to offer his opinions of American symphony orchestras. Steinberg concludes: "Wuorinen refused a bow, presumably not considering what had been played as sufficiently his, presumably also not curious to see if the orchestra would boo him again in front of 5000 people as they had in front of 100 at the dress rehearsal." *See:* W5, B166, B172

B159 Henahan, Donal. "Music Fete: New Works Bring Out Varying Reactions." The *New York Times*, 9 August 1972, p. 21.

An assessment of the 1972 Festival of Contemporary Music at Tanglewood, at which this work was premiered. Henahan reports that "at the final rehearsal, individual members and groups certainly expressed their displeasure with Mr. Wuorinen and their loathing for his piece by booing." He goes on to say that the controversy "soon became as highly amplified as the concerto itself." *See:* W5

B160 Noble, David. "Victory at Sea." *Patriot Ledger* [Quincy, Massachusetts], 9 August 1972.

Noble writes that the concerto's "harmonic density lay a little to the left of middle-period [Arnold] Schoenberg." *See:* W5

B161 Hinners, John. "Tanglewood." *Journal* [Lakeville, Connecticut], 10 August 1972.

"Back to the drawing board, please." *See:* W5

B162 Snyder, Louis. "Music: Wuorinen's Breakthrough." The *Christian Science Monitor*, 10 August 1972, p. 4.

A reprint of the same review that appeared three days earlier in the same tabloid, but titled "BSO — Amplified Wuorinen." *See:* W5

B163 Beaver, Martha. "Composer Charles Wuorinen Reflects On the Nature of His Craft." *Daily Hampshire Gazette* [Northampton, Massachusetts], 14 August 1972, p. 4.

This review of the world premiere includes interview material with Wuorinen. Beaver notes the technical demands of the work and praises Paul Zukofsky's violin playing. She also relates the circumstances of the rehearsals and performance and writes that an unidentified Boston Symphony musician admitted the premiere performance was merely a reading. Beaver states: "It must be said that conductor Michael Tilson Thomas seemed not to know how to use his rehearsal time to the best effect. Paul Fromm, co-sponsor of the Contemporary Music Festival, had also observed the disrespectful, unwarranted attitude and treatment accorded the composer's work." *See:* W5

B164 "Modern Maecenas." *Time*, 21 August 1972, p. 49.

An article about Paul Fromm and the Festival of Contemporary Music at Tanglewood. The writer mentions Wuorinen's concerto and states some players in the orchestra as well as audience members booed. *See:* W5

B165 Higgins, Joan. "Music: An SOS to the BSO." *Boston Magazine*, November 1972, pp. 28-34.

Higgins, a musician and music critic, had written an open letter to Seiji Ozawa about the Boston Symphony Orchestra's attitude toward the performance of contemporary music. In this letter she says the orchestra gave Wuorinen's concerto "what was from all accounts a rather rotten performance." (p. 30) She goes on to say that contemporary composers will probably continue to face this kind of treatment. *See:* W5

B166 Steinberg, Michael. "Celebration for Fromm Foundation: Some Major New Works, and Some Controversy, Mark Twentieth Anniversary." *High Fidelity/Musical America* 22, no. 11 (November 1972), pp. MA13, MA32.

Steinberg comments on the rehearsal and performance by noting that even though he had a score he could not offer much of an impression: "I am willing to predict that Wuorinen's new Concerto will be exciting when we can really hear it, but I think it makes no sense to offer a review at this point." *See:* W5, B158, B172

B167 Perlis, Vivian and Aaron Copland. *Copland Since 1943*. New York: St. Martins Press, 1989.

> The chapter titled "Around the World/1949-1953" includes an interview with the American soprano Phyllis Curtin, in which she describes her feelings about waiting to sing Copland's *Dickinson Songs* (the orchestrated version) at Tanglewood, while Wuorinen's *Concerto for Amplified Violin and Orchestra* was being rehearsed. Curtain said: "It was so loud I thought I would lose my mind. I finally said to Aaron I can't sit here and wait. I don't think I'll be able to hear when it gets to be my turn. Aaron kind of giggled and said, 'This is the first time I have ever felt like a nineteenth-century composer.'" (p. 166) The note citing this interview (p. 439) states Vivian Perlis interviewed Curtain on 5 August 1986 in Lenox, Massachusetts. *See:* W5

B168 Dwyer, John. "Thomas Loyal Throng Gets Its Stiffest Test." *Buffalo Evening News*, 2 April 1973.

> "It also had a human set of responses, for all the programmed materials and the nearest thing to melodic line I've detected in an adequate though incomplete survey of Wuorinen works." *See:* W5a

B169 Putnam, Thomas. "Wuorinen Concerto Anything But Boring." The *Buffalo Courier-Express*, 2 April 1973, p. 4.

> "Some 'coloristic' new music is boring, but the Wuorinen Concerto has sock." *See:* W5a

B170 Kerner, Leighton. "The Rustle & Splatter of Glass." *Village Voice*, 15 November 1973, pp. 47-49.

> Kerner writes that Wuorinen "has composed an intricate journey through an orderly jungle of musical ideas." *See:* W5b

B171 Saal, Hubert. "Music: Out of Tune With Today?" *Newsweek*, 24 December 1973, pp. 53-59.

> Saal compares the concerto to children in a play ground: "At the end, the meeting is called to order and the children's play ground turns out to be Pandemonium, that violin Lucifer himself, the orchestra his fellow fallen angels." *See:* W5b

B172 Steinberg, Michael. "Debuts & Reappearances: Buffalo Phil.: Wuorinen Concerto." *High Fidelity/Musical America* 24, no. 2 (February 1974), pp. MA20-MA21.

> Although Steinberg had written two articles about this concerto by this date, this one is the first in which he discusses the music itself. He comments favorably on the rhythm and texture of the piece: "The texture and the rhetoric are enlivened by rich, eruptive inner details, and it was particularly with respect to that feature that the Buffalo performance was so much more vivid than the Boston." (p. MA21) *See:* W5, W5a, B158, B166

B173 Commanday, Robert. "An Unusual Ojai Music Festival." *San Francisco Chronicle*, 3 June 1974, p. 47.

> Commanday says the amplification was the only important idea of the work in that it enabled the solo violin to compete with large orchestral forces. "So what, if the score is bereft of genuine musical impulse, as is true, I'm afraid, of other Wuorinen pieces I've heard." Commanday's criticism of Wuorinen's music changed to a much more positive kind when Wuorinen became composer-in-residence with the San Francisco Symphony in the 1980s. *See:* W5c

B174 Moran, Rita. "28th Ojai Festival Draws Record Crowd." *Star-Free Press* [Ventura, California], 3 June 1974, p. B-2.

Moran praises the performances of Paul Zukofsky, Michael Tilson Thomas and the Los Angeles Philharmonic. But she writes that the concerto's "jarring shrillness brought shouts of bravo from some and mutterings from others willing to strike a blow for the energy crisis by disconnecting the amplifiers." *See:* W5c

B175 Willard, Bert. "Ojai Music Festival Reflects Talents of Director-Conductor." *News-Press* [Santa Barbara, California], 3 June 1974.

"There were very few moments of lyricism; any moves toward sentimentality and coyness were blotted out." *See:* W5c

B176 Perlmutter, Donna. "Tilson Thomas and Ojai." *Herald-Examiner* [Los Angeles], 5 June 1974, p. B-2.

After saying that the performance of Igor Stravinsky's *Abraham and Isaac* offered no contrast to the performance of the *Five Pieces for Orchestra* by Arnold Schoenberg, Perlmutter writes it remained for Wuorinen's concerto "to provide the relieving dynamic outbursts which the orchestra handled with intense concentration and certainly under [Michael Tilson] Thomas' leadership." *See:* W5c

B177 Bernheimer, Martin. "Rags to Riches in Ojai." *Los Angeles Times*, 9 June 1974, pp. 1, 56.

Bernheimer notes that he may have been sitting too close to the orchestra but writes anyway that the amplification "allows the electrified fiddle, superbly played by [Paul] Zukofsky, to win a most unpleasant volume battle with a big, brassy, percussive orchestra." *See:* W5c

B178 *Music Of the Last Forty Years Not Yet Established In the Repertoire: A Survey Conducted By the Fromm Music Foundation at Harvard 1974-1975.* Cambridge, Massachusetts: The Foundation, 1975.

The survey lists *Concerto for Amplified Violin and Orchestra* as one of the twenty-four works by Wuorinen considered by the Fromm Music Foundation to be among "important but neglected or infrequently performed musical works dating from the last forty years." (l. 1) *See:* W5, B891

B179 Read Gardner. *Contemporary Instrumental Techniques.* New York: Schirmer Books, 1976.

In this book Read lists Wuorinen's concerto as a work that exploits extended ranges, idiomatic techniques and amplification: "And in Wuorinen's solo concerto a transducer, which is built into the violin bridge, is connected to a pre-amplifier controlled by an offstage technician." (p. 116) *See:* W5, B859

B180 Neubert, David. "Electronic Bowed String Works: Some Observations on Trends and Developments In the Instrumental/Electronic Medium." *Perspectives of New Music* 21 (Fall-Winter 1982, Spring-Summer 1983), pp. 540-566.

This brief article classifies electronic string works according to medium and means and discusses goals and trends of the medium. It concludes with a detailed list of bowed string works involving electronics; the list includes *Concerto for Amplified Violin and Orchestra. See:* W5

B181 Moore, David W. "Collections: Instrumental." *American Record Guide* 47, no. 5 (July 1984), p. 62.

> A review of the University of Iowa Press recording. Moore begins by saying "Wuorinen has composed a number of concertos in which the orchestra attempts to drown or otherwise maim the soloist." He goes on to say that this concerto and, in particular, this recording, reflect a situation in which the "battle sounds are evenly matched." *See:* D30

B182 *A Life For New Music. Selected Papers of Paul Fromm*. Ed. David Gable and Christoph Wolff. Cambridge, Massachusetts: Department of Music, Harvard University (Distributed by Harvard University Press), 1988.

> Describes the 1972 twentieth anniversary celebration of the Fromm Music Foundation. The following works had been commissioned: *Concertino*, by Roger Sessions; *Giardino Religioso*, by Bruno Maderna; *Music for Chamber Ensemble*, by Gunther Schuller; and *Concerto for Amplified Violin and Orchestra*, by Wuorinen. "With the exception of the Wuorinen, these works were all subsequently recorded." (p. xvi) Wuorinen's concerto was eventually recorded by the University of Iowa Press in 1983. *See:* D30, D80

Concerto for Violin and Orchestra

B183 *Music Of the Last Forty Years Not Yet Established In the Repertoire: A Survey Conducted By the Fromm Music Foundation at Harvard 1974-1975*. Cambridge, Massachusetts: The Foundation, 1975.

> The survey lists the *Violin Concerto* as one of the twenty-four works by Wuorinen considered by the Fromm Music Foundation to be among the "important but neglected or infrequently performed musical works dating the last forty years." (l. 1) This concerto is the early 1958 unpublished violin concerto that has never been performed. *See:* W6, B891

Consort from Instruments and Voices

B184 Salzman, Eric. "Music In Our Time Begins Its Season." The *New York Times*, 16 January 1961, p. 22.

> Salzman describes the work as "a tape splice, filter and feedback job" and says it is "a surrealistic instrumental piece." *See:* W158

B185 Baruch, David J. "Music In Our Time." *Musical America* 81, no. 2 (February 1961), p. 65.

> "Shock tactics were at a minimum and it was enjoyable, though whether as music is another question." *See:* W158

Consort of Four Trombones

B186 Flanagan, William. "Evening of Music Presented By Chamber Group." *New York Herald Tribune*, 5 April 1960.

> Flanagan writes "this work, like so many of the others, seems still that of a youngster who wants to be as 'mean' as possible to attract proportionate attention." *See:* W69

B187 Salzman, Eric. "New Chamber Group Gives Concert Here." The *New York Times*, 5 April 1960, p. 44.

The reviewer says the music "was as serious and about as interesting as a piece for four trombones could be." *See:* W69

Contrafactum

B188 Greene, Joseph. "Concert Keeps Promise." The *Daily Iowan* [Iowa City, Iowa], 21 November 1969, p. 8.

Greene praises James Dixon and the University of Iowa Symphony Orchestra for performing this work and offering the world premiere: "Many schools give lip service to modern music, but few have the nerve to attempt such a piece." *See:* W8

B189 Johnson, Harriet. "An Orchestra That Is Truly New." *New York Post*, 17 September 1975, p. 50.

The first of several reviews of the New York premiere. "The music, especially the last movement, 'Alive,' was alive far too long for my taste." *See:* W8a

B190 Henahan, Donal. "Music: A Mixed Debut: New Orchestra Under Wuorinen and Weisberg Bears Up to Grim Fare." The *New York Times*, 18 September 1975, p. 49.

"It seems obsessed with form and largely devoid of emotional expressiveness, whereas the best music balances those concerns delicately." Henahan praises the New Orchestra, however, the ensemble that debuted at this performance. *See:* W8a

B191 ["Music"] The *Westsider/The Villager* [New York City], 25 September 1975.

The reviewer says Wuorinen conducted with "intense conviction" but that the music did not offer "anything the listener could hold on to for more than a minute or so." *See:* W8a

B192 Jefferson, Margo. "Brave New Sounds." *Newsweek*, 29 September 29, 1975, p. 75.

Jefferson writes the music "filled the hall with rich percussive effects and moments of silence and explosive sound." *See:* W8a

B193 Kerner, Leighton. "A Brave New Orchestra Is Born." *Village Voice* [New York City], 29 September 1975, pp. 91-93.

The article is mostly about the creation, by Wuorinen and Arthur Weisberg, of the New Orchestra. Kerner says *Contrafactum* is not one of Wuorinen's best pieces. [P] *See:* W8a

B194 Smith, Patrick J. "Debuts & Reappearances: The New Orchestra." *High Fidelity/Musical America* 25, no. 12 (December 1975), pp. MA28-MA39.

In contrast to the review by Leighton Kerner, Smith says *Contrafactum* is definitely one of Wuorinen's best pieces, and describes it as "an extended gallery of musical pictures." Smith concludes: "Wuorinen's fertility of invention in his construction of the sections is amazing." (p. MA39) *See:* W8, W8a

B195 "Headliners." *Catalyst* [New York City], (Spring 1976), p. 4.

This publication of Affiliate Artists, Inc., merely mentions that the premiere took place and then discusses the New Orchestra. *See:* W8

B196 *Music of the Last Forty Years Not Yet Established In the Repertoire: A Survey Conducted By the Fromm Music Foundation at Harvard 1974-1975.* Cambridge, Massachusetts: The Foundation, 1975.

The survey lists *Contrafactum* as one of the twenty-four works by Wuorinen considered by the Fromm Music Foundation to be among the "important but neglected or infrequently performed musical works dating from the last forty years." (l. 1) *See:* W8, B891

Crossfire

B197 Monson, Karen. "BSO's Baltimore, N.Y. Concerts to Offer Wuorinen's 'Crossfire'." The *Sun* [Baltimore], 5 May 1985.

Pre-concert publicity for the premiere of *Crossfire. See:* W9

B198 Monson, Karen. "Debuts & Reappearances: Baltimore Symphony." *High Fidelity/Musical America* 35, no. 9 (September 1985), p. MA18.

"With regular rhythms and (in these performances) only modest dynamic spread, the work runs the risk of making its point within the first minute or two and having nothing more to say." *See:* W9

B199 Kresky, Jeffrey. "The Recent Music of Charles Wuorinen." *Perspectives of New Music* 25 nos. 1-2 (1987), pp. 410-417.

Crossfire is discussed in this important article. *See:* W9, B857

B200 Samuel, Rhian. ["Music Reviews."] *Music & Letters* 70, no. 4 (1989), pp. 597-598.

A review of the C.F. Peters edition. Samuel calls Wuorinen "a master of orchestral colour in modernist (nowadays, even conservative) vein." (p. 597) *See:* W9

Delight of the Muses

B201 Homzie, Hillary. "NYCB Season Honors W.A. Mozart." *Dance Magazine* 65 (November 1991), pp. 12-13.

Publicity concerning the premiere of *Delight of the Muses. See:* W10

B202 Kisselgoff, Anna. "A Playful Mozart Lives In a Premiere by Martins." The *New York Times*, 31 January 1992, p. B1.

Kisselgoff praises the dancers and Martins's choreography. Of Wuorinen's music she writes: "Only the hidebound might be unhappy with Mr. Wuorinen in his balloon-puncturing mood, typically bringing down a Mozartean motif with a resounding blast from the brass or racing through a finale at suspense-thriller speed." *See:* W10

B203 Berman, Janice. "Dance Review: Martins' Family Musings." *New York Newsday*, 25 February 1992.

"To paraphrase Queen Victoria, We are a-Mused." She also writes that the music and choreography are a great match. *See:* W10

B204 Tobias, Tobi. "Twyla Sharp and Peter Pan." *New York*, 17 February 1992, pp. 62-63.

Tobias writes that Wuorinen's music "sounds like Mozart having premonitions about the late twentieth century." (p. 63) She also pans Peter Martins's choreography, calling it boring and horrible. *See:* W10

B205 Dunning, Jennifer. "Ballet Closes Ranks and the Show Goes On." The *New York Times*, 24 July 1992, p. B6.

This article describes the controversy surrounding the arrest of New York City Ballet choreographer Peter Martins on a charge of wife-beating. (Upon appearing in court on 22 July 1992, the charge was dropped.) Dunning writes that a joke began to circulate in Saratoga Springs, New York: Bedřich Smetana's *The Battered Bride* would be added to the ballet company's repertory. Ms. Kistler (Peter Martins's wife) was a lead dancer in this performance of *Delight of the Muses*, which had taken place shortly after the event described above. Dunning says "the audience seemed to accept Ms. Kistler simply as one of the company's lead dancers, without special applause at her entrance." *See:* W10c

Divertimento for Alto Saxophone and Piano

B206 Page, Tim. "Music: In Review." The *New York Times*, 13 March 1983, p. 62.

Page says the work "continues an idiosyncratic and admirably single-minded odyssey into a new accessibility without, however, compromising the composer's cerebral austerity." *See:* W71

B207 McLellan, Joseph. "Performing Arts: Christopher Ford." The *Washington Post*, 11 April 1983, p. B11.

The reviewer writes that Wuorinen "uses the resources of the saxophone with a fine sense of color." *See:* W71a

B208 Cochran, Alfred W. "Music Reviews: Orchestral and Ensemble Music." *Notes* 49, no. 1 (September 1992), pp. 362-363.

A review of the C.F. Peters edition. The review discusses the rhythmic complexity and wide registral spread of the music. Cochran calls it an "uncompromising work and skillfully crafted music." (p. 363) *See:* W71

Doctor Faustus Lights the Lights

B209 Telberg, Lelia K. "Reviews of the Month." *Dance Observer* 24, no. 5 (May 1957), p. 74.

Telberg writes that Paul Sanasardo, Donya Feuer and Ellen Green "worked diligently with the script, but the words seemed to hamper the actors instead of becoming a springboard into a phantasy world." She calls Wuorinen's score "interesting." *See:* W73

Duo for Violin and Piano

B210 Fleming, Shirley. "Debuts & Reappearances: Paul Zukofsky, Violin." *High Fidelity/Musical America* 19 (February 1969), p. MA25.

"Though a certain pithiness was present in the spasmodic, heavily punctuated, tone-clustery interaction of the two instruments, the sum total of these three movements, rather undifferentiated in themselves, seemed to me one of increasing tedium." *See:* W76a

B211 Henahan, Donal. "Recordings: New Music as Public Art?" The *New York Times*, 3 January 1971, *(Arts & Leisure)*, p. 22D.
A review of the Acoustic Research recording. Henahan says the piece is "as prodigiously skilled in the performing as the writing." *See:* D9

B212 Rockwell, John. "Birth and Death of an Idea." *Los Angeles Times*, 29 August 1971, *(Calendar)*, p. 54.
A review of the Acoustic Research recording. He states the recording contains "an authoritative version by Paul Zukofsky and Charles Wuorinen of this piece." *See:* D9

B213 Chittum, Donald. "Reviews of Records." *Musical Quarterly* 58, no. 3 (July 1972), pp. 501-509.
A review of the Acoustic Research recording. Chittum writes, in part, "Wuorinen quite ably supports his contention that the last words regarding rhythmic complexity for live players are yet to be uttered." (p. 506) *See:* D9

B214 *Music of the Last Forty Years Not Yet Established In the Repertoire: A Survey Conducted By the Fromm Music Foundation at Harvard 1974-1975.* Cambridge, Massachusetts: The Foundation, 1975.
The survey lists *Duo for Violin and Piano* as one of the twenty-four works by Wuorinen considered by the Fromm Music Foundation to be among "important but neglected or infrequently performed musical works dating from the last forty years." (l. 1) *See:* W76

B215 Bloch, Robert S. "Reviews of Music: Ensemble and Solo Instrumental Music." *Notes* 33, no. 2 (December 1976), pp. 411-412.
A review of the C.F. Peters edition. Bloch calls it "a huge and thorny work whose accessibility is not aided by the printing." (p. 411) *See:* W76

B216 Lange, Art. "Charles Wuorinen and Benjamin Hudson." The *Reader* [Chicago], 24 March 1978, pp. 34-35.
"Unfortunately, the piece contained a limited amount of timbral color; the stark, skeletal outline displayed only the construction instead of the total edifice." *See:* W76c

Duuiensela

B217 Armstrong, George E. "Young Cellist Performs In Recital Here." *New Haven Register*, 1 May 1962, p. 34.
A review of the premiere performance. Armstrong calls the work "derivative" and says it "is one of the most avant garde pieces ever to be performed here." *See:* W77

B218 Breurer, Robert. "Welt der Musik: Drei Mahlzeiten täglich mit Zwölfton-musik: ein Wochenende mit der Amerikanischen Avantgarde." *Aufbau* [New York City], 24 August 1962, pp. 11, 17.
Breurer writes that the performance "confirmed, though with perhaps some too explosive effects, this composer's inner passion to elicit the most amazing and elementary forces from the score." (p. 17) *See:* W77b

B219 Breurer, Robert. "Drei Tage mit Amerikas Komponistennachwuchs."
Melos: Zeitschrift für Neue Musik 30, no. 2 (February 1963), pp. 64-65.
A reprint of the same article first published in *Aufbau* but under a different title.
See: W77b, B218

B220 Cott, Jonathan. "Electronic Music: How Many Flutes Was That?"
Columbia Daily Spectator [New York City], 9 May 1963.
"[*Duuiensela* is] a work that combines a despair and vitality to produce such a
staggering emotional effect that one must call the piece revolutionary." *See:* W77d

B221 Mellers, Wilfred. *Music In a New Found Land: Themes and Developments
In the History of American Music*. London: Carrie and Rockliff, 1964.
Of *Duuiensela* Mellers writes that Wuorinen used "Earle Brown's time-notation
and other semi-improvised techniques." (p. 232) *See:* W77

B222 *Music Of the Last Forty Years Not Yet Established In the Repertoire: A
Survey Conducted By the Fromm Music Foundation at Harvard 1974-1975.*
Cambridge, Massachusetts: The Foundation, 1975.
The survey lists *Duuiensela* as one of the twenty-four works by Wuorinen
considered by the Fromm Music Foundation to be "important or infrequently performed
musical works dating from the last forty years." (l. 1) *See:* W77

B223 Weinstein, Alan. "Music Reviews." *Notes* 46, no. 2 (December 1989), pp.
506-507.
"The rhythmic complexities make the piece quite challenging to any but
experienced performers." (p. 507) *See:* W77

Ecclesiastical Symphonies

B224 Forsman, Folke. "En hel kväll med Charles Wuorinen." *Hufvudstadsbladet*,
17 October 1981.
This is a Swedish-language newspaper published in Helsinki. In the review, titled
"A Whole Evening With Charles Wuorinen," Forsman (a concert organist) writes "one
could not grasp anything that one could call thematics, but the music lives entirely upon
its simple rhythm and upon the differentiated orchestration where the percussion section
takes a central place." *See:* W11a

B225 Tawaststjerna, Erik. "Epäilijä tulen sfäärissa." *Helsingen Sanomat Arkisto*,
18 October 1981.
In this review titled "A Doubter In the Sphere of Five" Tawaststjerna comments
on the movement 'About Resurrection': "[It] is somehow associated with [Olivier]
Messiaen's superfluous colority. Wuorinen does not write dense texture or superimpose
harmonics, but rather — the opposite — he lets the miracle of resurrection be reflected
in the wide linear movements of woodwinds and piano." *See:* W11a

B226 Hako, Pekka. "Lahoavaa Taidetta." *Sosialidemokraatti Demari* [Helsinki],
21 October 1981.
Titled "Rotting Art," the reviewer says: "If Charles Wuorinen intended to
describe things and feelings that are related to the titles of these symphonies, then in
Wuorinen's heaven, hardly anything happens. There rules a timeless and tensionless state
where all movement is, in the end, very slow and without special significance. It is like

sailing above the clouds while the hull of the boat is dangerously close to the earth."
See: W11a

Eight Variations for Violin and Harpsichord

B227 Purswell, Joan. "20th-Century Chamber Music for Harpsichord, Part II."
Clavier 19, no. 5 (May-June 1980), pp. 36-38.
A listing of contemporary harpsichord music; includes this piece. (p. 38) *See:*
W78

Evolutio: Organ

B228 Bingham, Seth. "Recitals and Concerts." *American Organist* 45, no. 10
(October 1962), pp. 14-15, 32-34.
"The man's music reveals here a potentially great talent, but spilling all the beans
on every second page is not the Via Gloria." (p. 33) *See:* W147a

B229 Bingham, Seth. "Recitals and Concerts." *American Organist* 51, no. 1
(January 1968), pp. 12-13.
"But our impression is that the vehicle of expression should be the orchestra and
not the organ, or possibly the orchestra with the organ where the latter can speak with
its own peculiar language." (p. 13) *See:* W147b

B230 Page, Tim. "Recital: New Music In Village." The *New York Times,* 22
April 1985, p. C18.
Page calls *Evolutio: Organ* one of Wuorinen's "most effective early composi-
tions." He does not identify the organist. *See:* W147c

Evolutio Transcripta

B231 Salzman, Eric. "Music: Rural Workshop." The *New York Times,* 21 August
1961, p. 18.
Salzman writes that Wuorinen "is a prolific if undisciplined young composer and
no composer of 23 ever sowed such wild oats." *See:* W47

B232 Tate, Lisa. "There's Sound and Music At Composers Conference."
Bennington Evening Banner [Bennington, Vermont], 23 August 1961.
"Yet for all its tenseness, and maybe due to it, the sound seemed to sear the ear,
with memorable effect." *See:* W47

B233 Strongin, Theodore. ["Music Review."] The *Knickerbocker News* [Albany,
New York], 29 August 1961.
"Music like this clears the air because Mr. Wuorinen scored his beating-out nobly
and registered it as if for a gigantic organ." *See:* W47

B234 Brozen, Michael. "Music In Our Time." *Musical America* 82, no. 3
(February 1962), p. 40.
Brozen writes that the music "contains some pretty pyramids for chamber
orchestra but lacks whatever it is that carries a piece from beginning to end." *See:* W47

B235 Mellers, Wilfred. *Music In a New Found Land: Themes and Developments In the History of American Music.* London: Carrie and Rockliff, 1964.

Mellers writes that in *Evolutio Transcripta* Wuorinen "is using a Carter-like evolutionary polyphony and polyrhythm, with aggressive Ivesian note-clusters." (p. 232) *See:* W47

B236 Tawa, Nicholas. *A Most Wondrous Babble: American Art Composers, Their Music, and the American Scene, 1950-1985.* Westport, Connecticut: Greenwood Press, 1987.

"The work sounds as if between two styles and shows the composer in search of an identity. The music plunges vehemently ahead from one set of thematic ideas to the next. The profusion of new departures gives the impression of undiscipline." (p. 98) *See:* W47

Fantasia

B237 Galkin, Elliott W. "Twentieth Century Music Performed at the Museum." The *Sun* [Baltimore], 15 December 1975.

"Historically, it could be proposed that its [the fantasia's] sparseness of timbre and exploitation of textural clarity might be considered logical extensions of [Igor] Stravinsky's contributions." *See:* W80

B238 Horowitz, Joseph. "Music: Xenakis, Wuorinen, et. al." The *New York Times*, 4 February 1977, *(Section 3)*, p. 18.

Horowitz describes how he perceived the rhythmic aspect of the music and talks about shifting meters. He concludes: "On first hearing, it seemed abstruse." *See:* W80a

B239 Artner, Alan. "Wuorinen Pleases All But One." *Chicago Tribune*, 13 March 1978, *(Section 3)*, p. 7.

Artner calls Benjamin Hudson's violin playing "brilliant, at times dazzling, but also dry as dust." Of Wuorinen's music, he writes: "If it indeed represented the music of the future, Wuorinen and his band of admirers can have it." *See:* W80b

B240 Lange, Art. "Charles Wuorinen and Benjamin Hudson." The *Reader* [Chicago], 24 March 1978, pp. 34-35.

"[Benjamin] Hudson's forceful attack helped stress the music's violent nature, though again there were contrasting lyrical passages to balance the work and hold the listener's attention." *See:* W80b

B241 Considine, J.D. "Music Review: Some Shining Moments in Chamber Concerts." The *News American* [Baltimore], 9 March 1981, p. 4D.

"Rather than intensify the dryness of Wourinen's [*sic*] thematic content, the performance instead emphasized the work's rhythmic and textural development." *See:* W80c

B242 Berrett, Joshua. "Record Reviews." *American Music* 8 (1990), pp. 121-123.

A review of the Bridge recording. Berrett compares the piece to Arnold Schoenberg's *Phantasy* and writes "it develops into a composition of characteristic nervous energy." (p. 123) *See:* D35

Fast Fantasy

B243 Kenyon, Nicholas. "Musical Events: Politics." The *New Yorker*, 4 February 1980, pp. 115-116.
    Kenyon praises Fred Sherry's performance but calls the music "intense and arid." (p. 115) He also recounts a post-concert discussion at which critic John Rockwell asked John Cage and Wuorinen to offer their views on the labels uptown and downtown composers. The composers proceeded to discuss their postal Zip Codes. *See:* W81a

B244 Roberts Ed. "The Compelling Wuorinen Premiere." The *Washington Post*, 26 November 1988, p. C3.
    The critic calls it a "strongly accented and driven work" but that there were "clearly identifiable points of repose." *See:* W81b

Five: Concerto for Amplified Cello and Orchestra

B245 Schwarz, K. Robert. "American Music's Vitality." The *New York Times*, 24 April 1988 *(Arts & Leisure)*, p. 27.
    Pre-concert publicity about *Five* and the New York City Ballet's *American Music Festival*. Schwarz discusses the philosophies of several composers, including Wuorinen, who is quoted as saying: "When I work with dance I'm struck by how wonderful it is to be in an environment where the new is taken for granted." [P] *See:* W13, W13a, W13b

B246 Kisselgoff, Anna. "A Ballet By Bonnefoux With a Wuorinen Score." The *New York Times*, 30 April 1988, p. 14.
    A review of the premiere. Kisselgoff writes "one can only be sorry that Mr. Bonnefoux's ballet could not match him [Wuorinen] on the same level." She also describes cellist Fred Sherry as "formidable". *See:* W13, W13b

B247 Henahan, Donal. "Music: St. Lukes Is Conducted by Composers of 2 Pieces." The *New York Times*, 8 November 1989, p. C23.
    Henahan says of this first concert performance that aside from some appealing moments and the virtuosic performance of Fred Sherry, the piece "provided few other compelling reasons for hearing it again." *See:* W13d

B248 Porter, Andrew. "Musical Events: Through Every Passion Ranging." The *New Yorker*, 4 December 1989, pp. 144-149.
    Porter calls the music "energetic yet refined invention." (p. 145) He notes that the performance was spoiled by a loudspeaker malfunction. *See:* W13d

B249 Rooney, Dennis D. "Concert Notes." The *Strad* 101, (March 1990), p. 168.
    Rooney notes there were problems with the amplification equipment during the performance: "This proved not only an intolerable distraction but had the further effect of bathing Sherry's tone in a harsh electronic glare." *See:* W13d

B250 Commanday, Robert. "Symphony Serves a New-Unusual Dazzler." *San Francisco Chronicle*, 2 April 1990, Section F, p. 2.
    The critic says "writing for the dance may well have helped release some of the composer's self-consciousness." Commanday also praises Fred Sherry's cello playing. *See:* W13e

B251 Glackin, William. "Accent on Unusual." The *Sacramento Bee* [Sacramento, California], 2 April 1990.

"The music sounds serial; it also sounds passionate." The reviewer comments favorably on Fred Sherry's cello playing. *See:* W13e

B252 Ulrich, Allan. "Symphony NUMS Ends With a Winner: Strong Repertoire, Lush Instrumentation in Half-Empty Herbst Theatre." *San Francisco Examiner*, 3 April 1990, p. 2.

Ulrich writes "the fluency and variety of the string writing and the tonal nuance with which Wuorinen infused his structure often contradicted the image of the austere mandarin the composer presents to the all-too susceptible media." *See:* W13e

Flute Variations I

B253 Ericson, Raymond. "Music: 4 Contemporary Americans." The *New York Times*, 19 December 1963, p. 41.

Ericson says the work had "explosive and contrasting sounds." *See:* W82

B254 Salzman, Eric. "New Music at Donnell." *New York Herald Tribune*, 19 December 1963.

Salzman calls it "a work of great tonal imagination, a piece of fantasy shaped by accent and color." *See:* W82

B255 Strongin, Theodore. "Sophie Sollberger Plays Flute Works." The *New York Times*, 10 November 1964, p. 57.

Strongin briefly mentions this work as one "spitting with energy, but tender at times, too." *See:* W82c

B256 *Music of the Last Forty Years Not Yet Established In the Repertoire: A Survey Conducted By the Fromm Music Foundation at Harvard 1974-1975.* Cambridge, Massachusetts: The Foundation, 1975.

The survey lists *Flute Variations I* as one of twenty-four works by Wuorinen considered by the Fromm Music Foundation to be among the "important but neglected or infrequently performed musical works dating from the last forty years." (l. 1) *See:* W82, B891

B257 Cohn, Arthur. *Recorded Classical Music. A Critical Guide to Compositions and Performances.* New York: Schirmer Books, 1981.

A review of the Nonesuch recording. Cohn writes the music "is serial styled but not in any way arid or rigid for the sake of the technical system." (p. 2109) *See:* D17

Flute Variations II

B258 Rosenfeld, Jay C. "Music Review: Musical High Jinks at Wheatleigh." The *Berkshire Eagle* [Berkshire, Massachusetts], 28 July 1974.

Rosenfeld merely expresses his opinion that the work should have been called "inflections." *See:* W83d

B259 Salisbury, Wilma. "A New Turn for Music Theater." The *Plain Dealer* [Cleveland], 25 August 1974, p. 4-F.

She writes that the work took the flutist "far beyond the normal limits of flute performance." *See:* W83d

B260 Frankenstein, Alfred. "Classical." *High Fidelity/Musical America* 25, no. 9 (September 1975), pp. 102-103.

Frankenstein merely mentions the work and says it is one of the few works on the Nonesuch recording to hold one's interest.   He praises Harvey Sollberger's "consummate musicality." (p. 102) *See:* D17

B261 Risatti, Howard. *New Music Vocabulary. A Guide to Notational Signs for Contemporary Music.* Urbana: University of Illinois Press, 1975.

A brief mention and notational illustration of "Trill from harmonic to natural, same pitch," (p. 153) which Wuorinen used in this work. *See:* W83

B262 Swift, Richard. "Music Reviews: Instrumental Solo and Ensemble Music." *Notes* 34, no. 3 (March 1978), pp. 722-723.

A review of the C.F. Peters edition. Swift writes that the instrumental techniques and "the control over a broad field of dynamics and modes of articulation demanded of the performer are essential to the full realization of the musical processes of the composition." (p. 723) *See:* W83

B263 Cohn, Arthur. *Recorded Classical Music. A Critical Guide to Compositions and Performances.* New York: Schirmer Books, 1981.

A review of the Nonesuch recording. "Mr. [Harvey] Sollberger cannot fail to make a believer out of anyone that listens to his playing." (p. 2109) *See:* D17

B264 Bondurant, Kathleen A. *Twentieth Century Flute Performance Techniques in Selected Compositions.* (Ph.D. dissertation) New York: New York University, 1984.

The section of the dissertation featuring an interview with Harvey Sollberger includes a discussion of Sollberger's professional relationship with Wuorinen. *Flute Variations II* is mentioned in her appendix (p. 234) where flutist Robert Dick lists the work as being noteworthy. Bondurant had undertaken a poll of three individuals — Robert Dick, Julius Baker, and John Heiss — to gather their responses concerning important compositions for flute. *See:* W83

B265 Austin, Larry and Thomas Clark. *Learning To Compose. Modes, Materials and Models of Musical Invention.* Dubuque, Iowa: William C. Brown, 1989.

This textbook on musical composition includes the statement that works such as Wuorinen's *Flute Variations II* "continued in an American vein to advance the medium [music for solo flute], confirming and extending the idioms of their predecessors." (p. 34) *See:* W83

B266 Ward, Charles. "Composer Prefers to Let Music Speak for Itself." *Houston Chronicle*, 11 May 1990.

Ward calls the piece "a well-written example of serial-oriented American music." *See:* W83e

Fortune

B267 Foil, David. "Contemporary Music CAN Be Rich, Pleasant to Hear." *Morning Advocate* [Baton Rouge, Louisiana], 19 February 1981, Section C, pp. 1-C, 10-C.

Foil writes the piece "emerged as a work full of wonderfully varied tension." Earlier that day, Wuorinen lectured about contemporary music and made the following statement: "People who criticize the way I write in 1981 generally don't use as a basis for that criticism the way I wrote in 1979. They're thinking of 1879. And I can't see what is necessarily better about writing in a style that was extensively explored by composers who were dead before most of the audience were born." *See:* W84a

Genesis

B268 "Lifeline: Beginning Music." *USA Today*, 25 September 1991.

Pre-concert publicity for the premiere. *See:* W163

B269 Ulrich, Allan. "Symphony and Chorus Wrestle With Creation." *San Francisco Examiner*, 27 September 1991, p. D-16.

"The thought, care and craftsmanship indicate that he [Wuorinen] does not take lightly the task of writing for massed voices." [P] *See:* W163

B270 Commanday, Robert. "Blomstedt's Faith Sustains New Work." *San Francisco Chronicle*, 28 September 1991, p. C3.

A mixed review that describes the music's textures as "too dense with detail" and the choral writing as "ungrateful, not unvocal but muddy in the voicing, remarkably lacking in contrast and in individualization of expressive ideas." Of the conductor, Commanday writes: "All praise to [Herbert] Blomstedt, whose command of Wuorinen's atomic web of rhythm channels the energies as if they were forces of nature." *See:* W163

B271 Hertelendy, Paul. "Wuorinen's Genesis Begins to Show the Gentler Side of a Genius." *Mercury News* [San Jose, California], 28 September 1991.

The critic writes Wuorinen "thinks so big that the vastness of the universe and of recorded time may not be quite enough to contain his ideas." Hertelendy also states Genesis "is reminiscent of Igor Stravinsky's mid-career work" and that the composition is "an interesting but aloof exercise." [P] *See:* W163

B272 Kiraly, Philippa. "1991/1992 Premieres: Composer Cameos." *Symphony* [Washington, D.C.]. (September-October 1991), p. 27.

Noteworthy in that this item features a photoreproduction of a manuscript page from the Cosmology part of Genesis (copyright 1990 by C.F. Peters Corp.). This is an excellent visual example of Wuorinen's musical penmanship. *See:* W163

B273 Porter, Andrew. "Musical Events: Creation, Revival." The *New Yorker*, 21 October 1991, p. 110.

"Impelled by counterpoint, challenging in its harmonies, it is richly and intently wrought and exhilarating to hear." *See:* W163

B274 Porter, Andrew. "New Music in America." *Financial Times* [London], 7 November 1991.

Porter says the work is "exhilarating, it might be a hit at the Proms." *See:* W163

B275 Dinwiddie, Richard D. "Songs to a Higher Power." *Christianity Today* 35 (25 November 1991), p. 64.

"Wuorinen's dense compositional style stands opposite the minimalist trend evident in so much concert music today." *See:* W163

B276 Anthony, Michael. "Wuorinen's 'Genesis' Powerfully Performed." *Star Tribune* [Minneapolis], 20 November 1992, p. 20E.

Anthony praises *Genesis* as a complex and erudite work. He also writes: "If he [Wuorinen] were a novelist, he would be John Barth or James Joyce rather than a straightforward realist like James Jones or Nelson Algren." *See:* W163a

The Golden Dance

B277 Commanday, Robert. "An Overview of the S.F. Symphony's 1986-87 Season." *San Francisco Chronicle*, 9 March 1986, *(Review)*, pp. 14-15.

This article discusses the composer-in-residence program of the San Francisco Symphony and mentions that Wuorinen's work in progress at that time — *The Golden Dance* — would be taken on tour by Herbert Blomstedt and the San Francisco Symphony between 12 February and 17 March 1987. The article includes a fair amount of interview material. Wuorinen is quoted as saying: "The 18th century public consisted of people who were musically trained. Our audience [today] consists of people who have suffered the kind of musical education produced in our public schools. Musical literacy should be the kind of universal goal verbal literacy is." *See:* W14 - W14e

B278 Kresky, Jeffrey. "The Recent Music of Charles Wuorinen." *Perspectives of New Music* 25, nos. 1-2 (1987), pp. 410-417.

The Golden Dance is discussed in this important article. *See:* W14, B857

B279 Holland, Bernard. "Music: Wuorinen Piece By the San Francisco." The *New York Times*, 15 February 1987, *(Arts & Leisure)*, p. 77.

A review of the New York City premiere. Holland notes that the piece was played first on the program, perhaps to placate listeners with other works by Igor Stravinsky and Johannes Brahms after listening to the Wuorinen. He describes *The Golden Dance* as "the kind of joyous, sometimes grating, din we associate with a busy New York street." *See:* W14a

B280 Greenfield, Edward. "Golden Dancers." The *Guardian* [London], 18 February 1987, p. 28.

A review of the London premiere. "What rather prevented the whole piece from adding up to the sum of its parts was the relentless evenness of pulse in both movements and the persistent busy-ness of textures." *See:* W14b

B281 Cairns, David. "A Festival of Finns: Music." The *Sunday Times* [London], 22 February 1987, p. 53.

A review of the London premiere. Cairns writes that the work "was less remarkable for what it had to say than for its ability to say it." *See:* W14b

B282 Lettner, Franz. "Das San Francisco Symphony Orchestra im Brucknerhaus: Ein sensationeller Nachmittag." *Obersteirisches Tagblatt* [Leoben, Austria], 24 February 1987.
     A review of the European premiere (the Austrian concert had been billed as the European premiere, even though the London concert had come first.) The article is subtitled "A Sensational Afternoon." The reviewer writes: "It is a two-part composition, musically structured in proportion to its rule, as difficult to play as it is to listen to." *See:* W14b, W14c

B283 Geitel, Klaus. "Charles Wuorinen un sein Goldener Tanz in der Philharmonie: Musikgefühle der Spätromantik." *Berliner Morgenpost*, 26 February 1987, p. 12.
     A review of the Berlin premiere. "Wuorinen proves himself to be a musician full of ideas and aware of musical effects, and he knows how to keep the listener occupied with successive attractions." Geitel also writes of Herbert Blomstedt: "His correct, simple and purposeful conducting style reminds one of the unforgettable Hans Rosbaud. Blomstedt demonstrated himself to be a director whose future has just begun to develop toward its full greatness." *See:* W14d

B284 Von Jena, Hans-Joerg. "Das San Francisco Symphony Orchestra unter der Leitung von Herbert Blomstedt in der Philharmonie: Beseeltes Musizieren statt Oberflächenschimmer." *Volksblatt Berlin*, 26 February 1987, p. 21.
     A review of the Berlin premiere. Subtitled "Inspired Performance Instead of Superficial Glitter" the critic writes: "It is a twenty-minute piece, clearly structured, which to the listener reflects pop music in the language of concert music. If it did not provoke an inappropriate comparison with [Ludwig van] Beethoven or [Maurice] Ravel, one could call the piece the 'apotheosis of the dance'." *See:* W14d

B285 Wilkening, Martin. "Triumph mit Brahms: Das San Francisco's Symphony Orchestra in der Phiharmonie." *Der Tagesspeigel* [Berlin], 26 February 1987.
     A review of the Berlin premiere. "But the musical impression of the work of strong images (a sort of ballet music) remains rather empty, too calculating and geared for a one-dimensional effect. Despite its eclecticism, Wuorinen's music shows original and independent traits." *See:* W14d

B286 Moor, Paul. "Debuts & Reappearances: San Francisco." *Musical America* 107, no. 1 (March 1987), pp. 29-30.
     A late review of the premiere performance, in San Francisco. "This quite brilliant work's first part, which progressively creates an atmosphere of mysterious anticipation, alternates between chamber-music transparency and sophisticated exploitation of that old style full symphony orchestra sound upon which so many of today's composers have turned their backs." Moor also praised Herbert Blomstedt's conducting. [P] *See:* W14

B287 Davis, Peter G. "Sound Sense." *New York*, 2 March 1987, p. 104.
     A review of the New York premiere. "Much of this score's appeal depends on how an orchestra copes with its virtuoso demands, a challenge that the San Francisco Symphony dealt with brilliantly." *See:* W14a

B288 Kerner, Leighton. "Victims of Circumstance." *Village Voice*, 3 March 1987, p. 76.

A review of the New York premiere. Kerner writes the work "drifts from dreamy but restless hints of tumult to clashing outbursts of street-struts." *See:* W14a

B289 "La stagione del Communale: San Francisco Symphony: Herbert Blomstedt dirige Stravinsky e Brahms." *La Citta* [Florence], 5 March 1987.
    A review of the Italian premiere. "Beyond its programmatic intents, the piece allows the orchestra to exhibit itself in a vast range of virtuoso displays of great effect which involve all the instrumental families. The result: polite applause and a few yawns." *See:* W14e

B290 Pinzauti, Leonardo. "Quell'orchestra così «europea»." *Nazione Firenze* [Florence], 5 March 1987.
    A review of the Italian premiere. Pinzauti applauds the first-desk players by saying their performance was so good "even the twenty minutes of Wuorinen's music, entitled *The Golden Dance*, among the least inviting and the most useless that can be imagined (Wuorinen, according to the program notes, is the composer-in-residence, but we don't think that's such a coup), managed to retain one's attention primarily for the bravura of the instrumentalists." *See:* W14e

B291 Kohlhaas, Ellen. "Goldene Brücken gebaut: Die Europatournee des San Francisco Symphony Orchestra." *Frankfurter Allgemeine* [Frankfurt], 9 March 1987.
    A general article about the San Francisco Symphony's 1987 European tour that featured Wuorinen's *Golden Dance*. Kohlhaas briefly mentions Wuorinen's work was included and states the orchestra likes to display emancipation, particularly by employing female players. *See:* W14d

B292 Millington, Barry. "Music in London: Orchestral." The *Musical Times*, 128 (April 1987), p. 217.
    A review of the London premiere. "The piece consists of a quarter-hour movement full of striking gestures and expectant pauses, followed by a dance of exhilarating rhythms that positively exude East Coast bustle and self-confidence. (Wuorinen is the man who admits to having misjudged an oboe note, once, 12 years ago.)" *See:* W14b

B293 Saari, Seppo. "Mitä enemmän sävellän — sitä vähemmän tekee mieleni puhua sävellyksistäni." *Rondo* [Helsinki] 26, no. 3 (8 April 1988), pp. 11-12.
    This brief article titled "The More I Compose — The Less I Want to Talk About My Compositions" is a condensed version of an informal interview Seppo Saari had with Wuorinen after a concert appearance at the University of Illinois at Urbana-Champaign in 1986. The article includes some biographical information and mentions a few of Wuorinen's pieces. In discussing *The Golden Dance*, Saari writes "Wuorinen said that he knew some of Arvo Pärt's music, which also borrows medieval musical ideas, as do so many other musical works of our century." (p. 12) *See:* W14

B294 Moor, Paul. "San Francisco's Sonic Boom." *High Fidelity/Musical America* 38, no. 6 (June 1988), pp. 58-59.
    This article discusses the surge in recording activity by the San Francisco Symphony under Herbert Blomstedt's leadership. The Nonesuch recording of *The Golden Dance* is mentioned. *See:* D36

B295 Ulrich, Allan. "Bay Area Sounds on Tape and Disc." *San Francisco Sunday Examiner and Chronicle*, 5 February 1989, *(Style)*, p. E-5.
    A review of the Nonesuch recording. "This is either music for dancers of superhuman stamina, or an attempt at computer-age ritual, or a glorious orchestral workout, or a bit of all three." Ulrich also praises Michael Steinberg's annotations on the recording and says it is the best recording ever to come from Davies Symphony Hall. *See:* D36

B296 Ulrich, Allan. "Sound of Music in S.F. Sure to Change." *San Francisco Examiner*, 21 May 1989, p. E-3.
    In this article Ulrich discusses Wuorinen's term as composer-in-residence of the San Francisco Symphony. He says: "In many ways, Wuorinen's tenure has been exemplary." Ulrich especially mentions Wuorinen's ability to compose in many forms, and cites the recording of *Golden Dance. See:* D36

B297 Pincus, Andrew L. "The Wizardry that Makes the Most of the Music." The *New York Times*, 18 June 1989, *(Section 2)*, p. 23.
    A review of the Nonesuch recording. It merely mentions the work. *See:* D36

B298 Moor, Paul. "Review: Wuorinen." *High Fidelity* 39 (July 1989), pp. 62-63.
    A review of the Nonesuch recording. Moor calls it an "energetic reading by [Herbert] Blomstedt" and says it holds its own as vital, at times exciting music. *See:* D36

B299 Kozinn, Allan. "Critics Pick Some Favorites of the Year." The *New York Times*, 26 November 1989, *(Arts & Leisure)*, p. 26.
    A review of the Nonesuch recording. Kozinn writes the performance is the "tightest, most colorful and most emotional" of Wuorinen's music on disk. *See:* D36

Grand Bamboula

B300 Belt, Byron. "Music and Magnificence at U. of Iowa: A New Center for the Arts is a Students Dream." *High Fidelity/Musical America* 23, no. 1 (January 1973), pp. MA24-MA26.
    A review of the premiere performance. "It is sufficiently brief and attractive that composer and publisher should reap considerable and justified reward in coming seasons." (p. MA26) *See:* W49

B301 *Music of the Last Forty Years Not Yet Established In the Repertoire: A Survey Conducted By the Fromm Music Foundation at Harvard 1974-1975.* Cambridge, Massachusetts: The Foundation, 1975.
    The survey lists *Grand Bamboula* as one of the twenty-four works by Wuorinen considered by the Fromm Music Foundation to be among the "important but neglected or infrequently performed musical works dating from the last forty years." (l. 1) *See:* W49, B891

B302 Cohn, Arthur. *Recorded Classical Music. A Critical Guide to Compositions and Performances.* New York: Schirmer Books, 1981.
    A review of the Nonesuch recording. "It may be said that if Albert Roussel had written serially designed music this is the way it would have sounded." (p. 2107) Cohn goes on to say that *Grand Bamboula* may well be Wuorinen's most exciting piece and that the performance is excellent. *See:* D16

B303 Commanday, Robert. "Parlante Orchestra Has What it Takes." *San Francisco Chronicle*, (15 May 1985), *(Datebook)*, p. 56.

Commanday describes the piece as hyperactive but says it made the concert program "explode out of the box." *See:* W49b

B304 Watkins, Glen. *Soundings: Music in the Twentieth Century*. New York: Schirmer Books, 1988.

The section "Postwar Serialism and the Rise of an International Avant-Garde" mentions *Grand Bamboula* as a work "indicative of a loosening attitude [towards serialism] without forfeiture." (p. 536) *See:* W49

B305 Baumgartner, Edwin. "Culture: American Music in Vienna." *Wiener Zeitung*, 10 November 1989, p. 6.

The "forcefully modern [piece] did not really catch the ear." *See:* W49h

B306 Heinz, Otmar. "New and Newest Music in the Minoritsensaal in Graz." *Neue Zeit* [Graz, Austria], 10 November 1989.

Heinz says the music "is a model of increasingly denser rhythms, entering without difficulty into the spheres of aggressivity." *See:* W49g

B307 Newmann, Walther. "Culture: U.S. Sounds." *Kleine Zeitung* [Klagenfurt, Austria], 10 November 1989, p. 117.

Newmann merely states that he liked *Grand Bamboula* more than any other work on the program. *See:* W49g

Grand Union

B308 Monson, Karen. "Debuts & Reappearances: Speculum Musicae: Wuorinen." *High Fidelity/Musical America* 24, no. 2 (February 1974), p. MA17.

"The problem with *Grand Union* is that it brazenly takes seventeen minutes to say what could have been said in seven." *See:* W85

B309 Rosenfeld, Jay C. "Music Review: Musical High Jinks at Wheatleigh." The *Berkshire Eagle* [Berkshire, Massachusetts], 28 July 1974.

Rosenfeld merely mentions that the work was played at the concert, and calls Fred Sherry a brilliant cellist. Of the entire concert (titled *Charles Wuorinen: Profile of a Composer*) Rosenfeld says it featured "...the most sophisticated musical high jinks since Victor Borge or P.D.Q. Bach...." *See:* W85a

B310 Salisbury, Wilma. "A New Turn for Music Theater." The *Plain Dealer* [Cleveland], 25 August 1974, p. 4-F.

She describes the work as "a furious contest of complex rhythmic patterns." *See:* W85a

Harp Variations

B311 Porter, Andrew. "Musical Events: Potpourri." The *New Yorker*, 28 April 1973, p. 135.

"This struck me as a slightly arid, schematic work in which the composer concentrates on the harp's ability to define single notes and is determined to avoid the voluptuous swirls and the tinkling melodic prettiness usually associated with the instrument." This review is subsequently reprinted in Porter's book *A Musical Season. A Critic From Abroad in America* (New York: Viking Press, 1972). *See:* W86

Harpsichord Divisions

B312 Thorp, Keith Andrew. *The Twentieth-Century Harpsichord: Approaches to Composition and Performance Practice as Evidenced by the Contemporary Repertoire.* (D.M.A. dissertation) Urbana: University of Illinois at Urbana-Champaign, 1981.

Chapter nine, "National Trends — The United States" discusses music by Nicolas Roussakis and mentions Wuorinen's *Harpsichord Divisions*: "[The work] makes similar use of twelve-tone techniques, but in a style peculiar to that composer, avoids any periodic redundancies." (p. 193) *See:* W146

Horn Trio

B313 Porter, Andrew. "Musical Events: Feast of Reason, Flow of Soul." The *New Yorker*, 2 May 1983, p. 96.

This review is devoted completely to music by Wuorinen. Of the *Horn Trio* Porter says: "The first epithet that occurs to me is 'Haydnish,' by which I would indicate a play of musical ideas so dexterous, inventive, and happy that a listener to them smiles with pleasure." *See:* W87

Hyperion

B314 Silsbury, Elizabeth. "Forty Years of Modern Music." *The Advertiser* [Adelaide, Australia], 22 March 1976.

"It is a highly cerebral and technically difficult work, conventionally notated and phythmically [*sic*] divisive within a square frame." *See:* W50

B315 Prerauer, Maria. "Opening Ears to a New World." The *Australian* [Adelaide, Australia], 23 March 1976.

"On this evidence the composer could well emerge as one of the handful that will survive." *See:* W50

B316 Porter, Andrew. "Musical Events: Festival City." The *New Yorker*, 12 April 1976, p. 134.

Porter writes that the piece "sounded dense, sometimes sparky, mainly clotted — a satyr to [Arthur] Berger's elegantly wrought *Septet*, which preceded it on the program." *See:* W50

B317 Heikinheimo, Seppo. "Musiikki: Nykymusiikkia kryptassa." *Helsingen Sanomat Arkisto* [Helsinki], 22 October 1976.

Titled "Contemporary Music in a Crypt," the review describes the music as follows: "*[Hyperion]* is a work that has an instrumental image as rough as that of Varése, but a general character as boring as, say [Paul] Hindemith or [John] Cage." *See:* W50a

B318 Rockwell, John. "Music Plays 2nd Fiddle." The *New York Times*, 9 March 1977, p. C25.

A review of the New York premiere. Rockwell says it has "surging energy and virtuosic deployment of the instruments to recommend it." *See:* W50b

B319 Porter, Andrew. "Musical Events: Introductions." The *New Yorker*, 24 April 1978, pp. 136-144.
This article is about radio programs that offer interviews with composers prior to concert performances of their works. Porter refers briefly to a radio broadcast of *Hyperion* and says he underrated the work at its premiere: "It flowered as a bright, lyrical, and exuberant piece." (p. 139) *See:* W50, B316

Janissary Music

B320 Hollister, David. "Concert Goers Were Well Rewarded." The *Daily Iowan* [Iowa City, Iowa], 21 January 1967.
"Adroitly and with disarming calm, William Parsons performed the Wuorinen — which needs at least an octopus among its multitude of percussion instruments — like a dodecapus, a new breed of musician often found silently counting very rapidly in demisemiquavers (in multiples of twelve)." *See:* W152a

B321 Michaelides, Peter. "Critic Sees Appreciation Gap: 150 Hear Exploration of New Musical Structures." *Waterloo Courier* [Waterloo, Iowa], 30 January 1967.
"To say that exceptional coordination and unusual sensitivity are needed to perform this work is an understatement — the skill and accuracy with which Mr. Parsons wove and struck his way in and around his instrumental forest offered ample proof of his remarkable ability." *See:* W152b

B322 Arlen, Walter. "Monday Concert at the Bing Center." *Los Angeles Times*, 29 November 1967, *(Part IV)*, p. 31.
"Its two parts comprised a collection of seemingly random, rather unconvincing percussion sounds which Kenneth Watson ticked off with four dexterously handled mallets." *See:* W152e

B323 Frank, Peter. "Age of Idea." *Columbia Daily Spectator* [New York City], 3 December 1968, pp. 4-5.
"The writing for (and performing on) the various drums was tense, colorful, and generally impressive." *See:* W152f

B324 Klein, Howard. "Recordings: A New Look for an Old Label." The *New York Times*, 23 March 1969, *(Arts & Leisure)*, p. 32D.
An article about the history of Composers Recordings, Inc., containing a discography that includes the CRI recording of Janissary Music. *See:* D6

B325 Jack, Adrian. ["Record Review."] *Records and Recording* (June 1975).
A review of the CRI recording. "Perhaps it is praise to say that one never suspects from the cool and uncluttered sounds that [Raymond] DesRoches took 18 months to master and 13 hours to record them." *See:* D6

B326 Combs, F. Michael. "Reviews." *Percussive Notes* 18, no. 3 (Spring-Summer 1980), p. 57.

A review of the C.F. Peters edition. "Although the notation is specific and somewhat complex, the good quality printing helps facilitate reading the score." *See:* W152

B327 O'Neill, John C. "Recent Trends In Percussion Notation." *Percussionist*, 18, no. 1 (Fall 1980), pp. 20-55.

This article includes a discussion, with musical examples, of the percussion techniques used in *Janissary Music*. O'Neill writes that the notation "coupled with the intricacies of its musical ideas, makes it one of the most complex writings for percussion to date." (p. 25) In the same section of the article, O'Neill also mentions a personal discussion he had with Wuorinen at a branch of the University of California in 1976, when Wuorinen stated that at the time of composing *Janissary Music* "he believed in writing parts of high complexity so that they had to be memorized, thus demanding adequate rehearsal time." (p. 27) *See:* W152

B328 Cohn, Arthur. *Recorded Classical Music. A Critical Guide to Compositions and Performances*. New York: Schirmer Books, 1981.

A review of the CRI recording. "If percussion music can be termed intimately responsive then this is it." (p. 2107) *See:* D6

B329 Adams, Daniel Clifford. *Striking Implement and Surface Area Specification in Unaccompanied Multiple Percussion Solos: Its Compositional Significance.* (D.M.A. dissertation) Urbana, Illinois: University of Illinois at Urbana-Champaign, 1985.

This dissertation includes a 12 page discussion of *Janissary Music*. (pp. 76-88) Wuorinen's method of indicating striking implements, use of surface areas and changes, associations of those changes with other musical elements, and the compositional significance of striking implement and surface area contrasts are discussed in detail. "Wuorinen's notation, while very precisely defining musical parameters, provides no detail regarding the physical gestures of the performer." (p. 87) *See:* W152

B330 Tircuit, Heuwell. "Percussionists Display — Wuorinen Stands Out." *San Francisco Chronicle*, 8 October 1985.

The reviewer writes that Wuorinen's approach to percussion vocabulary "plus a handsome feeling for inventive patterns, made for an absorbing experience." *See:* W152g

B331 François, Jean-Charles. *Percussion et Musique Contemporaine*. Paris: Klincksieck, 1991.

One of the few European imprints to include a discussion of Wuorinen's music, this monograph features a lengthy discussion of the percussion techniques — including diagrams and notational excerpts — used in *Janissary Music* (Chapter 3, "La percussion et les structures de hauters," (pp. 96-107), and chapter 6, "Percussion et notation" (pp. 196-201)). *See:* W152

Joan's

B332 Rockwell, John. "Music: Da Capo Players." *The New York Times*, 28 March 1980, p. C29.

Rockwell used one word to describe the piece: "gray." *See:* W89

B333 Page, Tim. "A Feather in Da Capo." The *Soho News* [New York City], 2 April 1980.

Page says this new piece "was interesting only in its singular lack of interest." He mentions the awards Wuorinen had won and comments: "I can only add that his music bores me to tears; it is bone dry, humorless, passionless and contrived." *See:* W89

B334 Sandow, Gregory. "Da Capo: Just Fine." *Village Voice* [New York City], 21 April 1980, p. 71.

Sandow states his view that Wuorinen's music is underrated and criticized as being cerebral. "To me it's passionate and committed, though the passion is an inner, almost secret longing, fixed on the growth and flowering of musical ideas rather than the expression of poetic emotion, which is what people usually look for when they want feeling in music." *See:* W89

B335 Commanday, Robert. "Music: Through the Windows of New Style." *San Francisco Chronicle*, 7 February 1982, *(Review)*, pp. 16-19.

A review of the CRI recording. "Each time [hearing], more subtleties emerge in the melodic transformations as the piece is carried to a mysterious and affecting close." (p. 17) *See:* D25

B336 Donner, Jay M. "Chamber Music." The *New Records* 50, no. 2 (April 1982), pp. 7-8.

A review of the CRI recording. "[The work] is less intriguing and fluent than his large-scale works." (p. 7) *See:* D25

B337 Ditsky, John. "Classical Recordings: Ensemble." *Fanfare* 6, no. 2 (November/December 1982), p. 302.

A review of the CRI recording. The reviewer describes Wuorinen's compositional style as "a bit forbidding." *See:* D25

The Long and the Short

B338 Baron, John H. "Music Reviews." *Notes* 29, no. 4 (June 1973), p. 819.

A review of the C.F. Peters edition. "The details of notation give the performer almost no freedom of interpretation, but Wuorinen understands the violin; and, if he follows the details, the violinist will discover that the composer has notated what he, the interpreter, customarily adds to under-notated music." *See:* W90

B339 Morgan, Robert P. "Classical." *High Fidelity/Musical America* 24, no. 1 (June 1974), p. 82.

A review of the Mainstream recording. Morgan writes the work exploits "different rates of speed." *See:* D12

B340 *Music of the Last Forty Years Not Yet Established In the Repertoire: A Survey Conducted By the Fromm Music Foundation at Harvard 1974-1975.* Cambridge, Massachusetts: The Foundation, 1975.

The survey lists *The Long and the Short* as one of the twenty-four works by Wuorinen considered by the Fromm Music Foundation to be among the "important but neglected or infrequently performed musical works dating from the last forty years." (l. 1) *See:* W90, B891

B341 Lange, Art. "Charles Wuorinen and Benjamin Hudson." The *Reader* [Chicago], 24 March 1978, pp. 34-35.

"[Benjamin] Hudson brought out its glissandi and timbral events nicely, emphasized a legato phrasing within the work's svelte though rhapsodic character, and danced through a difficult display of Bachian double stops." *See:* W90e

B342 Cohn, Arthur. *Recorded Classical Music. A Critical Guide to Compositions and Performances.* New York: Schirmer Books, 1981.

A review of the Mainstream recording. Cohn calls the music an "expressionistic inquiry." He adds: "Composers who write for a solo fiddle find their music in the high-risk category; that is, unless they have a [Paul] Zukofsky to play it, technically conquer it, and intellectually define it." (p. 2110) *See:* D12

B343 Berrett, Joshua. "Record Reviews." *American Music* 8 (1990), pp. 121-123.

A review of the Bridge recording. Berrett calls the work a "tour de force" and says Benjamin Hudson played it "in commanding fashion." (p. 123) *See:* D35

Machault Mon Chou

B344 Ulrich, Allan. "Symphony Season Looks Promising." *San Francisco Sunday Examiner and Chronicle*, 4 September 1988, *(Style)*, p. E-1, E-5.

An overview of the 1988-89 season of the San Francisco Symphony. Wuorinen is mentioned concerning the premiere of this work, which is described as "a punning title for a suite of transcriptions of the 14th century composer-poet, Guillaume de Machault." (p. E-5) *See:* W15

B345 Dierks, Donald. "First Pulitzer Concert at UCSD is a Prize-Winner." *San Diego Union*, 12 January 1990.

Dierks praises the performance and writes: "This proved to be a work of unusual power and appeal, with it [sic] wonderful rhythms and haunting harmonies, sometimes harmonies that are open and morose." *See:* W15a

B346 Herman, Kenneth. "Visceral Offering by Wuorinen Redeems Avant-Garde Concert." *Los Angeles Times* [San Diego County Edition], 13 January 1990.

Herman says the orchestration "made about as much sense as, say, a concert band arrangement of [Wolfgang Amadeus] Mozart's 'Requiem'." *See:* W15a

B347 Henry, Derrick. "Comet's Debut With ASO Shows Poise, Lacks Spirit." *Atlanta Journal/Constitution*, 4 January 1991.

Henry writes that the concert was poorly attended but that Wuorinen "has crafted a charming, evocative, colorful piece." *See:* W15c

B348 Webster, Daniel. "Review: Music." The *Philadelphia Inquirer*, 19 January 1991, p. 7-D.

Webster terms the piece "a brilliantly orchestrated 20th-century recollection of the bold musical manner of the 14th-century composer." *See:* W15d

The Magic Art

B349 Anthony, Michael. "St. Paul Chamber Orchestra Offers a Blend of Henry Purcell's Music." *Minneapolis Tribune*, 29 September 1979.
Anthony says the piece is "cleverly constructed." [P] *See:* W52

B350 Aaltoila, Heikki. "Meikki vältti räikeyden." *Unsi Suomi* [Helsinki], 17 October 1981.
This article, titled "The Make-Up Avoided the Garish," mentions that *The Magic Art* was performed at Wuorinen's recent concert in Helsinki. *See:* W52a

B351 Forsman, Folke. "En hel kväll med Charles Wuorinen." *Hufvudstadsbladet*, 17 October 1981.
This is a Swedish-language newspaper published in Helsinki. Forsman, a concert organist, writes in this review titled "A Whole Evening With Charles Wuorinen" that Wuorinen's music reflects "peculiar whims, sometimes with intentional archaisms." **See:** W52a

B352 Tawaststjerna, Erik. "Epäilijä tulen sfäärissä." *Helsingen Sanomat Arkisto*, 18 October 1981.
Titled "A Doubter in the Sphere of Fire" the review states that "the beauty of the music was fascinating in every measure, and the section titled 'Celebration' especially carried the audience away." *See:* W52a

B353 Hako, Pekka. "Lahoavaa Taidetta." *Sosialidemokraatti Demari* [Helsinki], 21 October 1981.
Hako's article is titled "Rotting Art." He writes: "I can only imagine what this magic art entity (from which we heard only three segments) may evoke in a listener in the U.S., whose first acquaintance with [Henry] Purcell occurs through these cute arrangements. I would almost like to talk about a destructive art or even rotting art which will self-destruct." *See:* W52a

B354 Rautio, Matti. "Kaikuja Atlantin takaa." *Aamulehti*, 25 October 1981.
Titled "Echoes From Behind the Atlantic" the concert review states: "If the first movement of the work reminded you of the ritualistic chordal progressions found in some of the late works of [Igor] Stravinsky, the second and third movements, with their dark and aggressive nuances were closer to [Arnold] Schoenberg's strict, Old Testament world." *See:* W52b

B355 Holland, Bernard. "Music: Wuorinen Reworks Purcell." The *New York Times*, 15 December 1981, p. C8.
Holland writes that the Brooklyn Philharmonia's string players gave a poor performance and says that Henry Purcell's music "survived through Wuorinen's ears...."
See: W52d

B356 Johnson, Lawrence B. "Foss Directs Symphony in Unusual Treat." *Milwaukee Sentinel*, 13 February 1982.
Johnson states Wuorinen "eloquently, brightly and above all warmly recaptures the spirit of [Henry] Purcell by distinctively 20th century means." *See:* W52e

B357 Mootz, William. "Louisville Ballet at Kentucky Center for the Arts: 'Odalisque,' 'Courtly Dances,' and 'Tunes'." The *Courier-Journal* [Louisville], 5 October 1984, p. C3.

"Although Wuorinen has a reputation for writing some of today's thorniest music, this particular score takes the music of Henry Purcell and dresses it in chaste contemporary orchestration." *See:* W52f

B358 Kisselgoff, Anna. "Dance: By Bonnefoux." The *New York Times*, 7 February 1985, p. C16.

"It was a beautifully fashioned and well-bred piece." *See:* W52g

Making Ends Meet

B359 Kriegsman, Alan M. "Contemporary Music is Presented." The *Washington Post*, 20 May 1968, p. B6.

A review of the premiere. "Some of it is interesting, some of it is dull; to grapple with it can be an exhilarating experience. Whether it is possible to like such music, I can not say." *See:* W134

B360 Novik, Ylda. "Kurka is Best by Piano Team." The *Evening Star* [Washington, D.C.], 20 May 1968.

A review of the premiere. The critic briefly mentions that the piece was performed and calls it a "blood brother" of other works on the program she disliked. *See:* W134

B361 Strongin, Theodore. "Avant-Garde Series Presents Premiere of Wuorinen Work." The *New York Times*, 14 April 1969, p. 56.

A review of the New York premiere. "This was relatively mild Wuorinen, but in his individual style." *See:* W134c

B362 Ericson, Raymond. "Wentworths Offer New 4-Hand Works for Piano." The *New York Times*, 31 October 1969, p. 35.

Ericson writes the work "was a lean, transparent exercise that traveled through varying attitudes to its austere material." *See:* W134e

B363 Brooks, Muriel. "Wentworths in Concert at Center." *Patent Trader* [Cross River, N.Y.], 6 November 1969, p. 27.

"The Wentworths perform this music with a flourish. Their aims are laudable. I wish the results were more rewarding." *See:* W134e

B364 Kreisberg, Louisa. "Sights and Sounds: Wentworthiana at Tully Hall." *Herald Statesman* [Yonkers, N.Y.], 12 November 1969.

"A skilled craftsman, Wuorinen controls everything in a very complex manner." *See:* W134e

B365 Hiemenz, Jack. "Debuts & Reappearances: Jean, Kenneth Wentworth." *High Fidelity/Musical America* 20, no. 1 (January 1970), p. 20, 28.

Making Ends Meet "proved to be a total dud." Hiemenz also writes: "I felt as if I were witnessing a sordid domestic squabble, where wit lies low and passion peters out." (p. 20) *See:* W134e

B366 Henahan, Donal. "Wentworths Explore Moderns in Tully 4-Hand Piano Recital." The *New York Times*, 21 November 1970, p. 23.
The critic says the music evidences "logical progress." *See:* W134g

B367 Satz, Arthur. "Debuts & Reappearances: Jean and Kenneth Wentworth, pianists." *High Fidelity/Musical America* 21, no. 2 (February 1971), p. MA32.
"There was more serialization by Wuorinen, but with a greater exploitation of piano sonority to brighten the landscape a bit." *See:* W134g

B368 *Music of the Last Forty Years Not Yet Established In the Repertoire: A Survey Conducted By the Fromm Music Foundation at Harvard 1974-1975.* Cambridge, Massachusetts: The Foundation, 1975.
The survey lists *Making Ends Meet* as one of the twenty-four works by Wuorinen considered by the Fromm Music Foundation to be among the "important but neglected or infrequently performed musical works dating from the last forty years." (l. 1) *See:* W134, B891

B369 Cory, Eleanor. "Reviews of Records." The *Musical Quarterly* 61, no. 2 (April 1975), pp. 327-335.
A review of the Desto recording. "A number of compositional notions connected with the title *Making Ends Meet* appear as surface ornamentation to the fundamental structural concepts." *See:* D18

B370 Cohn, Arthur. *Recorded Classical Music. A Critical Guide to Compositions and Performances.* New York: Schirmer Books, 1981.
A review of the Desto recording. Cohn praises Jean and Kenneth Wentworth for having met "all of the superhuman demands of the composer." He also writes: "*Making Ends Meet* may sound like a fleeting improvisation, but it is planets removed from the unpredictable in its absolute, harnessed plan." (p. 2110) *See:* D18

Mannheim 87.87.87

B371 Belt, Byron. "Music in the Churches." *Music: The A.G.O. and R.C.C.O. Magazine* 7, no. 7 (July 1973), pp. 20-23.
"If the [William] Albright hymn seems destined for the most use, that by Charles Wuorinen would seem doomed for deserved oblivion." (p. 23) *See:* W169, B902

Mass

B372 Kresky, Jeffrey. "The Recent Music of Charles Wuorinen." *Perspectives of New Music* 25, no. 1-2 (1987), pp. 410-417.
Mass is discussed in this important article. *See:* W170, B857

Message to Denmark Hill

B373 Hughes, Allen. "Poet and Composer Join in a Recital." The *New York Times*, 25 December 1970, p. 34.
"To this listener's ears, at least, it actually robbed the poem of some of its original strength and added nothing in its place." *See:* W178a

Missa Brevis

B374 Ramirez, Antonio. "St. Ignatius Bridges Centuries With Music Premiere." The *Episcopal New Yorker* (January-February 1992), p. 4.

Pre-concert publicity for the premiere performance. Ramirez discusses Wuorinen, organist-choirmaster Dr. Harold Chaney, and the musical tradition at St. Ignatius of Antioch Episcopal Church in New York City. Wuorinen is quoted as saying: "This Little Mass is a partial answer to those who want the idea of the beauty of holiness to totally replace the holiness of beauty in the church, which has lost its mission to be a patron of good art." The article includes a photograph of Wuorinen, Chaney, and The Rev. Howard T. W. Stowe, Rector. (It is an unusual photograph of Charles Wuorinen in church). [P] *See:* W171

B375 Holland, Bernard. "Classical Music in Review: Wuorinen's Missa Brevis for his Church." The *New York Times*, 25 February 1992, p. C14.

"Skillful, fervent and sensitive to its environment, *[Missa Brevis]* will serve the church well." *See:* W171

Movers and Shakers

B376 Rosenberg, Donald. "Cleveland Will Play Host to Movers and Shakers." *Beacon Journal* [Akron, Ohio], 10 December 1984, pp. C5, C6.

Pre-concert publicity concerning the premiere. *See:* W16

B377 Finn, Robert. "A Premiere, New Era for Orchestra." The *Plain Dealer* [Cleveland], 12 December 1984.

Pre-concert publicity concerning the premiere. The article also contains general background information on Wuorinen's career and discusses his philosophy of music. *See:* W16

B378 Finn, Robert. "Dohnanyi Premieres New Piece." The *Plain Dealer* [Cleveland], 14 December 1984, p. 8B.

A review of the premiere. Finn writes "the piece held the interest continuously with its alternating moments of luminously orchestrated calm and energetic brilliance." *See:* W16

B379 Rosenberg, Donald. "Orchestra's Greatness Radiates Again." *Beacon Journal* [Akron, Ohio], 14 December 1984, p. B5.

A review of the premiere. "The music's communicative power lies in its rhythmic vitality, its economy of gesture and its extremes of mood." [P] *See:* W16

B380 Finn, Robert. "Dohnanyi Premiere of New Piece Proves Daring." The *Plain Dealer* [Cleveland], 15 December 1984.

A reprint of the 14 December 1984 article in the same tabloid reviewing this piece. *See:* W16

B381 Kiraly, Philippa. "Music: Meat and Potatoes at Severance." The *Cleveland Edition* [Cleveland], 20 December 1984 - 2 January 1985. *See:* W16

"This is a work which must be listened to in [Arnold] Schoenberg's terms; not for melodies, but for the spectrum of rhythm and tone colors, textures, dynamics and the juxtaposition of instruments."

B382 Hruby, Frank. "Debuts & Reappearances: Cleveland." *High Fidelity/Musical America* 35, no. 5 (May 1985), p. MA21.
A review of the premiere. "Would that composers desist from fragmenting their music to the point where nothing sticks in the mental musical memory." *See:* W16

B383 Shulgold, Marc. "Wuorinen: State of the Orchestra." *Los Angeles Times*, 6 February 1986, *(Part VI)*, p. 2.
Pre-concert publicity for the Los Angeles premiere. Contains interview material in which Wuorinen discusses his conception of the ideal concert program. Shulgold comments: "With contemporary composers receiving short shrift, Wuorinen suggests, the orchestra seemed headed for a home for the feeble and useless by the beginning of the next century." [P] *See:* W16b

B384 Fruchter, Rena. "Blomstedt in Return to Rutgers Podium." The *New York Times*, 2 March 1986.
A general article about Herbert Blomstedt and the San Francisco Symphony's concerts at Rutgers University. *Movers and Shakers* is discussed. *See:* W16c

B385 Redmond, Michael. "Charles Wuorinen Discusses His Art — And Does a Little Critic-Bashing Too." *Star-Ledger* [Union, N.J.], 2 March 1986.
This article mentions *Movers and Shakers* and contains interview material with Wuorinen. The composer offers his views about entertainment and art, and how critics confuse the two. Redmond writes: "Charles Wuorinen can be described as the North Star in the zodiac of American composers. Aside from being one of the brightest lights in that particular sky, Wuorinen is also a fixed luminary, by whose light one can chart a course through whatever weather happens to be prevailing in American music." *See:* W16

B386 Steinbrink, Mark. "San Francisco's New Conductor — A Man of Firm Beliefs." The *New York Times*, 9 March 1986.
A general article about Herbert Blomstedt and the San Francisco Symphony. Steinbrink quotes Blomstedt as saying of *Movers and Shakers*: "[It] is meant to be an abstract play of textures, harmonies and sounds that work according to laws that Mr. Wuorinen has created for himself." *See:* W16d

B387 Pontzious, Richard. "S.F. Symphony Sounds Good In New York." *San Francisco Examiner*, 10 March 1986, *(Section E)*, p. E-1.
A review of the New York premiere. "The acoustics of Carnegie Hall make it easy for an audience to hear every detail of even the most complicated score, and Wuorinen's piece is among those needing that benefit." *See:* W16d

B388 Zakariasen, Bill. "His Beethoven Beat Can't Be Beat." *New York Daily News*, 11 March 1986, p. 34.
A review of the New York premiere. "There's a lot of clangor to be heard, but more than a modicum of poetry as well, plus a nice sense of wit — punctuated by some virtuoso writing for the tuba." *See:* W16d

B389 Page, Tim. "Concert: San Francisco Symphony." The *New York Times*, 12 March 1986, p. C19.
"Mr. Wuorinen's harmonic language is still uncompromising, but 'Movers and Shakers' has passages of aching lyricism, and many moments of sheer, visceral excitement." *See:* W16d

B390 Kresky, Jeffrey. "The Recent Music of Charles Wuorinen." *Perspectives of New Music* 25, nos. 1-2 (1987), pp. 410-417.

> *Movers and Shakers* is discussed in this important article. *See:* W16, B857

Music for Orchestra

B391 Baruch, David J. "Premieres Given By Columbia Orchestra." *Musical America* 76, no. 16 (December 15, 1956), p. 27.

> Baruch claims Wuorinen is a new talent to be watched closely. Of the symphony, however, he writes: "Unfortunately it often sounded just like an electric generator station coming to life." *See:* W17

Nature's Concord

B392 *Music of the Last Forty Years Not Yet Established In the Repertoire: A Survey Conducted By the Fromm Music Foundation at Harvard 1974-1975.* Cambridge, Massachusetts: The Foundation, 1975.

> The survey lists *Nature's Concord* as one of the twenty-four works by Wuorinen considered by the Fromm Music Foundation to be among the "important but neglected or infrequently performed musical works dating from the last forty years." (l. 1) *See:* W92, B891

B393 Kosman, Joshua. "Classics: Modern Choral." The *Villager* [New York City], 11 March 1982, p. 9.

> "[The work] managed to overcome the theoretical contrivances on which it is based (at least as expounded in the composer's convoluted program notes) to provide sketches of serene beauty." Kosman praises the playing of Ronald Anderson and Louis Karchin. *See:* W92f

New York Notes

B394 Glackin, William. "New York Ensemble Makes 'New Music' Likable." The *Sacramento Bee* [Sacramento, California], 10 November 1982, p. C6.

> Glackin says the piece "not only demands respect for its propulsive energy and dynamic ideas but tugs at the affection as well." In the same review he reverses himself by writing Wuorinen's music "is fine for the concert hall, so to speak, but you wouldn't want to have it around the house." *See:* W93

B395 Rockwell, John. "Fractals: A Mystery Lingers." The *New York Times*, 26 April 1990, p. C24.

> This is a review of the Guggenheim Museum performance at which mathematician Benoit Mandelbrot was present for a panel discussion, and at which the music was accompanied by a slide show of images generated by fractal geometry. Rockwell writes: "Given the science-fantasy look of many of the pictures, early 1970's English art-rock might have been more appropriate." *See:* W93c, W93e, B855, B856, B858

B396 Ward, Charles. "Composer Prefers to Let Music Speak for Itself." *Houston Chronicle*, 11 May 1990.

> Ward says the music "had an emotional shape, variety and pacing that were impressive." *See:* W93d

B397 Oskamp, Jacqueline. "Eigentijdse muziek in de Verenigde Staten." *Mens & Melodie* 46, no. 2 (February 1991), pp. 100-106.

The reviewer says *New York Notes* "shows a complex motivic structure with minimalist influence: long pauses alternating with occasionally dense juxtaposition of tones; with regard to rhythm, [Igor] Stravinsky comes to mind." (p. 101) *See:* W93c

B398 Page, Tim. "Music Review: A Maestro On Piano." *New York Newsday*, 11 March 1991.

Page writes that although he admires Wuorinen's music he did not enjoy this piece. He says it is "to this taste, clever and skillfully made but also shrill, aggressive, and not very likable (I except some lambent, shimmering passages for computer which have an ethereal beauty)." *See:* W93e

B399 Ellis, William. "New York New Music Ensemble." *American Record Guide* 54, no. 4 (July-August 1991), p. 141.

A review of the Harmonia Mundi recording. Ellis says the work is "notable for its preoccupation with prolation games." *See:* D38

Octet

B400 Robison, Judith. "Concert Given By New York Chamber Society." *New York Herald Tribune*, 28 September 1962.

Robison states the piece was "a real rouser [that] with its two horns, considerably enlivened what was turning out to be a rather puttering occasion." *See:* W94

B401 "Work By Sydeman In Premiere Here." The *New York Times*, 28 September 1962, p. 29.

The writer calls the piece "scrappy and aggressive." *See:* W94

B402 Lowens, Irvin. "News of Music. A Persuasive Plea for the Avant-Garde." The *Evening Star* [Washington, D.C.], 12 March 1966, *(Religious News)*, p. A-9.

Lowens says that "while it was too complex to grasp completely in one single hearing, it was evidently the work of a musical intelligence of the highest order." The reviewer also notes that Wuorinen, then twenty-eight, "will have to be reckoned with in the future." *See:* W94d

B403 Taylor, Clifford. *Musical Idea and the Design Aesthetic in Contemporary Music: A Text for Discerning Appraisal of Musical Thought in Western Culture.* Lewiston, N.Y.: The Edwin Mellen Press, 1990.

This book is volume seven in the publisher's series, *Studies in the History and Interpretation of Music.* The chapter, "Dodecaphony and Pitch Stasis in a Design Aesthetic" includes these comments, by Taylor, about Wuorinen's *Octet*: "Historically referenced expressivity in the harmonic control of texture is obviously not at work in this music. What is left is pitch-rhythm patterning, given purpose of a kind by the demands that principles of design impose on the composer's aurally perceived textural juxtapositions. What becomes interesting replaces in this aesthetic what has been historically referenced and valued as expressive, meaningful, and relatable to the human drama directly, rather than what might be considered obliquely. Musical ideas and narrative serve this desire for direct relatability; sound design does not." (p. 56-57) *See:* W94

On Alligators

B404 Porter, Andrew. "Musical Events: Getting to Know You." The *New Yorker*, 10 February 1975, p. 113.
"His [Wuorinen's] music can sound undisciplined. He takes chances. When the recklessness pays off it does so handsomely — given performers as dexterous as Daniel Shulman's Light Fantastic Players; but I should hardly like to hear *On Alligators* snap and crackle from any ensemble less spirited." *See:* W54a

Orchestral and Electronic Exchanges

B405 Ericson, Raymond. "Stimulant and Challenge." The *New York Times*, 4 July 1965, *(Section 2)*, p. 9
An article about the New York Philharmonic's French-American Festival at which this work was premiered. *See:* W18

B406 Ericson, Raymond. "Music: Accent is American at Festival." The *New York Times*, 31 July 1965, p. 11.
"Its 20 minutes of juggled sounds were not without interest, but its constant complexity of rhythm and tonal combinations did not, on first hearing, have enough variety of texture or momentum to keep the interest constant." Ericson praises Lukas Foss's conducting. *See:* W18

B407 Gruen, John. "Premieres Ring at the Philharmonic." *New York Herald Tribune*, 31 July 1965, *(Amusements-General News)*, p. 6.
"A series of aural explosions formed imaginary abstract shapes — each of them organized by the composer with brilliant forethought and invention." *See:* W18

B408 Johnson, Harriet. "Words and Music. From Golden Brooms to Blasts." *New York Post*, 1 August 1965, *(Entertainment)*, p. 3.
Johnson calls the work a "boring, silly tirade for tape and orchestra." She concludes: "I would say an imaginative physicist-engineer could do similar jobs better." *See:* W18

B409 Lewando, Ralph. "New Works." *Music Journal* 23, no. 6 (September 1965), pp. 87-89.
"It *[Orchestral and Electronic Exchanges]* hews a path which may lead other similarly minded imaginative composers toward a new era." (p. 88) Lewando also praises Lukas Foss's conducting. *See:* W18

B410 Morgenstern, Dan. "Caught in the Act." *Downbeat* 32 (9 September 1965), p. 38.
"The electronic portions of the music would make a fine background score for a horror film, while the brisk orchestral passages, surprisingly tonal, emphasized percussion and brass." Morgenstern uses two words to sum up his opinion of the piece: "sterile" and "entertaining." *See:* W18

B411 Breurer, Robert. "New York bietet auch im Hochsommer Experimente." *Melos: Zeitschrift für Neue Musik* 32:11 (November 1965), pp. 414-415.
Breurer writes that the work will not be valued for its dialogue, but, rather, as an exchange of two fundamental dynamic structures that will be comprehensible to those that appreciate the twelve-tone material from which the work is constructed. *See:* W18

B412 Dufallo, Richard. *Trackings. Composers Speak with Richard Dufallo*. New York: Oxford University Press, 1989.

This book contains three brief references to Wuorinen, one of which is a mention of the world premiere of *Orchestral and Electronic Exchanges*. *See:* W18

B413 Black, Frederick. "Modern Composers' Works ISU Close [*sic*] Arts Festival." The *Terre Haute Star*, 12 May 1967, p. 12.

"One might say music in this has gone so way out as to raise the question is it music. But it was fascinating and not as blatantly strident as one might have feared." *See:* W18a

B414 Christie, John. "Christie Comments on Performance by Indianapolis Symphony at ISU." The *Indiana Statesman* [Terre Haute], 16 May 1967, p. 4.

Christie claims Wuorinen's purpose is to eventually eliminate the human performer. He also comments on audience reaction: "The electronic passages, programmed by RCA, elicited highly observable reactions from the audience. They were: dismayed, amazed conversation; chuckles, anger, much leg-crossing, but never indifference." *See:* W18a

B415 Vercoe, Barry. "Live Performance and Prerecorded Electronic Sounds Combined: A Repertoire." *Music Educators Journal* 55, no. 3 (November 1968), pp. 172-174.

This forty-title list includes *Orchestral and Electronic Exchanges*. *See:* W18

B416 Neubert, David. "Electronic Bowed String Works: Some Observations on Trends and Developments in the Instrumental/Electronic Medium." *Perspectives of New Music* 21 (Fall-Winter 1983), pp. 540-566.

The brief article classifies electronic string works according to medium and discusses goals and trends of the medium. (Abstract, p. 540) The article concludes with a detailed list of bowed string works involving electronics; *Orchestral and Electronic Exchanges* is listed. *See:* W18

Percussion Duo

B417 Meckna, Michael. "Collections: Instrumental." *American Record Guide* 46, no. 2 (December 1982), pp. 71-72.

A review of the CRI recording. "It goes somewhere and does so without faltering." (p. 72) Meckna praises the performances of James Avery and Steven Schick. *See:* D28

B418 Webber, David W. "Chamber Music." The *New Records* 50, no. 11 (January 1983), p. 6.

A review of the CRI recording. "The careful writing provides that the instrumental timbres are used in gorgeous combinations." *See:* D28

B419 François, Jean-Charles. "Music Reviews." *Notes* 39, no. 3 (March 1983), p. 699.

A review of the C.F. Peters edition. The writer states his opinion that Wuorinen's harmonic language is a synthesis of tonality, atonality and twelve-tone composition. He also writes that the melodic, harmonic and rhythmic elements of *Percussion Duo* are "reminiscent of a certain 1960s jazz idiom." François concludes "it is a disservice to this composer if performers are not completely involved with the piece for a very long time before meaningful performance can take place." *See:* W153

B420 "Miscellaneous." *Fanfare* 6 (March/April 1983), p. 343.
A review of the CRI recording. "Wuorinen has written better percussion music than this." *See:* D28

B421 François, Jean-Charles. *Percussion et Musique Contemporaine.* Paris: Klincksieck, 1991.
This book is volume 53 of the publisher's series *Collection d'esthetique.* It is also one of the few European imprints to include a discussion of Wuorinen's music. The brief bibliography lists *Percussion Duo. See:* W153

B422 Farley, Barbara C. Phillips. *A History of the Center for New Music at the University of Iowa, 1966-1991.* (D.M.A. thesis) Iowa City: University of Iowa, 1991.
Based on concert programs, program notes, concert reviews and oral history, this dissertation lists ten works by Wuorinen that were performed at the Center for New Music (University of Iowa) between 1961 and 1979, one of which was the first performance of *Percussion Duo. See:* W153

Percussion Symphony

B423 Rogers, Gary. "Entertainment: Charles Wourinen [*sic*] Percussion Symphony." *Seal Beach Journal* [Seal Beach, California], 25 October 1978.
A review of the Nonesuch recording. "The conciseness of sound peculiar to percussion, recorded here with a cleanliness of execution." *See:* D21, D33

B424 Hasden, Wes. ["Record Reviews."] The *Chattanooga Times* [Chattanooga, Tennessee], 5 November 1978.
A review of the Nonesuch recording. "Recorded in an old theater in New Jersey, the album is a fine example of the recording art, a disc that should satisfy the most discriminating audiophile." *See:* D21, D33

B425 "Wuorinen-Percussion Symphony." *San Bernadino Sun* [San Bernadino, California], 25 November 1978.
A review of the Nonesuch recording. "Only a few composers — [Igor] Stravinsky, [Edgard] Varese, [Alberto] Ginastera and [Carlos] Chavez among them — have handled percussion instruments as well as the Pulitzer Prize-winning American composer Charles Wuorinen." *See:* D21, D33

B426 "Contemporary." The *Oregonian* [Portland, Oregon], 15 December 1978.
A review of the Nonesuch recording. "Written for percussion ensemble, the music exploits the vast resources of the instruments in a work that is substantial and engrossing." *See:* D21, D33

B427 Oliva, Mark. "Oliva's Opus." *Journal Gazette* [Reno, Nevada], 17 December 1978.
A review of the Nonesuch recording. "What is important is the delicious palette of mind-expanding chromatic exploration Wuorinen offers in a new, exciting wonderland of musical color." *See:* D21, D33

B428 ["Record Reviews."] The *Sunday Oregonian* [Portland, Oregon], 17 December 1978.

A review of the Nonesuch recording. The writers says the New Jersey's Percussion Ensemble's performance on this recording exhibits "innovative musical styles." *See:* D21, D33

B429 Felson, Karl. "Classical Music." The *Sunday Record* [Troy, New York], 14 January 1979.

A review of the Nonesuch recording. "This is not one of those irreverent pieces for crashing cymbals, 20 tympanies and four car engines." *See:* D21, D33

B430 Devoe, E. David. "Classical." *Fort-Wayne News-Sentinel* [Fort Wayne, Indiana], 20 January 1979.

A review of the Nonesuch recording. Devoe writes that the piece "holds the attention for the whole time with its vast array of timbres." *See:* D21, D33

B431 Bronston, Levering. "Miscellaneous." The *New Records* 46, no. 11 (February 1979), p. 9.

A review of the Nonesuch recording. "If you have strong ears and an open mind, don't miss this." *See:* D21, D33

B432 Terry, Kenneth. "Record Reviews: Charles Wuorinen." *Downbeat* 46, no. 3 (8 February 1979), p. 24.

A review of the Nonesuch recording. Terry says the work is "a masterly synthesis of avant garde percussion techniques." *See:* D21, D33

B433 Rapoport, Paul. "Guide to Records." *American Record Guide* 42, no. 5 (March 1979), p. 48.

A review of the Nonesuch recording. "I doubt that it *[Percussion Symphony]* has many predecessors, but it surely deserves many successors." *See:* D21, D33

B434 Stephens, Kevin. "Recordguide: Orchestral." *Records and Recording* 22, no. 6 (March 1979), p. 95.

A review of the Nonesuch recording. Stephens writes that the music lacks "that imaginative leap which distinguishes good music from the merely routine." *See:* D21, D33

B435 Whittall, Arnold. "Reviews: Instrumental." *Gramophone* 56, no. 670 (March 1979), pp. 1584, 1589.

A review of the Nonesuch recording. "The Symphony is played with great precision and refinement under the composer's direction." Whittall concludes "it is a valuable introduction to a good composer who is far too little known." (p. 1589) *See:* D21, D33

B436 Salzman, Eric. "Classical Discs and Tapes. Recording of Special Merit." *Stereo Review* 42, no. 4 (April 1979), p. 154, 156.

A review of the Nonesuch recording. Salzman writes: "Charles Wuorinen is just about America's No. 1 incomprehensible serious music composer." (p. 154) He says Wuorinen composes "Gothic twelve-tone music," but praises the performance and the quality of the recording. *See:* D21, D33

B437 Lange, Art. "Record Reviews." *Fugue* 3, no. 11 (July/August 1979), p. 59.

    A review of the Nonesuch recording. Lange terms the work and quality of the recording an "enjoyable step in the development of percussion music in the twentieth century." *See:* D21, D33

B438 Fantel, Hans. "Sound." The *New York Times*, 16 August 1979, p. C7.

    A review of the Nonesuch recording. A brief section of this article lists this *Percussion Symphony* recording as having won an Audio Excellence Record Award for 1979. (These awards are sponsored by Audio Technica). *See:* D21, D33

B439 "Wuorinen: 'Percussion Symphony'." *Los Angeles Times*, 19 August 1979.

    A review of the Nonesuch recording. "Scored for 26 players, the work's endlessly fascinating textures and rhythmic diversity will stimulate even the grumpiest conservative and Nonesuch's recording should shatter windows in the next county." *See:* D21, D33

B440 "Charles Wuorinen: Percussion Symphony." *San Francisco Chronicle*, 2 September 1979.

    A review of the Nonesuch recording. "It's not so schizophrenic as you might think." *See:* D21, D33

B441 Shawn, Allen. "Music: Contemporary American Composers." *Atlantic* 247, no. 4 (April 1981), pp. 115-118.

    This article discusses contemporary symphonic and chamber music, and features biographical sketches of composers Shawn considers important: Elliott Carter, Leon Kirchner, Wuorinen, Philip Glass, Steve Reich, Frederic Rzewski, Earl Kim, George Crumb, John Harbison and Roger Sessions. He lists Wuorinen's *Percussion Symphony* in his brief discography and writes that Wuorinen "has added some extraordinary works to the growing body of eloquent percussion music." (p. 117) *See:* D21, D33

B442 Page, Tim. "Music: Percussion Group In Contemporary Works." The *New York Times*, 7 October 1984, p. 88.

    Page says "the symphony is virtuosic, expertly crafted, almost abrasively colorful — and ultimately rather chilly." *See:* W154b

B443 Davis, Peter G. "Music: The Elite Beat." *New York*, 22 October 1984, pp. 143-147.

    Davis says the work is "an astonishing piece" that keeps the listener sustained. *See:* W154b

B444 Tawa, Nicholas. *A Most Wondrous Babble: American Art Composers, Their Music, and the American Scene, 1950-1985.* Westport, Connecticut: Greenwood Press, 1987.

    This book is volume 9 in the publisher's series *Contributions to the Study of Music and Dance*. Tawa makes the following comments: "At the time he [Wuorinen] wrote the composition [*Percussion Symphony*], much in evidence was a decrease in the dissonant content of contemporary works. (Consonance and triadic harmonies occur in this piece.) At the same time, some composers were taking interest in gamelanlike percussive sounds, like those associated with Java. (They occur in this symphony.) An inclination to reclaim music from Europe's past, for use in new settings, was gaining in popularity. (Music from the early Renaissance is found in the work.)" (p. 100) *See:* W154

B445 Watkins, Glen. *Soundings: Music in the Twentieth Century*. New York: Schirmer Books, 1988.

In the chapter "Uses of the Past," Watkins comments that *Percussion Symphony* reflects Wuorinen's "'hobby' of reworking old music." Watkins also says: "The last movement, which is infused to a degree with reminiscences of the preceding interlude, is a disarming finale that, for all its dodecaphonic base, sounds like a fusion of early [John] Cage, a Broadway [Milton] Babbitt, and the George Shearing Quintet." (p. 642) *See:* W154

B446 François, Jean-Charles. *Percussion et Musique Contemporaine*. Paris: Klincksieck, 1991.

This book is volume 53 of the publisher's series *Collection d'esthetique*. One of the few European imprints to include a discussion of Wuorinen's music, the book lists *Percussion Symphony* in a brief bibliography of works composed principally for solo percussion and percussion ensemble. *See:* W154

Piano Concerto No. 1

B447 Steinberg, Michael. "Where's the Action? Babbitt and Wuorinen Visit the Middle West." *Boston Sunday Globe*, 15 May 1966.

A review of the premiere performance. Steinberg writes that drama is "suggested by music in which explosive and intense activity is often followed by, or startlingly unprepared by, broad stretches of dying vibration or silence." *See:* W19

B448 Dwyer, John. "Foss and Moderns: Big Range of Styles, Traditional to Hip." *Buffalo Evening News*, 2 October 1967.

Dwyer says the work is "a sinewy and somewhat mordant work on a serial basis, where de-tuned percussion seems to carry out a rhythmic counterpart of the tone-row evolvement." *See:* W19a

B449 Putnam, Thomas. "At Music Hall: Five Composers Heard." *Buffalo Courier-Express*, 2 October 1967.

"But the music has a boldness, an athleticism, which shows the composer's debt to Varese." *See:* W19a

B450 Rossi, Nick and Robert A. Choate. *Music Of Our Time. An Anthology of Works of Selected Contemporary Composers of the 20th Century*. Boston: Crescendo Publishing Company, 1969.

This book concludes with a six-page (pp. 380-386) chapter devoted exclusively to Wuorinen; it consists of biographical and interview material. The *Piano Concerto No. 1* is analyzed in some depth. The chapter features a letter from Wuorinen to Rossi about the concerto. Rossi describes Wuorinen as "reminiscent of the 18th century musical virtuoso-of-all-trades. At an age when most composers are just finding themselves, he made his mark as a composer, performer, teacher, impresario, writer on subjects musical, and musical commentator." [P] *See:* W19

B451 Cohn, Arthur. "...More on Ben Weber and Wuorinen." *American Record Guide* 35, no. 11 (July 1969), pp. 1040-1041.

A review of the CRI recording. "Wuorinen's is another dish of tea — somewhat cool, minus any sugar." Cohn subsequently rewrote a portion of this review for his 1981 guide to classical sound recordings. *See:* D7, B455

B452 Henahan, Donal. "Reviews of Records." The *Musical Quarterly* 55, no. 3 (July 1969), pp. 424-426.

A review of the CRI recording. "It is a piano concerto based and built upon the composer's own technical achievements and temperamental complexities. The musical line could hardly fall on the page more differently, and yet one is continually put in mind of Beethoven and his productive rages." (p. 424) *See:* D7

B453 "The Year's Best Recordings." *Saturday Review*, 6 December 1969, pp. 76-77.

The CRI recording is listed as one of the year's best and is recommended to Christmas shoppers. *See:* D7

B454 *Music of the Last Forty Years Not Yet Established In the Repertoire: A Survey Conducted By the Fromm Music Foundation at Harvard 1974-1975.* Cambridge, Massachusetts: The Foundation, 1975.

The survey lists *Piano Concerto No. 1* as one of the twenty-four works by Wuorinen considered by the Fromm Music Foundation to be among the "important but neglected or infrequently performed musical works dating from the last forty years." (l. 1) *See:* W19, B891

B455 Cohn, Arthur. *Recorded Classical Music. A Critical Guide to Compositions and Performances.* New York: Schirmer Books, 1981.

A review of the CRI recording. "Wuorinen uses a great amount of percussion and uses it frequently; it almost rivals the solo piano in importance. This sort of timbre clutch is fine in pithy pieces: in a twenty-minute time span it may well be argued that such post-Webern focus fuzzes the ear." *See:* D7, B451

Piano Concerto No. 2

B456 "Baldwin Amplified Grand In New York World Premiere." The *Music Trades* 122, no. 12 (December 1974), p. 32.

A brief article discussing the premiere performance, but with no critical commentary. Includes some information on the history of the Baldwin ED-1 electronically amplified concert grand piano. *See:* W20

B457 Ericson, Raymond. "The Philharmonic Meets an Electronic Piano." The *New York Times*, 1 December 1974, *(Section 2)*, p. 21.

Pre-concert publicity about the premiere. Ericson writes that Wuorinen seems to be optimistic about the performance. *See:* W20

B458 Iachetta, Michael. "The Thing Comes to Fisher Hall." *New York Daily News* (2 December 1974).

Pre-concert publicity about the premiere. [P] *See:* W20

B459 Ericson, Raymond. "Music: New Wuorinen." The *New York Times*, 7 December 1974, p. 22.

"For all its intellectual rigor, the concerto seems to misfire." Ericson does, however, praise Wuorinen's solo performance as well as Erich Leinsdorf's conducting. *See:* W20

B460 Saal, Hubert. "Amplifying the New Music." *Newsweek*, 16 December 1974, p. 71.

A review of the premiere. "The concerto itself is brassy, percussive, peppery, mercurial in its tempos, muscular and insistently powerful." *See:* W20

B461 "Klavierkonzert mit Verstärker." *Instrumentenbau* 29 (1975), p. 516.

A one-paragraph report on the premiere performance. *See:* W20

B462 *Music of the Last Forty Years Not Yet Established In the Repertoire: A Survey Conducted By the Fromm Music Foundation at Harvard 1974-1975.* Cambridge, Massachusetts: The Foundation, 1975.

The survey lists *Piano Concerto No. 2* as one of the twenty-four works by Wuorinen considered by the Fromm Music Foundation to be among the "important but neglected or infrequently performed musical works dating from the last forty years." (1. 1) *See:* W20, B891

B463 Cumming, Robert. "The Journal Reviews: Fisher Hall." *Music Journal* 33, no. 2 (February 1975), p. 42.

"Wuorinen, as usual, was greeted with bravos and boos alike — as have other important composers throughout history." *See:* W20

B464 Porter, Andrew. "Musical Events: Getting to Know You." The *New Yorker*, 10 February 1975, pp. 111-112.

A review of the premiere. "In the event, the Electropiano made pungent, painful, and horribly distorted noises. And this was a pity, for the score of the concerto reveals many striking and potent musical inventions." This review was subsequently reprinted in Porter's book *Music of Three Seasons: 1974-1977* (New York: Farrar, Straus, Giroux, 1978). *See:* W20

B465 Smith, Patrick J. "Debuts & Reappearances: N.Y. Phil.: Wuorinen Piano Cto." *High Fidelity/Musical America* 25, no. 3 (March 1975), pp. MA30-MA31.

A review of the premiere. Smith writes: "I can't help feeling that, for all the musical expertise in the score, Wuorinen has not faced up to the consequences of the acoustical demands he has made." (p. MA31) The review features a photograph of Wuorinen with Erich Leinsdorf and Jack Romann of the Baldwin Piano Company. [P] *See:* W20

B466 Smith, Patrick J. "New York." The *Musical Times* 116 (April 1975), pp. 362-363.

A review of the premiere. "Whatever merits were in the score (the concerto's idea is that the orchestra is the obedient handmaiden of the piano) were obliterated by the inadequacy of Avery Fisher Hall's sound system, which reproduced the piano as incessant and monotonous clangour." *See:* W20

B467 Dydo, Stephen. "Charles Wuorinen's Second Piano Concerto: A Preliminary Examination." *Contemporary Music Newsletter* 9, nos. 2-3 (May-June 1975), pp. 3-5.

This article analyzes the work in terms of pitch content, rhythm, and compositional procedure. Dydo concludes that "the notion of the set as a factor operating very much in the background is perhaps one of the basic concepts in any study of Wuorinen's music, and this is quite clear from the lower level procedures in the *Second Piano Concerto.*" *See:* W20

B468 Willis, Thomas. "Two Musical Jewels Sparkle in One Night." *Chicago Tribune*, 20 October 1975, *(Section 3)*, p. 19.

This is a review of a Chicago performance at which a normal concert grand piano was used, but with four speaker enclosures fed by microphones placed near the piano's strings. "The surface sheen of sound is often impressive, particularly in the carefully scaled climaxes where the planes and levels of interacting rhythms and pitch levels mesh powerfully." *See:* W20a

B469 Slonimsky, Nicolas. *Supplement to Music Since 1900.* New York: Charles Scribner's Sons, 1986.

Surprisingly, this is the first edition or part of Slonimsky's chronology to mention Wuorinen. The fourth edition, published in 1971, appeared a year after Wuorinen won the Pulitzer Prize for music, yet it contained not one entry on him. Of *Piano Concerto No. 2*, Slonimsky writes it is scored for "an electronically amplified piano exercising a sonic hegemony, with the orchestra functioning as a duplicator, fragmentor and integrator of the discordant musical materials." (p. 88) *See:* W20

Piano Concerto No. 3

B470 Cantrell, Scott. "Drawing on Music's Participatory Effect." *Sunday Times Union* [Albany, New York], 29 April 1984.

Pre-concert publicity about the premiere; includes interview material with Wuorinen. *See:* W21

B471 LeBrun, Fred. "Tailor-made Music Costly." *Sunday Times Union* [Albany, New York], 29 April 1974.

Pre-concert publicity about the premiere. The article includes a discussion about the financial aspects of commissioning new music. *See:* W21

B472 Purvin, Robin. "World Premiere in Troy." The *Times Herald Record* [Albany, New York], 4 May 1984.

Pre-concert publicity about the premiere; includes interview material with Garrick Ohlsson. *See:* W21

B473 Webb, Steve. "Anatomy of a Concerto." *Knickerbocker News* [Albany, New York], 4 May 1984, pp. 1, 15.

Pre-concert publicity about the premiere; also includes background information on how the collaboration between Wuorinen and Garrick Ohlsson came about. [P] *See:* W21

B474 Cantrell, Scott. "Reviews: Premiere Ends Music Series on a High Note." *Sunday Times Union* [Albany, New York], 6 May 1984.

A review of the premiere performance. "This proved to be an exciting and surprisingly engaging work, quite brilliantly written for the piano." *See:* W21

B475 Nilsson, B.A. "Entertainment: New Concerto Most Original for Piano Since Bartok." *Knickerbocker News* [Albany, New York], 7 May 1984.

A review of the premiere performance. "The piano writing is extremely difficult. Often it sounds like [Sergei] Prokofiev on Benzedrine." *See:* W21

B476 Suter, Noel. "ASO Ends Season in Style." *Schenectady Gazette* [Schenectady, New York], 7 May 1984, p. 15.
"Wuorinen's music proved to be a masterful piece of orchestration with its fair share of majesty and mystery." *See:* W21

B477 Cantrell, Scott. "Debuts & Reappearances: Albany." *High Fidelity/Musical America* 34, no. 9 (September 1984), p. MA22.
A review of the premiere performance. "Overall, the effect is more openly ingratiating, more 'public', than in much of Wuorinen's output." Cantrell also praises Garrick Ohlsson's piano playing and Julius Hegyi's conducting. *See:* W21

B478 Shulgold, Marc. "Music and Dance News: Pianist Ohlsson: A Soft Spot for Chopin." *Los Angeles Times*, 9 September 1984, p. C44.
This brief article about Garrick Ohlsson mentions he will perform as the soloist in an upcoming Hollywood Bowl performance of *Piano Concerto No. 3*. Ohlsson comments: "Charles [Wuorinen] considers it a great bowl piece. He told me he thought it had lots of nice Hollywood melodies in it." *See:* W21

B479 Porter, Andrew. "Musical Events: Roundup." The *New Yorker*, 3 September 1984, pp. 85-86.
A review of the premiere performance. "It's energetic, packed with ideas, exhilarating." (p. 85) *See:* W21

B480 McLean, Priscilla. "The Albany Symphony's Daring Path." *High Fidelity/Musical America* 35, no. 4 (April 1985), pp. MA28-MA29.
An article about the Albany Symphony, its director, Peter Kermani, and its conductor, Julius Hegyi. McLean reports that several performers praised Wuorinen's *Piano Concerto No. 3* because it displayed "musical strength and integrity." (p. 29) Wuorinen is also quoted as saying that Hegyi is "a marvelous musician, a superb conductor." *See:* W21

B481 Goldstein, Jeffrey. "Sidlin Was a Master With Complex Composition." *New Haven Register* [New Haven, Connecticut], 30 October 1985.
"Tepid applause followed and conversations overheard during intermission were less restrained in their dislike." *See:* W21a

B482 Wiser, John D. "Pianist Solos for HVP." The *Times Herald Record* [Albany, New York], 19 May 1986.
"Always amazingly deft in technique, Wuorinen, now 48, has deepened and matured into a musical communicator of uncompromising strength and security." *See:* W21b

B483 Gerber, Leslie. "My Ears Hear Wuorinen." *Woodstock Times* [Woodstock, New York], 22 May 1986, p. 23.
"The big surprise was hearing a thrilling new piece, one of the most exciting discoveries in years." *See:* W21b

B484 Heresniak, M.F. "HVP Symphony Series Concludes." *Poughkeepsie Journal* [Poughkeepsie, New York], 20 May 1986, p. 4D.
"This is an intelligent and magnificent work with a thrilling, captivating sound." Heresniak also discusses the controversy surrounding the alleged remarks of conductor Imre Pallo about modern music. Pallo had been quoted as saying after intermission that

listeners should be thanked for putting up with modern music. Heresniak later asserted in this same tabloid that Pallo had actually said listeners should be thanked for being adventuresome. *See:* W21b

B485 Montgomery, Kitty. "Soloist Puts Power in Piano." *Daily Freeman* [Kingston, New York], 22 May 1986, p. 35.
"The music committee that arranges these affairs apparently chose this overly familiar work [Peter Ilich Tchaikovsky's *Pathetique Symphony*] as an antidote to Wuorinen's far out concerto. One man's sweetness is another man's saccharine." *See:* W21b

B486 Kupferman, Meyer. "Letters to Enjoy. Reader Supports Maestro Pallo." *Poughkeepsie Journal* [Poughkeepsie, New York], 23 May 1986.
This letter to the editor from composer Meyer Kupferman was a response to conductor Imre Pallo's comments to the audience attending the 18 May 1986 performance of Wuorinen's *Piano Concerto No. 3*, at which Pallo conducted and allegedly made disparaging remarks about contemporary music. Kupferman claims the remarks were supportive of modern music and had been misinterpreted. *See:* W21b, B484

B487 Kresky, Jeffrey. "The Recent Music of Charles Wuorinen." *Perspectives of New Music* 25, nos. 1-2 (1987), pp. 410-417.
Piano Concerto No. 3 is discussed in this important article. *See:* W21, B857

B488 Mach, Elyse. *Great Pianists Speak for Themselves. Volume 2.* New York: Dodd, Mead & Co., 1988.
The chapter featuring comments by Garrick Ohlsson includes two remarks on Wuorinen and his *Piano Concerto No. 3*: "But the piece is a very brilliant piece, and it's full of very great display for piano and orchestra; it's full of brilliant and great athleticism. Wuorinen in a sense is very much a spiritual descendent of [Igor] Stravinsky in many ways, especially in the physical vitality and rhythmic energy displayed in so much of Stravinsky's work. It's also very difficult music, but that does not make it unapproachable. It can be performed, and it can be done well, and although the audiences haven't danced in the aisles over it yet, the reception has been better than good, and someday you might just see that dancing." (pp.190-191) *See:* W21

B489 Moor, Paul. "San Francisco's Sonic Boom." *High Fidelity/Musical America* 38, no. 6 (June 1988), pp. 58-59.
This article discusses the surge in recording activity by the San Francisco Symphony under Herbert Blomstedt's leadership. Wuorinen is mentioned: "Blomstedt revived the orchestra's recording activities in late 1986 with a one-shot Nonesuch gig combining two works by Charles Wuorinen." (p. 59) (One of the works was *Piano Concerto No. 3*.) *See:* D36

B490 Wiser, John. "A Conversation With Garrick Ohlsson." *Fanfare* 12, no. 3 (February 1989), pp. 76-79.
This brief interview concludes with Wiser and Ohlsson remarking how they both felt *Piano Concerto No. 3* reminds them of Bela Bartok's *Second Piano Concerto*. Ohlsson states: "And I think that Charles [Wuorinen] feels that his Third Concerto is *extremely* accessible." (p. 79) *See:* W21

B491 Ulrich, Allan. "Bay Area Sounds on Tape and Disc." *San Francisco Sunday Examiner and Chronicle*, 5 February 1989, *(Style)*, p. E-5.

A review of the Nonesuch recording. "The 30-minute piano concerto radiates a keen, urban edge and is redolent with quotations, especially from that late 12-tone convert, Igor Stravinsky." Ulrich also praises the quality of the recording and Michael Steinberg's container notes. [P] *See:* D36

B492 Pincus, Andrew L. "The Wizardry that Makes the Most of the Music." The *New York Times*, 18 June 1989, *(Section 2)*, p. 23.

A review of the Elektra/Nonesuch recording. "With its manic energy levels and shrapnel-like bursts of notes, the Stravinsky-tinged music has all the repose of a prison riot." *See:* D36

B493 Moor, Paul. "Review: Wuorinen." *High Fidelity* 39 (July 1989), pp. 62-63.

A review of the Nonesuch recording. "The virtuoso repertory holds no terrors for a pianist of [Garrick] Ohlsson's formidable technical endowment, but even he forthrightly calls that movement [the finale] 'hard as hell, a bit like an aerobics class'." (p. 63) *See:* D36

B494 Kozinn, Allan. "Critics Pick Some Favorites Of the Year." The *New York Times*, 26 November 1989, *(Arts & Leisure)*, p. 26.

A review of the Nonesuch recording. Kozinn says the performance is the best he has heard on compact disk. *See:* D36

Piano Sonata No. 1

B495 Kriegsman, Alan M. "Mandel's Fresh Light." The *Washington Post*, 15 December 1970, p. B8.

A review of the premiere performance. "This is root-canal music; listening to it is like feeling the drill hit pay dirt." *See:* W135

B496 Novik, Ylda. "Ragtime Exponent Packs House at American U." The *Evening Star* [Washington, D.C.], 15 December 1970.

A review of the premiere performance. "If Ragtime turned people on, it would not be inconceivable that this austere composition could turn them off." *See:* W135

B497 Hughes, Allen. "Poet and Composer Join in a Recital." The *New York Times*, 25 December 1970, p. 34.

Hughes says the work lacked "pianistic distinction." *See:* W135a

B498 Hughes, Allen. "5 Pianists at Finale of 'Hear America First' Series." The *New York Times*, 20 July 1972, p. 27.

Hughes calls the sonata an abstract piece that displays "severe intellectuality." *See:* W135g

B499 Hiemenz, Jack. "Debuts & Reappearances: Hear American First." *High Fidelity/Musical America* 22, no. 10 (October 1972), p. MA10.

Hiemenz writes that the sonata has "freezing serial networks" but that "Ursula Oppens played it with intense conviction." *See:* W135g

B500 Bronston, Levering. "Piano." The *New Records* 42, no. 3 (May 1974), p. 12.

A review of the CRI recording. "In other words (forgive the plagiarizing of Mr. Twain), it isn't that Mr. Wuorinen's music has anything wrong with it — it just doesn't sound good." *See:* D14

B501 Cook, David. "Release Offers Canadian Music." *Tallahassee Democrat*, 5 May 1974, p. 14E.
A review of the CRI recording. Cook says the sonata "falls on the ear crystal clear like cool spring water." *See:* D14

B502 *Music of the Last Forty Years Not Yet Established In the Repertoire: A Survey Conducted By the Fromm Music Foundation at Harvard 1974-1975.* Cambridge, Massachusetts: The Foundation, 1975.
The survey lists *Piano Sonata No. 1* as one of the twenty-four works by Wuorinen considered by the Fromm Music Foundation to be among the "important but neglected or infrequently performed musical works dating from the last forty years." (l. 1) *See:* W135, B891

B503 Cory, Eleanor. "Reviews of Records." The *Musical Quarterly* 61, no. 2 (April 1975), pp. 327-335.
A review of the CRI recording. Cory's review is more of an analysis of the work itself. In part, she writes: "Although the texture is often very dense, there are essentially only two structural voices." (p. 333) *See:* D14

B504 "Where Angels Fear To Tread." *I.S.A.M. [Institute for Studies in American Music] Newsletter* [Department of Music, Brooklyn College, City University of New York] 9, no. 1 (November 1979), pp. 4-5.
"The incredibly difficult, if not impossible, task of judging the lasting value of contemporary works was tackled by a distinguished group of musicians consulted by the Rockefeller Foundation. Their project was to prepare repertories of 20th-century American music for applicants to perform in the *International Competitions for Excellence* now underway at the John F. Kennedy Center for the Performing Arts in Washington." (p. 4) Wuorinen's *Piano Sonata No. 1* is listed as one of the works selected for the piano competition category. *See:* W135

B505 Bailey, Barbara Elliot. *A Historic and Stylistic Study of American Solo Piano Music Published from 1956 Through 1976.* (Ph.D. dissertation) Evanston, Illinois: Northwestern University, 1980.
Piano Sonata No. 1 "is typical of stylistically extreme works in which the composer's focus on processes and schemes of construction creates works of exceedingly complex relationships of all parameters." (p. 70) *See:* W135

B506 Cohn, Arthur. *Recorded Classical Music. A Critical Guide to Compositions and Performances.* New York: Schirmer Books, 1981.
A review of the CRI recording. "Wuorinen's piece (dedicated to him [Robert Miller]) offers no problems that he [Miller] has not mastered to the last agogic mark. It can be taken for granted that his performance is definitive." (p. 2110) *See:* D14

Piano Sonata No. 2

B507 McLellan, Joseph. "Swann: Technique Versatility and Dynamic Piano Resources." The *Washington Post*, 4 October 1976, p. D7.

A review of the premiere performance. "It is music clearly contemporary in form but not modern for the sake of modernity, often angular in its melodic lines but nonetheless emotionally expressive, ingenious in the way it uses silences as well as the more substantial dynamic resources of piano." *See:* W136

Piano Sonata No. 3

B508 Henahan, Donal. "An Evening of the Old and the New." The *New York Times*, 31 March 1989, p. C3.
A review of the premiere performance. Henahan writes "the percussive brilliance of the Wuorinen seemed garrulous and aimless." The critic describes Alan Feinberg as "a champion of new music." *See:* W137

B509 Kerner, Leighton. "Fathoming Five." *Village Voice*, 2 May 1989, p. 98.
A review of the premiere performance. Kerner characterizes the work as "incredibly exciting and affecting." *See:* W137

B510 Levinson, David. "Feinberg Plays Modern With Moxie." *Press-Telegram* [Long Beach, California], 2 April 1989, p. B3.
Levinson praises pianist Alan Feinberg for not being afraid of modern music, and writes of the sonata's third movement: "If Theolonious Monk had been blessed with Art Tatum's technique, this might have been the result." *See:* W137a

B511 Clements, Andrew. "Piano Recitals: Feinberg & Richter." *Financial Times* [London], 4 June 1992.
A review of the London premiere. "Wuorinen's sonata too buries most of its substance under a welter of notes." *See:* W137c

Piano Trio

B512 Redmond, Michael. "Wuorinen 'Trio' Premiere is Kean College Opener." The *Star-Ledger* [Union, N.J.], 3 October 1983, p. 21.
A review of the premiere performance. "The real surprise of the piece was its finale, which seemed to evoke tragic gestures — and which left one with a sense of wonder, in flashback, at the course of the work." *See:* W95

B513 Hughes, Allen. "Chamber Music: Arden Trio." The *New York Times*, 10 October 1983, p. C13.
The critic says the trio "represents a continuation of the composer's effort to relax his compositional style and make it more accessible to the listener." *See:* W95a

B514 Sommers, Pamela. "Performing Arts: Arden Trio." The *Washington Post*, 1 November 1983, p. B6.
"Alternately tortured and tremulous, the piece creates an argument and resolution made up of shrieks from the violin, hollow chords and sustained astringent passages." *See:* W95b

B515 Malltz, Nancy. "New Music Without an Old Handicap." The *Detroit News*, 5 December 1983.
"The Arden musicians [Arden Trio] played it as if they loved it, imbuing it with all the sensual beauty and theatrical pacing that is arguably in the score, and burdening

it with none of that 'second language' handicap that prevents too much contemporary music from surviving the translation." *See:* W95c

Piano Variations

B516 Boretz, Benjamin. "New Music and the American Mainstream." The *Nation*, 4 May 1964, pp. 466-467.

A substantive article about contemporary music performance in New York City. The bulk of the piece is devoted to a discussion of Milton Babbitt's music. Boretz selects Wuorinen's *Piano Variations* as one of the composer's "more self-disciplined and mature [compositions]." He also writes that the music "attempts to combine pure gesture and controlled pitch succession to a personal phraseology." (p. 468) *See:* W138

B517 Steinberg, Michael. "Contemporary Music Fete: Closing Night Program Stirs the Audience." The *Boston Globe*, 14 August 1964.

Steinberg says: "Wuorinen radiates an uncommon dramatic force, and the Variations in his own performance made one of the more meaningful moments of the festival." *See:* W138c

B518 Klein, Howard. "Music: At Tanglewood." The *New York Times*, 15 August 1964.

Klein simply writes that Wuorinen's performance of this work made a stronger impression than other works commissioned for the occasion. *See:* W138c

B519 Salzman, Eric. "Tanglewood: The Wrapup Six." *New York Herald Tribune*, 15 August 1964.

"The notes don't matter much at all, only the contours and textures, but the piece has real shape and power none the less." *See:* W138c

B520 Gruen, John. "Moaning Music-Fit To Curdle the Blood." *New York Herald Tribune*, 27 January 1965, p. 15.

Gruen calls the variations "frantic, brilliant evocations of schizophrenic states." *See:* W138d

B521 "Musica: Inicióse un Festival de Música en el I. Di Tella." *Clarin* [Buenos Aires], 29 August 1965, p. 30.

"The work itself, in spite of being composed in the form of variations, shows a conceptual logic and a balanced development." The reviewer praises pianist Carla Hübner's performance, but erroneously states that the performance was the world premiere. *See:* W138f

B522 "Zeitgenössische Musik im Instituto di Tella: Erstes Konzert." *Argentinisches Tageblatt* [Buenos Aires], 29 August 1965.

The critic writes that the *Piano Variations* constitute "a work completely under the influence of Pierre Boulez's *Third Piano Sonata*...[Wuorinen's] work makes use of the achievements of this modern French pioneer with persuasive power." *See:* W138f

B523 "Instituto di Tella." *Tribuna Musical* [Buenos Aires], September 1965.

"They *[Piano Variations]* are written with a direct expressive sense, and in their construction we find authenticity that is lacking in the work of [John] Cage *[Music of Changes IV]*, and expressive desire absent from the sonata *[Sonata No. 7, Op. 101]* by

[Jacopo] Ficher." The reviewer also states that pianist Carla Hübner was magnificent. *See:* W138f

B524 "Carla Hübner spielt Klaviermusik des XX. Jahrunderts." *Argentinisches Tageblatt* [Buenos Aires], 25 November 1965.

The critic describes the piece as "the only completely brittle, cramped, ringing work of the program" and erroneously says Wuorinen was born in 1906. *See:* W138g

B525 "Modernas Obras Para Piano Se Escucharon en Di Tella." *La Prensa* [Buenos Aires], 25 November 1965.

The reviewer says *Piano Variations* "is not too original as a resultant esthetic" and identifies Wuorinen as a composer at the University of Columbia [i.e., Columbia University.] *See:* W138g

B526 "Obras pianísticas del siglo XX oír Carla Hübner." *La Nation* [Buenos Aires], 26 November 1965.

"[It was music] that we previously heard during a recent occasion and that in this new opportunity interested us less than before, causing in more measure an insistent artificiality." *See:* W138g

B527 "Carla Hübner Dio un Notable Recital de Obras Para Piano." *Clarin* [Buenos Aires], 29 November 1965.

The critic says the variations "exhibit a considerable richness of ideas, yet their quality and elaboration suffer very pronounced highs and lows." *See:* W138g

B528 "Instituto di Tella." *Tribuna Musical* [Buenos Aires], November/December 1965, pp. 17-18.

The reviewer writes "in this second hearing *[Piano Variations]* seems less interesting to us than the first time, not because of the difference in execution, but because the work itself made the program last an unnecessarily long time." *See:* W138g

B529 Strongin, Theodore. "Recordings: Advance With the Serialists and the Far-Out Avant-Garde." The *New York Times*, 26 March 1967, *(Arts & Leisure)*, p. D25.

A review of the Advance recording. Strongin writes the *Piano Variations* are "full of explosive energy, expressed with exactitude." He also says "Wuorinen is wilder than Webern." *See:* D4

B530 Cohn, Arthur. "Gilt-edged Aural Securities." The *American Record Guide* 33, no. 9 (May 1967), pp. 731-732.

A review of the Advance recording. Cohn claims that he has yet to find a real personality in Wuorinen's music. "The variations heard here bind into a coherent whole, and yet no memory remains of their procedures. A certain amount of tension is woven into the fabric but it is plain, eclectic goods, of the serial kind that has been produced by the carload." (p. 732) Cohn later changes his mind and gives the *Piano Variations* a more favorable review in his 1981 book *Recorded Classical Music*. *See:* D4, B539

B531 Hitchcock, H. Wiley. *Music in the United States: A Historical Introduction.* Englewood Cliffs, New Jersey: Prentice-Hall, Inc., 1969.

In the final chapter, "Intersections, Interactions, Projections," Hitchcock discusses virtuoso performers, including pianists Paul Jacobs and Robert Miller, percussionist Raymond DesRoches, and flutist Harvey Sollberger. He states that their performing abilities have been extended by composers such as Wuorinen, whose *Piano Variations* is an example of "a music of ferocious intensity and furious activity, both responding to and demanding more of the new virtuosity, and approaching the outer limits of perception and comprehension." Hitchcock modified this sentence slightly for his second edition, which appeared in 1974. *See:* W138, B538

B532 Ivey, Jean Eichelberger. "Current Chronicle." The *Musical Quarterly* 55, no. 1 (January 1969), pp. 87-91.
An assessment of the second annual Summer Institute in Compositional Studies of the American Society of University Composers, held in Ann Arbor, Michigan. Ivey writes: "Hearing his *[Piano] Variations* made all the more relevant Charles Wuorinen's talk about his recent compositional practices. He believes that pitch is now at a low point in the interest of composers generally, but for him pitch is still the fundamental determinant. He is interested in twelve-tone relations and minor extensions thereof, as determining both the micro- and the macro structure of a work." (p. 87) *See:* W138

B533 Cole, Hugo. "A Rare Performance." The *Guardian* [London], 14 March 1969.
Cole says the *Piano Variations* are "pianistic in the modern sense, with loudly struck, slowly fading tones, set against fierce note-flurries with just two 'special effects' notes; single strings, plucked within the piano to produce the effects of a distant French carriage-clock." This review was subsequently reprinted in *American Musical Digest* 1, no. 1 (October 1969). *See:* W138j

B534 Doris, Hubert. "Some Music Reviews." The *Piano Quarterly* 68 (Summer 1969), pp. 2, 23.
A review of the McGinnis & Marx edition. The reviewer writes that "if you don't mind the notational stratosphere it's not as hard as it looks." (p. 23) *See:* W138

B535 Jenkins, Speight. "Zodiak Piano Cycle Receives N.Y. Premiere." The *New York Post*, 6 November 1973, p. 21.
Jenkins merely mentions that the work was performed on the program and calls it "angular, rather uncompromising." *See:* W138l

B536 Ericson, Raymond. "Burge Conjures Up a Mystical Collage of Music by Crumb." The *New York Times*, 7 November 1973, p. 53.
The critic calls Wuorinen's *Piano Variations* "austere and academic, but nonetheless strong." *See:* W138l

B537 Felton, James. "Pianist David Burge Plays Strong Avant-Garde Fare." The *Evening Bulletin* [Philadelphia], 7 November 1973.
Felton says the piece "mixes staccato and legato textures like mashed potatoes and marbles. They came out juicily nice and very pleasing." *See:* W138m

B538 Hitchcock, H. Wiley. *Music in the United States: A Historical Introduction.* 2nd ed. Englewood Cliffs, New Jersey: Prentice-Hall, Inc., 1974.
In this second edition of his book, Hitchcock refers to *Piano Variations* as he did in his first edition, but with the same sentence somewhat modified: "Wuorinen writes a music sometimes of ferocious intensity and furious activity, sometimes of a complex lacy delicacy, that both responds to and demands more of the new virtuosity, approaching at times the outer limits of interpretive possibility and perception." (p. 265) *See:* W138, B531

B539 Cohn, Arthur. *Recorded Classical Music. A Critical Guide to Compositions and Performances.* New York: Schirmer Books, 1981.
A review of the Advance recording. "As expected, the sentiment is cool. However, the logic that is found in Wuorinen's *Piano Variations* is not merely a carbon copy of a rigid technical system. In fact there is an excitement in the tensions that are built into the work by way of silences and registral differences." He also praises David Burge's piano playing. Cohn's comments are somewhat of a reversal of his remarks about the same piece in his review of May 1967, published in The *American Record Guide. See:* D4, B530

B540 Burge, David. *Twentieth-Century Piano Music.* New York: Schirmer Books, 1990.
This book contains seven references to Wuorinen. Chapter 21, "The American Avant-Garde," contains a brief section on him. In that section, Burge describes *Piano Variations* as Wuorinen's "first and most successful composition for piano," "a splendid, ringing piece of virtuoso writing." (p. 200) Burge also writes that Wuorinen's efforts in establishing the ASUC (American Society of University Composers) "did an enormous amount to bring composers together from all over the country for colloquia and concerts of their music." (p. 200) In an endnote to the chapter, Burge recounts a conversation he had with Wuorinen in which Wuorinen stated the ASUC was begun before foundations supported new music, and that when they applied for funding "they were rejected on the grounds that they were doing well enough on their own." (p. 272) *See:* W138

The Politics of Harmony

B541 Kresky, Jeffrey. "Colloquy and Review: University of Michigan: ASUC's Summer Institute in Compositional Studies." *Perspectives of New Music* 7, no. 1 (Fall-Winter 1968), pp. 147-149.
This brief article includes a discussion of a lecture given by Wuorinen during the summer institute. The lecture dealt with his use of pitch in a few compositions, one of which was *The Politics of Harmony.* Kresky notes Wuorinen stated that a section of the work was originally intended for electronic realization but that circumstances prevented that from happening. He concludes by writing that "pitch relations are for him [Wuorinen], yet the essential matter of music." (p. 149) *See:* W160

B542 Hibbard, William. "Younger American Composers: Charles Wuorinen: The Politics of Harmony." *Perspectives of New Music* 7, no. 2 (Spring-Summer 1969), pp. 155-166.
This article is a highly detailed analysis of the work. Hibbard examines scenario, pitch content, characterization, etc., of the masque, and concludes: "Much more can be written, and indeed should be written, about such matters as the masque's extraordinary orchestrational design, the pacing and positioning of the thirty-five sections, the structure of the text, the dramaturgical plan, methods of dynamic and musical continuity, and so forth. However, much of what could be said in those realms would be relatively meaningless without impractically massive quotes from the score. But I do wish, in conclusion, at least to express my belief that *The Politics of Harmony* is a major contribution to twentieth-century music drama." (pp. 165-166) *See:* W160

B543 Schonberg, Harold C. "Music: A New Series at Philharmonic." The *New York Times*, 3 October 1971, p. 82.
This review contains one of the most infamous comments on Wuorinen's music: "The Wuorinen was one of those academic post-serial drags, completely amelodic, awkwardly set for the three voices." The comment is cited in Joan Peyser's account of

the concert, published in her psychobiography *Boulez: Composer, Conductor, Enigma* (New York: Schirmer Books, 1976). *See:* W160a, B545, B552

B544 Kolodin, Irving. "Music to My Ears." *Saturday Review* 54 (16 October 1971), p. 38.

"The work itself has such obvious attributes of enjoyment and communication that a verbal dialogue was hardly required, and I departed without waiting for it." *See:* W160a

B545 Schonberg, Harold C. "Boulez Trips Up Downtown." The *New York Times*, 17 October 1971, *(Arts & Leisure)*, p. D17.

This is a Sunday edition follow-up to the critic's review of 3 October. "The work was played; it ran some forty dismal minutes, with the singers maltreating the English language in extended twelve-tone syllabic extensions, with the usual academic kind of organization, with a 1960's kind of athematicism, with virtually no personality, with not a trace of charm." This review was later reprinted in Schonberg's book *Facing the Music* (New York: Summit Books, 1981). *See:* W160, W160a, B543

B546 Hamilton, David. "Music." The *Nation*, 25 October 1971, pp. 413-414.

"And [Pierre] Boulez's little illustrated talk on Wuorinen's text setting was so generalized as to be applicable (with different illustrations, of course) to virtually any significant stage work of the last three centuries, and thus hardly informative with respect to this particular one." (p. 414) *See:* W160a

B547 Hiemenz, Jack. "Debuts & Reappearances: Boulez: Prospective Encounters." *High Fidelity/Musical America* 22, no 1 (January 1972), p. MA18-MA19.

"If there were a prize for tedium unleavened, I'd be happy to award it to the Wuorinen theater piece, *The Politics of Harmony*." (p. MA19) *See:* W160a

B548 "The First Village Prospective Encounter." *Concert Hall [John F. Kennedy Center Program Magazine]*, (November 1971), pp. 8-9.

This magazine was published by *Saturday Review*. The article mentions the performance of this work and features black and white photographs of the production; the original photographs are probably the only archival photographs of the production in existence. The article also appeared (with the same photographs) in the *New York Philharmonic Program Notes* (November 1971-1972 season), also published by *Saturday Review*. *See:* W160a

B549 *Dictionary of Contemporary Music.* Ed. John Vinton. New York: E.P. Dutton & Co., 1974.

The article titled "Text Setting and Usage," by Edward Levy, includes a discussion of relations between speech and timbre. Levy states that in parts of *The Politics of Harmony* Wuorinen has "phonemes and their order determine the choice of specific pitch classes, with word illustration one criterion for choosing register." (p. 741) *See:* W160, B952

B550 Kolodin, Irving. "Wuorinen and the New American String Quartet." *Saturday Review/World*, 26 January 1974, pp. 62-64.

An article comprising an overview of Wuorinen's career up to his thirty-sixth year. Kolodin writes of *The Politics of Harmony*: "In the context of time, it was clearly a parable of the unhappy adventure of the United States in Vietnam." (p. 62) **[P]** *See:* W160, B920

B551 *Music Of the Last Forty Years Not Yet Established In the Repertoire: A Survey Conducted By the Fromm Music Foundation at Harvard 1974-1975.* Cambridge, Massachusetts: The Foundation, 1975.

The survey lists *The Politics of Harmony* as one of the twenty-four works by Wuorinen considered by the Fromm Music Foundation to be among the "important but neglected or infrequently performed musical works dating from the last forty years." (l. 1) *See:* W160, B891

B552 Peyser, Joan. *Boulez: Composer, Conductor, Enigma.* New York: Schirmer Books, 1976.

This book includes an in-depth discussion — especially in terms of personality conflict and ego — of the New York Philharmonic's *Prospective Encounter* that featured Wuorinen's *The Politics of Harmony.* Peyser writes: "The tedium of the piece, set for three voices and chamber instruments, was not relieved by the mimes. But the audience was more imprisoned than any audience uptown. Those who tried to leave were impeded by a door that would not open easily. People pushed and scuffled around in embarrassment with the audience's eyes riveted on them as they tried to make their escape. Afterwards, when the discussion began, there was a mass exodus. [Pierre] Boulez asked Wuorinen to talk about the compositional principles of the work. Wuorinen said he didn't want to 'bore' anyone. Someone asked him if it were twelve-tone. Wuorinen replied, 'It is at least that.' When I [Joan Peyser] asked Boulez why he had chosen *The Politics of Harmony* he said it was because he believed the use of mimes would prove attractive to the audience." (pp. 200-201) Portions of this book had been excerpted prior to publication, and were published in the October 1976 issue of *High Fidelity. See:* W160, W160a, B543

B553 Griffiths, Paul. *Modern Music. The Avant Garde Since 1945.* New York: George Braziller, 1981.

Griffiths discusses *The Politics of Harmony* in some detail. "It is impossible in a short extract to give more than a faint impression of the manner in which Wuorinen weaves together his contrapuntal lines, often passing from instrument to instrument, and winds those lines through chords spaced with almost Stravinskyan finesse. Even so, it should be clear that his constructive procedures, which have been no more than sketched here, do not inhibit the creation of music that is poetically apt and fluently expressive. Indeed, it is entirely characteristic of Wuorinen that his music should appear, unlike that of [Milton] Babbitt or [Peter] Westergaard, quite spontaneous despite its evident density of working." (p. 163) *See:* W160

B554 Jameux, Dominique. *Pierre Boulez.* Paris: Fayard/Fondation SACEM, 1984.

In the chapter, "Boulez, chef d'orchestre [II] (1971-1974)," Jameux mentions Boulez featured a work by Wuorinen on the first program of the New York Philharmonic's *Prospective Encounters.* (The work was *The Politics of Harmony.*) *See:* W160a

B555 *Orientations: Collected Writings By Pierre Boulez.* Ed. Jean-Jacques Nattiez. Tr. Martin Cooper. Cambridge, Massachusetts: Harvard University Press, 1986.

In his essay titled "Freeing Music," included in this book's section "Composer and Audience," Boulez discusses his efforts in "going out to meet the public, not confining music to conventional concert halls." (p. 483) He states that he tried this in New York City, with his players "dressed in mufti." (p. 483) One of these occasions was the premiere of *The Politics of Harmony. See:* W160a

B556 Kresky, Jeffrey. "The Recent Music of Charles Wuorinen." *Perspectives of New Music* 25, nos. 1-2 (1987), pp. 410-417.
   The Politics of Harmony is discussed in this important article. *See:* W160, B857

The Prayer of Jonah

B557 Ericson, Raymond. "Choral Music Spanning Five Centuries. The *New York Times,* 12 September 1965, p. 30.
   A review of the Cambridge recording. Ericson writes that Wuorinen's employment of serial techniques did not prevent him from creating a "surprisingly liturgical atmosphere." *See:* D3

B558 Klein, Howard. "Records: Music Since the War." The *New York Times,* 3 March 1967, *(Arts & Leisure),* p. D25.
   A review of the Cambridge recording. In this brief article Klein writes that since the end of World War II, New York City "usurped the role formerly played by Vienna and Fountainbleau" as centers of activity for contemporary music. *The Prayer of Jonah* recording is listed in Klein's discography attached to this article. *See:* D3

Prelude and Fugue for Four Percussionists

B559 Klein, Howard. "Records: Music Since the War." The *New York Times,* 3 March 1967, *(Arts & Leisure),* p. D25.
   A mention of the Golden Crest recording — the recording is listed in the discography at the end of the article. *See:* D1

B560 Glowski, Eugeniusz. "W. Rudzinski 'Wariacje i fuga na perkus solo,' Ch. Wuorinen 'Preludiumi i fuga na 4-ch wykonawcow' — niektore problemy analizyporownawczej." *Zeszyty naukowe. Państwowa Wyższa Szkola Muzyczna w Gdańsku* 10 (1971), pp. 40-59.
   Wuorinen's *Prelude and Fugue for Four Percussionists* is one of two works analyzed in detail. This article probably constitutes the only analysis in Polish of any Wuorinen work. *See:* W155

B561 Cohn, Arthur. *Recorded Classical Music. A Critical Guide to* Compositions and Performances. New York: Schirmer Books, 1981.
   A review of the Golden Crest recording. Cohn blasts the packaging and production: "There are no liner notes for the work; the composer is credited only on the label and there his first name is substituted for by an initial; the performers are not identified. Finally, although the timing of the work is 5:38, the record label gives the ridiculous total of 2:50, while Wuorinen's score states the performance length as 6:15." (p. 2108) *See:* D1

Prelude to Kullervo

B562 Holland, Bernard. "Music: Finnish Tribute." The *New York Times,* 24 November 1985, p. 84.
   A review of the premiere performance. "Its tuba solos and its rich yet wonderfully clear orchestration have terseness and restraint, and they achieve by doing less just the baritonal melancholy that the Sibelius's [the tone-poem *Kullervo*] great weight and length cannot sustain." *See:* W22

Psalm 39

B563 Fain, Kenneth W. "Theater Chamber Players Return." The *Washington Star* [Washington, D.C.], 13 November 1979.
　　　　A review of the premiere. "Unfortunately, like much Baroque recitative, 'Psalm Thirty-Nine' is largely dull and annoying." *See:* W180

B564 Porter, Andrew. "Musical Events: Capital Fare." The *New Yorker*, 26 November 1979, pp. 142-168.
　　　　A review of the premiere. "An impressive piece." *See:* W180

B565 Harvey, David. "Recordings." *Tempo* 142 (September 1982), pp. 43-44.
　　　　A review of the Nonesuch recording. "The references to Anglican intoning which open and close the work are, at best, a gross misjudgment — perhaps they do not grate quite so much on American ears. Elsewhere, the vocal writing is blustery and unimaginative, the writing for guitar wooden." (p. 44) *See:* D26

A Reliquary for Igor Stravinsky

B566 Ericson, Raymond. "The Philharmonic Meets an Electronic Piano." The *New York Times*, 1 December 1974, p. 21.
　　　　This article includes a brief discussion of the origin of the piece. Wuorinen says in the article that he had a dream in which he heard many sixteenth notes on one of [Igor] Stravinsky's last fragments, set for trumpet: "Later someone noticed that among the notations on the fragment was a Russian word. It translated as 'bugle'!" He also tells Ericson: "I don't want to try to be Stravinsky, and I have conceived the setting as a kind of reliquary, a word that might become the title of the piece." *See:* W23

B567 Levinson, David. "Ojai Music Festival. In the Style of Stravinsky." *Independent* [Long Beach, California], 3 June 1975, p. A-10.
　　　　A review of the premiere. "The result was not a pastiche but a moving testament to [Igor] Stravinsky's art and an affirmation of the continuity of musical thought in our century." *See:* W23

B568 Bernheimer, Martin. "Ojai Festival: Still Stimulating Great Expectations." *Los Angeles Times*, 8 June 1975, *(Calendar)*, p. 1, 68.
　　　　A review of the premiere. "Regardless of its thematic source, this is a cleverly structured study in which a large orchestra shifts textural and coloristic gears with bravado." A somewhat revised version of this review appears in the September 1975 issue of *High Fidelity/Musical America. See:* W23

B569 Bernheimer, Martin. "Ojai Festival — An Antidote to Tired Conventions." *High Fidelity/Musical America* 25, no. 9 (September 1975), pp. MA29, MA40.
　　　　This is a slightly revised version of the Bernheimer review that appeared in the *Los Angeles Times* on 8 June 1975. *See:* W23, B568

B570 Horowitz, Joseph. "'Reliquary' By Wuorinen In Commemorative Mood." The *New York Times*, 30 January 1977, p. 49.
　　　　A review of the New York premiere. "Taken as a whole, 'Reliquary' has a tragic, commemorative cast that is most impressive." *See:* W23a

B571 Heikinheimo, Seppo. "Kokoillan annos modernia musiikkia." *Helsingen Sanomat Arkisto*, 8 February 1979.

Pre-concert publicity for the Helsinki premiere. The article is titled "An All Evening Dose of Modern Music." *See:* W23b

B572 Gagne, Cole and Tracy Caras. *Soundpieces: Interviews With American Composers*. Metuchen, New Jersey: Scarecrow Press, 1982.

Cole Gagne's interview with Wuorinen, dated 14 July 1975, is the last one in the book (pp. 384-418). Fourteen questions were asked of the composer and many have lengthy answers. The subjects covered include electronic music, the musical life of New York City, the performance of contemporary music, music education, jazz, aleatoric music, and elements of music, such as pitch. Gagne asked Wuorinen how he obtained Igor Stravinsky's last fragments (for Wuorinen's *A Reliquary for Igor Stravinsky*). Wuorinen replied: "Robert Craft showed them to me on one occasion when I was at the Stravinskys' — this was, of course, after the old man had died — and the idea came to mind that it would be interesting to do something with them. I proposed it and Madame [Vera] Stravinsky agreed, and we proceeded from there." (p. 395) [P] *See:* W23

B573 Henahan, Donal. "Music: Schuller Leads 'Horizons '83'." The *New York Times*, 16 June 1983, p. C20.

Henahan writes the piece lacks "continuity, shape and meaningful incident." He also questions why it had been programmed in a series devoted to Romanticism. *See:* W23c

B574 Breuer, Robert. "In New York unter die Lupe genommen: ein 'neuer Romantizismus'?" *Neue Zeitschrift für Musik* 144, no. 11 (November/December 1983), pp. 34-36.

An article about the New York Philharmonic's *New Romanticism* festival *('Horizons '83')*. Breuer briefly mentions that Wuorinen "paid homage to the man [Igor] Stravinsky." (p. 35) *See:* W23c

B575 Skei, Allen B. "Music Reviews: Orchestral Music." *Notes* 40, no. 3 (March 1984), p. 641.

A review of the C.F. Peters edition. Skei describes how Wuorinen uses the fragments and writes that in one section, "the fragments serve simply as a basis for Wuorinen's virtuosic flight of imagination." *See:* W23

B576 Craft, Robert. *Small Craft Advisories. Critical Articles 1984-1988. Art, Ballet, Music, Literature, Film*. London: Thames & Hudson, 1989.

Craft's discussion of the book *Confronting Stravinsky* includes a reference to the essay by Wuorinen and Jeffrey Kresky in that publication. Craft writes: "In 'The Significance of Stravinsky's Last Works,' Charles Wuorinen and Jeffrey Kresky contend that the late music, especially the 1966 fragments, the pediment of Wuorinen's own musical monument, *An Igor Stravinsky Reliquary*, will ultimately be seen as the most 'significant'." (p. 161) *See:* W23

Rhapsody for Violin and Orchestra

B577 Galardi, Susan. "Premieres: The Composer Speaks." *High Fidelity/Musical America* 35, no. 1 (January 1985), pp. MA13, MA25.

This brief article includes interview material concerning the work. Wuorinen commented: "The work was originally called *Rhapsody in Black* but I had to change it when I realized it's not dark or somber." (p. MA25) *See:* W24

B578 Ulrich, Allan. "Wuorinen's Intriguing Rhapsody." *San Francisco Examiner*, 17 January 1985.

A review of the premiere. "The confidence with which he [Wuorinen] arranges sound in successive blocks suggests those influences [Igor Stravinsky, Edgard Varèse] are abiding." *See:* W24

B579 Commanday, Robert. "A Bold, Outgoing Premiere at Davies." *San Francisco Chronicle*, 18 January 1985.

A review of the premiere. "I couldn't now begin to describe the work other than in terms of its effect — constant aliveness and purpose. Various ideas act like signals or pennants." *See:* W24

B580 Moor, Paul. "Debuts & Reappearances: San Francisco." *High Fidelity/Musical America* 35, no. 5 (May 1985), p. MA23.

A review of the premiere. "The score has exceptional strength and vitality, and adventurous fiddlers up to its musical and technical exigencies should welcome its existence." *See:* W24

B581 Kresky, Jeffrey. "The Recent Music of Charles Wuorinen." *Perspectives of New Music* 25, nos. 1-2 (1987), pp. 410-417.

Rhapsody for Violin and Orchestra is discussed in this important article. *See:* W24, B857

Ringing Changes

B582 Maconie, Robin. "Recordings." *Tempo* 103 (1972), pp. 54-62.

A review of the Nonesuch recording. "Though an organising intelligence is clearly evident, one misses the individual sensibility that emerges from even the most rigorously ordered music of a [Pierre] Boulez or a [Luigi] Nono." Later in the review, Maconie delivers this scathing remark: "His [Wuorinen's] ensembles seem arbitrary and unbalanced, his tempo mechanical, and his gestural vocabulary limited to the most elementary mannerisms of 19th century rhetoric — the flourish, the climax, and the pregnant pause. A computer could write it, and probably did." (p. 55) *See:* D10

B583 Cook, David. "Dvorak's Eighth Makes Bargain." *Tallahassee Democrat* [Tallahassee, Florida], 13 February 1972.

A review of the Nonesuch recording. "Wuorinen's *Rising* [sic] *Changes* (1969-70) was disappointing until I turned up the volume and found that it can be a rather shattering experience." *See:* D10

B584 Shupp, Enos E. "Miscellaneous." The *New Records* 40, no. 1 (March 1972), p. 15.

A review of the Nonesuch recording. Shupp says the piece may "enjoy a modest acceptance for at least awhile." *See:* D10

B585 Harrison, Max. "Records: American Composers." The *Times* [London], 20 January 1973, p. 9.

A review of the Nonesuch recording. He writes "the music is so eclectic as to lack any centre of identity." *See:* D10

B586 Henahan, Donal. "A Novel Idea in Drum-Tape Music." The *New York Times*, 2 April 1975, p. 24.

Henahan terms the work "a playground for expert percussionists." *See:* W156c

B587 Cohn, Arthur. *Recorded Classical Music. A Critical Guide to Compositions and Performances*. New York: Schirmer Books, 1981.

A review of the Nonesuch recording. Cohn says it "is the supreme logic of Wuorinen's discourse that is the expressive point, not the special palette he uses" and that the "thoroughness and toughness of the former provide its own personality point of reference." (p. 2108) *See:* D10

B588 "Wuorinen." *International Music Guide. 1981*. London: Tantivy Press, 1981.

A review of the C.F. Peters edition. The reviewer writes that the work "shows a sharp ear for effect and at the same time a fine sense of proportion in the deployment and dramatisation of its resources." (p. 290) *See:* W156

B589 Kresky, Jeffrey. "The Recent Music of Charles Wuorinen." *Perspectives of New Music* 25, nos. 1-2 (1987), pp. 410-417.

Ringing Changes is discussed in this important article. *See:* W156, B857

B590 François, Jean-Charles. *Percussion et Musique Contemporaine*. Paris: Klincksieck, 1991.

This book is volume 53 of the publisher's series *Collection d'estethique*. It is one of the few European imprints to include any mention of Wuorinen's music. *Ringing Changes* is listed in a brief bibliography of works written principally for solo percussion and percussion ensemble. *See:* W156

Scherzo for Piano

B591 Harrison, Jay S. "Glee Club Uses Classmates's Music." *New York Herald Tribune*, 14 May 1956.

A review of the premiere and one of the earliest concert reviews of Wuorinen's music. Harrison states the music reflects the influence of Darius Milhaud and that "one hopes Mr. Wuorinen's academic superiors [at Trinity School, New York City] will see to it that he is soon placed in the hands of a teacher who will allow him to develop along the lines indicated by his particular talent." *See:* W139

Self-Similar Waltz

B592 Palmer, Robert. "Music: 25 Waltzes at Kitchen." The *New York Times*, 5 February 1979, p. 14.

Palmer writes that the piece "packed a lot of action — contrasts of dynamics and density, percussive bravura passages — into its brief span." *See:* W140

Short Suite

B593 Salisbury, Wilma. "Musician's Notions Set Dancer in Motion." The *Plain Dealer* [Cleveland], 7 April 1985.

A general article and pre-concert publicity about the collaboration between Wuorinen and choreographer Alice Rubenstein. (Rubenstein's work *Discovery* used the music from Wuorinen's *Short Suite*.) Salisbury writes: "His intense music perfectly matches the mood of Rubenstein's dance, and the choreography explodes in dynamic movements that spring from the rich rhythms and textures of the score." *See:* W25a

B594 Snow, Jan C. "Plucky Footpath Troupe Reflects Zeal of Director." *Akron Beacon Journal*, 15 April 1985.

"Feline movements were contrasted with more human behavior. In some sections there was a wild animal nervousness about the dancers, in others, unbridled sensuality." *See:* W25a

B595 Salisbury, Wilma. "Eye On National Performance." *Dance Magazine* (July 1985).

The reviewer merely mentions that Wuorinen's score "establishes an intense mood for the dramatic dance." *See:* W25a

B596 Chute, James. "Music's Electricity Lights Up Concert." The *Milwaukee Journal*, 28 September 1985, p. 6.

"This is music somehow connected with the very life force, somehow vital and alive, making us also feel more vital and alive when we experience it." *See:* W25b

B597 Johnson, Lawrence B. "Symphony Breathes Life Into 'Zombie Concert'." *Milwaukee Sentinel*, 28 September 1985.

"Charles Wuorinen, a composer with the effrontery to be alive, crashed a typical symphonic zombie jamboree Friday night and demonstrated that you don't have to be dead to be interesting." *See:* W25b

B598 McElwain, Bill. "If You Don't Like Wuorinen's Music, Eat Your Words." *Daily Dispatch* [Moline, Illinois], 31 August 1986.

McElwain refers to a previous, unspecified performance of the work and says: "I seem to remember labeling it a trifling piece." The article is mostly about Wuorinen having won a MacArthur Foundation award, however, and contains comments on his appearances in the midwest. [P] *See:* W25

B599 Kresky, Jeffrey. "The Recent Music of Charles Wuorinen." *Perspectives of New Music* 25, nos. 1-2 (1987), pp. 410-417.

Short Suite is discussed in this important article. *See:* W25, B857

Six Pieces for Violin and Piano

B600 "Ausgesprochenes Raritätenprogram." *Badische Zeitung* [Freiburg], 19 May 1961.

A brief discussion of an unspecified performance. The reviewer calls it "six expressive pieces of great tension." *See:* W96

B601 "Where Angels Fear to Tread." *I.S.A.M. [Institute for Studies in American Music] Newsletter* [Department of Music, Brooklyn College, City University of New York] 9, no. 1 (November 1979), pp. 4-5.

"The incredibly difficult, if not impossible, task of judging the lasting value of contemporary works was tackled by a distinguished group of musicians consulted by the Rockefeller Foundation. Their project was to prepare repertories of 20th-century American music for applicants to perform in the *International Competitions for Excellence* now underway at the John F. Kennedy Center for the Performing Arts in Washington." (p. 4) Wuorinen's *Six Pieces for Violin and Piano* is listed as one of the works selected for the violin competition category. *See:* W96

B602 "Wuorinen." *International Music Guide. 1981.* London: Tantivy Press, 1981.

A review of the C.F. Peters edition. The reviewer offers few words about the piece but calls it "tersely complex." *See:* W96

B603 Griffiths, Paul. "Music Reviews: Mostly Cage." The *Musical Times* 72, no. 1658 (April 1981), p. 249.

A review of the C.F. Peters edition. "The music is fluent, well made and tricky, in a style that owes something to Babbitt, Carter, and Wolpe." *See:* W96

B604 Dove, Jonathan. "Music Reviews." The *Strad* 92, no. 1095 (July 1981), p. 208.

A review of the C.F. Peters edition. "But it is the refined beauties of the last two movements which will most reward the player for his efforts." *See:* W96

B605 Goodfriend, James. "Recording of Special Merit." *Stereo Review* 46, no. 12 (December 1981), p. 118.

A review of the Orion recording. Goodfriend writes that Wuorinen "has chosen to pay careful attention to such things as lyrical melody, and thus presents us, once again, with a real piece of music rather than an admirable but arid intellectual exercise." The recording is rated "Admirable," and the performance rated "Serviceable." *See:* D23

B606 Payne, Ifan. "Guide to Records." *American Record Guide* 45, no. 8 (June 1982), pp. 25-26.

A review of the Orion recording. "Although a performance of this work might ideally require a greater variety of tonal colors and dynamic range from the violinist, [John] Ferrell is at his best in the gentleness of the fifth and sixth piece." *See:* D23

B607 Ashby, Arved. "The Chicago Ensemble Radiates Love." The *Herald* [Chicago], 7 November 1984, p. 30.

"Although the procession of logic throughout these pieces may be initially difficult to follow, Wuorinen's train of thought is really quite simple and therefore rewards close attention." *See:* W96b

B608 Rooney, Dennis. "Record Reviews." The *Strad* 100, no. 1195 (1989), p. 985.

A review of the Bridge recording. Rooney writes it was one of the two "most diverting works on the compact disk" but that the entire recording displays "[Benjamin] Hudson's amazingly versatile fiddling." *See:* D35

B609 Berrett, Joshua. "Record Reviews." *American Music* 8 (1990), p. 121-123.

A review of the Bridge recording. Berrett compares the work to Elliott Carter's *Eight Etudes and a Fantasy for Woodwind Quartet*, and writes: "Benjamin Hudson and Garrick Ohlsson are to the manner born." (p. 123) *See:* D35

Sonata for Piano

B610 Hughes, Allan. "Shapey's 'Incantations' in Debut A + Finale of Composers Forum." The *New York Times*, 24 April 1961, p. 38.

Hughes calls Douglas Nordli "an expert soloist" and says the sonata is "skillfully wrought." *See:* W14d

Sonata for Violin and Piano

B611 Roberts, Ed. "The Compelling Wuorinen Premiere." The *Washington Post*, 26 November 1988, p. C3.

A review of the premiere. "The performance, by violinist Benjamin Hudson and pianist Garrick Ohlsson, was splendid, and set an enviable standard for future and hopefully frequent performances of this fine addition to the repertoire." *See:* W98

B612 Rooney, Dennis D. "Concert Notes." The *Strad* 101 (March 1990), p. 168.

A review of the New York City premiere. Rooney calls it "music to admire but not love." *See:* W98a

B613 Wager, Gregg. "Conservative Composer Mellows a Bit." *Los Angeles Times*, 5 April 1990, p. F1, F8.

Pre-concert publicity for the West coast premiere. Includes some interview material in which Wuorinen expresses some interest in composing for films. [P] *See:* W98a

B614 Bliss, Susan. "Music Review: A Stunning Coast Debut of Sonata in Orange." *Los Angeles Times*, 7 April 1990, p. F3.

A review of the West coast premiere. "The violin-piano duo, having been coached by the composer for several days before the concert, approached the piece with busy absorption and shrewd perception, urgently drawing their listeners into the mounting excitement." *See:* W98b

Song and Dance for Piano

B615 Harrison, Jay S. "Glee Club Uses Classmate's Music." *New York Herald Tribune*, 14 May 1956.

A review of the premiere and one of the earliest concert reviews of Wuorinen's music. "Though barely out of his childhood, he [Wuorinen] has a vigorous and adult imagination, an extraordinary technique and a gift for setting down notes in patterns that are both communicative and expressive." *See:* W142

Speculum Speculi

B616 "Speculum Musicae Slates Performance." *Grand Forks Herald* [Grand Forks, North Dakota], 11 January 1973.

Pre-concert publicity concerning the premiere. The article also reports that the three-day festival will include clinics, workshops and recital demonstrations. *See:* W101

B617 Hughes, Allan. "Music: Wuorinen's 'Speculum Speculi' in Debut." The *New York Times*, 23 February 1973, p. 19.

Hughes says the piece "reveals a Wuorinen who seems to have broken the bonds that circumscribed the content, structure and expressivity of his music previously." *See:* W101a

B618 Dyer, Richard. "There's No Lady Like the Nonesuch Lady." The *New York Times*, 24 November 1974, pp. 1, 8.

This article is about Teresa Sterne who was then director of Nonesuch Records. Dyer mentions the Nonesuch recording of *Speculum Speculi* and says Sterne was dissatisfied with the degree of surface noise on that particular recording. *See:* D15

B619 ["Record Reviews."] *Rutgers Daily Telegram*, 18 December 1974.

A review of the Nonesuch recording. "With the exception of that band of avant-garde composers who drop bricks from bridges and scream a lot and who are generally beyond anarchism and closer to madness, there is no composer with as much ability to unnerve as Wuorinen." *See:* D15

B620 *Music of the Last Forty Years Not Yet Established In the Repertoire: A Survey Conducted By the Fromm Music Foundation at Harvard 1974-1975.* Cambridge, Massachusetts: The Foundation, 1975.

The survey lists *Speculum Speculi* as one of the twenty-four works by Wuorinen considered by the Fromm Music Foundation to be among the "important but neglected or infrequently performed musical works dating from the last forty years." (l. 1) *See:* W101, B891

B621 McLellan, Joseph. "Composers: An Endangered Species." The *Washington Post*, 5 January 1975, *(Book World)*, p. 4.

A review of the Nonesuch recording. "In the actual sound, this is less cerebral than it looks on paper, but the process is fascinating to the mind as well as the ears." He also says the playing and recording quality are excellent. *See:* D15

B622 Salzman, Eric. "New Music: Uptown and Downtown." *Stereo Review* 34, no. 6 (June 1975), pp. 110-111.

This article discusses what had come to be termed the "uptown" and "downtown" composers of New York City. According to Salzman, the downtown group consisted of multi-media, pop, minimalist composers; the uptown group consisted of cerebral serial composers (of which Wuorinen is considered to be one). Salzman also writes *Speculum Speculi* "has a rhythmic quality that seems to punch through the abstract note manipulation." (p. 110) *See:* W101

B623 Wells, Tildren. "Record Label Promotes Americans." *Columbus Dispatch* [Columbus, Ohio], 24 August 1975.

A review of the Nonesuch recording. Wells says the work is the most appealing on the album. *See:* D15

B624 Pangaro, Lois. "Nonesuch as Nonesuch." The *Washington Times*, 26 September - 9 October 1975.

A review of the Nonesuch recording. Pangaro says the piece is wonderful "just to listen to the magical percussion." *See:* D15

B625 Rorem, Ned. *An Absolute Gift. A New Diary.* New York: Simon and Schuster, 1978.

This book includes a brief mention of the work. "Wuorinen's *Speculum Speculi* for six disparate instruments, which, despite a certain spikiness, was also kind of charming." (p. 150) The date of the Brooklyn Academy of Music performance is not mentioned. This is one of the few positive remarks Rorem has made concerning Wuorinen's music. The book also discusses two other works by Wuorinen. Those entries were subsequently reprinted in *The Nantucket Diary of Ned Rorem*, published in 1987. *See:* W101, B903

B626 Cohn, Arthur. *Recorded Classical Music. A Critical Guided to Compositions and Performances.* New York: Schirmer Books, 1981.

A review of the Nonesuch recording. "The serial style has Wuorinen's personality stamp, meaning that the properties are interesting, the logic positively clear, and the sonorities colorful." Cohn praises the quality of the performance. *See:* D15

B627 "Music: Giving New Composers a Hearing." *Time* 23 March 1981, p. 80.

An article celebrating the tenth anniversary of the ensemble *Speculum Musicae*. It mentions that Wuorinen is one of the many composers to be commissioned by this ensemble and that *Speculum Speculi* — the work commissioned — is performed fairly frequently. *See:* W101

B628 Post, Nora. "Monophonic Sound Resources for the Oboe." *Interface* 11, no. 3 (1982), pp. 131-176.

This article describes monophonic sounds used by contemporary composers in terms of oboe technique. *Speculum Speculi* is briefly mentioned as a work in which the oboe part includes an example of pitch bending. (p. 159) *See:* W101

B629 Stadlen, Peter. "Tricks of Time." The *Daily Telegraph* [London], 21 December 1985.

The critic writes "the serial obscurantism of 'Speculum Speculi' by the 47-year old New Yorker Charles Wuorinen could not be edited out by the performance of this Sextet. Alas, there seemed to be nothing else as far as I could hear, and so I kept wondering 'why?' — a classical experience." *See:* W101b

Spinoff

B630 Dreier, Ruth. "Debuts & Reappearances: New York: Speculum Musicae." *High Fidelity/Musical America* 33, no. 9 (September 1983), p. MA30.

The reviewer says "the piece is a supremely confident, and good-humored barrage of unrelenting rhythmic and harmonic energy." Dreier also says violinist Benjamin Hudson, bassist Donald Palma and percussionist Joseph Passaro were superb and that both the piece and the performance "took the pants off the evening." *See:* W102

B631 Ericson, Raymond. "Gershwin Stars in a Display of American Musical Variety." The *New York Times*, 18 August 1985, p. 19.

This article discusses new recordings featuring American music. *Spinoff* (the Bridge recording) is mentioned as a work recorded by Speculum Musicae for their fifteenth anniversary album. [P] *See:* D32, D35

B632 Gann, Kyle. "Classicals." *Fanfare* 9, no. 4 (March/April 1986), p. 178.
A review of the Bridge recording. Gann writes East Coast academic composers are trying to find ways of making their music "palatable" to the lay audience and that *Spinoff* has "essentially elitist, theoretical origins." Gann concludes: "How much you enjoy the result will depend on whether you staunchly insist that you really *like* post-Babbitt American 12-tone music, or whether you would prefer to go to some good, honest ethnic music for your rhythmic thrills." *See:* D32, D35

B633 Berrett, Joshua. "Record Reviews." *American Music* 8 (1990), pp. 121-123.
A review of the Bridge recording. Berrett writes that the piece "is interesting mainly for the unusual instrumental combination and the interplay of rhythmic motifs." (p. 123) *See:* D32, D35

B634 Cameron, Michael. "Chamber Music: Three Trios of Charles Wuorinen." *International Society of Bassists* 16, no. 2 (Winter 1990), pp. 33-34, 36-37.
This article analyzes three works by Wuorinen (one of which is *Spinoff*) from the perspective of double-bass performance practice. Cameron writes that, like the other trios he examines, *Spinoff* "requires real virtuosos to handle the technical difficulties"; he adds the piece "has the added worry of presenting the performer with extreme rhythmic complexities." (p. 36) *See:* W102, B764, B771

String Quartet No. 1

B635 Constantine, Peggy. "Fine Arts Quartet Received Warmly." *Chicago Sun-Times*, 12 October 1971, p. 54.
A review of the premiere. "The work obviously requires more than one hearing to understand its intent, but the audience, in spite of a couple of booers, accepted it kindly enough to bring the players and the composer, who attended the premiere, onstage for four curtain calls." *See:* W104

B636 Jacobson, Bernard. "Wuorinen Quartet in Memorable Premiere by Fine Arts." *Chicago Daily News*, 12 October 1971, p. 25.
A review of the premiere. "Wuorinen is clearly not trying to write music for Everyman. But for the purposes of a fairly narrow, highly cultivated audience, it is a valuable and supremely accomplished addition to the repertoire." *See:* W104

B637 Winer, Linda. "They All Work for Wuorinen." *Chicago Tribune*, 12 October 1971, p. 3.
A review of the premiere. Winer writes that the work "has a rewarding coherence easier to find than in many of the young composer's Columbia-Princeton colleagues." *See:* W104

B638 Winer, Linda. "What He Means Is..." *Chicago Tribune*, 17 October 17, 1971, *(Arts & Fun)*, p. 5.
Another review of the premiere by the same critic. She says the quartet "uses traditional instruments in fairly traditional ways which were mostly shocking in their conventionality." *See:* W104

B639 *Music of the Last Forty Years Not Yet Established In the Repertoire: A Survey Conducted By the Fromm Music Foundation at Harvard 1974-1975.* Cambridge, Massachusetts: The Foundation, 1975.

The survey lists *String Quartet No. 1* as one of the twenty-four works by Wuorinen considered by the Fromm Music Foundation to be among the "important but neglected or infrequently performed musical works dating from the last forty years." (l. 1) *See:* W104, B891

B640 Rockwell, John. "Speculum Musicae Plays Superb Music Superbly." The *New York Times*, 14 May 1975, p. 34.
Rockwell characterizes the quartet as "the most gripping blend of piece and performance." He calls the performance by Speculum Musicae "superb." *See:* W104a

B641 Cohn, Arthur. *Recorded Classical Music. A Critical Guide to Compositions and Performances*. New York: Schirmer Books, 1981.
A review of the Turnabout recording. "The laws of artistic balance could not be better served." (p. 2111) *See:* D11

String Quartet No. 2

B642 "Contemporary Music Ruggieri's Fascinating World." *Jackson Hole Guide*, 26 July 1979, p. A14.
Pre-concert publicity about the premiere. Includes interview material with Roger Ruggieri, double-bass player and coordinator of the series *Music in the Present Tense*, of which the concert featuring the Wuorinen work is one. *See:* W105

B643 "String Quartet to Premier Charles Wuorinen Composition Tonight." *Jackson Hole News*, 1 August 1979, p. 2.
Pre-concert publicity about the premiere. The cellist of the Columbia String Quartet, André Emelianoff, is quoted: "There are so many unknowns' when you are playing a piece for the first time." He also says "there are anxieties." *See:* W105

B644 Cariaga, Daniel. "Fifth Day of Cal-Arts Festival." *Los Angeles Times*, 11 March 1980, p. 2.
A review of the West Coast premiere. Cariaga says the piece "hits the ear as music of ordered violence, transparent in texture, weighty of substance and largely humorless." *See:* W105a

B645 Horowitz, Joseph. "Music: Foss Ends Series By Offering 8 Premieres." The *New York Times*, 13 April 1980, p. 48.
A review of the New York City premiere. "What commands attention, rather than particular materials or momentary effects, is the continuing evolutionary thrust." [P] *See:* W105b

B646 Kozinn, Allan. "Group for Contemporary Music." The *New York Times*, 23 April 1991, p. 14.
"The journey Mr. Wuorinen pursues is rich in contrasts." *See:* W105c

String Quartet No. 3

B647 Crutchfield, Will. "Concert: 4 Composers' New Works." The *New York Times*, 7 January 1988, p. C28.
Crutchfield writes the piece "left that impression of something intriguing to reinvestigate." *See:* W106a

B648 Porter, Andrew. "Musical Events: Quartets." The *New Yorker*, 11 April 1988, pp. 112-114.

> Porter writes of this unspecified concert that the quartet represents Wuorinen "in an unusually intimate vein, and it strikes me as a major contribution to the string-quartet repertory." (p. 113)

B649 Roberts, Ed. "The Compelling Wuorinen Premiere." The *Washington Post*, 26 November 1988, p. C3.

> "An incredibly fresh amalgam of romantic gestures, contemporary musical language and imaginative use of colors and dynamics, it proved that serial techniques still have enormous potential to generate beauty and meaning in music." *See:* W106b

String Sextet

B650 Oestreich, James R. "The Chamber Society Seeks to Prove a Musical Point." The *New York Times*, 20 November 1989, p. C16.

> A review of the New York premiere. "At length the work gathers its energies in an animated passage of jazzy syncopations and conjunct melodies, and the clotted textures ultimately thin out to grand unisons." *See:* W107

B651 "Wuorinen Sextet Premiered." The *Instrumentalist*, 44 (February 1990), p. 49.

> The brief article does not discuss the piece itself, but says that Fred Sherry, then the Artistic Director of the Chamber Music Society of Lincoln Center, programmed the work with pieces by Wolfgang Amadeus Mozart and Johannes Brahms "so listeners could perceive the similarities in the three works." *See:* W107g

B652 Rooney, Dennis D. "Concert Notes." The *Strad* 101 (March 1990), p. 168.

> Rooney terms the performance "an elegant account of a work that explores changing sonorous combinations in a characteristically austere style." *See:* W107g

B653 Rothstein, Edward. "Contemporary Composers Reflect Oddities of the Age." The *New York Times*, 5 October 1992, p. B3.

> Rothstein says the sextet is "compelling and vigorous as well as obsessed, a 20-minute expression of fury and overflowing energy." *See:* W107h

B654 Kerner, Leighton. "Piece Work." *Village Voice*, 14 October 1992, p. 84.

> "Melodic (okay, atonally melodic) and harmonic resources, together with rhythmic strength, constitute the game here, and the playing was championship stuff." *See:* W107h

String Trio

B655 Kriegsman, Alan. "Potomac Trio Even Better Now." *Washington Post*, 28 October 1968, p. D12.

> A review of the premiere. "The trio is a strange, corrosive, disturbing composition that I found repellent at first hearing." Kriegsman goes on to say that the music does, however, warrant repeated hearings. *See:* W108

B656 Oppens, Kurt. "Berichte: New York: Speculum Musicae." *Musica* 25, no. 5 (September-October 1971), pp. 478-479.

> Oppens writes that the highlight of the evening was the performance of this trio and that the work is one of "burning intensity." *See:* W108b

B657 Fennelly, Brian. "Music Reviews." *Notes* 30, no. 2 (December 1973), pp. 346-369.
A review of the C.F. Peters edition. Fennelly provides some analytical commentary on the music, and makes the following additional remark: "For once the copyist, here Nicolas Roussakis, receives proper credit for the beauty of his craft." The score "is an unusually attractive publication of a compelling and important work." (p. 357) *See:* W108

B658 Davis, Peter G. "12 Musicians Keen in Modern Works." The *New York Times*, 29 April 1974, p. 46.
The critic calls *String Trio* "one of the composer's most eloquent statements: characteristically biting and energetic, yet consistently and deeply expressive." *See:* W108c

B659 Hamilton, David. "Musical Events: The Mirror of Man." The *New Yorker*, 6 May 1974, pp. 116-118, 121, 124.
Hamilton compares the work to Arnold Schoenberg's *String Trio, Op. 45*, which was also performed on the program. He says Wuorinen's trio is a "metrically open contest, which resolves in an astounding and beautiful slow apotheosis of the single note that began the piece." (p. 116) *See:* W108c

B660 *Music of the Last Forty Years Not Yet Established In the Repertoire: A Survey Conducted By the Fromm Music Foundation at Harvard 1974-1975.* Cambridge, Massachusetts: The Foundation, 1975.
The survey lists *String Trio* as one of the twenty-four works by Wuorinen considered by the Fromm Music Foundation to be among the "important but neglected or infrequently performed musical works dating from the last forty years." (l. 1) *See:* W108, B891

B661 Cohn, Arthur. *Recorded Classical Music. A Critical Guide to Compositions and Performances.* New York: Schirmer Books, 1981.
A review of the Nonesuch recording. "Its prodigious power, of granitic force, makes it one of the most fascinating and exciting works in the string trio literature." *See:* D16

B662 Kuchera-Morin, Joann. *Structure in Charles Wuorinen's String Trio.* (Ph.D. dissertation) Rochester, New York: Eastman School of Music, 1984.
This is the only doctoral dissertation devoted exclusively to the analysis of one of Wuorinen's works. The purpose of her analysis is "to outline aspects of Wuorinen's own musical language and, in general, to illustrate basic procedures and applications of serial composition in recent twentieth-century music." And: "The analysis uncovers an abundance of intricate cross-relations which provide the piece with a high degree of musical unity." (Abstract) *See:* W108

B663 Kisselgoff, Anna. "Dance: By Bonnefoux." The *New York Times* 7 February 1985, p. C15.
"It is an avant-garde score, and Mr. Bonnefoux used it in its entirety, playing upon the unit of three among the musicians and the dancers." *See:* W108d

B664 Kresky, Jeffrey. "The Recent Music of Charles Wuorinen." *Perspectives of New Music* 25, nos. 1-2 (1987), pp. 410-417.
String Trio is discussed in this important article. *See:* W108, B857

Symphonia Sacra

B665 Schonberg, Harold C. "Music: Concert Without Performers." The *New York Times*, 10 May 1961, p. 53.

An important review of this historic concert. Schonberg describes the composers involved as "a bunch of bright children with new, complicated toys." He mentions that *Symphonia Sacra* was performed but says nothing descriptive or critical of the work. *See:* W175a

B666 Berry, Ray. "Concerts & Recitals." The *American Organist* 44, no. 6 (June 1961). p. 25.

"For me there was a personalized yet abstract quality which was utterly fascinating; but which at the same time left me wondering if I were hearing sounds which were but effects." *See:* W175a

B667 La Rue, Jan. "An Electronic Concert in New York." The *Music Review* 22, no. 3 (August 1961), pp. 223-225.

An important review of this historic concert. "I felt more easily in touch with his [Wuorinen's] style, possibly an undesirable reaction to a piece of 'advanced' music." (p. 225) *See:* W175a

B668 Mellers, Wilfrid. *Music in a New Found Land: Themes and Developments in the History of American Music*. London: Carrie and Rockliff, 1964.

Of *Symphonia Sacra*, Mellers writes it is composed "in a style that is chromatically serial, neo-medieval, and at the same time highly, if somewhat luridly, imaginative." (p. 232) *See:* W175

B669 Luening, Otto. "An Unfinished History of Electronic Music." *Music Educators Journal* 55, no. 3 (November 1968), pp. 43-49, 135-145.

In this overview of electronic music Luening describes the inaugural concerts of the Columbia-Princeton Electronic Music Center and mentions that Wuorinen's *Symphonia Sacra* was on the program. He says the program was well received and that the daily tabloids and some music magazines considered the event "of historic importance and wrote favorably of it." (p. 141) *See:* W175a

B670 Vercoe, Barry. "Live Performance and Prerecorded Electronic Sounds Combined: A Repertoire." *Music Educators Journal* 55, no. 3 (November 1968), pp. 172-174.

This forty-title list includes *Symphonia Sacra*. *See:* W175

B671 Holmes, Thomas B. *Electronic and Experimental Music*. New York: Charles Scribner's Sons, 1985.

Holmes discusses the RCA Mark II synthesizer as well as the Columbia-Princeton Electronic Music Center. He mentions the Center's first public performance, which included the first performance of *Symphonia Sacra* with electronic tape as the organ part. *See:* W175a

Symphony No. 2

B672 "4 Works Played First Time Here." *New York Herald Tribune*, 28 February 1959, p. 6.

A review of the premiere. "One factor [that made the concert less than successful] was the astonishingly banal character of the Wuorinen piece, a pretentious patchwork of sound effects." *See:* W26

B673 Schonberg, Harold C. "Music In Making At Cooper Union." The *New York Times*, 28 February 1959, p. 12.

Schonberg says Wuorinen composed the symphony "in an angry-young-man style, with great indignant outbursts." *See:* W26

Symphony No. 3

B674 Harrison, Jay S. "Concerto for Marimba Has Premiere." *New York Herald Tribune*, 12 November 1959.

A review of the premiere. Harrison calls it "a hulking blockbuster of a piece that is rather more pretentious than it is successful." He goes on to say that Wuorinen "will ripen and develop." *See:* W28

B675 Sargeant, Winthrop. "Music Events." The *New Yorker*, 21 November 1959, pp. 208-210.

A review of the premiere. Sargeant writes that Wuorinen "is too fascinated with the chromium-plated gadgetry of modern music." (p. 209) *See:* W28

B676 Kendall, Raymond. "New York Opera and Concert Beat." *Musical Courier* [New York City] 160, no. 6 (December 1959), p. 16.

A review of the premiere. "This promising novelty had a warm reception." *See:* W28

B677 Kammerer, Rafael. "Orchestra of America Gives Second Program." *Musical America* 79, no. 14 (December 1, 1959), p. 37.

A review of the premiere. "If he makes the orchestra sound at times like the bloated 'mammoth' organs that were once so popular, his symphony is written from an original and arresting angle." *See:* W28

B678 Johnson, Thomas. "Recordings. 3 More From CRI." *Musical America* 82, no. 6 (June 1962), pp. 25-30.

A review of the CRI recording. Johnson says the work "has its share of dull moments, but it also has one of the most arresting openings of any symphony since Beethoven's *Fifth* or, at least, Brahms' *First*." *See:* D2

B679 Stone, Kurt. "Reviews of Records." *Musical Quarterly* 48, no. 3 (July 1962), pp. 409-418.

A review of the CRI recording. "It is a wild and disorderly piece, it strikes angry, rebellious poses, it takes little time out to sing or reflect, it creates a compelling atmosphere the moment it begins, and unfortunately, it also commits a fantastic offense to good taste and propriety when, at the end, it commandeers none less than Josquin des Prez to provide chunks of his touching *Déploration de Johann Ockeghem* for Mr. Wuorinen to arrange for symphony orchestra and, thus improved, to serve him as coda to the work!" (p. 414) *See:* D2

B680 Rich, Alan. "Disks: Americans." The *New York Times*, 22 July 1962, *(Arts & Leisure)*, p. 8.

 A review of the CRI recording. Rich simply calls the work "tremendously energetic" and says the recording is worth owning. *See:* D2

B681 Diether, Jack. "Other Reviews." The *American Record Guide* 29, no. 5 (January 1963), pp. 350-395.

 A review of the CRI recording. "Indeed the harsh purity of the middle renaissance seems an excellent discipline and point of departure for the emerging Wuorinen, and may have been quite catalytic in regard to his astonishing development in the short succeeding years." (p. 395) *See:* D2

B682 "Record Reviews." *American Record Guide*, 29, no. 5 (January 1963), pp. 393-395.

 A review of the CRI recording. The reviewer says the symphony "is ideal for his [Wuorinen's] debut in Schwann." *See:* D2

B683 Mellers, Wilfred. *Music in a New Found Land: Themes and Developments in the History of American Music.* London: Carrie and Rockliff, 1964.

 Mellers describes the work as "a shatteringly sensational, brash, technicolored piece that brings [Aaron] Copland, [Roy] Harris and [Wallingford] Riegger up to date with superb irreverence." (p. 232) *See:* W28

B684 Helm, Everett. "Experimentelle Musik in den USA." *Melos: Zeitschrift für neue Musik* 4, no. 3 (April 1964), pp. 123-125.

 Helm writes that Wuorinen has attracted a great deal of public attention and is considered to be one of America's best hopes for a composer. He briefly describes *Symphony No. 3. See:* W28

B685 Helm, Everett. "Experimentelle Musik in den USA." *Orchester* 12 (June 1964), pp. 208-210.

 A reprint of the same article first published in *Melos: Zeitschrift für neue Musik* in April 1964. *See:* W28, B684

B686 Chase, Gilbert. *America's New Music From the Pilgrims to the Present.* 2nd ed. rev. New York: McGraw-Hill, 1966.

 The final chapter, titled "The Scene in the Sixties," concludes with a three-page biographical and critical discussion of Wuorinen. Chase states: "Wuorinen, both by his chronological situation and his technical-temperament equipment, is the type of composer who may bring about a new creative synthesis between traditional and electronic media in musical composition. In his Third Symphony he gave ample proof of his ability to communicate in terms of traditional compositional rhetoric, which aims at direct emotional-dramatic effect." And, later: "...he may indeed assume for his generation a commanding position and prestige comparable to those achieved by the leading American composers of the three preceding generations." (pp. 690-692) Wuorinen was not discussed at all in the first edition (1955) of this book. *See:* W28, B946

B687 Klein Howard. "Records: Music Since the War." The *New York Times*, 3 March 1967, *(Arts & Leisure)*, p. D25.

 In this article Klein writes that since World War II, New York City "usurped the role formerly played by Vienna and Fountainbleau" as centers of activity for contemporary music. The CRI recording of *Symphony No. 3* is listed in Klein's discography attached to this article. *See:* D2

Tashi (Chamber Version)

B688 Smith, Patrick J. "Debuts & Reappearances: Tashi: Wuorinen Premiere." *High Fidelity/Musical America* 26, no. 6 (June 1976), p. MA28.

A review of the New York premiere. Smith offers positive comments on the work but says: "Wuorinen, as a composer, is like the little girl with the curl: he is so prolific that his output varies widely as to quality." *See:* W110b

B689 Smith, Patrick J. "Reports: New York." The *Musical Times* 1600, vol. 117 (June 1976), p. 511.

An abbreviated version of Smith's review published in *High Fidelity/Musical America* the same month. Here Smith writes the music is a "high-spirited romp, but not unlike the play of a tangle of puppies." *See:* W110b, B688

B690 Ericson, Raymond. "Music: Tashi Plays 'Tashi' Premiere." The *New York Times*, 20 February 1976, p. 22.

A review of the New York premiere. Ericson says "it would help if he [Wuorinen] gave more thought to a greater variety of texture and to a more sensuous instrumental sound than he has here." Ericson erroneously reports this performance as the world premiere. *See:* W110b

B691 Wiser, John D. "A Conversation With Peter Serkin." *Fanfare* 8, no. 1 (September/October 1984), pp. 151-155.

In this review Peter Serkin mentions his performances with the ensemble Tashi and refers to Wuorinen's work of the same name (chamber version) as one of the most important pieces the ensemble had performed. *See:* W110

Tashi (Orchestral Version)

B692 Hruby, Frank. "Critic Takes Gulp of Today's Music." The *Cleveland Press*, 14 October 1976.

A review of the premiere. "Wuorinen permitted some conventional sounds to be heard, but in such a way as to give the impression he was doing it as a bit of a joke, or perhaps a nose-thumbing exercise, or even an oversight." *See:* W29

B693 Salisbury, Wilma. "Severance Hall is Rocked by 'Tashi'." *Cleveland Plain Dealer*, 15 October 1976.

A review of the premiere. "Brilliantly organized within a tight rhythmic structure, the dramatic music assaults the ear drums, tenses the nerves and ties the stomach in knots." *See:* W29

B694 Schwartz, Elliott. "The American Bicentenary." *Soundings: A Music Journal* [Cardiff, England] 6 (1977), pp. 88-93.

This article surveys the musical activities which took place in America during the bicentennial celebration. The premiere of the orchestral version of *Tashi* is mentioned as featuring Wuorinen's "driving, complex style in a 'chamber' situation for orchestral forces." (p. 90) Schwartz also writes that "the gestural and affective materials of tonality" have become prominent in Wuorinen's music since the early 1970s. *See:* W29

Te Decet Hymnus

B695 Harrison, Jay S. "Glee Club Uses Classmate's Music." *New York Herald Tribune*, 14 May 1956.

One of the earliest reviews of Wuorinen's music. Harrison writes the piece reflects the influence of Randall Thompson, but that Wuorinen's "grasp of the materials of compositions, save that of form, might easily be the envy of any one twice his age." *See:* W176

Tiento Sobre Cabézón

B696 Bedford, Frances. "A Survey of Twentieth Century Music for Woodwinds and Harpsichord." *Woodwind-Brass & Percussion* 16, no. 4 (July 1987), pp. 24-25, 36-37, 39.

The survey mentions the work is its list of published works. *See:* W114

B697 Purswell, Joan. "20th-Century Chamber Music for Harpsichord, Part II." *Clavier* 19, no. 5 (May-June 1980), pp. 36-38.

A listing of contemporary harpsichord music; includes this piece. *See:* W114

Time's Encomium

B698 Hamilton, David. "Records." The *Nation*, 1 September 1969, p. 190.

A review of the Nonesuch recording. Hamilton says "it is by far the most sophisticated work to result from the Nonesuch Records commissioning program." *See:* D8

B699 Strongin, Theodore. "Electronic — But With Soul." The *New York Times*, 7 September 1969, p. D40.

A review of the Nonesuch recording. Strongin writes the music "often bombards the nerve endings with high-tension particles of sound." [P] *See:* D8

B700 Kolodin, Irving. "Recordings Reports II: Miscellaneous. LPs." *Saturday Review*, September 27, 1969, p. 60.

A review of the Nonesuch recording. "The interest it arouses for me is in Wuorinen's refined sense of sonorities, which makes for a mingling of timbres with a fair range of fascination on their own." *See:* D8

B701 Winer, Linda. "Wuorinen's 'Time's Encomium'—Sound for the Mind and Ear." *Chicago Tribune*, 12 October 1969, *(Section 5)*, p. 6.

A review of the Nonesuch recording. "By processing the clearly-pitched synthesized sounds with reverberations, and by combining these sounds with superb stereo engineering, the composer has created a kind of musical Doppler effect with sounds coming toward and leaving the listener in many directions." Winer mistakenly says that Wuorinen is a painter as well as a composer. *See:* D8

B702 Daniel, Oliver. "If It Pleases." *Saturday Review*, 29 November 1969, pp. 71, 84.

A review of the Nonesuch recording. "It is all precisely calculated as a project in rocketry." (p. 84) [P] *See:* D8

B703 Wilson, Galen. "Reviews." The *Composer* [United States] 1, no. 4 (1970), pp. 170-171.
A review of the Nonesuch recording. Galen describes the work as "a lengthy piece (both sides LP) — post Webernish, pointillistic, contrived and 'old hat'." (p. 170) *See:* D8

B704 "Electronic Music." The *Gramophone* 47 (April 1970), p. 1644.
A review of the Nonesuch recording. "Wuorinen has pursued an extreme eclecticism, and here again one has the impression of a gifted young American composer." *See:* D8

B705 "Wuorinen Is Awarded Pulitzer Music Prize." *Gardner News* [Gardner, Massachusetts], 5 May 1970, p. 1.
An announcement that Wuorinen won the Pulitzer Prize for *Time's Encomium*. [P] *See:* W159

B706 "Kultuuri: Pulitzerin palinko My Lain paljastajalle." *Helsingen Sanomat Arkisto*, 6 May 1970, p. 18.
Titled "Pulitzer Prize for the Exposer of My Lai," this *New York Times* dispatch (in Finnish) includes a mention of Wuorinen having won the Pulitzer Prize for Music, for *Time's Encomium*. *See:* W159

B707 "The Pulitzer Awards." The *New York Times*, 6 May 1970, p. 48.
This announcement on the editorial page includes a very brief mention of Wuorinen's award. *See:* W159

B708 "Suomalaissyntyinen Pulitzer-voittaja." *Helsingen Sanomat Arkisto*, 7 May 1970.
An article discussing *Time's Encomium* and the Pulitzer Prize for music. It also includes material on Wuorinen's father, John Wuorinen. *See:* W159

B709 "Persistence Pays Off for a Reporter In the Annual Pulitzer Prize." The *National Observer, 11 May 1970, p. 17.*
An announcement of the 1970 Pulitzer Prizes, including: "Music — Charles Wuorinen for his work, Time's Encomium, played on the electronic synthesizer." *See:* W159

B710 "Electronic Work Wins Pulitzer Music Prize." *Variety*, 13 May 1970, p. 55.
An announcement that *Time's Encomium* won the Pulitzer Prize for music. *See:* W159

B711 "Charles Wuorinen: 'Work Toward Permanence'." *Entertainment World* [Hollywood, California], 15 May 1970, pp. 6-7.
A discussion of Wuorinen winning the Pulitzer Prize for music for *Time's Encomium*. The writer says: "Wuorinen says he wasn't surprised by the announcement, and seems genuinely unimpressed by the award." (p. 7) In talking about the RCA Mark II synthesizer, Wuorinen is quoted as having said: "I think it's really pathetic that we find it so enticing that we can get a machine to do moderately well what humans have been able to do exquisitely for hundreds of years." (p. 7) *See:* W159

B712 Pei, Emil. "Electronic Music Wins A Pulitzer." *Des Moines Register* [Des Moines, Iowa], 30 May 1970, p. 16.

This article describes *Time's Encomium* and mentions the Pulitzer Prize. The writer states: "Electronic music in the United States has outgrown its troublesome adolescent years and now has graduated to adulthood." *See:* W159

B713 *Electronic Music Special. BMI [Broadcast Music, Inc.]: The Many Worlds of Music* (Summer 1970), 46 p.

This issue of the regularly published BMI organ features several articles on electronic music as well as a discography of music composed in that medium. Wuorinen is mentioned several times, especially in terms of having won the Pulitzer Prize for *Time's Encomium. See:* D8

B714 "Awards/Contests." *Music & Artists* [New York City] 3, no. 3 (June-July 1970), p. 46.

Includes a brief mention of Wuorinen winning the Pulitzer Prize for music for *Time's Encomium.* Also featured is this comment: "A short discussion took place at the April 9 Advisory Board on the Pulitzer Prizes meeting on 'whether a computer could compose,' but the 13-member board decided to endorse the jury's recommendation." [P] *See:* W159

B715 Anderson, William. "Editorially Speaking: 'Bum, Beep, Deetely Doot.'" *Stereo Review* 25, no. 1 (July 1970), p. 4.

This editorial discusses Wuorinen's having won the Pulitzer Prize for *Time's Encomium.* Anderson mentions that Vermont C. Royster, Editor of The *Wall Street Journal* and a Pulitzer advisory board member, said at the judging session *Time's Encomium* "goes something like this: bum, beep, deetly doot" and that his impromptu comment gave Wuorinen's piece "the nod." Anderson concludes with a comment about the importance of Nonesuch Records: "This Pulitzer prize may be signalling the recording medium's long-overdue declaration of independence from the concert hall." *See:* D8

B716 "Charles Wuorinen Wins Pulitzer Prize." The *New England Conservatory of Music Alumni News* 2, no. 2 (July 1970), p. 8.

A brief article discussing *Time's Encomium;* it includes biographical information on Wuorinen. (At the time this article was written Wuorinen was teaching part-time at the New England Conservatory.) *See:* D8

B717 Henahan, Donal. "Pianist Adds Soul to Electronic Fete." The *New York Times*, 2 December 1970, p. 57.

Henahan states the hearing was under optimal conditions "in the theater's 360 degree sound." *See:* W159f

B718 Ewen, David. *Composers of Tomorrow's Music.* New York: Dodd, Mead & Company, 1971.

Time's Encomium is discussed in terms of having won the Pulitzer Prize for music. Ewen concludes his two paragraphs on Wuorinen by writing: "But he has unbounded faith in the future of electronic music, and specifically for music produced on the Mark II Synthesizer." (p. 133) *See:* W159

B719 "Panel Discussion: The Nature of Continuity in Music." *Proceedings of the Sixth Annual Conference, April 1971*. American Society of University Composers 6, pp. 49-82.

This discussion, published in print form in these proceedings, was chaired by Benjamin Boretz. The participants were Harold Oliver, Barney Childs, and Charles Whittenberg. Whittenberg, in presenting his paper, states: "The followers of both Arnold Schönberg and John Cage are musical conservatives, if indeed they wish to extend and transform the possibilities present in both open and closed systems." A footnote to this sentence reads: "The editor has been informed by the author that, at the time of this lecture, he had not completed analytical studies of what he now believes to be four tradition-transforming and system-preserving masterpieces: [Pierre] Boulez' *Pli Selon Pli*, George Crumb's *Of Time and the River*, Charles Wuorinen's *Time's Encomium*, and Benjamin Britten's (1958!) *Nocturne*. 'The death of [Igor] Stravinsky,' writes Professor Whittenberg, 'almost paralyzed my entire musical activity for several months.'" (p. 70) *See:* W159

B720 Cloud, David. "The Classical Touch." *Free Press* [Los Angeles], 27 August 1971, p. 48.

A review of the Nonesuch recording. Cloud writes that the piece "might be termed a conservative avant-garde piece (if that's not too severe a contradiction in terms)." *See:* D8

B721 Chasins, Abram. *Music at the Crossroads*. New York: MacMillan, 1972.

The chapter on sound recordings contains a reference to Wuorinen in which the composer refers to the "suicidal unawareness" of recording the same musical works again and again for fifty years. (pp. 162-163) The chapter "Straws in the Wind" contains a reference to the Columbia-Princeton Electronic Music Center's tenth anniversary celebration. Chasins writes: "The occasion was notable not alone for the fact that Charles Wuorinen's *Time's Encomium* was awarded the first Pulitzer music prize ever bestowed on a purely electronic composition, but also for proof positive that electronic music is a firmly established part of every aspect of our musical life." (p. 186) *See:* D8

B722 Russcol, Herbert. *The Liberation of Sound. An Introduction to Electronic Music*. Englewood Cliffs, New Jersey: Prentice-Hall, 1972.

Wuorinen is discussed six times in the book, especially in terms of his work at the Columbia-Princeton Electronic Music Center. Russcol also reviews the Nonesuch recording: "From the evidence of this recording, Wuorinen ranks as one of the few composers who have succeeded in mastering the secrets of that notoriously complex leviathan [the RCA MARK II synthesizer]." (p. 232) "Wuorinen is one of the new breed of young composers who move with ease and assurance from compositions for live performers to electronic works; in *Time's Encomium* he has delivered a satisfying, provocative example of what electronic music can be in the hands of a capable and thoroughly musical composer." (p. 233) Russcol also calls Nonesuch Records "the Count Esterhazy of contemporary music." (p. 233) *See:* D8

B723 Hopkins, G.W. "Records: Nonesuch Finds." *New Statesman* [London], 11 February 1972.

A review of the Nonesuch recording. Hopkins says the piece "offers itself more readily as a delightful introduction to the world of synthesized sound, whose increasing flexibility as a medium is still not sufficiently recognised." *See:* D8

B724 Schwartz, Elliott. *Electronic Music: A Listener's Guide*. New York: Praeger, 1973.

Wuorinen is mentioned six times. In the section titled "The Musical Past, 1906-60," Schwartz writes: "All composers learn from one another; Wuorinen has learned as much from [Anton von] Webern as, say, [Johannes] Brahms learned from [Ludwig van] Beethoven or [Robert] Schumann from [Johann Sebastian] Bach." (p. 36) The section titled "The Musical Present, 1960-70" includes a paragraph that describes Wuorinen as follows: "He's now a leading figure among the younger American composers, best known for his ability to extract the maximum dramatic thrust from a self-restricted body of material. Like [Milton] Babbitt, he prefers to retain control over all relationships, although the surface gestures of his work are more extroverted; his earlier music is, in fact, often highly charged and intense in a manner reminiscent of [Edgard] Varèse." (p. 136) The same section of the book mentions *Time's Encomium* as "another milestone in the history of electronic music." (p. 136) Featured in the book is a partial reprint of Wuorinen's "Towards Good Vibrations," originally published in the journal *Prose*. *See:* W159

B725 Mayer, Martin. "Recordings." *Esquire*, July 1973, pp. 14, 22, 33.

A general article about Wuorinen and other contemporary composers. It mentions that *Time's Encomium* had been commissioned by Nonesuch Records and had won a Pulitzer Prize for music. Wuorinen discusses his views about performing for a university audience as opposed to performing for the public. Mayer concludes: "Because Wuorinen considers himself a radical (though he isn't), this department happily awards him a Right On! with oak cluster." (p. 33) *See:* D8

B726 *The Development and Practice of Electronic Music.* Jon H. Appleton and Ronald C. Perera, eds. Englewood Cliffs, New Jersey: Prentice-Hall, Inc., 1975.

The book mentions Wuorinen several times in relation to *Time's Encomium* and the Columbia-Princeton Electronic Music Center. Includes a reprint (pages 135-136) of most of Wuorinen's container notes on the same piece for the Nonesuch recording. *See:* D8

B727 *Music of the Last Forty Years Not Yet Established In the Repertoire: A Survey Conducted By the Fromm Music Foundation at Harvard, 1974-1975.* Cambridge, Massachusetts: The Foundation, 1975.

The survey lists *Time's Encomium* as one of the twenty-four works by Wuorinen considered by the Fromm Music Foundation to be among the "important but neglected or infrequently performed musical works dating from the last forty years." (l. 1) *See:* W159, B891

B728 Schuller, Gunther. "Amerikas Avantgarde — zwischen Tradition und Experiment." *Oesterreichische Musikzeitschrift* 31 (October 1976), pp. 482-489.

Schuller describes Wuorinen as a productive American composer who possesses a pure technique and stark intellectual talent. He also writes that *Time's Encomium* is evidence of Wuorinen's master composer status. *See:* W159

B729 Cope, David. *New Music Composition.* New York: Schirmer Books, 1977.
Time's Encomium is listed as a work for analysis. *See:* W159

B730 Ernst, David. *The Evolution of Electronic Music.* New York: Schirmer Books, 1977.

The book includes a brief discussion of *Time's Encomium*: "As [Milton] Babbitt did with the Mark II synthesizer, Wuorinen developed many instrumental-type timbres, particularly the keyboardlike sounds of the piano, harpsichord, and organ. The electronic synthesis of instrumental timbres was one direction taken by composers working primarily with synthesizers." (p. 77) *See:* W159

B731 Davidson, Jerry. "The Evolution of Electronic Music." *Clavier* 16, no. 8 (November 1977), pp. 18-19.
    A brief article on the evolution of electronic music; mentions the Nonesuch recording of *Time's Encomium* as a work that can help musicians become familiar with the medium. *See:* D8

B732 Schwartz, Elliott. "Electronic Music: A Thirty-Year Retrospective." *Music Educators Journal* 64, no. 7 (March 1978), pp. 37-41.
    This survey mentions Wuorinen as an important twentieth century composer and reviews the Nonesuch recording: "He [Wuorinen] is concerned with fine degrees of articulation and ways of producing subtle, quasi-human rubato in electronically manufactured phrases." (p. 41) *See:* D8

B733 Austin, Larry. "New Romanticism: An Emerging Aesthetic for Electronic Music, Part Two." *Mundus Artium* 12 & 13 (1980 & 1981), pp. 206-212.
    A brief article discussing the contexts and styles of electronic music composition. *Time's Encomium* is mentioned as having been the first exclusively electronic work to have won the Pulitzer Prize. *See:* W159

B734 Cohn, Arthur. *Recorded Classical Music. A Critical Guide to Compositions and Performances.* New York: Schirmer Books, 1981.
    A review of the Nonesuch recording. "*Time's Encomium* has pitch and intervallic, chordal, and temporal lineation, rather than the assorted punctuations, tidal tremolos, and explosive tidbits heard in the average electronic score." (p. 2112) *See:* D8

B735 Cope, David. H. *New Directions in Music.* 3rd ed. Dubuque, Iowa: William C. Brown Co., 1981.
    Wuorinen has an entry in the biographical appendix as well as two bibliographical references. The section on electronic music includes a brief paragraph on *Time's Encomium. See:* W159, B738, B950

B736 Schrader, Barry. *Introduction to Electro-Acoustic Music.* Englewood Cliffs, New Jersey: Prentice-Hall, Inc., 1982.
    The chapter titled "Electronic Music Synthesizers" lists *Time's Encomium* as a work in the "For Further Listening" list and includes a brief description of it. (p. 148) *See:* D8

B737 Boulanger, Richard. "Interview with Roger Reynolds, Joji Yuasa, and Charles Wuorinen." *Computer Music Journal* 8, no. 4 (Winter 1984), pp. 45-54.
    This interview took place on 9 March 1984 at the University of California, San Diego (Center for Music Experiment). Wuorinen was in residence finishing the computer-generated tape portion of *Bamboula Squared.* Boulanger's questions were about tape music, use of space, interaction with sound, use of metaphor and randomness, limiting synthesis possibilities, unpredictable algorithms, music and science, and commercial music technology. Boulanger also asked what is was like to work with the RCA Mark II synthesizer. Wuorinen replied: "I think enough rust has probably accumulated on that machine by this point that one can say without any fear of damaging

anyone that working on it was a perfect nightmare." (p. 48) Wuorinen then described in specific terms how the synthesizer worked and how tweezers were required to straighten out bent brushes that made contact with a metal roller over which passed paper with punched holes. He also stated: "When I began to use the machine I restricted both my rhythmic and timbral expectations to a very limited palette because I knew that I would be spending the rest of my life there if I didn't. This explains why the entirety of *Time's Encomium* is not synthesized. Only the core material of the composition is. This core was then subjected to much looser kinds of analog studio transformations." (p. 48) *See:* W4, W159, B899

B738 Cope, David H. *New Directions in Music.* 4th ed. Dubuque, Iowa: William C. Brown Co., 1984.

Includes several references to Wuorinen — bibliographical, biographical (in Appendix II) and some brief discussion of *Time's Encomium* as in the third edition. *See:* W159, B735, B950

B739 Holmes, Thomas B. *Electronic and Experimental Music.* New York: Charles Scribner's Sons, 1985.

The discography includes *Time's Encomium.* Holmes writes that "Wuorinen's chief contribution in this piece was the freedom with which he varied the temporal scale and rhythm of the music with the ease and complex control that is intrinsic to the medium." (p. 225) *See:* D8

B740 Manning, Peter. *Electronic and Computer Music.* Oxford, England: Oxford University Press, 1985.

Manning discusses *Time's Encomium* as probably the most important work to come from the Columbia-Princeton Electronic Music Center during the 1960s. *See:* W159

B741 Mason. R.M. *Modern Methods of Music Analysis Using Computers.* Peterborough, New Hampshire: Schoolhouse Press, 1985.

This textbook "describes a simple means of utilizing a digital computer to analyze music." (Preface) The introductory section of the book includes this statement: "Although much of today's music, its impact dulled a bit by many more striking achievements of the space age, sometimes tries to compensate with programmed cacophony for what it still lacks in inspiration, once in awhile in the realm of electronic music can be heard an incipient strength or a nascent grace that could foreshadow the rebirth of true musical majesty." (pp. 2-3) Mason then states *Time's Encomium* is an excellent example of such a work. *See:* W159

B742 Slawson, Wayne. *Sound Color.* Berkeley: University of California Press, 1985.

The chapter titled "Musical Evidence: Sound Color in Electronic Music," includes a brief reference to *Time's Encomium*: "Almost any electronic piece that has a 'note-like' character — from 'switched-on' versions of instrumental music to pieces like Wuorinen's *Time's Encomium* (1969) — contain passages with filters used in this way [color as a factor in contrapuntal differentiation]." (p. 170) *See:* W159

B743 Simms, Bryan R. *Music of the Twentieth Century: Style and Structure.* New York: Schirmer Books, 1986.

The chapter titled "Electronic Music" mentions *Time's Encomium*: "The work, over half an hour in duration, uses the twelve tempered pitch classes and serialized structures favored by [Milton] Babbitt. But it relies more heavily upon sonorous effects.

Synthesized sounds, for example, alternate with the same passages electronically modified, most obviously by the addition of reverberation." (p. 389) *See:* W159

B744 Tawa, Nicholas. *A Most Wondrous Babble: American Art Composers, Their Music, and the American Scene, 1950-1985.* Westport, Connecticut: Greenwood Press, 1987.

This book is volume 9 in the publisher's series *Contributions to the Study of Music and Dance.* Tawa makes the following comment about *Time's Encomium*: "The composition can be interesting to hear if the listener has an interest in unusual sound combinations. At times purely electronic sound bursts or less strident bleeps come through the speakers; at times the simulated tones of a music instrument, particularly of the vibraphone, take over. Familiarity produces the strange effect of not remembering the actual music but of being able to anticipate the general effect of specific spots in the music." (p. 99) *See:* W159

B745 Watkins, Glen. *Soundings: Music in the Twentieth Century.* New York: Schirmer Books, 1988.

The section titled "The Quest for New Sounds" includes this statement: "By the time Charles Wuorinen's *Time's Encomium* (1969) had won a Pulitzer Prize in 1970, the natural compatibility of well-tempered dodecaphonic serialism had been forcefully demonstrated. Various types of electronic music had not only come of age but had, apparently, settled into a comfortable niche of respectability." (p. 599) *See:* W159

B746 Austin, Larry and Thomas Clark. *Learning to Compose. Modes, Materials and Models of Musical Invention.* Dubuque, Iowa: William C. Brown Co., 1989.

This textbook on composition uses *Time's Encomium* as the first example following this statement: "The great importance of time in the image of a musical work, especially in contemporary styles, is suggested by the number of pieces referring to time in their titles." (p. 131) *See:* W159

B747 Schwarz, K. Robert. "An American Sampler. Part II: Arnold Schoenberg and the Twelve-Tone School." *Ovation* 10 (March 1989), pp. 20-22.

An article about Schoenberg's twelve-tone system, how it was extended by Milton Babbitt, and the precision that electronics can bring to serial music. *Time's Encomium* is mentioned as being "uncharacteristic of Wuorinen's output as a whole, which has been predominantly for acoustical instruments." (p. 22) *See:* W159

Trio for Bass Instruments

B748 Page, Tim. "Concert: Styles Sampler By New Music Consort." *The New York Times*, 17 April 1983, p. 54.

A review of the premiere. Page calls it "a good-humored growl of a work that brought the house down." *See:* W116

B749 Porter, Andrew. "Musical Events: Feast of Reason, Flow of Soul." *The New Yorker*, 2 May 1983, p. 96.

A review of the premiere. "It is eight minutes of lively, diverting Stravinskian play — not an important piece but an attractive one, and lighter in touch than the forces involved would suggest." *See:* W116

B750 Ward, Charles. "Composer Prefers to Let Music Speak for Itself." *Houston Chronicle*, 11 May 1990.

Ward writes the musicians "tried to give slow-speaking instruments the same dexterity as high-pitched ones." *See:* W116a

B751 Cameron, Michael. "Chamber Music: Three Trios of Charles Wuorinen." *International Society of Bassists* 16, no. 2 (Winter 1990), pp. 33-34, 36-37.

This article analyzes several trios by Wuorinen. Of the *Trio for Bass Instruments*, Cameron writes: "This work presents the bass in a positive, virtuosic role with not a single gesture being unplayable." (p. 36) *See:* W116, B634, B771

Trio [No. 1 for Flute, Cello and Piano]

B752 "Welt der Musik: Zwei Komponisten-Ehrungen." *Aufbau* [New York City], 28 December 1962.

Titled "Two Composers Honors," this article is about the 60th birthday concert that honored Stefan Wolpe. Of Wuorinen's *Trio*, the reviewer says the music "is inclined to express strong contrasts through rigorously worked ideas." *See:* W118c

Trio No. 2 for Flute, Cello and Piano

B753 Schonberg, Harold C. "Music: Wired for Sound." The *New York Times*, 7 May 1963, p. 47.

A review of the premiere. Schonberg calls Wuorinen an "angry young-old man" and says the trio was "extremely boring." This comment is virtually identical to Schonberg's comment on Wuorinen's *Symphony No. 2*, which he had reviewed in the same tabloid on 28 February 1959. *See:* W119, B673

B754 Cott, Jonathan. "Electronic Music: How Many Flutes Was That?" *Columbia Daily Spectator* [New York City], 9 May 1963.

A review of the premiere. "Wuorinen does not indulge himself in sentimental or mellow heartbreak. His music courageously propels itself forward without forfeiting intense musical feelings and challenges us to an acceptance of these feelings by its insistent and imposing distinction." *See:* W119

B755 Ericson, Raymond. "Concert Offers Young Composers." The *New York Times*, 22 May 1963, p. 37.

Ericson calls the piece "wildly turbulent" and writes: "Using extremes of sounds from the three instruments, the music was sometimes brilliant, sometimes gossamer in quality. It was never dull." *See:* W119c

B756 Gruen, John. "And Now Music to Set One's Teeth on Edge." *New York Herald Tribune*, 22 May 1963, p. 16.

"The Trio contains passages of electrifying momentum — wild rhythmic convolutions that set one's teeth on edge, a kind of hysteria suggesting the inner torments of someone deranged. It is music written as if the composer were possessed of the very devil himself." *See:* W119c

B757 Stone, Kurt. "Current Chronicle." *Musical Quarterly* 49, no. 3 (July 1963), pp. 358-383.

A review of the premiere. "With these fine characteristics [relentless emotional drive, musical imagination and sincerity, technical resourcefulness] went his [Wuorinen's]

equally customary tendency towards overdoing things, of writing more notes and inventing more ecstatic musical gestures than are needed to make a point." (p. 373) *See:* W119

B758 Tate, Lisa. "Music Review: From Haydn to 'Radical' In the Carriage Barn." *Bennington Evening Banner* [Bennington, Vermont], 19 August 1963, p. 5.

"His [Wuorinen's] was the only true radical piece of contemporary music on the program, and, like it or not, the only piece that gave the listener a taste of things to come." *See:* W119e

B759 Salzman, Eric. "Smuggled Avant-Garde — Music the Soviet Bars." *New York Herald Tribune*, 14 March 1964.

Salzman says the piece "is one of the composer's best works, wild Wuorinen, vehement, strong, action music, a universe of possibilities and realizations opened up in its driving, carefully free construction of dynamic and linear intersections." *See:* W119f

B760 "Music Festival Set Feb 10." The *Colorado Daily* [Boulder, Colorado], 7 February 1967, p. 2

Pre-concert publicity for the second Festival of Contemporary Music held in Boulder, 10-17 February 1967. Wuorinen and Harvey Sollberger both appeared in concert. An open rehearsal of *Trio No. 2* took place on 15 February. *See:* W119g

B761 Burge, David. "Toward A Higher Standard of Performance." *American Society of University Composers. Proceedings of the Third Annual Conference, April, 1968 and the Second Summer Institute in Compositional Studies* 3 (August 1968) pp. 64-73.

Burge's lecture, presented in print form in these proceedings, discusses various aspects of contemporary music performance practice. Burge mentions *Trio No. 2* as a work that requires intense rehearsal and excellent young players. *See:* W119

B762 Porter, Andrew. "Musical Events: Further Events." The *New Yorker*, 10 December 1979, pp. 192-206.

Porter writes about an unspecified concert honoring the oboist Josef Marx, at which the *Trio No. 2* was played. He says the piece was one of several that "even to someone who had not known Marx and his circle, seemed to draw the portrait of an enthusiastic, lovable, and inspiring musician." (p. 206)

B763 Von Rhein, John. "Manhattan Ensemble Satisfies in Ravinia Debut." *Chicago Tribune*, 1 September 1991, *(Tempo)*, p. 4.

The reviewer says the music "suggests highly charged particles of sound hurtling through space." *See:* W119j

Trio No. 3 for Flute, Cello and Piano

B764 Rockwell, John. "Charles Wuorinen, Harvey Sollberger at Cultural Center." The *New York Times*, 30 March 1973, p. 26.

A review of the premiere. "One was conscious of a remarkable number of ingenious devices operating at several levels, most notably a complex juxtaposition of tempos for the three instruments." *See:* W120

Triptych

B765 Parmenter, Ross. "Music: In Our Time." The *New York Times*, 20 January 1958, p. 18.
A review of the premiere. The critic describes the scoring and says "the 19-year-old composer skillfully used the unusual sonorities for genuinely expressive purposes." *See:* W121

B766 Hughes, Allan. "Shapey's 'Incantations' in Debut At Finale of Composers Forum." The *New York Times*, 24 April 1961, p. 38.
Hughes praises pianist Douglas Nordli's piano technique. (In this piece, the pianist is required to use mallets directly on the piano strings.) Hughes also says Wuorinen is a gifted young composer. *See:* W121b

Turetzky Pieces

B767 Bernheimer, Martin. "Chamber Music Is Played at Living Theater." *New York Herald Tribune*, 8 October 1960.
The critic says the work "had original thematic ideas that got lost in occasionally muddy instrumental textures." *See:* W123b

B768 Sabin, Robert. "Living Theatre Presents Works By Young Composers." *Musical America* 80, no. 13 (December 1960), p. 82.
A review of the New York premiere. "Of all the composers on the program, Mr. Wuorinen exhibited the most technical surety and powers of organization. But unfortunately, his music did not sound nearly as impressive as his program note." *See:* W123b

B769 Glackin, William C. "Arts In Review: Bassist Delights." The *Sacramento Bee*, 1 June 1972. p. D8.
"[The pieces] have a bright charm and strongly melodic character that speaks for an authoritative talent." *See:* W123f

B770 Turetzky, Bertram. *The Contemporary Contrabass*. Rev. ed. Berkeley: University of California Press, 1989.
The chapter titled "Harmonics" contains an excerpt from *Turetzky Pieces* with the following comment: "Wuorinen's well-conceived polyphonic texture, a colorful mix of natural and artificial harmonics, plus an occasional stopped note, produces an absolutely unique texture that is quite evocative of early instruments." (pp. 126-127) *See:* W123

B771 Cameron, Michael. "Chamber Music: Three Trios of Charles Wuorinen." *International Society of Bassists* 16, no. 2 (Winter 1990), pp. 33-34, 36-37.
This article analyzes several trios by Wuorinen. Of this work, Cameron writes: "Most composers would be happy to claim this fine work as a point of their careers, and the fact that Wuorinen penned the *Turetzky Pieces* at such a tender age is monument to his skill and imagination." (p. 34) *See:* W124, B634, B764

Twang

B772 Kozinn, Allan. "New York New Music Ensemble." The *New York Times*, 20 October 1992, p. C14.
    Kozinn merely says the work is "a short, appealing setting" of a section of a Wallace Stevens poem. *See:* W184

Twelve Short Pieces

B773 "Charles Wuorinen: Twelve Short Pieces." *Clavier* 19 (October 1980), p. 46.
    A brief review of the C.F. Peters edition. The work is merely described as a "splendid collection" for people interested in twelve-tone compositions. *See:* W144

B774 Wiseman, Steve. *Contemporary American Piano Music for the Beginning Student: A Study of Selected Composers and Materials.* (M.A. thesis) Kirksville, Missouri: Northeast Missouri State University, 1981.
    A study of "pedagogical problems related to the study of beginning contemporary piano literature." [Abstract] The thesis includes an analysis of the first piece from *Twelve Short Pieces* for piano. Wiseman states: "Although this piece is quite short, the more intellectually-minded student may appreciate the compactness of the work and its interpretive complexity." (p. 84) *See:* W144

B775 *Twentieth Century Music Scores.* Ed. Thomas DeLio and Stuart Saunders Smith. Englewood Cliffs, New Jersey: Prentice Hall, 1989.
    An anthology presenting "a generous selection of scores by many of the most important composers of European and American music of the twentieth century." (p. vii) The anthology includes pieces No. 3 and No. 11 from the *Twelve Short Pieces*. *See:* W144

Two-Part Symphony

B776 Henahan, Donal. "'Two-Part Symphony' in a Debut." The *New York Times*, 12 December 1978, p. 8.
    A review of the premiere. "The result was often what might be called a panchromatic grayness, if the idea can be allowed." *See:* W30

B777 Porter, Andrew. "Musical Events: Intuitions." The *New Yorker*, 15 January 1979, pp. 94-96.
    A review of the premiere. Porter says the piece impressed him "as being one of Wuorinen's larger but not one of his 'major' or most intensely imagined compositions." (p. 94) *See:* W30

B778 Wechsler, Bert. "Classical: Live: New York." *Music Journal* 37, no. 2 (February 1979), p. 41.
    A review of the premiere. "Even though it began with a 'ylem,' it turned out to be well put together, if busy, with a driving force and respect for both instruments and sonorities." *See:* W30

B779 Ericson, Raymond. "Music Notes: With An American Accent." The *New York Times*, 28 October 1979, *(Arts & Leisure)*, p. D21.

A brief article about the American Composers Orchestra. Ericson mentions that a new recording of a work by Wuorinen *(Two-Part Symphony)* is due to be released by Composers Recordings, Inc. *See:* D22

B780 "Music Is Clear, Complex." *Los Alamos Monitor* [Los Alamos, New Mexico], 31 January 1980, p. B-2.
A review of the CRI recording. "Wuorinen's music always seems to become so involved with its own complexity that it forgets to perform for the listener, and this is no exception." *See:* D22

B781 "New Noteworthy Recordings." The *Kansas City Star* [Kansas City, Missouri], 17 February 1980.
A review of the CRI recording. The reviewer says he liked the *Two-Part Symphony* for "its perky rhythms and invigorating contrasts." *See:* D22

B782 Davis, Peter G. "A Vivid Rendering Of a Modern Opera." The *New York Times*, 24 February 1980, p. D20.
A review of the CRI recording. Davis says the work "is wholly characteristic in its coiled-spring intensity, propulsive energy and gestural precision." *See:* D22

B783 Tircuit, Heuwell. "Classical Records." *San Francisco Sunday Examiner and Chronicle*, 9 March 1980, *(This World)*, p. 39.
A review of the CRI recording. "There is a totally unexpected series of hints at Roger Sessions' style — serial, but not doctrinaire." *See:* D22

B784 Monson, Karen. "Classical Reviews." *High Fidelity* 30, no. 4 (April 1980), pp. 75-102.
A review of the CRI recording. "Understandable as it is that such a switch in style could cause an identity crisis, one must conclude that the newly tamed composer still hasn't found a way to purr differently from anyone else." (p. 82) Monson also praises the performances of Dennis Russell Davies and the American Composers Orchestra. *See:* D22

B785 Salzman, Eric. "John Cage." *Stereo Review* 44, no. 4 (April 1980), pp. 124-126, 128, 131.
A review of the CRI recording. "Wuorinen, like many other composers of his generation, is working closer to the tradition all the time. For better or worse, this music sounds like updated [Paul] Hindemith." (p. 124) Salzman goes on to write that the *Two-Part Symphony* is impressively performed and well recorded. *See:* D22

B786 Shupp, Enos E. "Symphonic." The *New Records*, 48, no. 2 (April 1980), pp. 3-4.
A review of the CRI recording. Shupp writes that the piece "is like a coiled spring, full of tension and very busy, with piquant scoring spiced with tuned percussion." (p. 3) *See:* D22

B787 ["Record Reviews."] *Daily Press* [Newport News, Virginia], 10 April 1980.
A review of the CRI recording. The reviewer says Wuorinen possesses "superb craftsmanship" and that the music "mixes modernistic beauty with harshness." *See:* D22

B788 Sargent, David. "What's News, What's Coming: Music." *Vogue* May 1980, p. 70.

> A review of the CRI recording. Sargent calls the *Two-Part Symphony* "driving and exciting" and says it is somewhat reminiscent of Igor Stravinsky's music. *See:* D22

B789 Grueninger, Walter F. "Recorded Music in Review." *Consumer's Research Magazine*, (July 1980), p. 43.

> A review of the CRI recording. "It's highly charged music not difficult to grasp." *See:* D22

B790 Rapoport, Paul. "Guide to Records." *American Record Guide* 43, no. 9 (July/August 1980), p. 20.

> A review of the CRI recording. "Most of the symphony's gestures are short and punctuate each other in a constant interplay which is hard to follow at first but yields more on each hearing." Rapoport also praises the quality of the performance. *See:* D22

B791 Terry, Kenneth. "Record Reviews: John Cage/Charles Wuorinen." *Downbeat* 47, no. 10 (October 1980), p. 44.

> A review of the CRI recording. "Indeed, despite the unfailingly well-balanced ensemble effects in this work, one suspects that the continually shifting, syncopated rhythms camouflage the composer's lack of anything to say." Terry praises the performers and gives the recording four stars (a rating of *very good*). *See:* D22

B792 Canby, Edward. T. ["Record Reviews."] *Audio* 64 (December 1980), pp. 87-88.

> A review of the CRI recording. Canby calls the *Two-Part Symphony* "a mature and ripe work of its sort" and says: "What counts in a general way, is the sonic impact, and here this music excels." (p. 88) *See:* D22

B793 Shere, Charles. "Conductor Davies Makes Excellent Bow in S.F." *Tribune* [Oakland, California], 19 November 1981, p. D-3.

> Shere says the *Two-Part Symphony* "is often abrupt, though never jerky." *See:* W30b

Violin Variations

B794 Henahan, Donal. "Music: Computer's Role." The *New York Times*, 16 May 1972, p. 50.

> A review of the premiere. Henahan writes that the piece "made much use of microtones and also alluded frequently to the classics" but "to little apparent point." *See:* W125

B795 Henahan, Donal. "Music: Homage to 'Pierrot'." The *New York Times*, 9 December 1977, p. 18.

> "Mr. Wuorinen's piece, played with grim brilliance by Linda Quan, had the usual workmanship associated with this composer, but sounded fragmented and short-winded, as perhaps any 11-minute set of variations must." Henahan mistakenly writes that this was the first New York City performance. Apparently he forgot that his review of the premiere appeared in the *New York Times* five years earlier. *See:* W125a, B794

B796 Lange, Art. "Charles Wuorinen and Benjamin Hudson." The *Reader* [Chicago], 24 March 1978, pp. 34-35.

A review of the Chicago premiere. "The piece, containing a complete catalog of violinistic effects, held its urgency and propulsion solely on the strength of Hudson's virtuosity." *See:* W125b

B797 Foil, David. "Contemporary Music CAN Be Rich, Pleasant to Hear." *Morning Advocate* [Baton Rouge, Louisiana], 19 February 1981.

"*[Violin Variations]* appears to strike upon motives (and bits of motives) from [Ludwig van] Beethoven and [Wolfgang Amadeus] Mozart like so many bolts of lightening." *See:* W125d

The W. of Babylon

B798 Rosenfeld, Jay C. "Music Review: Musical High Jinks at Wheatleigh." The *Berkshire Eagle* [Berkshire, Massachusetts], 28 July 1974.

A review of a vocal duet from the work, sung by Wuorinen and soprano Catherine Rowe (the duet between the Baron and the Chinese Princess). The text of the duet had first been read at the concert by Fred Sherry. Rosenfeld writes it was "sung with deep pathos." *See:* W161a

B799 Salisbury, Wilma. "A New Turn for Music Theater." The *Plain Dealer* [Cleveland], 25 August 1974., p. 4-F.

A review of a vocal duet from the work, sung by Wuorinen and soprano Catherine Rowe (the duet between the Baron and the Chinese Princess). The text of the duet had first been read by Fred Sherry. Salisbury merely writes that Wuorinen "spoke brilliantly for a few moments about his risque new opera." *See:* W161a

B800 Henahan, Donal. "Opera: 'W. of Babylon'." The *New York Times*, 17 December 1975, p. 38.

A review of the preview excerpt program in New York City. "The point of their amorous comings and goings [the operatic characters], so to speak, was not always evident from the performance, but a narrative of sorts was sustained by Coburn Britton, listed as the 'explainer,' in an arch manner, that probably was intended to be hilariously high camp." *See:* W161

B801 Porter, Andrew. "Musical Events: Muses." The *New Yorker*, 29 December 1975, p. 46.

A review of the preview excerpt program in New York City. "Entertainment on a locker-room level! Renaud Bruce's libretto suggests a Ronald Firbank story stripped of its elegance and retold, heavily, by a smutty-minded schoolboy. Wuorinen has set it to leaping vocal lines that made the words largely inaudible. Such jokes as could be heard were concerned with anatomical dimensions." *See:* W161

B802 Wadsworth, Stephan. "Reports: U.S.: New York." *Opera News* 40, no. 14 (February 1976), pp. 46-47.

A review of the preview excerpt program in New York City. "Wuorinen's amorphous score has nothing to illuminate in Renaud Bruce's offensive libretto, which abounds in monstrous racial indiscretions and lamentable bathroom metaphor." *See:* W161

B803 "Ray Luke's 'Medea' Wins Prize as Original Opera." The *New York Times*, 11 February 1979, p. 61.

This brief unsigned notice about prizes for an opera composition competition mentions that Wuorinen had won the third prize of $1,500 for *The W. of Babylon*. The article mistakenly prints the title of the opera as *The Whore of Babylon*. The competition was sponsored by the Rockefeller Foundation and the New England Conservatory. *See:* W161

B804 Rorem, Ned. *The Nantucket Diary of Ned Rorem, 1973-1985*. San Francisco: North Point Press, 1987.

Rorem recounts his impressions from having attended the preview excerpt performance, in New York City, of *The W. Of Babylon*. In the entry dated 16 December 1975, he writes: "Wuorinen too is on the wrong path, a path all the more uncomfortable in being paved with coy intentions." (p. 155) "I used to feel I missed the might of Wuorinen's art — it was my lack. But there *is* no might; it's bluff." (p. 155) This material appeared earlier, in Rorem's book *An Absolute Gift* (New York: Simon and Shuster, 1978). *See:* W161, B625, B903

B805 Kosman, Joshua. "S.F. Premiere: Wuorinen's Opera — Erotic 'Babylon'." *San Francisco Chronicle*, 20 January 1989, p. C4.

Pre-concert publicity about the San Francisco concert performance. Includes interview material. [P] *See:* W161b

B806 "S.F. Symphony Bringing Up 'Babylon'." *San Francisco Examiner*, 21 January 1989.

A review of the San Francisco concert performance. "'The W. of Babylon' is something like 'Dangerous Liaisons' recast with the Marx Brothers and Margaret Dumont." The reviewer also writes that Wuorinen "conducted with certifiable verve." *See:* W161b

B807 Kosman, Joshua. "'Babylon' — Lascivious But Lacking." *San Francisco Chronicle*, 23 January 1989, p. F3.

A review of the San Francisco concert performance. "There is music for us in 'W.,' writing that is right up there among Wuorinen's best. But for the listener who does not share Wuorinen's enthusiasm for elaborate pitch structures, much of the opera is rough sledding." [P] *See:* W161b

B808 Von Buchau, Stephanie. "In Review: From Around the World: San Francisco." *Opera News* 53, no. 15 (April 1989), pp. 33-34.

A review of the San Francisco concert performance. Merely a mention that "Wuorinen's vocal music tends toward crabby abstraction of the dodecaphonic school" but that the work is witty. (p. 34) *See:* W161b

B809 Moor, Paul. "Debuts & Reappearances: San Francisco." *Musical America* 109, no. 4 (July 1989), pp. 46-47.

A review of the San Francisco concert performance. "Problem children, we know, sometimes enjoy an inordinate portion of parental affection. Charles Wuorinen's numerous other accomplishments let us easily forgive him his ill-starred championing of *The W. of Babylon*." (p. 47) *See:* W161b

Wind Quintet

B810 Horowitz, Joseph. "Boehm Offers Wuorinen's Quintet." The *New York Times*, 26 February 1978, p. 49.

A review of the premiere. Horowitz writes that the piece "marks a striking departure from the thorny, rigorously intellectual style with which Mr. Wuorinen is commonly associated." *See:* W126

B811 "Commissioners." *American Record Guide* 41, no. 7 (May 1978), pp. 30-31.

A very brief one-paragraph mention that the Boehm Quintette recently presented the world premiere of the work. A large photograph of Wuorinen and the players of the quintet, all drinking cocktails, appears across both pages. [P] *See:* W126

B812 Hruby, Frank. "Boehm Quintette Lights Up Art Museum." The *Cleveland Press*, 19 June 1980.

Although the critic praises the musicianship of the Boehm Quintette, he makes the following assessment: "Yet, ultimately, the piece ended up being somewhat boring, because the framework and structure were neither evident (which is all right) nor even discernible (which is not)." *See:* W126a

B813 Finn, Robert. "No Ill Winds Here; Boehm Quintet Blows Well." The *Plain Dealer* [Cleveland], 20 June 1980.

"No small part of this piece's appeal is its virtuoso aspect. It is a real showpiece, and the Boehm Quintet appeared to do it real justice." *See:* W126a

B814 Heglund, Gerald. "Music In Review." The *Chautauquan Daily* [Chautauqua, N.Y.], 9 July 1980.

Although Heglund writes positively about the work's harmony and tone colors, he concludes with this statement: "But with the world crying out for melodies that can possibly touch even the most calloused heart, this musical creation seemed almost a wasted effort." *See:* W126b

The Winds

B815 Ericson, Raymond. "Parnassus Chamber Ensemble Gives Premiere of Wuorinen's 'Winds'." The *New York Times*, 21 May 1977, p. 18.

A review of the premiere. "It demanded considerable virtuosity on the part of the players, which was amply supplied, and this formed part of the music's attractiveness." *See:* W57

B816 Porter, Andrew. "Musical Events: Intuitions." The *New Yorker*, 15 January 1979, pp. 94-96.

Porter calls it a "brilliant, animated stretch of music." (p. 94) *See:* W57a

B817 Salzman, Eric. "New Music: The New York School(s)." *Stereo Review* 46, no. 5 (May 1981), p. 80.

A review of the New World recording. Along with Mario Davidovsky, Wuorinen is described as having taken "the rebellious, avant-garde ideas of the immigrants and domesticated them with great skill." Salzman does not discuss *The Winds* or the recording aside from writing that all of the pieces are well played. *See:* D24

OTHER CATEGORIES

Academia

B818 "A Columbia Group Bids 4 Get Tenure." The *New York Times*, 18 March 1971, p. 43.
This article reports that eight members of the Columbia University music teaching faculty and thirty-two students had sent a letter to Columbia's President, William J. McGill, asking that Wuorinen and three other music colleagues be retained and given tenure. The article includes a reply from George Fraenkel, Dean of the Graduate School of Arts and Sciences, who said "it would take an incredible amount of money" to retain three talented young composers indefinitely through the tenure stage. *See:* B819, B822, B824, B825, B871, B1062

B819 Henahan, Donal. "Columbia Music Unit Faces Extinction." The *New York Times*, 20 May 1971, p. 47.
This article reports that the Group for Contemporary Music, based at Columbia University, faces possible extinction due to Columbia's decision to deny tenure to Wuorinen. The composer is quoted in the article as saying his tenure rejection was linked to disagreement in the music department over the philosophical differences between faculty of music theory, musicology, and composition. He also says his militant stand during the 1968 Columbia campus riots contributed to his termination. *See:* B818, B822, B824, B825, B871, B1062

B820 Jacoby, Hugh William. *Selected American Composers Affiliated With American Colleges and Universities: Biographical Sketches, Their Productivity, Professional Status, Performances of Works and Attitudes Towards University Patronage.* (Ph.D. dissertation) St. Louis: Washington University, 1974.
This dissertation attempts "to survey the job, family, social and professional characteristics of American composers at colleges and universities to examine factors that might affect, or not affect, the productivity of such composers." (p. 8) The dissertation examines 492 American composers in academia; lists Wuorinen.

B821 Keller, Anthony. "Composers on Campus: Can a Modern Mozart Spring from the Groves of Academe?" *High Fidelity/Musical America* 16, no. 10, (October 1966), pp. 104-107.
Examines the role played by the American university in patronizing new music; includes an overview of composer/university relationships from the end of the nineteenth century. Keller writes that at the university the composer "is unmolested by public tastes or commercial pressures, and encouraged, by the presence of numerous equally analytical and scholarly disciplines, to intellectualize his creative efforts." Keller states that Wuorinen "at twenty-seven probably exemplifies the new trend as well as anyone in the country — both as a composer and as an active spokesman." Wuorinen is quoted as saying that American universities are finally beginning to resemble "a true community of minds, an atmosphere comparable to that of the medieval university." (p. 105) [P]

B822 Lang, Paul Henry. "Music at Columbia Will Endure Even Without Wuorinen." The *New York Times*, 29 August 1971, pp. 11, 18, 22.
This lengthy article is a both a part of the public controversy surrounding Columbia University's denial of tenure to Wuorinen and a response to Wuorinen's 8 August *New York Times* article "Are the Arts Doomed on Campus?" Lang claims Wuorinen went on a vicious attack against Columbia University in that article, and says:

"Mr. Wuorinen's manifesto was a sorry display of spleen and vindictiveness, apparently the expression of an artistic Oedipus complex." (p. 11) Letters from Lewis Lockwood, Dr. Israel Kugler, Philip Friedheim, Alvin Etler and others followed Lang's response, either in support or opposition to Wuorinen's position. The letter from Kugler (President of the United Federation of College Teachers, Local 1460, AFT, AFL-CIO, New York City) included this statement: "It is to be hoped that all of this ['the right of a non-tenured faculty member to know the reasons for his dismissal'] may soon be resolved in a case which will come to the United States Supreme Court." (p. 18) Wuorinen's reply to Lang also appears here. Wuorinen writes, in part: "Often when you overturn a stone, you cause the little creatures crawling beneath it to scurry around furiously, in indignation and alarm." (p. 22) *See:* B818, B819, B824, B825, B871, B1062

B823 McKnight, Mark. "Book Reviews." *Notes* 45, no. 3 (March 1989), pp. 496-499.

McKnight reviews Nicholas Tawa's books *A Most Wondrous Babble* and *Art Music in the American Society*, and mentions Wuorinen briefly: "In their struggle to break from the past, postwar composers — especially those of the serial and atonal schools (the avant-garde) — left mainstream audiences behind. This alienation continued as the leading modernists — Milton Babbitt, Charles Wuorinen, Elliott Carter, and others — isolated themselves in their various academic communities." (pp. 496-497) *See:* B825

B824 Rich, Alan. "Higher Learning Lowers the Boom." *New York*, 6 September 1971, pp. 56-57.

An article about musical life in academia and the conflicts between composers and musicologists in university music departments. Much of the article discusses Columbia University's denial of tenure to Wuorinen. Rich notes: "It must have been rather galling to his [Wuorinen's] Columbia colleagues when he won a Pulitzer Prize a year ago, administered by that very university, the first genuinely progressive composer to be so honored." (p. 56) *See:* B818, B819, B822, B825, B871, B1062

B825 Tawa, Nicholas. *A Most Wondrous Babble: American Art Composers, Their Music, and the American Scene, 1950-1985.* Westport, Connecticut: Greenwood Press, 1987.

This book is volume nine in the publisher's series *Contributions to the Study of Music and Dance.* In the section titled "The World of the Modern Composer: Support Systems," Tawa discusses at length the denial of tenure to Wuorinen by Columbia University. (This is the only book to discuss this issue specifically in relation to Wuorinen.) Tawa writes: "Every now and again a composer heady over his own importance openly criticized his academic colleagues, scorning the principle of collegiality. I know of several composers who have operated thusly, some of whom were quietly invited to leave. Perhaps the most widely bruited instance of a composer who found himself dismissed because of his acerbic personality took place in 1971, when Columbia University fired Charles Wuorinen and ceased sponsoring the Group for Contemporary Music." (p. 69) Tawa continues by describing some of the specific articles and letters appearing in the press; those items are represented individually in this bio-bibliography. *See:* B818, B819, B822 - B824, B871, B1062

Awards

B826 Allison, Virginia. "Report of the 1978 Young Composers Contest." *Music Clubs Magazine* 58, no. 1 (Autumn 1978), pp. 30-32, 34.

An article about the 39th Annual Young Composers Contest of the National Federation of Music Clubs. Wuorinen participated as a judge. Contains biographical information. [P]

B827 "American Academy Elects Four Members." The *New York Times*, 9 February 1985, p. 13.

This brief unsigned article announces that Wuorinen and George Rochberg have been elected to the American Academy and Institute of Arts and Letters. Formal induction took place on 15 May 1985.

B828 "Arts Institute to Give $2,500 Grants to 4 Composers." The *New York Times*, 29 March 1967, p. 38.

A brief unsigned article announcing that Wuorinen, George Crumb, Donald Martino and Julian Orbon have been selected "to receive $2,500 grants on May 24 at the annual joint ceremonial of the institute and its affiliate, the American Academy of Arts and Letters." Wuorinen was the only native New Yorker among the winners.

B829 "BMI News." *BMI [Broadcast Music, Inc.] Newsletter* 3 (1984), p. 20.

A brief column announcing Wuorinen's two-year residency with the Louisville Orchestra, under the Meet the Composer/Orchestra Residencies Program.

B830 "BMI News." *BMI [Broadcast Music, Inc.] Newsletter* 2 (1986), p. 78.

A brief announcement that Wuorinen won a MacArthur Foundation award. [P]

B831 "Brandeis Lauds Two Generations in Arts Awards." The *New York Times*, 18 May 1970, p. 38.

An unsigned article announcing that Brandeis University has awarded Wuorinen a citation for achievement in music.

B832 "Charles Wuorinen Composer, Will Receive Coveted Award." *Gardner News* [Gardner, Massachusetts], 3 April 1967, pp. 1-2.

An article announcing that Wuorinen had won a National Institute of Arts and Letters award. "He is known as one for whom the act of composing is concerned with the problems and possibilities of ultimate performance." (p. 2) [P]

B833 "Composer-in-Residence for Symphony." *San Francisco Chronicle*, 30 January 1985, p. 55.

This article announces Wuorinen's appointment to a two-year term as composer-in-residence with the San Francisco Symphony. It also mentions that Wuorinen will direct the symphony's *New and Unusual Music Series* and recommend new scores to Herbert Blomstedt, the orchestra's music director. [P]

B834 Fleming, Shirley. "Music Notes: Piano Commissions." The *New York Times*, 9 March 1975, p. 21.

A brief piece discussing the new commissions for piano works resulting from sponsorship by the Edyth Bush Charitable Foundation. Each commission was for $3,000 and was offered to a composer chosen by a young pianist. The article mentions pianist Jeffrey Swan had commissioned a new work from Wuorinen. *See:* W136

B835 Fleming, Shirley. "Music Notes: Pulitzer Prize Composers Have Their Hands Full." The *New York Times*, 23 February 1975, p. 21.

The article features brief conversations with some winners of the Pulitzer Prize for music and mentions then current work being done by each composer. In addition to Wuorinen, the other composers discussed are Elliott Carter, George Crumb and Jacob Druckman.

B836 "$407,276 in Grants to Go to Composers." The *New York Times*, 11 February 1974, p. 46.

A brief article announcing that Wuorinen was one of thirteen composers to receive a grant under a new program started by the National Endowment for the Arts. Wuorinen's grant is for $3,500.

B837 "Gibson to Receive Degree." The *New York Times*, 6 June 1971, p. 52.

A brief announcement that Mayor Kenneth A. Gibson of Newark, New Jersey, and Wuorinen would receive honorary degrees at the commencement (the next day) of Jersey City State College. Wuorinen received an honorary doctorate.

B838 Holland, Bernard. "How 3 'Geniuses' View Their Prizes." The *New York Times*, 16 July 1986, p. C17.

Holland interviewed Milton Babbitt, George Perle and Wuorinen concerning their recent MacArthur Foundation awards. The commentary on Wuorinen corrected the academic affiliation that the tabloid erroneously reported in its 15 July 1986 article. (By 1986 Wuorinen had joined the faculty at Rutgers University.) Holland also writes: "Mr. Wuorinen recently completed, with the help of computers at Bell Laboratories, a philosophical study of musical structure." (See the *Interview* section of this bio-bibliography for clarification of that project.) When asked what he would do with the $236,000, Wuorinen replied that he would save it. [P] *See:* B847

B839 Hume, Paul. "The Arts: At the Pianists' Request." The *Washington Post*, 19 February 1975, p. C6.

The brief article announces the new commissions established by the Edyth Bush Charitable Foundation, and states that pianist Jeffrey Swan commissioned a new work by Wuorinen. *See:* W136

B840 Jepson, Barbara. "After the Pulitzer, Then What?" The *New York Times*, 28 October 1984, *(Arts & Leisure)*, p. 23.

A lengthy article discussing the Pulitzer Prize for music. Jepson mentions that in addition to having won the award, Wuorinen also served as a juror during other years. Includes interview material. [P] *See:* W159

B841 Kihss, Peter. "Report of Songmy Incident Wins a Pulitzer for Hersh." The *New York Times*, 5 May 1970, pp. 1, 48.

This front-page article — appearing with the headline article announcing "4 Kent State Students Killed By Troops" — reports that Seymour Hersh's work on the alleged Songmy (Mylai) massacre of Vietnamese civilians by U.S. soldiers has won a Pulitzer Prize. The third paragraph of the article announces that Wuorinen won a Pulitzer Prize for *Time's Encomium*. A biographical sketch of Wuorinen is included. [P] *See:* W159

B842 Nakao, Annie. "S.F. Composer, Two on UC Faculty Win 'Genius' Awards." *San Francisco Examiner*, 15 July 1986, p. A-4.

A brief mention of Wuorinen's MacArthur Foundation award.

B843 "Onstage: A Platform for Music & Musicians." *Symphony Magazine* 35, no. 5 (October/November 1984), pp. 55-56.

The section of the article titled "Resident Composer Program Expands: Louisville Added," announces that the Meet the Composer program has added the Louisville Orchestra and that Wuorinen had accepted a two-year term as composer-in-residence. Due to a labor dispute, Wuorinen left shortly after his term of appointment began and was immediately appointed composer-in-residence with the San Francisco Symphony.

B844 "Onstage: A Platform for Music & Musicians." *Symphony Magazine* 37, no. 4 (August/September 1986), p. 57.
A brief mention announcing Wuorinen's MacArthur Foundation award.

B845 "The Pulitzer Prizes: Profiles of Past Winners." *BMI [Broadcast Music, Inc.]: The Many Worlds of Music* 2 (1974), pp. 20-27.
Includes a brief biography of Wuorinen. [P] *See:* W159

B846 Rothstein, Edward. "In the Fracas Over a Prize, No One Won." The *New York Times*, 19 April 1992, *(Arts & Leisure)*, p. 25.
Discusses the controversy surrounding the 1992 Pulitzer Prize for music in which Wayne Peterson was awarded the prize over the Pulitzer jury's recommendation of Ralph Shapey. The article mentions that the jury consisted of George Perle, Roger Reynolds, and Harvey Sollberger, and that they had unanimously agreed Shapey should receive the award. Rothstein examines the issues involved and mentions jurors for this award have often been composers who were previous winners. He lists Wuorinen as the first of those composers. *See:* W159

B847 Teltsch, Kathleen. "Magician Makes the List of 25 'Genius' Winners." The *New York Times*, 15 July 1986, p.15.
An article announcing the winners of the MacArthur Foundation grants to "outstandingly talented" people. The tax-free grants are "intended to free the recipient from economic pressures so they can devote themselves to research or scholarship, or the creative arts." Wuorinen is erroneously listed as being an instructor at the Manhattan School of Music (Wuorinen left that institution well before receiving this award). The amount of the award is not mentioned but is later reported to be $236,000. Two other composers — Milton Babbitt and George Perle — were also recipients of these awards, the same year. *See:* B838

B848 Tircuit, Heuwell. "Enviable Record of the Composers' Competition." *San Francisco Sunday Examiner and Chronicle*, 27 May 1973, *(This World)*, p. 26.
The article is devoted to the history of the annual BMI [Broadcast Music, Inc.] awards to student composers. "Men like George Crumb, Mario Davidovsky, and Charles Wuorinen all came to the fore through the BMI Awards — and while they were still students."

B849 "2 Composers, Violinist Join Conservatory." *Herald Traveller* [Boston], 22 October 1968, p. 22.
A brief unsigned article announcing that composers Wuorinen and Alexander Goehr as well as violinist Paul Zukofsky have joined the faculty of the New England Conservatory.

B850 Ulrich, Allan. "Jingle of Award Dollars is Music to the Ears." *San Francisco Examiner*, 15 July 1986, p. A-4.
An article announcing Wuorinen's MacArthur Foundation award. Wuorinen is quoted as making the following remark in a telephone interview: "The award to all three of us [George Perle and Milton Babbitt being the other two] suggests an attempt at preservation of the most important values in Western music."

B851 White, Evelyn C. "3 in Bay Area Get 'Genius' Awards." *San Francisco Chronicle*, 15 July 1986, p. 2.

An announcement about Wuorinen's MacArthur Foundation award. The composer is quoted as saying: "I am glad the committee found my activities promising enough to support. I intend to have a good time." [P]

B852 "Winners Named by Guggenheim." The *New York Times*, 7 April 1972, p. 25.

A brief article announcing the winners of the 48th annual John Simon Guggenheim Memorial Foundation fellowship awards. Wuorinen and George Russell were the two composers to win.

B853 Witcher, Gregory. "'Genius Grants' Awarded to 25 by MacArthur Foundation." The *Boston Globe*, 15 July 1986, p. 24.

This account of Wuorinen's MacArthur Foundation award lists the amount of the award at $45,600 and says Wuorinen is from San Francisco. The correct amount was $236,000; Wuorinen is a native New Yorker.

Compositional Theory and Analysis

B854 Balzano, Gerald J. "What Are Musical Pitch and Timbre?" *Music Perception* 3, no. 3 (Spring 1986), pp. 297-314.

This article is an exposition of a pitch system that divides the octave into twenty parts. Balzano describes how he and Wuorinen have explored this system together to establish voice-leading rules for different chord progressions. Balzano writes: "We have found the audible results of generating some simple progressions on the computer to be unusual but not at all unpleasant. It turns out to be not at all difficult to get a sense of the trajectory of, even develop expectancies for, a simple 'circle of fifths'-type of chord progression." (p. 308) An earlier discussion of this and other related pitch systems appeared in Balzano's article "The Group Theoretic Description of 12-Fold and Microtonal Pitch Systems" (*Computer Music Journal* 4, no. 4 (Winter 1980), pp. 66-84); Wuorinen was not mentioned in that article.

B855 Brown, Malcolm W. "In a Musical Invention, Bach + Fractals = New Compositions." The *New York Times*, 16 April 1991, pp. C1, C5.

A discussion of fractals and their use in music composition. Wuorinen and György Ligeti are mentioned as two contemporary composers who have worked with fractals: "Both Mr. Wuorinen and Mr. Ligeti, whose music generally draws mixed reviews from critics, contend that composers conceive music in large forms, later filling in the details with ever smaller reductions of the large forms. Many musicians dispute this idea, however." (p. C5) *See:* W93c, W93e, B395, B856, B858

B856 Kendall, Robert. "Great Performances: Three Special Composers." *PC Computing* 3, no. 1 (January 1990), pp. 95-101.

Kendall's section on Wuorinen is subtitled "Charles Wuorinen: Explorer of the Mathematics of Music," and discusses the composer's interest in fractals and computers. Kendall writes: "Charles Wuorinen applies principles of fractal geometry to his music, achieving motifs similar to those found in nature." Kendall also discusses Wuorinen's work with the music software *SCORE*: "In large-scale orchestral pieces where the initial draft is difficult to enter into *SCORE*, he uses the program later in the process to eliminate time-consuming copying and proofreading. When all is done, the work goes to his publisher, C.F. Peters — on disk, not on paper." (p. 100) *See:* W93c, W93e, B395, B855, B858

B857 Kresky, Jeffrey. "The Recent Music of Charles Wuorinen." *Perspectives of New Music* 25, nos. 1-2 (1987), pp. 410-417.

This important article is one of the few scholarly pieces to be devoted exclusively to Wuorinen's music. Any reader seeking to gain written material on Wuorinen and analysis of his compositional technique is strongly encouraged to read this article. The works discussed, some with examples, are *Arabia Felix, Chamber Concerto for Violoncello and Ten Players, Ringing Changes, String Trio, Piano Concerto No. 3, Short Suite, Mass, Bamboula Squared, Movers and Shakers, Concertino, Rhapsody for Violin and Orchestra, Crossfire, Golden Dance,* and *The Politics of Harmony.* Kresky's statements include the following: "For the return to pulse, tune and the like in music such as Wuorinen's may be emblematic of a restoration of some of the most cherished outward features of tonality that it may have been necessary to eschew for a time, in order to confront and project with any chance of success the radically different backgrounds, grammars and even fundamental premises being adopted or attempted since Schönberg." (p. 416) "It is much to put one's hopes in, in terms of what Godfrey Winham once disturbingly referred to as 'the not improbable circumstance of the failure of serious music to survive.' No composer fights more against that unacceptable possibility directly through his music than Wuorinen." (p. 417) *See:* W4, W9, W14, W16, W21, W24, W25, W38, W45, W60, W108, W156, W160, W170, B14, B40, B130, B151, B199, B278, B372, B390, B487, B556, B581, B589, B599, B664

B858 Lisella, Julia. "Computer Music Moves Into the Fractal Void." *Village Voice*, 25 November 1986, *(Fast Forward),* pp. 17-20.

An article about fractal geometry and how it has been applied to music composition. Wuorinen is mentioned several times as a composer who has used fractal geometry. In discussing the implications of fractal geometry for contemporary music he is quoted as saying: "Most contemporary musicians are illiterate. They use computers to compensate for their lack of training." (p. 20) *See:* W93c, W93e, B395, B855, B856, B858

B859 Read, Gardner. *Modern Rhythmic Notation.* Bloomington: Indiana University Press, 1978.

This book on music notation contains references to nine Wuorinen compositions, most of which occur in the appendix, titled "Nonstandard Time Signatures." In the chapter "Traditional Rhythmic Notation in New Guises," Read comments: "Elliott Carter and Charles Wuorinen have also availed themselves of notehead denominators, but only when compound durational groupings were required." (p. 18) *See:* B179

B860 Smith, Patrick J. "Debuts & Reappearances: New York: Meet the Moderns (Foss)." *High Fidelity/Musical America* 31, no. 6 (June 1981), pp. MA33-MA34.

This was a review of a performance of *Four Fragments of 1/f Music*, a brief bit of music Wuorinen created but that he does not consider to be a musical composition. Smith says the fragments were witty but that the ones ending with a computer elicited "Bronx cheers." (p. MA33) *See:* B900

B861 Stone, Kurt and Gerald Warfield. "Report on the International Conference on New Music Notation. Proceedings of the Ninth Annual Conference, February 1974." *American Society of University Composers*, nos. 9-10, pp. 56-78.

This was a lecture presented in print form in these published proceedings. Wuorinen was one of many prominent composers to attend the conference, held at the Institute of Psycho-Acoustics and Electronic Music at the University of Ghent, Belgium.

Stone's discussion includes background information on the conference as well as examples of new music notation. Warfield's part of the lecture addresses the conclusions of the conference and presents a sampling of notational results that were endorsed by a two-thirds majority of the attendees.

B862 Warfield, Gerald. *Writings on Contemporary Music Notation: An Annotated Bibliography.* (*MLA Index and Bibliography Series*, No. 16) Ann Arbor, Michigan: Music Library Association, 1976.

    Wuorinen has one entry in this bibliography (no. 447). It concerns his article "Notes on the Performance of Contemporary Music" (*Perspectives of New Music* 3, no. 1, (1964), pp. 10-21). Warfield's annotation reads: "Primarily concerned with aspects of the realization of ensemble rhythm. Examines notation of rhythmic complexities and compares some 15th- and 16th-century examples with contemporary notation." (p. 90) *See:* B863, B1077

B863 Winick, Steven D. *Rhythm: An Annotated Bibliography.* Metuchen, New Jersey: The Scarecrow Press, 1974.

    This bibliography includes one entry on Wuorinen — an annotation on his article "Notes on the Performance of Contemporary Music" (*Perspectives of New Music* 3, no. 1, (1964), pp. 10-21): "Suggests that difficulty in reading and performing complex rhythmic patterns is not inherent but rather cultural in origin and due to habits acquired by most players in their training. Recommends a way for the performer to learn to execute the 'irrational' rhythms of contemporary music." (pp. 90-91) *See:* B862, B1077

Ensembles — Group for Contemporary Music

B864 Blechner, Mark. "The Group for Contemporary Music: Performing is Not a 'Lower Form of Activity'." *High Fidelity/Musical America* 27, no. 11 (November 1977), pp. MA24-MA25.

    A general article about the history of the Group for Contemporary Music. Wuorinen is quoted as saying: "Some composers may think we are discriminating against C major. But discrimination is not taking place against C major; it's taking place against a lack of quality. And that is a form of intolerance that we will adhere to." (p. MA25)

B865 Boretz, Benjamin. "Music." The *Nation*, 26 February 1968, pp. 283-285.

    This article criticizes music journalists and, in particular, the music policies of the *New York Times* for having evidenced "an intense belief in the virtues of amateurism." Boretz says the tabloid has a poor record with regard to the coverage of new music performance events in New York City. According to Boretz, performing groups frequently ignored by the tabloid include the Group for Contemporary Music.

B866 Boretz, Benjamin. "Music." The *Nation*, 17 June 1968, pp. 802-805.

    This article is an important discussion of contemporary music performance groups and their associated financial costs, fund-raising, and sponsor problems. The Group for Contemporary Music is one of the ensembles discussed. Wuorinen's association with that ensemble is also discussed. In a parenthetical statement Boretz says Wuorinen "virtually developed a new set of pianistic modes of articulation [along with Easley Blackwood]" (p. 804)

B867 Borroff, Edith. *Music in Europe and the United States. A History.* Englewood Cliffs, New Jersey: Prentice-Hall, Inc., 1971.

    Wuorinen is one of eight composers mentioned as being "representative of the several hundred American composers of virtually all styles who were enriching the musical art at American universities in 1970." Further, she states: "The need for a new concept of the performing group was answered by such innovations as the Columbia University Group for Contemporary Music (founded in 1962), which performed over 100 twentieth-century works in its first four years, and the Monday Evening Concerts in Los Angeles." (p. 670)

B868 Cantrell, Scott. "The Hills Are Alive With the Sound of New Music." The *New York Times*, 18 September 1988, *(Arts & Leisure)*, pp. H27, H38.

An article about a touring new music festival arranged by the New York State New Music Network, which included performances by the Group for Contemporary Music. The problems of attracting audiences and financing concerts are discussed. Wuorinen states his opposition to government support for the arts and says having the composer Philip Glass as part of this tour is "the equivalent of using public funds to support a rock concert."

B869 "...courante." *American Composers Alliance Bulletin* 11, no. 1 (June 1963), pp. 9-10.

This one paragraph article mentions the high standards set by the then new ensemble, the Group for Contemporary Music. "Charles Wuorinen is not only one of our most gifted young composers; he is also a man who feels social responsibility for the presentation of the works of others." The writer goes on to say that American musical culture could change quickly if all American universities would encourage the creation of such ensembles.

B870 Estevan, Pilar. *Talking With Flutists. Volume 1*. New York: Edu-tainment, 1976.

This volume of interviews with various flutists includes an undated interview with Harvey Sollberger, in which he discusses the Group for Contemporary Music: "Charles Wuorinen and I are not just interested in more performances of new music, but in performances of a certain quality. Since our involvement with the ensemble is primarily as composers who perform, we feel that our performances can speak with a certain legitimacy and authority that is not always present in performances of new works." (p. 61)

B871 Henahan, Donal. "Columbia Music Unit Faces Extinction." The *New York Times*, 20 May 1971, p. 47.

This article reports that the Group for Contemporary Music, based at Columbia University, faces possible extinction as a university-sponsored ensemble due to Columbia's decision to deny tenure to Wuorinen. Henahan says the ensemble "became the prototype for hundreds of such university-connected ensembles." *See:* B818, B819, B822, B824, B825, B1062

B872 Henahan, Donal. "The Grand Old Teen-agers of Contemporary Music." The *New York Times*, 13 February 1977, p. 21.

This article discusses the goals and activities of the Group for Contemporary Music, based at the Manhattan School of Music. Henahan also comments on the roles of Wuorinen, Nicolas Roussakis and Harvey Sollberger, in terms of the ensemble's history and success. A number of statements by Wuorinen are featured; most concern the plight of the young composer.

B873 Kozinn, Allan. "For Contemporary Music, Times Are Hard." The *New York Times*, 8 June 1991, p. C11.

The piece discusses reductions in grant funding for new music performance and mentions that the Group for Contemporary Music suffered a 60% cut in grant funding in 1990. Wuorinen argues that popular culture and commercial success have displaced artistic merit: "We don't distinguish between the committed, passionate audience and the trend-seeking yuppie audience. We just count bodies and measure sales."

B874 *Newsletter of the Group for Contemporary Music at Columbia University* 1, no. 1 (December 1967).

The first issue of the ensemble's newsletter. It is a two-page announcement about activities and personnel. The newsletter is timed to appear with the first concert of the ensemble's sixth season and is intended to be issued prior to each regularly scheduled concert. This issue also announces the affiliation of the Group for Contemporary Music with the Columbia-Princeton Electronic Music Center. The newsletter features the following statement: "We hope, shortly, to take notice of various matters of topical concern, the sort of which ought to be dealt with by daily music journalism but which, lamentably, are not."

B875 Peyser, Joan. "The New Music." *Vogue*, 1 February 1966, pp. 176-177, 196.

A general article about new music and the Group for Contemporary Music. Peyser writes about Wuorinen, Harvey Sollberger, and others, and says the spirit of their music is far removed from that of "the fraternity of composers who flocked around Nadia Boulanger in Paris a generation ago." (p. 196)

B876 Porter, Andrew. "Musical Events: Babbitt on Broadway." The *New Yorker*, 15 March 1982, pp. 126, 129-134.

Porter writes at length about many new music concerts that took place in Manhattan during the winter of 1982. Some of those concerts were by the Group for Contemporary Music. In a parenthetical, he asks: "What has happened to those Group for Contemporary Music events in the students' café of the Manhattan School — candles burning, wine flowing — of a few years ago?" (p. 126)

B877 Porter, Andrew. "Musical Events: Opportunities." The *New Yorker*, 7 July 1975, p. 66.

Porter discusses the professionalism of The Fires of London, a new music ensemble in England. He mentions the Group for Contemporary Music as an American new music ensemble that has a similar standing but that has not yet developed a comparable repertory.

B878 Tawa, Nicholas. *A Most Wondrous Babble: American Art Composers, Their Music, and the American Scene, 1950-1985.* Westport, Connecticut: Greenwood Press, 1987.

This book is volume 9 in the publisher's series *Contributions to the Study of Music and the Dance.* Tawa discusses the Group for Contemporary Music's rapport with music by its founders (Wuorinen, Nicolas Roussakis, Harvey Sollberger), and other composers whose styles were similar. Tawa states: "When John Corigliano accused the ensemble of refusing his works because he was not radical enough a composer, Charles Wuorinen claimed the ensemble's discrimination was solely against music that lacked quality and confessed that this was a form of intolerance the players intended to continue cultivating. Wuorinen's music, in turn, would have seemed to lack quality to the ONCE Group, formed by [Robert] Ashley in 1963." (pp. 64-65)

Ensembles — Other Ensembles

B879 *A Celebration of American Music: Words and Music in Honor of H. Wiley Hitchcock.* Ed. Richard Crawford, R. Allen Loft, and Carol J. Ota. Ann Arbor: University of Michigan Press, 1990.

The chapter on the American Composers Orchestra, by Francis Thorne, mentions Wuorinen as a composer who has had works premiered by that orchestra.

B880 Commanday, Robert. "Cultivating an Audience for American Music." *San Francisco Sunday Examiner and Chronicle*, 5 February 1989, *(Review)*, pp. 14-15.

An article about John Duffy, director of the Meet the Composer program and its history. Wuorinen is discussed in terms of his residency with the San Francisco Symphony, which, according to Commanday, paid him $40,000 per year. Commanday writes that Wuorinen "was criticized for dividing his time during his three years of residency, spending more of it working in New York than here." (p. 14) Commanday also mentions that Herbert Blomstedt, conductor of the San Francisco Symphony, specifically wanted Wuorinen to become composer-in-residence with that orchestra. *See:* B829, B843, B1007, B1038

B881 Commanday, Robert. "Music for People Willing to Take a Risk." *San Francisco Chronicle*, 12 March 1988, p. C4.

This article discusses the San Francisco Symphony's *New and Unusual Music Series.* Commanday says Wuorinen is "cool, penetrating and anything but defensive about predicting the results or guaranteeing satisfaction." [P]

B882 Commanday, Robert. "Sweet and Sour Notes on the New Season." *San Francisco Chronicle*, 12 March 1989, *(Review)*, p. 12.

A brief piece about Herbert Blomstedt and the programming of concerts at the San Francisco Symphony. Commanday mentions that Wuorinen has completed his residency and that Michael Steinberg is leaving as Artistic Director: "Steinberg and Wuorinen were exceptionally well-equipped, independent and self-assured advisors. Nothing less can help the Symphony hold the walls against the ceaseless tides of commercialism."

B883 Ericson, Raymond. "New Orchestra Making Its Debut Here." The *New York Times*, 15 September 1975, p. 13.

This article discusses the formation of the New Orchestra. Both Wuorinen and Arthur Weisberg had planned the creation of an orchestra devoted exclusively to contemporary music and decided to combine their efforts to produce this one.

B884 Henahan, Donal. "Music View: A New Tune at the Chamber Music Society." The *New York Times*, 4 December 1988, p. 27.

An article about cellist Fred Sherry being named director of the Chamber Music Society of Lincoln Center, succeeding Charles Wadsworth. Henahan mentions that Wuorinen is one of a few composers to already have a work scheduled for performance under Sherry's new leadership.

B885 Kosman, Joshua. "Snags in Symphony's Resident Composer Program." *San Francisco Chronicle*, 19 June 1989, p. E3.

An article about the composer-in-residence program with the San Francisco Symphony. Kosman says Peter Lieberson and Donald Martino withdrew their names from consideration because they did not wish to relocate to the Bay Area. Wuorinen is mentioned as having spent 40% of his time in San Francisco while he held the post.

B886 *Symphony Orchestras of the United States: Selected Profiles.* Ed. Robert R. Craven. New York: Greenwood Press, 1986.

Wuorinen is briefly mentioned in profiles of four orchestras: the Louisville Orchestra, the Springfield [Massachusetts] Symphony Orchestra, the Albany [New York] Symphony Orchestra, and the American Composers Orchestra [New York City].

B887 Terry, Kenneth. "New Orchestra to Stress Music of 20th Century." *Kite* [Schenectady, New York] 5, no. 49 (3 December 1975), pp. 1, 3.

An article discussing the formation of the New Orchestra, by Wuorinen and Arthur Weisberg. Wuorinen says existing institutions do not adequately serve contemporary music.

B888 Waleson, Heidi. "Speculum Musicae at 15." *High Fidelity/Musical America* 36, no. 5 (May 1986), pp. MA13-MA15.

A brief history of the ensemble Speculum Musicae. Waleson states: "Once firmly wedded only to the New York composers such as Milton Babbitt, Elliott Carter, and Charles Wuorinen, in recent years its horizons have begun to broaden." (p. MA14)

Fromm Music Foundation

B889 Gelles, George. "Conspicuous Composers Who Deserve Attention." The *Washington Star*, 1 June 1975, p. H-20.

This article discusses the results of the Fromm Music Foundation survey which attempted to assess critical gaps in the performance of contemporary music. The foundation hoped to list "important but neglected or infrequently performed musical works from the last forty years." Gelles says of Wuorinen: "In terms of mere numbers of titles, a dark horse is the winner." *See:* B3, B57, B66, B105, B117, B125, B178, B183, B196, B214, B222, B256, B301, B340, B368, B392, B454, B462, B502, B551, B620, B639, B660, B727, B891, B893

B890 Henahan, Donal. "Music: A New Way of Looking at the New And the Old." The *New York Times*, 16 July 1972, *(Arts & Leisure)*, p. D11.

An article about Paul Fromm and the Fromm Music Foundation. Henahan discusses the change of direction the foundation implemented — away from Princeton University and serialism, toward Harvard University and more traditional attitudes about musical composition. Henahan writes: "In new music circles, this is like moving the Papacy from Rome to Avignon."

B891 *Music of the Last Forty Years Not Yet Established In the Repertoire: A Survey Conducted By the Fromm Music Foundation at Harvard 1974-1975.* Cambridge, Massachusetts: The Foundation, 1975.

In September 1974 the Fromm Music Foundation invited 1,600 members of the music community to participate in a survey. The purpose of the survey was to identify works composed since about 1935 that could fill the gap between the classics composed since 1900 and works composed since the early 1970s. Fromm's introduction describes the survey methodology and states that the survey population consisted of the Fromm Foundation's list of 600 composers, conductors, performers, music critics and educators, combined with the 1,000 individuals who made up the American Music Center's membership at that time. The survey letter states the results would be used "to encourage orchestra conductors, chamber ensemble groups and recitalists to use the list as a means of extending their 20th century repertoire." Wuorinen is represented by twenty-four works on the final list. In terms of number of works listed per composer, Wuorinen came in sixth. The first five composers were Paul Hindemith, Igor Stravinsky, Bela Bartok, Arnold Schoenberg, and Sergei Prokofiev. *See:* B3, B57, B66, B105, B117, B125, B178, B183, B196, B214, B222, B256, B301, B340, B368, B392, B454, B462, B502, B551, B620, B639, B660, B727, B889, B893

B892 Parmenter, Ross. "Music World: Parting Is No Sweet Sorrow." The *New York Times*, 20 October 1963, p. 11.

An article featuring a small section titled "Nonet," which announced Paul Fromm's creation of the *Festival of Contemporary Music* at the *Berkshire Music Festival*. The nine composers selected for the first festival were Wuorinen, Randolph Coleman, Mario Davidovsky, Donald Martino, Robert Nowell, John MacIvor Perkins, Loren Rush, Harvey Sollberger, and David Del Tredici.

B893 Safford, Edwin. "Fromm's a Friend of Neglected Music." *Providence Sunday Journal* [Providence, Rhode Island], 25 May 1975, *(Arts & Travel)*, p. H-26.

Safford writes about the Fromm survey of contemporary music not yet established in the repertoire. He mentions Wuorinen had many entries. *See:* B3, B57, B66, B105, B117, B125, B178, B183, B196, B214, B222, B256, B301, B340, B368, B392, B454, B462, B502, B551, B620, B639, B660, B727, B889, B891

Genre — Electronic Music

B894 Appleton, Jon. "Live and In Concert: Composer/Performer Views of Real-Time Performance Systems." *Computer Music Journal* 8, no. 1 (Spring 1984), pp. 48-51.

This article discusses electronic music and several American composers. Appleton writes: "Some of the composers who made important early contributions to electroacoustic music, for example, Luciano Berio, Mario Davidovsky, and Charles Wuorinen, now claim that tape music is dead." (p. 48)

B895 "Current and Prospective Visitors." *CME [Center for Music Experiment] Roster* [University of California, San Diego], 1 March 1984.

An occasional publication, this newsletter includes a mention of Wuorinen's activities at the Computer Audio Research Laboratory (CARL), University of California, San Diego. The newsletter states Wuorinen is "working on research leading to a computer music composition relying on digital synthesis only. He intends to produce a research paper on the subject of computer composition techniques for controlled random processes relevant to musical composition which will be suitable for publication in the 'Computer Music Journal'." (p. 3)

B896 Davis, Deta S. *Computer Applications in Music. A Bibliography*. Madison, Wisconsin: A-R Editions, 1988.

This book is volume 4 of the *Computer Music and Digital Audio Series*. Although there is no mention of Charles Wuorinen, there is one entry (#3114) citing a piece co-authored by his brother, John Wuorinen: Kinsel, Tracy S., and John H. Wuorinen. "A Digital Signal Generator." *IEEE Micro* 1 (November 1981), pp. 6-15. This entry comes under the category "Sound Generation for Music — Hardware," and is on page 258.

B897 McLean, Priscilla. "Fire and Ice: A Query." *Perspectives of New Music* 16 (Fall/Winter 1977), pp. 205-211.

A discussion of electronic music "as a sonic experience that is neither a continuation of the traditional abstractions (melodic-rhythmic groupings with timbres and textures as primary or secondary considerations) nor 'kidnapped' environmental aura, but a sonorous occurrence somewhere in between." (p. 205) McLean discusses the ideas expressed in Wuorinen's article "Toward Good Vibrations" and compares those ideas to views expressed by the composer Jon Appleton, who included sound sources "from the urban environment" in his music. Further, McLean writes that Luciano Berio's *Visage* is a powerful dramatic work that "seems to be a refutation of Wuorinen's argument that non-pitched material cannot form strong syntactical relationships." (p. 207) *See:* B1090

B898 *Music in the Modern Age.* Ed. F.W. Sternfeld. New York: Praeger Publishers, 1973.

This book is volume 5 of the series *A History of Western Music.* Wuorinen is mentioned twice, first as a composer of the younger generation (p. 388), and second, as follows: "Of figures mentioned earlier in this essay only Milton Babbitt, Charles Wuorinen, John Cage and the most recent generation of experimentalists have worked extensively with electronic sounds." (p. 390)

B899 *The Music Machine. Selected Readings from Computer Music Journal.* Ed. Curtis Roads. Cambridge, Massachusetts: The MIT Press, 1989.

This monograph includes a number of references to Wuorinen, one of which is a reprint of Richard Boulanger's interview with Wuorinen, Roger Reynolds and Joji Yuasa. Another reference is the appearance of a quotation by Wuorinen from that same interview, reprinted in D. Gareth Loy's piece "Musicians Make a Standard: The MIDI Phenomenon." Yet another reference is a comment by Curtis Roads, in the section titled "Overview," which refers to Wuorinen's comments in the Boulanger interview. Roads writes: "Wuorinen conveys strongly held views on various topics, ranging from the use of compositional algorithms to the problems of composing for electronic media. His eye-opening recollections of the RCA synthesizer (installed at the Columbia-Princeton studios in the 1950s and 1960s) put the brave composers who used this difficult instrument in a new light." (p. 3) *See:* B737

B900 Sandow, Gregory. "But Is It Art?" *Village Voice*, 4 March 1981, p. 63.

An article questioning which kinds of music constitute art. "Wuorinen's computer pieces have a real voice of their own, as if someone — or something — were deciding whimsically or even sulkily where the music would go next." This is actually a concert review of Wuorinen's 4 Fragments on 1/f Music. *See:* B860

B901 Stockhausen, Karlheinz. *Texte zur Musik 1963-1970. Band 3. Einführungen und Projekte Kurse, Sendungen, Standpunkte Nebennoten.* Koln: Verlag M. Du Mont Schauberg, 1971.

In the section that discusses electronic music studios "die Amerikaner Charles Wuorinen" is mentioned (p. 261) along with others working at the Columbia-Princeton Electronic Music Center.

Genre — Sacred Music

B902 Belt, Byron. "Music in the Churches." *Music: The A.G.O. and R.C.C.O. Magazine* 7, no. 7 (July 1973), pp. 20-23.

This article is an overview of the 30 April - 2 May 1973 workshop titled "Music in the Church ... A Long View" held at the Cathedral of St. John the Divine in New

York City. Belt discusses the difficulties of composing accessible music for those attending worship services. "Wuorinen indicated his own difficulties by admitting that a relatively simple congregational hymn resulted in his 'most compromised and rudimentary' composition." (p. 22) *See:* W169, B371

B903 Rorem, Ned. *The Nantucket Diary of Ned Rorem, 1973-1985.* San Francisco: North Point Press, 1987.
　　　　The entry dated 2 May 1973 describes the two-day symposium titled "Music in the Church ... A Long View" held at the Cathedral of St. John the Divine in New York City. Rorem offers his views of the event. In another entry dated "Sans date, 1974," Rorem writes: "Charles Wuorinen and I have nothing in common, not even music. Yet for a brief minute, during a composers' panel at Saint John the Divine, we exchange glances of complicity when the question of money is touched. Because as artists we want the rewards of Mammon, we become lambs for those Philistines who believe only in God." (p. 111) This statement also appeared earlier, in Rorem's book *An Absolute Gift* (New York: Simon and Schuster, 1978). *See:* B625

References — General Citations

B904 Caldwell, Jan. "Music 'Messiah'?" *Thursday's Drummer*, 24 December 1970, p. 12.
　　　　Caldwell recounts a conversation he had with Otto Luening in which Caldwell said modern music needed another Igor Stravinsky or a Pablo Picasso "to pull everything together." Caldwell writes: "'Charles Wuorinen may be your man,' predicted Otto Luening. That was two years ago." The article discusses several Wuorinen works and includes a brief discography.

B905 "Composers in Focus." *BMI [Broadcast Music, Inc.]: The Many Worlds of Music* (Winter 1976), pp. 15-33.
　　　　The last page of the article is devoted to Wuorinen and includes biographical information, and concert review material. [P]

B906 Downs, Joan. "New Music Man." *Life*, 12 November 1971, pp. 41-48.
　　　　This article is about Pierre Boulez during his years in New York City. It includes a large photograph of Wuorinen with Boulez and the pianist Paul Jacobs. (p. 42) Wuorinen is not mentioned in the text. [P]

B907 Gagnard, Frank. "Prankish Composer to Conduct at LSU Fest." The *Times-Picayune* [New Orleans], 7 January 1981, p. 9.
　　　　A brief article discussing Wuorinen's participation in Louisiana State University's 36th Festival of Contemporary Music. Gagnard asks: "Charles Wuorinen — devil, or merely *little* devil?"

B908 Kastendieck, Miles. "Charles Wuorinen." *BMI [Broadcast Music, Inc.]: The Many Worlds of Music* (December 1969), p. 15.
　　　　A general one-page article on Wuorinen that includes the following statement: "In the van of contemporary music Charles Wuorinen finds himself in an enviable position. He provides constantly fascinating sound experiences. Also he cogently represents everything avant-garde: distinctive individualism, atonalism and electronicism." [P]

B909 Kerner, Leighton. "Industrial Report." *Village Voice*, 20 January 1982, p. 68.

Kerner writes about the symphony orchestra business in New York City and mentions a luncheon at which Wuorinen discouraged young conductors from blindly following the standard fare of symphonic programming. Wuorinen is quoted as saying the *Mostly Mozart Festival* has helped "in keeping some of our musicians off the streets in summer," and that it gave tourists another option when they "couldn't get tickets to Broadway shows," but that he is opposed to the endless regurgitation of the same musical pieces performed again and again.

B910 Maguire, Jan. "20th-Century Music in a Contemporary Way." *New York Herald Tribune*, 28 September 1963.

This article, dispatched from Paris, discusses the musical efforts of Keith Humble, musical director of the Centre de Musique at the American Students and Arts Center. Maguire writes that Humble plans to perform works of Wuorinen, Milton Babbitt, Ralph Shapey, Harvey Sollberger, and Gunther Schuller during the upcoming season.

B911 Manoff, Tom. "Run Into Any Mozarts Lately?" The *New York Times*, 17 November 1991, *(Arts & Leisure)*, pp. 27-28.

An article about musical genius and success in modern times. Wuorinen is one of several composers discussed. Manoff writes: "[Wuorinen's] proudly elitist sensibility has been crucial in defining his musical language, which, because of its relatively high levels of dissonance and complexity, has been called 'difficult music'." (p. 28) [P]

B912 Maxfield, Richard. "The Mail Pouch: Readers Name Composers." The *New York Times*, 4 February 1962, *(Arts & Leisure)*, p. 9.

A brief collection of responses to Harold C. Schonberg's *New York Times* article in which he asked for the identities of young composers working seriously. Maxfield, a faculty member of the New School for Social Research (New York City), named Earle Brown, Morton Feldman, John McDowell, Terry Riley, Gunther Schuller, Ralph Shapey, Ezra Sims, Christian Wolff, La Monte Young, and Wuorinen.

B913 McLellan, Joseph. "Performing Arts: Charles Wuorinen." The *Washington Post*, 25 October 1984, p. D4.

A review of an all-Wuorinen, all violin music concert of works composed between 1967 and 1977. The concert was held at the Kennedy Center for the Performing Arts on 24 October 1984, as part of a contemporary music series. McLellan writes: "It confirmed what Wuorinen watchers have suspected for some time: that this composer — one of the high priests of serialism and tight, intricate, objective music — has been subtly changing his style."

B914 "Music Journal's 1972 Gallery of Living Composers." *Music Review* 30 (1972 Annual), p. 62.

An article containing a biography of Wuorinen. [P]

B915 "New Yorker Neuigkeiten." *Frankfurter Allgemeine*, 20 July 1979.

Subtitled "Between the Chairs, Beyond the Established/A Festival of Experimental Music Downtown," the article merely mentions that Wuorinen is thought of in New York City as "an up-town composer."

B916 Nuortio, Antti. "Säveltäjä Charles Wuorinen: Vakava musiikki ei ole rock und rollia." *Unsi Suomi* [Helsinki], 13 October 1981.

Titled "Composer Charles Wuorinen: Serious Music is Not Rock and Roll," the article features a brief interview with Wuorinen.

B917 Page, Tim. "The Alluring Soundscapes of Philip Glass." The *Wall Street Journal*, 17 April 1981, p. 21.

This article is about the emergence of Philip Glass as a New York composer. Page states: "Audiences began to get bored with the pedantic, often strident music by establishment composers like Charles Wuorinen...." He asserts they drifted to music they found more pleasing to listen to.

B918 Page, Tim. "In the Interest of American Music." The *New York Times*, 2 February 1986, p. 24.

Page writes about various musical events in America to be held in the near future. One is the first composer-conductor workshop formed by Wuorinen and Harold Farberman, to be held in Morgantown, West Virginia. The two-week workshop was devoted to six young American conductors and six composers.

B919 Peyser, Joan. "It's a Big Week for Wuorinen." The *New York Times*, 10 April 1983, pp. 21, 24.

The article mentions Wuorinen's then current compositions and performances: "...five different compositions, two of which are world premieres, performed by five different organizations in a period of six days in New York." Peyser concludes: "Mr. Wuorinen has a large ego; he sees himself central to the new era and believes his music will endure. No one knows if he is right or not, and if he is wrong he will never know it. Meanwhile the fact that five of his pieces will be played in New York in less than a week means at least some people think he is right." Includes biographical information. [P]

B920 Pitkanen, Allan M. "Letters From Readers: Great Finnish Notes." *Saturday Review/World*, 6 April 1974, p. 8.

An appreciation of Irving Kolodin's article "Wuorinen and the New American String Quartet," published in the January 1974 issue of this magazine. Pitkanen writes, in part: "Recognition of Finnish musical genius is long due. Perhaps Wuorinen's ascendancy will expose the names of other Finnish geniuses that are unfamiliar to insular Americans." *See:* B550

B921 Powell, Jean. "Dinner for President Kekkonen. MacGregor Set for 'Horse Race'." The *Evening Star* [Washington, D.C.], 24 July 1970, *(Woman's World)*, pp. C1, C5.

This article is about the White House state dinner for President Kekkonen of Finland, which was hosted by President and Mrs. Richard M. Nixon on 23 July 1970. Powell reports Nixon's comments, which included remarks that Kekkonen had been in office longer than any other elected leader in the world, and that although he lost his first election, he lost none after that. Nixon then stated that he wished he had been as fortunate. Wuorinen attended the dinner as an invited guest, as did Abraham Kaplan, who conducted the Camerata Singers in a half-hour of songs in six languages, including Finnish. Wuorinen was seated at a table for three; his dinner companions were the conservative columnist William Rusher, and the physicist Edward Teller, father of the hydrogen bomb. The *horse race* in the title of this article refers to the Rep. Clark MacGregor (Republican, Minnesota)/Hubert Humphrey senatorial race in Minnesota; MacGregor was also an invited guest at the dinner.

B922 Pury, Marianne de. "Musique: Jacques Guyonnet decouvre l'Amerique." *La Tribune de Geneve*, April 3-4, 1965, p. V.

This article is about Jacques Guyonnet — an organizer of concerts, composer, and conductor who visited New York City to learn something about contemporary American music. Pury writes of Guyonnet's experiences, both as a musician and tourist: "Charles Wuorinen, the 'cock' of contemporary American music, is not pleased. At 26 he has the reputation of being one of the most interesting, if not *the* most interesting young American composers of today. Everyone knows (and he makes little effort to deny) that he is hostile to whatever comes from Europe, stating he wants it well understood that America can get along very well without the old continent, that all his relationships with European musicians have been very painful (clarifying that these are musicians who make enemies wherever they go, whether in America or Europe), and that while he is always glad to have new European works to direct, he can't say the same for those European musicians who despise anything American. (On this point he is perhaps not entirely wrong.)"

B923 Rorem, Ned. *The Nantucket Diary of Ned Rorem, 1973-1985*. San Francisco: North Point Press, 1987.

    The entry dated 1 June 1985 opens with this comment: "Andrew Porter gives Wuorinen the whole first paragraph without offering a value judgement, merely a brief description. With me he doesn't even bother with the brief description. (He doesn't bother to say I'm not worth bothering with.)" (p. 572)

B924 Rorem, Ned. *Setting the Tone. Essays and a Diary*. New York: Coward-McCann, Inc., 1983.

    This book includes two references to Wuorinen. The first discusses composers who are also pianists: "At random, a few: Leon Kirchner, Robert Helps, David Del Tredici, Charles Wuorinen, Lukas Foss. They all play their own music dazzlingly, as well as that of contemporaries." (p. 30) The second reference appears in a section about Vera Stravinsky and Robert Craft's book *Stravinsky: In Pictures and Documents*; Rorem's review of the book is dated December 1978. Rorem writes: "The single youngish current composer of any nationality whom Craft finds worth quoting is Charles Wuorinen who in 1961 wrote to Stravinsky: 'Your recent magnificent serial compositions ... [Rorem's ellipses] are inspirations to all reasonable musicians'. The implication is the True Way is actually less fallacious than the idea of a 'reasonable musician'." (pp. 188-189) Note: Rorem's index mistakenly refers the reader to page 187 for this entry. *See:* B982

B925 Sachs, David. "CRI at 30: Celebration and Challenge." *Fanfare* 8, no. 1 (September/October 1984), pp. 146-150.

    An article about the history of Composers Recordings, Inc., (CRI). Sachs mentions that Wuorinen is one of "the better known (or less ignored) names to be found on CRI." (p. 146) The article includes details about recording costs and financing.

B926 Salzman, Eric. "Performers Aid Creators On Mountain." The *New York Times*, 27 August 1961, *(Arts & Leisure)*, p. 9.

    An article about the history of the Bennington Composers Conference. Wuorinen is not discussed but is featured in a photograph with Charles Russo and Charles Whittenberg. [P]

B927 Schonberg, Harold C. "Our Changing Musical Language." The *New York Times*, 31 January 1965, *(Arts & Leisure)*, p. 11.

    An editorial in which Schonberg expresses his opinion of where contemporary music is going and why. He argues that over the centuries composers have evolved a musical vocabulary that has served well. He concludes by naming Wuorinen as one of many contemporary composers who "may be on the road to nowhere."

B928 Steinberg, Michael. "Tanglewood. An Attempt to Appraise Modern Music Festival." The *Boston Globe*, 23 August 1964.

This article is an assessment of the Festival of Contemporary Music at Tanglewood. He notes that there were six concerts that included 13 premieres in less than 100 hours. "Del Tredici's music and Wuorinen's were both indicative of strong personalities, perhaps at this point more latent than actual in the case of Del Tredici." (Steinberg does not name the works performed.)

B929 "The Tiger's Roar: Charles P. Wuorinen '56." The *Trinity Alumni Review* (Winter 1984), pp. 11-12.

A biographical article on Wuorinen containing information on his years at Trinity School, as well as his professional career.

B930 Ulrich, Allan. "Play It Again, Please." *San Francisco Sunday Examiner and Chronicle*, 4 December 1988, *(Style)*, pp. E-1, E-4.

This commentary includes a remark on the San Francisco Symphony's *New and Unusual Music* series: "Under both John Adams and current composer-in-residence Charles Wuorinen, the project has never escaped the 'ghetto mentality' (though Adams and Wuorinen hail from vastly different artistic ghettos.)"

B931 Wierzbicki, James. "Opus: Record Reviews." *Musical America* 109, no. 4 (July 1989), p. 85.

A review of the Nonesuch and Bridge compact disk recordings of various violin pieces by Wuorinen. "Charles Wuorinen's classically formulated 12-tone music, at any rate, continues to sound viable in this unfocused age of minimalism, neo-Romanticism, and eclectic This-and-That-ism." *See:* D16, D35

B932 Ylänne, Kari. "Pulitzer-säveltäjä jälleen Suomessa Charles Wuorinen Finlandia-talossa." *Ilta-Sanomat* [Helsinki], 15 October 1981.

This article, titled "Pulitzer Composer Visited Finland Again: Charles Wuorinen in Finlandia Hall," consists of background information on the composer to coincide with one of his visits to Finland.

B933 Zailian, Marian. "A Feisty Composer Who Scores the Unusual." *San Francisco Chronicle*, 15 December 1985, *(Datebook)*, p. 44.

A look at Wuorinen's leadership of the San Francisco Symphony's *New and Unusual Music* series. Zailian describes Wuorinen as a "blend of ice and fire." She also writes: "Critics say there has been a subtle change in his musical and personal style: it is warmer, less academic. Friends say he's mellowed since he left his brownstone in Manhattan and took up residence here [San Francisco]." Includes biographical and interview material. [P]

References — Scholarly Citations

B934 *Amerikanische Musik seit Charles Ives: Interpretationen, Quellentexte, Komponistenmonographien.* Herausg. Hermann Danuser, Dietrich Kämper und Paul Terse. Laaber: Laaber-Verlag, 1987.

This book contains a number of articles on contemporary American music, some of which are analytical studies and biographies. Wuorinen is mentioned in passing in two different places (pp. 97, 128); a brief biography and partial list of his works are included at the end of the book (pp. 398-399).

B935 Anderson, Ruth. *Contemporary American Composers: A Biographical Dictionary*. 2nd ed. Boston: G.K. Hall, 1982.
This biographical dictionary contains an entry on Wuorinen (p. 569).

B936 *Baker's Biographical Dictionary of Musicians*. 6th ed. Rev. Nicolas Slonimsky. New York: Schirmer Books, 1978.
This biographical dictionary contains an entry on Wuorinen (p. 1919).

B937 *Baker's Biographical Dictionary of Musicians*. 7th ed. Rev. Nicolas Slonimsky. New York: Schirmer Books, 1984.
This biographical dictionary contains an entry on Wuorinen (pp. 2533-2534).

B938 *Baker's Biographical Dictionary of Musicians*. 8th ed. Rev. Nicolas Slonimsky. New York: Schirmer Books. 1992.
This biographical dictionary contains an entry on Wuorinen (pp. 2078-2079).

B939 Breurer, Robert. "Die Avantgarde in den Vereinigten Staten." *Melos: Zeitschrift für Neue Musik* 30, no. 3 (March 1963), pp. 77-79.
Breurer states that Wuorinen's character lends itself "to the expression of a self-centered art." Later on, Breurer writes: "He [Wuorinen] disapproves of applying the term 'young, modern composers' to 40 to 50 year-old composers who write 'strong vertical and highly tonal music'; although this opinion can be considered to have come from a compositional toddler, it is substantiated by the large number of his works that have been performed in the New York [City] concert halls alone — not a bad balance for an avant-garde baby!" (p. 79)

B940 Brindle, Reginald Smith. *The New Music: The Avant-Garde Since 1945*. 2nd ed. Oxford: Oxford University Press, 1987.
In the chapter titled "The Search Outwards — The Orient, Jazz, Archaisms," Wuorinen is briefly mentioned. Brindle states Peter Maxwell Davies has worked to incorporate the past in a modern idiom and that John Tavener and Wuorinen have sporadically attempted to do the same thing. "There is no doubt that this is a fairly fertile field, the first fruits of which have barely been seen, but it is also a dangerous one, for the successful fusion of such contrasting idioms calls for great artistic discrimination." (p. 141)

B941 Burbank, Richard. *Charles Wuorinen. A Bio-Bibliography*. Westport, Connecticut: Greenwood Press, 1993.
This is the only full-length book on Wuorinen and is the most comprehensive collection of bibliographic information about the composer. It is a volume in the publisher's series *Bio-Bibliographies in Music*. It contains biographical material, details on the composer's compositions, chronological listings of important performances, entries for concert reviews, a discography (including video recordings), entries for scholarly and other writings about Wuorinen, and a full register of articles and essays by Wuorinen. Any musicologist or scholar studying Wuorinen's music should consult this book as a point of departure.

B942 Burbank, Richard. *Twentieth Century Music. Orchestral, Chamber, Operatic & Dance Music 1900-1980*. New York: Facts On File, 1984.
This chronology includes thirty-four entries on Wuorinen that document premieres, awards and other events in his career through 1980.

B943 Burge, David. "ASUC: Six Years. Proceedings of the Sixth Annual Conference, April 1971." American Society of University Composers 6, pp. 5-12.

This article was originally presented as a lecture at the annual conference of the ASUC, held at the University of Houston. It describes the origin and history of the society. Burge states: "The American Society of University Composers was conceived and formed in 1956 by a group of composers living in and around New York City. These seven men, Benjamin Boretz, Donald Martino, J.K. Randall, Claudio Spies, Harry Weinberg, Peter Westergaard, and Charles Wuorinen, acting as the first Executive Committee, sent out invitations to numerous composers throughout the country to become founding members, to which some fifty-six responded affirmatively. It was then announced that the American Society of University Composers was formed 'as a professional organization for composers in American universities.'" (p. 5)

B944 Burkholder, J. Peter. "Museum Pieces: The Historicist Mainstream In Music of the Last Hundred Years." The *Journal of Musicology* 2, no. 2 (Spring 1983), pp. 115-134.

Burkholder defines historicist composers as those "writing music for a museum, for that is what the concert hall has become." (p. 116) He identifies Wuorinen as a historicist composer whose music "will be understood well only in the context of Schoenberg and Webern; Wuorinen has commented himself that his music will not become widely known until the music of Berg and Schoenberg is performed as often as Brahms is now. The view of music sketched out in this paper suggests that may very well never happen." (fn., p. 126)

B945 *Charles Wuorinen: Profile of a Composer.* New York: C.F. Peters Corp., 1994.

Part of the publisher's series on contemporary composers whose works are published by C.F. Peters, this volume on Wuorinen includes brief articles by a number of other composers and scholars. These publications are in a magazine-sized format and are designed as introductory material for students and professionals.

B946 Chase, Gilbert. *America's Music: From the Pilgrims to the Present.* 3rd ed. Urbana: University of Illinois Press, 1987.

This third edition of the book includes a two-page discussion of Wuorinen and his work. In the section titled "America and the World," the chapter titled "Creative Systems," Chase describes Wuorinen as "the most prolific and articulate latter-day disciple of [Arnold] Schoenberg and [Milton] Babbitt." (p. 587) Chase also includes biographical material, brief interview excerpts, and snippets from critical reviews. Chase writes: "Actually, the personal imprint is always there, but it is continually transformed by an apparently inexhaustible capacity for recombining the components at various levels (such as foreground and background) and in ever-changing configurations." (p. 588) Wuorinen was also discussed in the second edition of this book (1966), but not in the first edition (1955). *See:* B686

B947 Claghorn, Charles Eugene. *Biographical Dictionary of American Music.* West Nyack, N.Y.: Parker Publishing Co., 1973.

This biographical dictionary contains an entry on Wuorinen (p. 485).

B948 *Confronting Stravinsky: Man, Musician, and Modernist.* Ed. Jan Pasler. Berkeley: University of California Press, 1986.

This monograph is an anthology of essays that grew out of the first *International Stravinsky Symposium* held 10-14 September 1982 at the University of California, San

Diego. Pasler's preface mentions Wuorinen four times. The section of the book titled "Compositional Practices in the Late Music" includes Milton Babbitt's essay "Order, Symmetry, and Centricity in Late Stravinsky," which footnotes Wuorinen's book *Simple Composition* as a source of discussion of *order transposition*, particularly in relation to Stravinsky's music. (p. 251) Also included is the essay/address "On the Significance of Stravinsky's Last Works," by Wuorinen and Jeffrey Kresky, in which they make the following remarks: "Most journalists and critics — among so many others — prefer to see in Stravinsky's stylistic periods a youthful exuberance, followed by an elegant and controlled middle age, all culminating in a disappointing experimental dotage. But some of us, as composers, have been so profoundly affected by the late works, in which are first exhibited techniques and devices we have extracted to employ and extend, as to want to predict what that the final chapter of his output will be the most significant in the long run." (p. 262) Wuorinen and Kresky then proceed to discuss several of Stravinsky's late works in detail, and conclude by stating that the practices exhibited in those late works "may then show the possibility of convergence and direct continuity between the diatonic past and what can in a very general way be called the chromatic present — with these remarkable, spare last works of the master as the precious link. To be sure, such a convergence would be so much more definitively important than, say, the low-grade neotonality that is often expressed these days in semipop or trancelike terms involving diatonic figures, and that is perhaps a relatively transient phenomenon. It is an intriguing matter to realize that it was only after Schoenberg's death that Stravinsky came to express his own concerns through his colleague's procedures: for we can never know what Schoenberg's response, musical and otherwise, might have been." (p. 270) *See:* B969, B1048, B1087

B949 *Contemporary Composers.* Ed. Morton, Brian and Pamela Collins. Chicago: St. James Press, 1992.
  This biographical dictionary contains an article on Wuorinen by Christian Hertzog (pages 977-980). Hertzog writes, in part: "Wuorinen has done more than any other composer since Aaron Copland to advocate the idea of concert music composition as an earnest profession in the United States." (p. 318)

B950 Cope, David. *New Directions in Music.* Dubuque, Iowa: William C. Brown Co., 1971.
  Wuorinen is mentioned in the preface and in a biographical appendix. Subsequent editions of this book expanded coverage of him. *See:* B735, B738

B951 *Current Biography Yearbook: 1972.* New York: H.W. Wilson Co., 1972.
  This biographical dictionary contains an entry on Wuorinen (pp. 451-454).

B952 *Dictionary of Contemporary Music.* Ed. John Vinton. New York: E.P. Dutton & Co., 1974.
  This dictionary contains an article on Wuorinen, written by Harvey Sollberger (pages 823-824). Sollberger writes: "Influenced neither by folkloristic Americana music nor by aleatoric efforts, the music of Wuorinen occupies a radical middle ground where the main tasks are the traditional ones of assimilation and extension through new works of a living musical tradition, in this case that growing from the work of [Arnold] Schoenberg and [Igor] Stravinsky." (p. 823) The articles "Recording," "Text Setting and Usage," and "United States," also feature references to or brief mentions of Wuorinen's works. The dictionary also contains an article titled "Performance," which was partially written by Wuorinen with research assistance from Jeffrey Kresky. *See:* B549, B994, B1079

B953 Dreyfus, Laurence. "Early Music Defended Against its Devotees: A Theory of Historical Performance in the Twentieth Century." *Musical Quarterly* 69, no. 3 (Summer 1983), pp. 297-322.

In his section titled "Early Music and the Aesthetic of Novelty," Dreyfus writes: "Thus, although the stylistic development of the avant-garde was conceived as eminently rational (the Schoenbergs and Co. continually insisted on their direct links with the past) the European middle classes took the path of least resistance and dedicated themselves to a predictable standard repertory." Dreyfus then cites Wuorinen in a footnote to this sentence: "Or, as Charles Wuorinen put it in 1975: 'Credo in unam musicam.'" (p. 314)

B954 Engle, Eloise. *The Finns in America*. Minneapolis: Lerner Publications, 1977.

This book is a volume in the publisher's *In America Series*. The section called "Contributions to American Life" includes comments on music teacher Martii Nisonen, vocalist Kaija Juusela, and composer Charles Wuorinen. (p. 95)

B955 Ewen, David. *American Composers: A Biographical Dictionary*. New York: G.P. Putnam's Sons, 1982.

This biographical dictionary contains an entry on Wuorinen (pp. 729-733).

B956 Ewen, David. *Composers Since 1900: A Biographical and Critical Guide*. 1st supp. New York: H.W. Wilson Co., 1981.

This biographical dictionary contains an entry on Wuorinen (pp. 318-322).

B957 *The Grawemeyer Collection of Contemporary Music 1985-1991. A Catalog*. Ed. Richard Griscom. Louisville, Kentucky: University of Louisville School of Music, 1992.

This catalog lists all of the scores submitted to the Grawemeyer Award committee. The award was established in 1984 by Charles Grawemeyer, whose goal was to create an international award for musical composition that would be equivalent to a Nobel Prize for music. The award offers the most lucrative prize of any award in this field. All submissions for consideration become the property of The Grawemeyer Collection of Contemporary Music. The catalog reveals that Wuorinen submitted six works between 1985 and 1991. This is probably the only major award Wuorinen has not won.

B958 Greene, David Mason. *Greene's Biographical Encyclopedia of Composers*. New York: Doubleday, 1985.

This biographical dictionary contains an entry on Wuorinen (pp. 1344-1345).

B959 Griffiths, Paul. *The Thames & Hudson Encyclopædiea of 20th-Century Music*. London: Thames & Hudson, 1986.

This reference book contains an entry on Wuorinen (p. 194).

B960 Grout, Donald J. and Claude V. Palisca. *A History of Western Music*. 3rd ed. New York: W.W. Norton & Co., 1980.

Wuorinen appears in a photograph with Pierre Boulez taken during a discussion period at a New York Philharmonic Prospective Encounter. (p. 751) There is no discussion of Wuorinen's music in the text. This is the only edition of Grout that includes a mention of Wuorinen, despite a blind reference in the index to the fourth edition. [P] *See:* B961

B961 Grout, Donald J. and Claude V. Palisca. *A History of Western Music.* 4th ed. New York: W.W. Norton & Co., 1980.

A blind reference in the index indicates there is an illustration or photograph of Wuorinen on page 880, yet that page and surrounding pages feature no such illustration or discussion of his music. The text of the area is largely the same as the text surrounding page 751 of the third edition of this book, where a photograph of Wuorinen did indeed appear. For some reason, the photograph was not carried over to the fourth edition, but its corresponding index entry was erroneously carried over. *See:* B960

B962 Hall, Charles J. *A Twentieth-Century Musical Chronicle: Events 1900-1980.* Westport, Connecticut: Greenwood Press, 1989.

This chronology is Number 20 in the publisher's series *Music Reference Collection.* It contains fourteen entries on Wuorinen, mostly for premiere performances, listed by year.

B963 Hansen, Peter S. *An Introduction to Twentieth Century Music.* 4th ed. Boston: Allyn and Bacon, Inc., 1978.

The chapter titled "Representative Composers, 1950-1975" includes a brief biography of Wuorinen (pp. 406-407). Another chapter opens with a photograph of Yannis Xenakis paired with a question posed by Wuorinen: "How can you make a revolution when the revolution before last has already said anything goes?" (p. 370)

B964 Hartsock, Ralph. *Otto Luening: A Bio-Bibliography.* Westport, Connecticut: Greenwood Press, 1991.

This book is Number 35 in the publisher's series *Bio-Bibliographies in Music.* The book contains eleven references (including concert reviews) to performances of works by Wuorinen.

B965 Hellau, Laurence. *La guittare en concert: catalogue des oeuvres ave guittare de XX° siecle.* Paris: Editions musicales transatlantique, 1988.

Lists three works by Wuorinen that include scoring for a guitar.

B966 Howard, John Tasker. *Our American Music. A Comprehensive History from 1620 to the Present.* 4th ed. New York: Thomas Y. Crowell Co., 1965.

Includes a brief biographical account of Wuorinen and concert review quotes for some of his early compositions.

B967 Jablonski, Edward. *The Encyclopedia of American Music.* New York: Doubleday, 1981.

This reference work contains an entry on Wuorinen (p. 577).

B968 Jacoby, Hugh Williams. *Contemporary American Composers Based at American Colleges and Universities.* Paradise, Ca.: Paradise Arts Publishers, 1975.

This reference book contains an entry on Wuorinen (p. 229).

B969 Kielian-Gilbert, Marianne. "In Counterpoint: Two Stravinsky Books." *Perspectives of New Music* 27, no. 1 (Winter 1989), pp. 246-262.

This is a book review of *Confronting Stravinsky.* That book featured an essay by Wuorinen and Jeffrey Kresky. The reviewer writes: "They [Wuorinen and Kresky] offer the familiar solution — the view that the echo of the tonal in the serial (and the serial in the tonal) is another example of the continuities which span Stravinsky's diverse stylistic ventures." Further on, Kielan-Gilbert writes: "Finally, Stravinsky's exploration of new kinds of continuity by writing his verticals out horizontally is a window into recent extensions by Wuorinen and others, namely the practice of generating rotational arrays from previously linearized verticals. Such procedures, not found in Stravinsky's work, provide the means to achieve different and perhaps richer alternatives to current repetitive practices of neotonality." (pp. 256-257) *See:* B948

B970 Kinney, Michael. *Perceptions of Developmental Influences as Contributing Factors to the Motivation for Musical Creativity of Eminent Twentieth Century Living American Composers.* (Ed.D. dissertation) Syracuse, New York: Syracuse University, 1990.
    "This qualitative study examines eminent living American composers' perceptions of factors considered pivotal to their creative development." (Abstract) Wuorinen appeared as number twenty-one on a list of such composers. Only the first fourteen composers participated in this study, however.

B971 Kober, Barbara Negley. *An Examination of the Music and Newspaper Coverage of Five Contemporary American Composers in Five Major United States Cities During the Period of January 1, 1982 and December 31, 1986.* (M.A. thesis) Washington, D.C.: The American University, 1987.
    This thesis examines newspaper coverage in New York City, Washington, D.C., Chicago, Philadelphia, and Boston to see whether or not concert reviews were positive or negative for Wuorinen, Elliott Carter, Philip Glass, Ned Rorem, and one other composer. Kober concludes: "The examination shows that critics have welcomed the performances of contemporary music, have been fair and objective, and have attempted to educate and inform." (Abstract) The bulk of entries in this bio-bibliography and Wuorinen's comments in the Interview section of this book would seem to indicate otherwise.

B972 Machlis, Joseph. *Introduction to Contemporary Music.* 2nd ed. New York: W.W. Norton & Co., 1979.
    Wuorinen's name appears several times in the book, most often in the "Dictionary of Contemporary Composers and Their Recorded Works." Wuorinen's music is not discussed in the text, however. The first edition of this standard text includes no mention of Wuorinen.

B973 Minnear, Carolyn Cockrum. *The Works of Charles Wuorinen. An Annotated Bibliography.* (M.A. thesis) Talahassee: Florida State University, 1977.
    "My purpose is to make readily available information about this composer and access to Wuorinen compositions of the last-quarter century." (p. 2) The thesis features a chronology and discography of Wuorinen's works to 1977.

B974 *The New American Arts.* Ed. Richard Kostelanetz. New York: Horizon Press, 1965.
    The final essay in the book — "The New American Music" — by Eric Salzman, includes comments on Wuorinen. Of the composer's pianistic abilities, Salzman writes: "The close relationship between the creative and the performing style of a young musician like Charles Wuorinen is typical [of a whole group of younger people whose performing and compositional activities are almost inseparable]: an exceptional pianist, he has developed an extraordinary range of piano activities and techniques." Salzman also comments on Wuorinen's music: "Wuorinen's own music (with or without a piano) has a highly improvisatory manner, expressive and free; even when open-form and improvisatory techniques are not used, the source of strength is the sense of controlled

wildness. His structures, not unlike those of [Elliott] Carter and [Stephan] Wolpe, grow out of an on-going opposition between fixed and free, thrust and stasis, violent energy and intense calm." (p. 255)   The discography at the end of the book lists two works by Wuorinen.

B975 *The New Grove Dictionary of American Music.* Ed. H. Wiley Hitchcock and Stanley Sadie. New York: Grove's Dictionaries of Music, 1986.
>   This reference work contains an article on Wuorinen, written by Richard Swift (pp. 568-570).

B976 *The New Grove Dictionary of Music and Musicians.* Ed. Stanley Sadie. London: MacMillan, 1980.
>   This reference tool includes an article on Wuorinen, written by Richard Swift (page 548).

B977 *The Orchestra. Origins and Transformations.* Ed. Joan Peyser. New York: Charles Scribner's Sons, 1986.
>   This book of twenty-three essays on the orchestra includes two that mention Wuorinen's music. The first is J. Peter Burkholder's essay "The Twentieth Century and the Orchestra as Museum." Burkholder writes: "Some younger serial composers have returned to classical forms; Charles Wuorinen, for instance, has written two symphonies [*sic*], two piano concertos, a concerto for amplified violin and orchestra, several concertos for soloist and chamber ensemble, and other works in classical genres." (p. 426)   The second essay is Rufus Hallmark's "The Star Conductor and Musical Virtuosity" which mentions Wuorinen along with Ralph Shapey, Peter Maxwell Davies, Karlheinz Stockhausen and Philip Glass as composer-conductors specializing in contemporary music: "These musicians have ventured into a repertoire with a following even more sparse than that of early music and pursue it — perhaps for that reason — with even more dogged conviction." (p. 577) *See:* B1084

B978 Perone, Karen L. *Lukas Foss: A Bio-Bibliography.* Westport, Connecticut: Greenwood Press, 1991.
>   This book is volume 37 in the publisher's series *Bio-Bibliographies in Music.* It contains four entries relating to Wuorinen's recordings, concert reviews, and performing activities.

B979 Post, Nora. "Varese, Wolpe and the Oboe." *Perspectives of New Music* 20 (Fall/Winter 1981 - Spring/Summer 1982), pp. 135-148.
>   "Wolpe's utilization of extreme contrasts in both dynamics and articulations is mirrored in the oboe music of Wuorinen, and Harvey Sollberger, as well as in Babbitt's own *Woodwind Quartet*." (p. 146)

B980 Rockwell, John. *All American Music. Composition in the Late Twentieth Century.* New York: Alfred A. Knopf, 1983.
>   Wuorinen is mentioned seven times in discussions of music by Milton Babbitt, Robert Ashley, and Philip Glass. Rockwell says "the juices of inspiration still run strong" in Babbitt and that the "same is true of Charles Wuorinen and George Perle, both of whom have contributed learned theoretical studies and both of whom write music that can appeal to the non-specialist." (p. 30) In the chapter on Ashley, Rockwell states: "The sponsors of the annual New Music America festivals have also struggled to define the term [experimental music], if only so they can figure out whom to exclude. These festivals are supposedly all-inclusive, theoretically open to Babbitt, Wuorinen and any of

the other Northeastern hard-liners. Yet those composers have not so far participated, and nobody seems to have made a very strenuous effort to invite them." (p. 97)

B981   Siron, Paul Louis. *Aspects de la musique contemporaine 1960-1981.* Lausanne: Editions de l'Aire, 1981.

One of the few European books to include a mention of Wuorinen. The chapter "Les Americains" mentions about fifteen American composers. Wuorinen is described as "un auteur prolifique." (p. 98) A comment by Wuorinen is also featured in a French translation.

B982   Stravinsky, Vera and Robert Craft. *Stravinsky In Pictures and Documents.* New York: Simon and Schuster, 1978.

In the chapter titled "The United States, 1939-1971" (Part Three), Wuorinen is mentioned: "One young composer, Charles Wuorinen, writing to thank [Igor] Stravinsky for his participation in the Lili Boulanger Award, which Wuorinen had won, added that 'Your recent magnificent serial compositions ... are inspirations to all reasonable musicians.' [Letter of April 1961]" (p. 454) *See:* B924

B983   Tawa, Nicholas E. *Art Music in the American Society: The Condition of Art Music in the Late Twentieth Century.* Metuchen, New Jersey: The Scarecrow Press, 1987.

In the chapter titled "The Public's Canons of Musical Taste" Tawa makes the following comment: "Ours is a society where the freedom allowed composers to explore whatever styles they wish has come to be associated in the public's mind with widespread and unrelieved aesthetic and stylistic confusion. Who is to say what recent music compositions possess excellence and result from urgent creative drives? Surely, not Milton Babbitt on Cage's works, nor John Cage on Milton Babbitt's works, nor Charles Wuorinen on Philip Glass's work. Although, on the one hand, a yardstick about what constitutes music and musical worth seems essential; on the other, the creative person wishes to work untrammeled by authoritative rules to which he or she does not subscribe." (p. 47)

B984   Thomson, Virgil. *American Music Since 1910.* New York: Holt, Reinhart and Winston, 1971.

This book is the first volume of the publisher's series *Twentieth-Century Composers,* edited by Anna Kallin and Nicholas Nabokov. The section titled "106 American Composers" includes a biography of Wuorinen. Thomson mentioned Wuorinen was president of the Serious Music Society and concluded by calling him "A composer of amazing fecundity but still unclear profile." (pp. 184-185)

B985   *Who's Who In American Music: Classical.* 2nd ed. Ed. Jacques Cattell. London: Bowker, 1983.

This biographical dictionary includes an entry on Wuorinen (p. 654).

B986   Willemze, Theo. *Composistenlexicon.* Utrecht: Spectrum, 1981.

This is one of the few European reference books on composers to include an entry on Wuorinen (p. 609).

Simple Composition

B987 Adams, Robert Train. *Music Composition for Beginners*. Dubuque, Iowa: William C. Brown, 1986.

This textbook includes two references to *Simple Composition*, one of which says Wuorinen's book "is not actually simple. He sets out a method of 12-tone composition, which includes aesthetic considerations applicable to electronic music." (p. 190) *See:* B1087

B988 "Best Buys In Books." *I.S.A.M. [Institute for Studies in American Music] Newsletter* [Department of Music, Brooklyn College, City University of New York] 9, no. 1 (November 1979), p. 9.

"Now comes a book which, although aimed at a different audience (students of composition), can tell us plain and simple observers of the modern music scene a great deal." The reviewer concludes by writing: "In about 150 pages of tight, elegant, and crystal-clear prose, with plenty of enlightening music examples, Wuorinen really lets us know the ins and outs of writing from the serial standpoint." *See:* B1087

B989 Joyce, Mary Ann. "Book Reviews." *Journal of Musicological Research* 5, nos. 1-3 (1984), pp. 265-267.

"He [Wuorinen] does not probe the question of why composers of the past intended to evoke human emotion while composers of 12-tone music generally do not." (p. 267) *See:* B1087

B990 Karlins, M. Williams. "Freedom and Control in Twentieth-Century Music." *TriQuarterly* 52 (Fall 1981), pp. 244-259.

"As obscenities and other kinds of words and expressions become neutralized, the power to express without recourse to a new language or to the absurd becomes difficult. The composer finds himself in this position to an extreme degree. Charles Wuorinen makes this point in his book *Simple Composition*." (p. 249) *See:* B1087

B991 Kolman, Barbara. "Reviews: Books." The *American Music Teacher* 33, no. 3 (January 1984), p. 62.

"For the most part, Dr. Wuorinen presents his material in a clear, easily comprehensible fashion." *See:* B1087

B992 Le Fanu, Nicola. "Reviews: Charles Wuorinen: Simple Composition." *Music Analysis* 1, no. 1 (March 1982), pp. 108-112.

"I think that in this book Wuorinen the author has done a disservice to Wuorinen the composer. I wonder why, in the midst of an active and successful composing career, he was tempted to pontificate, to command 'the applause of listening senates' rather than resting mute, an inglorious [John] Milton? Certainly his music deserves better than to be described as yielding 'nothing special'." (p. 112) *See:* B1087

B993 Marvin, Elizabeth West. *A Generalized Theory of Musical Contour: Its Application to Melodic and Rhythmic Analysis of Non-Tonal Music and Its Perceptual and Pedagogical Implications*. (Ph.D. dissertation) Rochester, New York: University of Rochester, 1988.

Chapter One, "Music Perception and Non-Tonal Music Theory," mentions *Simple Composition* as a textbook concerned with musical surface and underlying pitch-class relationships. Wuorinen's name is misspelled "Wourinen". *See:* B1087

B994 Morris, Robert. "Book Review: Simple Composition." *Theory and Practice: Newsletter-Journal of the Music Theory Society of New York State* 5, no. 1 (July 1980), pp. 66-72.

This lengthy review opens by stating Wuorinen's book "is certainly superior to David Cope's *New Music Composition*" and that it "avoids the speculative and 'calisthenic' pitfalls of Hindemith's *The Craft of Musical Composition*." (p. 66) Morris writes: "I know of no other good up-to-date elementary description of this area of compositional craft besides Brian Fennelly's contribution to [John] Vinton's *Dictionary Dictionary of Contemporary Music*, New York: E.P. Dutton, 1974]." After discussing the book in detail and criticizing it on a few points (including the omission of any discussion of electronic music and "its lack of examples from the literature of twelve-tone music to demonstrate many of the constructs and techniques discussed" (p. 69), Morris concludes: "My only regret is that we have had to wait for so long for such a work to appear." (p. 72) *See:* B729, B994, B1087

B995 Orr, Buxton. "Sensible and Readable." *Composer* [London], no. 73 (Summer 1981), p. 27.

"To those colleagues who have recoiled either in fear or in anger from Milton Babbitry, or the casting of Perles, I would strongly recommend this eminently sensible and readable book." *See:* B1087

B996 Perle, George. *The Listening Composer*. Berkeley: University of California Press, 1990.

In his discussion of a work by Arnold Schoenberg, Perle refers to words from page twenty-two of *Simple Composition*: "A manual on twelve-tone composition finds an analogy between melody and the twelve-tone row, in that melodies, too, 'will constitute ordered successions of tones.'" (p. 60) *See:* B1087

B997 Phipps, Graham H. "Comprehending Twelve-tone Music as an Extension of the Primary Musical Language of Tonality." *College Music Symposium* 24, no. 2 (Fall 1984), pp. 35-54.

This article is devoted to a discussion of Arnold Schoenberg's music. It includes a footnote on page fifty-one that refers to Wuorinen's *Simple Composition* as a current pedagogical approach to twelve-tone composition. *See:* B1087

B998 Pope, Conrad. "Reviews." *Journal of Music Theory* 24, no. 2 (Fall 1980), pp. 253-268.

A lengthy and mostly unfavorable review of the book. "*Simple Composition* is intended to provide the thread of 'idea continuity' but it never extends beyond the boundaries of the original definition of Wuorinen's twelve-tone system. Because *Simple Composition's* twelve-tone concept remains static, it never comes to enfold the other operations, rather, they become merely a foil to it. In this way, the book erodes not only the potency of its definition through its lack of a unifying concept but it weakens the ability of its exercises to be suggestive of anything greater than their local solution." (p. 267) *See:* B1097

B999 Rahn, John. *Basic Atonal Theory*. New York: Longman, 1980.

This text includes three references to Wuorinen. The first calls him a distinguished composer and mentions *Simple Composition* (p. viii). The second reference names Wuorinen as one of the contemporary American composers whose work has been part of the "relatively coherent tradition from [Richard] Wagner, [Johannes] Brahms, and [Gustav] Mahler; through [Arnold] Schoenberg and his pupils [Anton von] Webern and [Alban] Berg" (p. 2). The third reference suggests *Simple Composition* be used in conjunction with writings by George Perle, Milton Babbitt, and Peter Westergaard. (p. 120) *See:* B1087

B1000 Samuel, Rhian. ["Music Reviews."] *Music & Letters* 70, no. 4 (1989), pp. 597-598.

Samuel writes *Simple Composition* works "like a dose of salts...on traditionally-minded composition students, who thus far may have produced only turgid music of the kind [Harrison] Birtwistle describes (in deprecating reference to his own early attempts) as 'sub-Vaughan Williams'." (p. 597) *See:* B1087

B1001 Sandow, Gregory. "Lost Generation." *Village Voice* [New York City], 24 January 1984, pp. 78-79.

Sandow argues that contemporary music is at a turning point and mentions *Simple Composition* is an "otherwise wonderful textbook" (p. 79) in which Wuorinen asserts tonal music is no longer written by mainstream composers. *See:* B1087

B1002 Sandow, Gregory. "Other People's Words." *Village Voice* [New York City], 18 September 1984, pp. 81-82.

"His insistence that composers work on all parts of a piece at once instead of proceeding from the beginning to the end seems perverse, though, like his rules for writing melody, well-explained and vastly intriguing." (p. 82) Sandow concludes by saying the book provides "invaluable discipline." (p. 82) [P] *See:* B1087

B1003 Standford, Patric. "How to Compose." The *Musical Times* 122 (December 1981), p. 824.

A brief, favorable review. Standford raises one objection, however, in that "there seems to be no real concern about harmonic movement or the implications of the sound of music revealed through Wuorinen's ever-inventive flow of innumerable illustrations." *See:* B1087

B1004 Stucky, Steven. "Book Reviews." *Notes* 36, no. 4 (June 1980), pp. 895-896.

"Wuorinen demonstrates that precise writing about twelve-tone theory need not be couched in that clotted, obfuscatory prose style we have come to dread. His writing is readable, occasionally lively, and studded with welcome nuggets of practical advice born of experience." (p. 895) Later on, Stucky writes: "Although it was not the author's purpose, his explanations are so lucid as to make the book a good introduction to the twelve-tone system for the general reader. Indeed, it may well prove to be a more convenient (certainly more nearly 'state-of-the-art') reference than the standard [George] Perle, *Serial Composition and Atonality* (4th ed.; Berkeley, 1977) and the now quaint [Josef] Rufer, *Composition with Twelve Notes* (New York, 1954)." (p. 896) *See:* B1087

B1005 Taylor, Clifford. *Musical Idea and the Design Aesthetic in Contemporary Music: A Text for Discerning Appraisal of Musical Thought in Western Culture.* Lewiston, New York: The Edward Mellen Press, 1990.

This book is volume seven in the publisher's series *Studies in the History and Interpretation of Music.* Taylor writes: "Charles Wuorinen's tendency, in his book *Simple Composition...*, to relegate pertinent compositional aspects of the medium other than pitch, and possibly rhythm, to supportive positions in the compositional process, serves to verify his avoidance of simultaneous interaction in preference for the constructivist effort to harness within musical parameters that immense and volatile force of emotional energy that has been the essential heritage of twentieth-century posture and artistic practice, involving the objective control of pitch and rhythm not simultaneously integrated with the other essential aspects to much of the educational process in this country, if not throughout the Western world, and, in a significant if not a more subtle way, in the results of compositional activity itself." (p. 3) *See:* B1087

Viewpoints

B1006 Burge, David. "Instrumental Solo and Ensemble Music By John Corigliano." *Notes* 46, no. 4 (June 1990), pp. 1074-1075.

In reviewing two works by John Corigliano, Burge cites an interview with Wuorinen published in the *Los Angeles Times* in which Wuorinen gave his views of what Burge terms *the minimalist phenomenon*: "Wuorinen, never one to back off from a fight, comments: 'People have stopped trying to be civilized. What we have is...the need for instant self-gratification. And that accounts for this utterly unchallenging, unprovocative kind of music.'" (p. 1074)

B1007 Campbell, Karen. "Meet the Composer Orchestra Residency Program." *Ovation* 9 (September 1988), pp. 24-29.

The article is an overview of the Meet the Composer Program after seven years of existence. It contains commentary by John Duffy, founder and president of the program. Wuorinen comments on his concern about publicity and marketing activities of orchestras versus the intrinsic value of art. Of the composers interviewed in this article, Wuorinen is quoted the most. In discussing audiences and the cultural climate, Wuorinen states: "I think we are in danger of seeing a complete eclipse of serious music in the Western musical tradition." (p. 29) He mentions deceased conductors (Serge Koussevitzky, Carl Reiner, Dimitri Mitropoulos) who championed new music of their day and says Michael Tilson Thomas is perhaps the only major living conductor to follow that path. Wuorinen also notes a conversation he had with composer Jacob Druckman, who noted that "the average age of the New York Philharmonic audience was sixty-two and a half." (p. 29) Wuorinen comments that the aging population is not, by and large, being replaced. [P]

B1008 "Colloquy and Review: Communications: From Daniel Goode." *Perspectives of New Music* 5, no. 2 (Spring/Summer 1967), pp. 170-171.

This letter is a commentary on Wuorinen's review of Mario Davidovsky's *Contrastes No. 1* for string orchestra and electronic sounds. Goode calls for a new kind of analysis that would "reach out for a conceptual integration on a high level of what I would like to call the sculptural aspects of music...." (p. 170) *See:* B1066, B1069

B1009 "Composer and Critic: Two Views of Their Responsibility to the Art of Music and Its Public." *I.S.A.M. [Institute of American Music] Newsletter* [Department of Music, Brooklyn College, City University of New York] 10, no. 2 (May 1981), pp. 1, 8-11.

Excerpts from a public debate between *New York Times* music critic John Rockwell and Wuorinen, which took place on 13 April 1981 at Symphony Space in New York City. The debate focused on art versus entertainment, standards for composers, ignorance and education. There are illustrations with an unidentified concert-goer depicting facial expressions labeled "pain," "painful concentration," and "disdain."

B1010 *Contemporary Composers on Contemporary Music.* Ed. Schwartz, Elliott and Barney Childs. New York: Holt, Rinehart and Winston, 1967.

This book of interviews with composers contains a revised version of "What Concerns Me Is Music," which was first published in *Genesis West* in 1962. The interview includes a number of questions on various subjects, e.g., jazz, *Gebrauchsmusik.*

In response to a question about how much he cares about the "average" audience for major symphony orchestra concerts, Wuorinen replies: "...I can say that I care no more about them and their reactions than I do about the audience for juke boxes in bars. Indeed the latter are preferable because they really enjoy what they hear (I think), and in any case are not under the impression that their passive reception of 'music' qualifies them for literate judgement. Besides this, one can drink in bars; symphony orchestras, whose programs are enough to drive any sensible man to drink, unfortunately do not provide alcoholic anesthesia during performances, as they should — but then considering the amount of sleeping at symphony orchestra programs that gets done by our 'normal concert-going audience' I suppose the orchestras may be excused for not seeing the need." *See:* B1092

B1011 Craig, Dale A. "Colloquy and Review: Communications." *Perspectives of New Music* 6, no. 1 (Fall/Winter 1967), pp. 156-157.

This letter criticizes Wuorinen's review of Larry Austin's book *Music in the Twentieth Century*: "Wuorinen's peevish critique of Austin's great contribution reflects exactly the limited viewpoint that has plagued so many earlier histories of modern music and that Austin succeeded so admirably in ignoring." (p. 157) *See:* B1065, B1068

B1012 Daniel, Oliver. *Stokowski: A Counterpoint of View.* New York: Dodd, Mead & Company, 1982.

Daniel's chapter titled "Oedipus Le Pas d'Acier, *and* Pierrot Lunaire" closes with a reference to Wuorinen's container notes for a Nonesuch recording of that work (Nonesuch H71251): "On reading the far from favorable reviews for the Schoenberg [reprinted in *Musical America*, 25 April 1931, p. 42], I was reminded of a remark made by composer Charles Wuorinen on listening to *Pierrot Lunaire*, which, after all, dates back to 1912, just thirty-six years before Charles was born. He remarked that 'even at this late date [1971], listening to it occasionally reminds one of attempts to befriend a porcupine.'" (p. 272) *See:* D44

B1013 Dirks, Lee E. "New Faces, New Sounds. Is Music Entering a Rich New Era?" The *National Observer* 3, no. 33 (17 August 1964), pp. 1, 14.

This article is a general overview of the Festival of Contemporary American Music held at Tanglewood under the auspices of the Fromm Music Foundation. Dirks mentions what he terms "the growing self-confidence of American composers," and quotes Wuorinen: "'It must make the Europeans furious that we've suddenly burst forth,' muses Mr. Wuorinen over a glass of brandy. 'But notice that despite their long-standing patronizing attitude, you're starting to see them furtively showing up over here.'" Dirks also writes Wuorinen commands a greater following as a composer than any of his peers.

B1014 Fleming, Shirley. "Musician of the Month: Charles Wuorinen." *High Fidelity/Musical America* 20, no. 9 (September 1970), pp. MA8-MA9.

This article mentions a few works by Wuorinen and includes some interview material. Wuorinen discusses a number of topics. [P]

B1015 Green, Harris. "Are Today's Composers Adrift In a Void?" The *New York Times*, 1 October 1972, *(Arts & Leisure)*, pp. 17, 24.

Green writes about what he feels is the quandary of the contemporary composer and the characteristics of new music. He discusses the ideas of Pierre Boulez and Wuorinen and urges a detailed study of the music of the past. In part, he concludes: "Contemporary music merely reminds me of the void. The composers seem to be fearless voyagers into the unknown, all right, astronauts whose lifelines snapped during a needless space walk and who are now adrift." (p. 24) This article was praised in a letter to the editor, by Walter Simmons, which appeared in the 15 October 1972 issue of the *New York Times*. *See:* B1026

B1016 Hall, Carla. "The Sound Barrier." The *Washington Post*, 16 September 1981, p. B7.

A review of a 14 September 1981 event called *American Town Meeting on the Arts*, held at the Music Recital Hall, Catholic University, Washington, D.C. Wuorinen is quoted: "In 1790, Bach — who died in 1750 — was considered old-fashioned, obsolete.... Now, that may have been too much in the other direction, but [today] we've gone entirely too much toward death worship."

B1017 Hastings, Ross. "Letters: Serious Music: A Bleak Future?" The *New York Times*, 31 July 1988, *(Arts & Leisure)*, p. 13.

This letter to the editor was in response to Joan Peyser's article titled "Wuorinen's Bleak View of the Future." Hastings writes that Wuorinen's future, not serious music's, is the bleak one: "...this is the most encouraging news I have heard about contemporary music in years." *See:* B1025, B1028

B1018 Heikinheimo, Seppo. "Säveltäjäpury koolla Helsingissa." *Helsingen Sanomat Arkisto*, 13 October 1977.

Titled "A Jury of Composers Meet in Helsinki," the article discusses the ISCM [International Society of Contemporary Music] competition. Heikinheimo writes: "Charles Wuorinen thinks that the selection principles with regard to the ISCM Festival programs are unfortunate; the jury can choose only from those compositions sent by individual composers and selected by national juries." Wuorinen is quoted as saying: "It is unthinkable that, for example, such an American grand old man in music as Elliott Carter would send his compositions to be considered by two different juries, and possibly rejected." [P]

B1019 Henahan, Donal. "Try a Little Taoism." The *New York Times*, 7 June 1970, *(Arts & Leisure)*, pp. 13, 24.

This article is the result of an interview with Wuorinen. The topics discussed include Wuorinen's philosophy of various subjects and issues, such as Chinese philosophy (Taosim), the importance of orchestral instruments, twelve-tone music, and politics.

B1020 Julius, Ruth. "Edgard Varese: An Oral History Project, Some Preliminary Conclusions." *Current Musicology* 25 (1978), pp. 39-49.

This written "interpretation" of the oral history project (which included a 3 January 1977 interview with Wuorinen) features a number of comments by Wuorinen concerning Varèse. In terms of Varèse's music and other art forms, Wuorinen says "metaphors are useless, misleading, false, and dangerous, because they are too often used as a substitute for cognitive musical thought, information and skill." (p. 43) Further, Julius writes: "Even Wuorinen, the only composer interviewed who cannot include Varèse in the 'pantheon of great composers because of his relative indifference to pitch relational matters,' firmly believes that Varèse's major innovation was in dealing with musical time. He sees Varèse's contribution as 'his proposal to mark the passage of musical time by juxtapositional means rather than by developmental ones from the past. The music proceeds according to the juxtaposition of differentiated elements, rather than the inter-connection of evolutionary related elements.' Wuorinen cites *Octandre* and *Ionisation* as the most successful pieces in this respect." (p. 45) Further on, Julius writes: "Wuorinen has conducted *Deserts* several times in the complete instrumental and tape version, and has always been baffled by the relationship between the tape part and the instrumental part. He would like to perform it with only its instrumental sections (a possibility suggested by the score), to see whether the work might not present a more coherent entity without the tape." (p. 48)

B1021 Kraft, William. "Letters: The Wuorinen Hassle." *High Fidelity/Musical America* 25, no. 8 (August 1975), pp. M2-M4.
This letter to the editor was a response in support of Wuorinen's article "We Spit on the Dead," published in an earlier issue of this magazine. Kraft writes, in part: "I am sure that many of my colleagues were offended, as I was, by the remarks made by Mr. Upgren and Mr. Santuccio.... The issue is not the degree of marketability of contemporary music but primarily whether the composer deserves to exist as a professional, deriving his income from the practice of his profession as do those in other fields with comparable amounts of skill and training." (p. MA2) *See:* B1022, B1076, B1091

B1022 "Letters: Wuorinen's Case: For and Against." *High Fidelity/Musical America* 25, no. 3 (March 1975), p. MA2-MA4.
These letters to the editor were a response to Wuorinen's essay "We Spit On the Dead," published in an earlier issue of this journal. Arthur R. Upgren writes that even though Arnold Schoenberg is often called one of the most influential composers of the twentieth century, "he won by a wide margin a poll asking for the composer one could most easily do without (conducted last year by the Schwann Record and Tape Guide)." John A. Santuccio writes, in part: "Mr. Wuorinen seems to know the great value of his own work, and I assume that it is on the basis of his overvaluation he feels he should be compensated." *See:* B1021, B1076, B1091

B1023 Liebman, Stuart. "Charles Wuorinen: The Academy in Peril." The *Boston Phoenix*, 24 April 1973, pp. 18-19, 34.
An interview with Wuorinen consisting of fifteen questions about success, music at the university, the performance of contemporary music, orchestral music, recording versus live performance, and the identity of American music. In terms of the last topic, Wuorinen states: "The European influence, in a word, deparochialized American music. But what we have now is unquestionably the richest and most proliferate and varied compositional scene that this century has yet witnessed. Indeed, as perhaps had ever existed anywhere in Western music." (p. 34) [P]

B1024 Määttänen, Sakari. "Toisen polven Finnin Charles Wuorinen ylistyspuheet ja haukut." *Helsingen Sanomat Arkisto*, 10 February 1979.
This article features biographical material about Wuorinen. Written by a non-specialist who was a former New York City correspondent for this tabloid, the article also features some of Wuorinen's political opinions, ranging from Jimmy Carter to Gerald Ford, Iran to China, Chile to the then Soviet Union, [Ronald] Reagan to the Central Intelligence Agency. Wuorinen is quoted as saying: "What I like most in music does not exist." [P]

B1025 McKean, James N. "Letters: Serious Music: A Bleak Future?" The *New York Times*, 31 July 1988, *(Arts & Leisure)*, p. 13.
This letter to the editor was in response to Joan Peyser's 3 June 1988 *New York Times* article "Wuorinen's Bleak View of the Future." McKean writes Wuorinen has an "elitist view of the world...." *See:* B1017, B1028

B1026 "Music Mailbag: Often Forgotten." The *New York Times*, 15 October 1972, *(Arts & Leisure)*, p. 18.

This letter to the editor from Walter Simmons was in response to Morris Green's 1 October 1972 *New York Times* article "Are Today's Composers Adrift in a Void?" Simmons praises Green's article and writes: "He [Green] does well to expose the pretentious, self-serving rationalizations of the likes of [Pierre] Boulez and Wuorinen." *See:* B1015

B1027 "Music Mailbag: 'Why We Won't Buy Wuorinen'." The *New York Times*, 11 October 1970, *(Arts & Leisure)*, pp. 15, 32.

This letter to the editor column features three responses to Wuorinen's article "The Public Wants Only Beethoven? 'It's Not True!'," which appeared in the same newspaper on 3 September 1970. The first response, from Robert Claiborne, is a negative rebuttal. He writes, in part: "In the light of the dismal track record of 'contemporary' music over half a century, the recording companies (whatever their other sins) may conceivably know something Wuorinen and his colleagues don't know: people aren't buying his kind of music because they don't like it." (p. 15) The other two letters — from Martin J. Burne, O.S.B., and John Holt — praise Wuorinen for having had the courage to speak out against the recording companies. *See:* B1081

B1028   Peyser, Joan. "Wuorinen's Bleak View of the Future." The *New York Times*, 3 June 1988, p. 27.

An important article that describes Wuorinen's views on contemporary music. The article coincided with Wuorinen's fiftieth birthday and includes historical background about the Group for Contemporary Music and the controversy created when the New York State Council on the Arts cut funding for the ensemble on the grounds that the group's concert programs did not promote music of women and African-American composers. Wuorinen also speaks of what he terms a "professional malaise" in the serious music world: "A great work like a Beethoven symphony becomes like a blob of toothpaste." (In a subsequent conversation with Richard Burbank, Wuorinen restated this view and, as an example, referred to the 4 December 1988 London concert event at which Lorin Maazel conducted three different orchestras in all nine Beethoven symphonies. A 6 December 1988 *New York Times* review of that event quoted Maazel as having said "I was looking for something rather spectacular to attract attention.") Parts of this interview were quoted by Jacques Barzun in his dialog-form piece "Overheard at Glimmerglass ('Famous Last Words')" *(Berlioz Studies*. Ed. Peter Bloom. Cambridge: Cambridge University Press, 1992 (pp. 259, 270)). Peyser's article also mentions the controversy concerning Wuorinen's 1986 resignation as chairman of the American Composers Orchestra, during which conductor Paul Dunkel stated "music in New York would die if it were left in Wuorinen's hands." Peyser's last paragraphs include the statement "the current haute couture is definitely not with Mr. Wuorinen"; that Johann Sebastian Bach was eclipsed by the more modern music of his own sons, and "we all know how it turned out with Bach." Two letters to the editor (reactions to this article) subsequently appeared in the *New York Times. See:* B1017, B1025

B1029 Pontzious, Richard. "Wuorinen Speaks Out On the Role of Contemporary Music." *San Francisco Examiner*, 10 October 1986.

An article featuring Wuorinen's opinions on contemporary music and its importance in American culture.

B1030 Rich, Alan. "A Federal Case." *New York Herald Tribune*, 13 February 1966, p. 31.

An article about government support for the arts and a meeting of the National Music Council, held in January, 1966. Rich reports comments Wuorinen made, though it is unclear from the article whether Wuorinen attended the meeting.

B1031 Rockwell, John. "Today's Composers and Players May Yet Be Allies."
The *New York Times*, 7 August 1983, *(Arts & Leisure)*, pp. 17, 20.
This article describes a panel discussion sponsored by the Music Critics
Association that was devoted to the relationship between the recording industry and
contemporary music activities. Rockwell expresses his point of view that ambitious
performers may well have an important impact on how new music is composed.

B1032 Schwarz, K. Robert. "American Music Today: As Seen By Five
Composers." *Encore* [New York City] 3, no. 1 (March 1988).
A brief, unpaged article consisting of an overview of contemporary American
music and featuring comments of five composers (Wuorinen, John Adams, Ellen Zwilich,
Steve Reich, and William Bolcom). Schwarz says: "Wuorinen sees himself as the
defender of high culture, holding the fort against the onslaught of popular music." [P]

B1033 "Status Seeker. Talk of the Alumni." *Columbia College Today* [Columbia
University] (Fall 1970), pp. 57-58.
A brief article in a Columbia University alumni publication that includes
viewpoints by Wuorinen. "He [Wuorinen] predicts that the next major phase [of musical
development] will be the 'integration of Western music and world music,' due in large
part to what he describes as 'a confrontation with the high music cultures of the Far
East.'"

B1034 Taubman, Howard. "Adriatic Music Seminar." The *New York Times*, 20
July 1968, p. 16.
A report on the *Yugoslav-American Seminar on Music* held at Sveti Stefan,
Yugoslavia, 6-14 July 1968. Taubman says the views Wuorinen expressed at the
conference "could not but have been distasteful to the more conservative among the host
composers, but they heard him out with respect." *See:* B1086, B1088

B1035 Tawa, Nicholas. *A Most Wondrous Babble: American Art Composers,
Their Music, and the American Scene, 1950-1985.* Westport, Connecticut:
Greenwood Press, 1987.
This book is volume nine of the publisher's series *Contributions to the Study of
Music and Dance.* In the section of the book titled "Postwar Turbulence and Change:
The Role of Fashion," Tawa comments on Wuorinen: "The inconsistency of writers on
the contemporary music scene increased even as the rise of stylistic change accelerated
after 1960. Charles Wuorinen, irked when his serial music became passé, stated: 'When
I started out, my music was always characterized as being "explosive," "chaotic,"
"barbaric," "angry," etc. Which makes you wonder about the status of these reporters
who now characterize the same music as "academic," "grim," "dry," "freezing,"
"austere."' (p. 24) In the section titled "The World of the Modern Composer:
Predjudice, Pride, and Frustration," Tawa writes: "Charles Wuorinen, who insisted on
going his own way, said the public deserved to be spat upon for neglecting him. William
Kraft hastened to defend Wuorinen's statement, saying, whether the public liked it or not,
all composers deserved support as professional artists. Because Wuorinen aimed at the
profound and spiritual and did not stoop to entertainment, he represented the best in
American civilization." (p. 45) Later in the same chapter, Tawa writes: "Egocentrism
and isolation encouraged a musician like Wuorinen to urge composers to 'rise up and
demand' an end to the attacks on them and on their music, and an end to 'inadequate
compensation' for the act of composing. Revolt was necessary." (p. 49) "The protest
was pathetic and the revolt meaningless, if the outside world took notice. Referring
specifically to composers like Wuorinen, Abram Chasins once remarked about the
unwillingness to realize that noncommunication had left composers without any public.

Unable to face reality or 'to read a balance sheet' they lived a fantasy life in limbo, sputtering bitter charges that have little validity." (p. 49) *See:* B721, B1021, B1091

B1036 Terry, Kenneth. "Atonal Tonalities." *Downbeat* 48, no. 2 (February 1981), pp. 16-18.
       This article discusses various aspects of Wuorinen's work and philosophy of musical composition. The article is noteworthy in that it presents Wuorinen's frank opinions about a number of composers and their musics, including Frederic Rzewski, Steve Reich, La Monte Young. Terry writes: "When I point out that such minimalist composers as Steve Reich and La Monte Young reject the mainstream tradition because of its fixation on Western music since 1700, Wuorinen shoots back, 'That's bullshit. These people don't know anything. By and large, they don't know musical history. The articulate, known tradition of Western music, with identifiable composers of great worth and magnitude, goes back 750 years.'" (p. 17)

B1037 Ulrich, Allan. "New Music This Side of the Fringe." *San Francisco Examiner*, 4 November 1988.
       Discusses Wuorinen's leadership of the San Francisco Symphony's *New and Unusual Music Series*. Ulrich writes that Wuorinen "has never heard a Philip Glass work he liked...." Wuorinen is quoted: "When I'm convinced a piece is truly worthless, I can't put it on a program simply because it exists."

B1038 Waleson, Heidi. "Composers Meet the Orchestra." *Symphony Magazine* 38, no. 5 (October/November 1987), pp. 13-15, 48, 52.
       This article assesses the Meet the Composer's Orchestra Residencies Program at the halfway point of its projected ten-year life. Waleson writes: "For Wuorinen, the issue comes down to leadership — something he sees as dangerously absent, given today's absentee music directors." (p. 52)

B1039 Weinstein, Robert V. "Interview — Charles Wuorinen." *FM Guide: The Music Book* [Greater New York Edition] 11, no. 11 (November 1973), pp. 35-36.
       This interview includes a discussion of various topics, such as contemporary music and audiences, and symphony orchestra conductors. Weinstein cites a comment by Eugene Ormandy in which he said rehearsal time and audience keep orchestras away from contemporary music. Wuorinen replies: "I think one has to take these objections from men like that with a good deal of reservation because there you are speaking to someone who has never manifested any interest in twentieth century music or any sense of responsibility to his own time." (p. 36) Wuorinen goes on to say that Leopold Stokowski exhibited a "sense of moral leadership" because "he insisted on performing works which were then problematic because he felt that it was his artistic responsibility to educate his public." (p. 36)

B1040 "Where Is 20th-Century Music Now?" The *New York Times*, 24 June 1984, *(Arts & Leisure)*, p. 1.
       This article, largely of an interview nature, features five questions on contemporary music and the responses of five composers, one of which was Wuorinen. *New York Times* critic John Rockwell moderated the interview (though he did not sign the article) for the *Arts & Leisure* section of this tabloid. The questions concern comparing contemporary music with that of the past, accessibility of new music, the impact of technology on new music composition, and contemporary music in different parts of America. The other participants in the panel were Morton Subotnick, Morton Feldman, Laurie Anderson, and Anthony Davis.

Wuorinen as Performer

B1041 Archibald, Bruce. "Reviews of Records." *Musical Quarterly* 58, no. 2 (April 1972), pp. 333-335.

   A review of a CRI recording featuring works by Chou Wên-Chung (CRI 251). "For me it *[Cursive]* is the most beautiful of the four [works] recorded here, and it is excellently performed by Harvey Sollberger and Charles Wuorinen." (p. 335) *See:* D43

B1042 Commanday, Robert. "Carter New-Music Program Goes Over Big." *San Francisco Chronicle*, 22 November 1988, Section E, p. 1.

   A review of a 20 November 1988 concert of chamber music by Elliott Carter, part of the *New and Unusual Music Series* billed as a "Salute to Elliott Carter." Wuorinen and cellist Fred Sherry performed Carter's *Sonata for Cello and Piano.* Commanday writes: "Sherry and Wuorinen played this with a command at the level that frees the interpretive spirit." The event also included a panel discussion featuring Wuorinen, Carter and music critic Michael Steinberg.

B1043 Commanday, Robert. "A Stylized Premiere at Davies Hall." *San Francisco Chronicle*, 13 October 1986, p. 59.

   This concert review merely mentions that Wuorinen conducted an 11 October 1986 concert (*New and Unusual Music Series*, Davies Hall, San Francisco) featuring John Cage's ballet score *The Seasons* and Sylvestre Revueltas's *Homenaje a Federico Garcia Lorca.*

B1044 Dierks, Donald. "First Pulitzer Concert at UCSD is a Prize-Winner." *San Diego Union*, 12 January 1990.

   A concert review of the 11 January 1990 UCSD [University of California, San Diego] concert at which Wuorinen conducted Igor Stravinsky's *Dumbarton Oaks Concerto* and *Monumentum pro Gesualdo di Venosa.* Wuorinen also conducted his own *Bamboula Squared* and *Machault Mon Chou.* "The performances by Wuorinen and the orchestra were both solid and controlled, perhaps a little too stiff and lacking in a spirit of spontaneity at times." *See:* W4c, W15a, B44, B45, B345

B1045 Frank, Peter. "Contemporary Music. 2½ concerts." *Columbia Daily Spectator* [New York City] 113, no. 74 (25 February 1969), p. 2.

   A review of a 10 February 1969 Group for Contemporary Music concert at which Wuorinen and Nicholas England played Igor Stravinsky's *Sonata for Two Pianos.* "Both did a beautiful job of this ordinarily attractive piece, performing at the same time with clarity and with lushness."

B1046 Hamilton, David. "Music." The *Nation*, 19 January 1974, p. 93.

   A review of a 17 December 1973 performance of Elliott Carter's *Double Concerto*, by the Group for Contemporary Music (Ursula Oppens, harpsichord; Robert Miller, piano; Wuorinen, conducting). Hamilton says it "struck me as the most confident performance to date...." *See:* B1052

B1047 Hassen, Marjorie. "Record Reviews." *American Music* 6, no. 4 (1988), pp. 478-480.

   A review of the New World Records recording of Milton Babbitt's *Concerto for Piano and Orchestra*, Wuorinen conducting (New World 346). Hassen says the performers "served Babbitt admirably indeed." (p. 479) *See:* D54

B1048 Herman, Andrea. "Stravinsky Symposium: City's Gift to the World." *Evening Tribune* [San Diego], 15 September 1982.

A review of the five-day *International Stravinsky Symposium* (10-14 September 1982) held at the University of California, San Diego. Among other works, Wuorinen performed the world premiere of two fragment pieces by Igor Stravinsky: *Berceuses à 2 mains* for piano (1940) and *Boris Godunov* excerpt transcribed for piano (1918). Herman writes that Wuorinen played "with sprightly temperament; the playing nicely combined articulateness and craftsmanship." *See:* B948

B1049 Morgan, Robert P. "The Recordings of Edgard Varèse." *High Fidelity/Musical America* 27, no. 2 (February 1977), pp. 82-83.

A review of the CRI recording of Varèse's *Deserts* (CRI 268). "[Wuorinen's] reading with the Group for Contemporary music is much the tightest and most accurate, although it is a bit on the stiff side." (p. 83) *See:* D50

B1050 Page, Tim. "Music: Noted in Brief: Composers Orchestra Offers Diverse Concert." The *New York Times*, 21 1986, p. C20.

A review of an American Composers Orchestra concert at which Wuorinen conducted John Cage's *The Seasons*. Page writes: "Mr. Wuorinen's conducting was precise and knowledgeable."

B1051 Robinson, Harlow. "The ACO at 10: Still Making History." *High Fidelity/Musical America* 35, no. (October 1985), pp. MA25-MA26.

This article is an overview of the American Composers Orchestra. Wuorinen is mentioned once, as a conductor of the orchestra.

B1052 Rockwell, John. "Music: Contemporary Group Displays Charm." The *New York Times*, 19 December 1973, p. 54.

A review of a 17 December 1973 Group for Contemporary Music concert featuring Elliott Carter's *Double Concerto*. Wuorinen conducted. After calling the work a masterpiece, Rockwell says "the performance it received under Mr. Wuorinen's leadership sounded precise and committed, despite an imbalance between the two solo instruments and a less than ideal separation between the two chamber groups." *See:* B1046

B1053 Rockwell, John. "Opera: Feldman Event." The *New York Times*, 23 November 1978, p. 19.

This review of Morton Feldman's opera *Neither* (the American premiere) says "Mr. Wuorinen's direction sounded carefully prepared and scrupulously executed...." *See:* D78

B1054 Rockwell, John. "Zukofsky Is Effective in Recital Of Contemporary Violin Music." The *New York Times*, 14 April 1976, p. 31.

A review of a Group for Contemporary Music concert at Hubbard Recital Hall, Manhattan School of Music, New York City, held on 12 April 1976. Wuorinen performed as a pianist in works by Igor Stravinsky. Rockwell writes Wuorinen's playing was of a "far livelier and more sensitive sort than usual."

B1055 Rothstein, Joel. "Record Reviews: Music for Oboe." *Downbeat* 48, no. 6 (June 1981), p. 38.

A review of a Composers Recordings, Inc., recording of oboe music (CRI SD 423). Rothstein says Wuorinen (on piano) provided "sympathetic support" to oboist James Ostryniec. *See:* D51

B1056 Strongin, Theodore. "Divergent Works of Music Played." The *New York Times*, 20 January 1964, p. 21.

Robert Stewart's *Five Miniatures for Piano* was performed on 18 January 1964, at the Donnell Library, New York City. Wuorinen was the soloist. Henry Cowell moderated a discussion after the concert. Strongin writes that Wuorinen offered "a magnificent solo performance."

B1057 Strongin, Theodore. "Haphazard Treatment." The *New York Times*, 29 November 1964, *(Arts & Leisure)*, p. 24.

An article about recording contemporary music for commercial release, and focusing on Lukas Foss. It mentions that Wuorinen and the Group for Contemporary Music recorded *Echoi* for the Epic label. *See:* 42

B1058 Tucker, Marilyn. "Welcome Changes for New-Unusual Series." *San Francisco Chronicle*, 23 December 1985, p. 55.

A review of the season opening concert of the San Francisco Symphony's *New and Unusual Music Series*, held at Grace Cathedral, San Francisco, 20 December 1985. Tucker comments on the differences between Wuorinen's approach to programming, calling it refreshing. Of Wuorinen's conducting, Tucker writes he "kept the spirit light and unmuddied."

B1059 "Wuorinen's Music Featured At Tanglewood Youth Week." *Gardner News* [Gardner, Massachusetts], 14 August 1964, p. 1.

A novelty item in that this front-page story about Wuorinen performing some of his compositions at Tanglewood the preceding week is adjacent to a story headlined: "UN Secretary General Requests More Troops for Cyprus, Tension Increases."

Writings by Wuorinen

B1060 "…agitato: Letter to the Editor." American Composers Alliance Bulletin 10, no. 1 (1961), pp. 8, 22.

In this letter Wuorinen writes about the bleak situation in New York City concerning avenues of finance and performance for new music. He states that the previous generation of American composers came together to make things happen, but that if the current generation fails to act, musicians "will then have to start from the bottom again, and the effort of a third of a century will have been wasted." (p. 32)

B1061 "An Appreciation." *Perspectives of New Music* 15, no. 2 (1976), pp. 41-42.

This two-page tribute to Milton Babbitt constitutes Wuorinen's contribution to a special issue of this journal. The issue is subtitled "Sounds and Words: A Critical Celebration of Milton Babbitt at 60." Wuorinen writes, in part: "Many striking adjectives could be marshalled for service in one's encomiastic armada, but chief of all the things that strike me about it [Babbitt's music] is the sense of his music's permanence. One hears the works, both early and late, with an equal sense of their freshness and yet permanent relevance. They are masterworks." (p. 41)

B1062 "Are the Arts Doomed on Campus?" The *New York Times*, 8 August 1971, *(Arts & Leisure)*, p. D11.

In this article Wuorinen discusses his termination as a member of the music faculty of Columbia University. He writes that his dismissal was part of an increasing indifference to the arts among university administrators faced with financial crises. He also asserts university-based artists have mistakenly interpreted financial support from their institutions to mean genuine interest in such activity, when, in reality, such support had been based on a financial prosperity which allowed universities to expand their facilities. Further, he says universities should have the courage to support the arts despite diminishing revenues. Wuorinen concludes: "The saddest irony in the United States is that just when the artistic, the musical, culture is coming to its greatest flowering, the boobs who run the institutions we depend on would cut us down and cast us out." Paul Henry Lang wrote a response to this article, titled "Music at Columbia Will Endure, Even Without Wuorinen." The response appeared in The *New York Times* on 29 August 1971. *See:* B818, B819, B822, B824, B825, B871, B1062

B1063 "The Bulk of Hostility to New Music Would Pass If..." The *New York Times*, 10 September 1972, *(Arts & Leisure)*, p. 25.

This article is a result of and response to a 6 August 1972 *New York Times* article by Pierre Boulez on the functions of the music director. Wuorinen asserts that Boulez discusses the present orchestral conditions inimical to new music but fails to expose them explicitly. He also writes that limited rehearsal time and restrictive union regulations make the satisfactory performance of contemporary music impossible because current practice does not give performers adequate time to familiarize themselves with new music. He contends new music is not more difficult to perform than the standard repertoire and that the failure to appreciate contemporary music is a result of too few performances. At one point in the article, Wuorinen asks: "Why, for instance, should state and federal funds be poured into endless regurgitations of the 'standard repertoire,' endless bailings-out of sinking institutions, when every other country in the world emphasizes in its governmental support for music, first, the contemporary music of its nationals?"

B1064 "Campus Focus: The Composer in Academia: Reflections on a Theme of Stravinsky." *College Music Symposium* 10, (Fall 1970), pp. 57-98.

This presentation of twenty-three brief essays is the result of a survey of composers who had been in and out of academia, and their degrees of success in either environment. The survey was inspired by the advice Igor Stravinsky offered young composers concerning teaching activities. Wuorinen's two-paragraph essay appears on page 98. He asserts it is distracting for a composer to spend time away from his work and that students, universities, and society all prefer composers to teach so they can get "privileged information" — information of a nature that cannot be gained by study.

B1065 "Colloquy and Review: Communications: A Reply to Dale A. Craig." *Perspectives of New Music* 6, no. 1 (Fall/Winter 1967), pp. 157-158.

In this letter Wuorinen replies to Dale A. Craig's letter which criticized Wuorinen's review of Larry Austin's book *Music in the Twentieth Century*. Wuorinen's letter to Craig concludes with this comment: "I must apologize if my 'critique of Larry Austin's contribution' seems 'peevish.' It was not meant to; it was meant to be outraged." (p. 158) *See:* B1011, B1068

B1066 "Colloquy and Review: A Reply to Daniel Goode." *Perspectives of New Music* 6, no. 1 (Fall/Winter 1967), pp. 159-160.

Wuorinen comments on Goode's letter, which was about Wuorinen's discussion of Mario Davidovsky's *Contrastes No. 1* for string orchestra and electronic sounds. Wuorinen writes, in part: "I am sure Mr. Goode would not want to indulge in the formless association-mongering that used to pass for macrostructural description." (p. 159) *See:* B1008, B1069

B1067 "Colloquy and Review: Reports: Tanglewood: A Composer's View." *Perspectives of New Music* 3, no. 2 (Spring/Summer 1965), pp. 167-168.

In this brief article Wuorinen offers his assessment of a Festival of Contemporary Music at Tanglewood. He discusses some of the conditions under which new works were performed and describes how performers were overburdened. He asserts that contemporary music is segregated by the larger sphere of conventional music and that "our culture will have to grow up a good deal" (p. 168) before new music can be presented naturally.

B1068 "Colloquy and Review: [Reviews of Books]." *Perspectives of New Music* 5, no. 1 (Fall/Winter 1966), pp. 142-147.

This is a review of Larry Austin's book *Music in the Twentieth Century* (the final volume of the *Norton History of Music Series*). Wuorinen's review is lengthy and extremely unfavorable. Wuorinen states that the volume will probably become influential because it is part of an established series. He concludes: "Contemplation of the vapid irrelevancies thus to be perpetuated, embalmed, and hallowed must be utterly demoralizing to any music professional." (p. 147) *See:* B1011, B1065

B1069 "Colloquy and Review: Younger American Composers: Mario Davidovsky: Contrastes No. 1." *Perspectives of New Music* 4, no. 2 (Spring/Summer 1966), pp. 144-149.

This article is a discussion of Mario Davidovsky's *Contrastes No. 1* for string orchestra and electronic sounds, particularly in terms of electronic music. In his final paragraph, Wuorinen raises the question of what constitutes improvised compositional control in fully composed music where "characteristics [are] determined by spontaneous, rather than premeditated decision." (p. 149) Daniel Goode subsequently commented on this article. *See:* B1008, B1066

B1070 "Comment on Fred Coulter." *American Society of University Composers. Proceedings of the Second Annual Conference* (April 1967), pp. 45-48.

This comment, published in these proceedings, addressed a lecture by Fred Coulter titled "Simplification of Complex Musical Structures," given at the same conference. Coulter proposed a simplified method of music analysis that would assist lay people in understanding complicated musical notation and make performance easier. Coulter discussed his approach using works by Karlheinz Stockhausen as examples. Wuorinen comments that Stockhausen's notation has been criticized in this regard. Wuorinen states: "This being so, one would think it a part of the teacher-of-rhythmic simplification-method's primary responsibility to demonstrate whether the notational 'difficulties' are motivated by the need to express compositional relations that are uniquely representable in that and only that way, or whether, on the other hand, the intent is to impress, bamboozle, and obfuscate." (p. 48)

B1071 "The Composer and the Outside World." The *New York Times*, 5 March 1967, *(Arts & Leisure)*, p. 28D.

A general article in which Wuorinen discusses the university environment and the musical public. He concludes: "For without the composer at the center of musical culture, there can be no musical culture." [P]

B1072 "Composing the Future." *Newsweek*, 24 December 1973, p. 54.

This is a brief piece in which Wuorinen makes the following statement: "Critics and journalists don't know anything. Imagine if The *New York Times* covered every important new musical event. In a short time *that* would be the musical world. Make no mistake: if my friends and I decide today that there will be no orchestras, there won't be in 50 years. Our influence is long-range. We are the future."

B1073 *Contemporary Music Catalog: 1982 Catalog.* New York: C.F. Peters, 1982.

The section on Wuorinen is prefaced by this original comment from the composer: "My career in composition is directed toward integrating myself into my work, and my work into the world; so that both of us can disappear together." (p. 90)

B1074 "Conversation with Otto Luening." *Perspectives of New Music* 9, no. 2,/10, no. 1 (Spring/Summer, Fall/Winter 1971), pp. 200-208.

This special double-issue of the journal includes this transcript of an interview from August 1970. Wuorinen asked Luening nine questions about teaching composition, music critics, kinds and styles of music, the composer at the university, the performance of contemporary music, and professional standards for composers.

B1075 In Memoriam: Stefan Wolpe (1902-1972)." *Perspectives of New Music* 11, no. 1 (Fall/Winter 1972), pp. 3-10.

A group of praiseworthy comments in memory of Wolpe, containing this four-sentence appreciation by Wuorinen: "Stefan Wolpe's insights into composition were profound and original; I am indebted to him on both counts. His 'originality' lay in his special notions of musical continuity, which root in tradition but branch unexpectedly and indirectly. His 'profundity' lay in his use of traditional means, values, and materials to achieve his special continuity. There are many for whom the confrontation with the results of his efforts meant an incalculable broadening of compositional capacity, and in them as well as in his own remarkable music, the inner balances that supported his external volatility will endure." (p. 6)

B1076   "Letters: Wuorinen's Case For and Against." *High Fidelity/Musical America* 25, no. 3 (March 1975), p. MA4.

Wuorinen responded here to the letter to the editor from Arthur R. Upgren, which was about Wuorinen's essay "We Spit on the Dead," published in an earlier issue of this journal. Wuorinen expresses his distaste for those who insist that music not currently liked will never be liked. *See:* B1021, B1022, B1091

B1077   "Notes on the Performance of Contemporary Music." *Perspectives of New Music* 3, no. 1 (Fall/Winter 1964), pp. 10-21.

In this article Wuorinen discusses problems of contemporary music performance practice, concentrating on rhythmic problems. He says these problems are the result of the performer "having been trained in a tradition of no relevance to its performance requirements." (p. 10) Examples and discussions of music by Matheus de Perusio (c. 1400), Thomas Morley, Milton Babbitt, Karlheinz Stockhausen, Stefan Wolpe, Donald Martino, and Peter Westergaard are included in the article. Wuorinen asserts that accurate and meaningful realization of ensemble rhythm is a crucial aspect of contemporary music performance and is only remotely related to "degrees of 'complexity' as they appear on paper." (p. 14) In a footnote to that statement, Wuorinen writes: "If it were necessary, this alone would demonstrate the complete imbecility of the premises on which, for example, [Karlheinz] Stockhausen's *Klavierstuck XI* is based." (p. 14) He concludes: "It is only when, in this most mundane domain, basic circumstances are questioned, as they are in the acts of composition and performance themselves, that we can approach representations of music (both modern and ancient) worthy of the compositional efforts that have called the music into being. And the present activities of various groups and individuals who manifest such a questioning attitude show how vast and fruitful a field lies before us." (p. 21) *See:* B862, B863

B1078   "The Outlook for Young Composers." *Perspectives of New Music* 1, no. 2 (Spring 1963), pp. 54-61.

Wuorinen discusses the problems faced by young composers and the kinds of musical composition that present the greatest challenge to them. He also writes about the lack of adequate training for vocalists in terms of the contemporary music repertoire. Of the contemporary composers who have had an influence on the younger generation, Wuorinen mentions John Cage, Elliott Carter, and Stefan Wolpe. Finally, after discussing the isolation many young composers face from their older colleagues and from an uncaring public, Wuorinen states: "It is difficult to be optimistic about the future. The often cited increase in amateur music making, the erection of 'cultural' centers for the official enthronement of the standard repertoire, etc., do not seem healthy signs. For they are clearly not so much the manifestations of a culture's growing concern for art as indications of the progressive encroachments of vulgarity." (pp. 60-61)

B1079 "Performance." *Dictionary of Contemporary Music.* Ed. John Vinton. New York: E.P. Dutton & Co., 1971.

Wuorinen wrote the first half of this article, titled "Performance," with the subheadings "General Conditions," and "Performance Problems in the Seminal Literature." (Jeffrey Kresky provided research assistance.) Wuorinen discusses the music of Igor Stravinsky and Arnold Schoenberg, among others, and points out that textual problems have posed a serious problem for performance. For example, he mentions that the published score of Edgard Varèse's *Déserts* contains about 300 textual errors. Wuorinen also comments on the commercial concert world: "Performances by orchestras and opera companies suffer not only from indifference among the players but from the preoccupation of conductors with public acclaim. Two recent exceptions are James Dixon, conductor of the State Univ.[ersity] of Iowa Orchestra, and Hans Rosbaud, late conductor of the Baden-Baden radio orchestra. Opera houses generally have the poorest standards partly for the reasons mentioned, partly because of the concentration on staging, and especially because performance levels in the standard literature are lower than those of orchestras." (p. 563) Wuorinen was on the Board of Advisors for this important reference tool. His own music is discussed in the articles "Recording," "Text Setting and Usage," "United States," and the biographical article about him, written by Harvey Sollberger. *See:* B549, B952

B1080 "Performance of New Music in American Universities." *The American Society of University Composers. Proceedings of the First Annual Conference* (April 1966), pp. 20-22.

Wuorinen gave a lecture at this conference which was published in these proceedings. He discussed contemporary music performance activity. He states: "There seems no general disposition on the part of 'serious music' institutions in this country to assume genuine responsibility to contemporary composers, or indeed to significant twentieth century music altogether." (p. 21) He praises the American Society of University Composers for disseminating new music.

B1081 "The Public Wants Only Beethoven? 'It's Not True!'" The *New York Times*, 13 September 1970, *(Arts & Leisure)*, pp. 1, 3.

In this article Wuorinen criticizes recording companies for not recording enough contemporary music. He writes: "How can one blame them [the young] when they call rock 'contemporary music,' unaware in their pathetic ignorance of the living body of contemporary serious music?" Wuorinen accuses the recording companies of being the worst offender in that they abdicate responsibility in this regard. The article sparked a response from readers, which appeared in this tabloid on 11 October 1970, with three letters to the editor from Robert Claiborne, Martin J. Burne, O.S.B., and John Holt. *See:* B1027

B1082 "Reviews of Books: Computer Music Journal: Vol. IV, 1-4." The *Musical Quarterly* 67, no. 3 (July 1982), pp. 424-427.

A review of the first four volumes of *Computer Music Journal.* Wuorinen writes: "Here we have silly technocratic self-congratulation set next to truly important work, but what is both heartening and a tribute to the efforts of the editor is the fact that several really provocative essays have here found their way into print." (p. 425) Of volume three, Wuorinen writes: "If you want a really fatuous collection of superficialities about music, cloaked up in smart-boy jargon, consult the interview with Marvin Minsky...." (p. 426)

B1083 "Reviews of Books: David Schiff: The Music of Elliott Carter." The *Musical Quarterly* 64, no. 4 (Fall 1983), pp. 606-607.

This is Wuorinen's review of the first book devoted exclusively to the music of Elliott Carter (Schiff, David. *The Music of Elliott Carter.* New York: Da Capo Press, 1983). Wuorinen writes: "Reading like nothing so much as a nightmarishly long program note, it substitutes adoring panegyrics for objective criticism." (p. 606) Further on, he states: "Another aspect of the author's attempt to make Carter the Greatest Composer the Solar System has Ever Seen leads to many preposterous assertions, and not a little fudging of historical detail." (p. 607)

B1084 "Reviews of Books: *The Orchestra: Origins and Transformations.* Ed. Joan Peyser." The *Musical Quarterly* 72, no. 4 (1986), pp. 535-539.

This book, edited by Peyser, was published in 1986 (New York: Charles Scribner's Sons). Wuorinen gives the book a rather favorable review. He discusses in detail how Peyser edited this collection of essays about what Wuorinen terms "the first manifestations of the ensemble we now know as the symphony orchestra to its present show-biz apotheosis." (p. 535) In part, Wuorinen concludes with this statement: "The pathetic gallery of grotesque publicity pictures, where ensembles about to play the string quartets of [Ludwig van] Beethoven, [Milton] Babbitt or [Elliott] Carter, don costumes and idiot grins at the urging of their publicists, bears sad and eloquent witness to what has become of serious music making." (p. 538) *See:* B977

B1085 "The Role of the Creative Artist." *National Music Council Bulletin* 26, no. 2 (Winter 1965-1966), p. 9.

This report constitutes part of a general meeting of the National Music Council. The published, unsigned report is a summary of comments made by Wuorinen. The eight-paragraph piece focuses largely on problems associated with the funding of contemporary music projects.

B1086 "The Schooling of Young Composers in the United States." *Papers of the Yugoslav-American Seminar on Music.* Ed. Malcolm H. Brown. Bloomington, Indiana: Indiana University, 1970.

These papers represent the opinions and ideas exchanged at the Yugoslav-American Seminar on Music, held at Sveti Stefan, Yugoslavia, 6-14 July 1968. Wuorinen's paper appears on pages 26-34. He writes: "The problems are many: within, they emerge from the condition of universities themselves and the endemic, specific problems they pose to the education of the young composer; without, they emerge from the still massive indifference of U.S. society to cultural concerns, specifically manifested by the unenlightened behavior of the publishing, recording, and journalizing industries." (p. 31) Wuorinen then proposes specific changes to the American educational system for young composers. The changes include a tutorial arrangement proceeding from and related to the student's individual needs (as evidenced by his creative work); the opportunity to work with performing groups; the inclusion of electronic resources, both in terms of instruction in the synthesis and generation of electronic sound as well as ear-training; and the study of counterpoint for "calisthenic" reasons. Wuorinen also submits that composition "be made the beginning of any intended composer's undergraduate curriculum, instead of being deferred until he is thought 'ready.'" (p. 32) *See:* B1034, B1088

B1087 *Simple Composition.* New York: Longman, 1979. 168 pp., ill. *(Longman Music Series).* ISBN: 0-582-28059-1. Series editor: Gerald Warfield; Cover design by Jahnus Vizon; Developmental editor: Gordon T.R. Anderson; Design: Patricia Smythe; Manufacturing and production supervisor: Louis

Gabor; Composition: A & S Graphics, Inc.; Printing & binding: Crest Litho, Inc.

This is Wuorinen's only book and is a textbook on musical composition. The acknowledgements include Milton Babbitt, Benjamin Boretz, and Gerald Warfield. The book contains a misprint: Example 56 (p. 83) lists the first interval class (in semitones) as 2; it should be interval class 1. The illustrations consist of musical examples, charts and graphs. Wuorinen closes his Valedictory with the following statement: "This seductive notion of self-expression, merchandized to those who have as yet no self to express, is the most dangerous and destructive idea to corrupt a young composer. Remember always that freedom can be had only if it is earned; in art it is earned by prior submission to discipline. And remember too that freedom means nothing unless there are co-ordinates, fixed and clear, whose very immobility allows the one who is free to measure the unfetterdness of his flight." (p. 164) The book was reprinted in 1988 by Schirmer Books (New York City) and Collier MacMillan (London). In 1992, it was taken over by C.F. Peters, and, at the time of this writing, plans were being made for publication in China (in Chinese). *See:* B948, B987 - B1005

B1088 "Školovanje mladih kompozitora u SAD." *ZVUK, Jugoslovenska muzička revija* 87-88 (1968), pp. 376-381.

This article, titled "The Schooling of Young Composers in the United States," was Wuorinen's address given during the Yugoslav-American Seminar on Music, held at Sveti Stefan, Yugoslavia, 6-14 July 1968. Included is a one-page summary of his lecture. A full English translation of the whole lecture was later published in the translated papers of the whole seminar (Bloomington, Indiana University, 1970). *See:* B1034, B1086

B1089 "Stravinsky (1882-1971): A Composer's Memorial." *Perspectives of New Music* 9, no. 2/10, no. 1 (Spring/Summer, Fall/Winter 1971), pp. 128-129.

This special, double issue of the journal includes a brief statement by Wuorinen in honor of Igor Stravinsky: "His demonstration, in the great works of his old age, of the fact that the twelve-tone system is as much a continuation of the tonal past as a break with it, has set the stage for a union of the western musical past with its present; and thus, had advanced the moment when western music, heard as a unified fabric, can begin realistically the process of confronting the musics of the rest of the world." (p. 129)

B1090 "Toward Good Vibrations." *Prose* 2 (Spring 1971), pp. 205-213.

Wuorinen discusses electronic music after twenty-five years of its existence. He states his purpose is to reflect on issues brought out by a medium which does not include the participation of live performers. These issues include the temporal unfolding of music, musical notation, the differences between live performance and electronic realization, and aleatoric music. Wuorinen's discussion is in the context of his compositional creative processes for *Time's Encomium* and *Contrafactum*, both works that dealt with various relations between pitch and time — "precise quantitative means" later "illuminated by a matrix of stresses and unstressed pulses...." (p. 209) After further discussion of the imprecise versus the precise in music, Wuorinen writes: "It is gratuitous to speak of creating circumstances in which composers can realize every musical event 'exactly' as they want, since no composer ever *has* known exactly how he wants it, and since even the most exact vision of the event at the moment of realization will alter with time." (p. 210) Of aleatoric music, he states: "But since all composition asserts only generalities, the relation of the aleatoric to the fully composed is really that of the unfinished to the finished...." (p. 211) Finally, Wuorinen's concluding paragraphs feature this comment: "Music itself can never be said to exist; it has either just happened, or is about to. And at that instant when music is sounding, it is merely using acoustic actuality to assert and define a set of related intervals of time and pitch, intervals that are themselves only 'empty space.'" (p. 212) *See:* W8, W159

B1091 "We Spit on the Dead." *High Fidelity/Musical America* 24, no. 12 (December 1974), pp. MA16-MA17.

This is probably Wuorinen's most infamous article, at least in terms of the reaction it provoked. Wuorinen opens with the following statement: "We have developed a special way of honoring the dead: we spit on them. I notice, in this centennial year of [Arnold] Schoenberg, a spate of articles appearing which denigrate the worth of his music, the significance of his ideas, and the importance of his influence. And the same is true of [Igor] Stravinsky, though he does not yet have a centennial to arouse the wrath of the living: the great works of his old age are contemptuously belittled, his life achievement scorned. It is as if the vision of these dead men in their unstoppable progress to the pantheon of the greatest figures in history enrages beyond endurance the petty commentators who survive them. It is enough to make anyone sick; and if you are a composer, nausea will be neither a stranger nor solace of recourse to you. But the prospect of enduring a lifetime of calumny, succeeded by posthumous defilement, urges on us the need for some form of adequate compensation in this life, now, for the work and art of composition." (p. MA16) [P] *See:* B1021, B1022, B1076

B1092 "What Concerns Me Is Music." *Genesis West* [New York City], (Fall 1962), pp. 11-18.

An interview with Wuorinen. It was later republished in *Contemporary Composers On Contemporary Music*, edited by Elliott Schwartz and Barney Childs. *See:* B1010

Appendix I:
Chronological
List of Works

1953
O Filiet Filiae
Scherzo

1954
Te Decet Hymnus

1955
Hommage à Bach
Prelude and Fugue for 4 Percussionists
Song and Dance

1956
Concertpiece for Piano and String Orchestra
Faire, If You Expect Admiring, and Turne Backe, You Wanton Flyer
Into the Organ Pipes and Steeples
Music for Orchestra
Sonatina for Woodwind Quartet
Subversion
Two Tranquil Pieces
Wind Quintet No. 1

1957
Alternating Currents
Be Merry All That Be Present
Concertante 1
Dr. Faustus Lights the Lights
String Quartet
Summer Music
3 Mass Movements
Triptych
Wandering in this Place

1958

Concertante II
Concerto for Violin and Orchestra
Movement for Wind Quintet
Sonata for Piano
Spectrum
Symphony No. 1
Three Pieces for String Quartet
Three Prepositions for Piano
Trio Concertante
Wind Quintet No. 2

1959

Concertante III
Concertante IV
Musica Duarum Partium Ecclesiastica
Symphony No. 2
Symphony No. 3

1960

Concertone for Brass Quintet and Orchestra
Consort of Four Trombones
The Door In the Wall
8 Variations
Madrigale Spirituale Sopra Salmo Secundo
On the Raft
Sonata for Flute and Piano
Turetzky Pieces

1961

Concert for Double Bass Alone
Consort from Instruments and Voices
An Educator's "Wachet Auf"
Evolutio: Organ
Evolutio Transcripta
Symphonia Sacra
Tiento Sobre Cabézón
Trio [No. 1 for Flute, Cello and Piano]

1962

Bearbeitungen über das Glogauer Liederbuch
Duuiensela
Invention for Percussion Quintet
Octet
The Prayer of Jonah
Trio No. 2 for Flute, Cello and Piano

1963
Chamber Concerto for Cello and Ten Players
Flute Variations I
Piano Variations

1964
Chamber Concerto for Flute and Ten Instruments
Composition for Violin and Ten Instruments
Cycle of Elaborations
Super Salutem
Variations à deux

1965
Chamber Concerto for Oboe and Ten Instruments
Composition for Oboe and Piano
Orchestral and Electronic Exchanges

1966
The Bells
Bicinium
Harpsichord Divisions
Janissary Music
Making Ends Meet
Piano Concerto No. 1
Salve Regina: John Bull

1967
Duo for Violin and Piano
The Politics of Harmony

1968
Flute Variations II
String Trio

1969
Adapting to the Times
Contrafactum
The Long and the Short
Nature's Concord
Piano Sonata No. 1
Time's Encomium

1970
Cello Variations I
Chamber Concerto for Tuba
A Message to Denmark Hill
Ringing Changes
A Song to the Lute in Musicke

Wind Quintet

1971
Canzona
Grand Bamboula
String Quartet No. 1

1972
Bassoon Variations
Concerto for Amplified Violin and Orchestra
Harp Variations
On Alligators
Speculum Speculi
Violin Variations

1973
Arabia Felix
Grand Union
Mannheim 87.87.87
Trio No. 3 for Flute, Cello and Piano
Twelve Short Pieces

1974
An Anthem for Epiphany
Fantasia
Piano Concerto No. 2

1975
Cello Variations II
Hyperion
A Reliquary for Igor Stravinsky
Tashi (Chamber Version)
The W. Of Babylon

1976
Album Leaf (Violin and Piano)
Percussion Symphony
Piano Sonata No. 2
Tashi (Orchestral Version)

1977
Archangel
Fast Fantasy
Self-Similar Waltz
6 Pieces for Violin and Piano
Six Songs for Two Voices
Wind Quintet
The Winds

1978
Ancestors
Archaeopteryx
Two-Part Symphony

1979
Fortune
Joan's
The Magic Art
Percussion Duo
Psalm 39
String Quartet No. 2
3 Songs for Tenor and Piano

1980
Beast 708
The Blue Bamboula
The Celestial Sphere
Ecclesiastical Symphonies

1981
Capriccio
Horn Trio
Short Suite
Trio for Bass Instruments

1982
Divertimento for Alto Saxophone and Piano
Divertimento for String Quartet
Mass
New York Notes

1983
Piano Concerto No. 3
Piano Trio
Rhapsody for Violin and Orchestra
Spinoff

1984
Album Leaf (Piano)
Bamboula Squared
Concertino
Crossfire
Movers and Shakers

1985
Double Solo for Horn Trio
Horn Trio Continued
Natural Fantasy
Prelude to Kullervo
Trombone Trio

1986
A Doleful Dompe on Deborah's Departure As Well As Borda's Bawdy Badinage
Fanfare for Rutgers University
Fanfare for the Houston Symphony
The Golden Dance
Piano Sonata No. 3

1987
Bamboula Beach
Five: Concerto for Amplified Cello and Orchestra
Galliard
String Quartet No. 3

1988
Another Happy Birthday
Bagatelle
Josquin: Ave Christe
Machault Mon Chou
Sonata for Violin and Piano

1989
A Solis Ortu
Genesis
String Sextet
Twang

1990
Astra

1991
Delight of the Muses

1992
Missa Brevis
A Winter's Tale

Appendix II:
Alphabetical
List of Works

A Solis Ortu
Adapting to the Times
Album Leaf (Piano)
Album Leaf (Violin and Piano)
Alternating Currents
Ancestors
Another Happy Birthday
An Anthem for Epiphany
Arabia Felix
Archaeopteryx
Archangel
Astra

Bagatelle
Bamboula Beach
Bamboula Squared
Bassoon Variations
Be Merry All That Be Present
Bearbeitungen über das Glogauer Liederbuch
Beast 708
The Bells
Bicinium
The Blue Bamboula

Canzona
Capriccio
The Celestial Sphere
Cello Variations I
Cello Variations II
Chamber Concerto for Flute and Ten Instruments
Chamber Concerto for Oboe and Ten Instruments
Chamber Concerto for Tuba

Chamber Concerto for Violoncello and Ten Players
Composition for Oboe and Piano
Composition for Violin and Ten Instruments
Concert for Double-bass Alone
Concertante I
Concertante II
Concertante III
Concertante IV
Concertino
Concerto for Amplified Violin and Orchestra
Concerto for Violin and Orchestra
Concertone for Brass Quintet and Orchestra
Concert-Piece for Piano and String Orchestra
Consort from Instruments and Voices
Consort of Four Trombones
Contrafactum
Crossfire
Cycle of Elaborations

Delight of the Muses
Divertimento for Alto Saxophone and Piano
Divertimento for String Quartet
Doctor Faustus Lights the Lights
A Doleful Dompe On Deborah's Departure As Well As Borda's Bawdy Badinage
The Door In the Wall
Double Solo for Horn Trio
Duo for Violin and Piano
Duuiensela

Ecclesiastical Symphonies
An Educator's "Wachet Auf"
8 Variations
Evolutio: Organ
Evolutio Transcripta

Faire, If You Expect Admiring, and Turne Backe, You Wanton Flyer
Fanfare for Rutgers University
Fanfare for the Houston Symphony
Fantasia
Fast Fantasy
Five: Concerto for Amplified Cello and Orchestra
Flute Variations I
Flute Variations II
Fortune

Galliard
Genesis
The Golden Dance
Grand Bamboula
Grand Union

Harp Variations
Harpsichord Divisions
Hommage à Bach
Horn Trio
Horn Trio Continued
Hyperion

Into the Organ Pipes and Steeples
Invention for Percussion Quintet

Janissary Music
Joan's
Josquin: Ave Christe

The Long and the Short

Machault Mon Chou
Madrigale Spirituale Sopra Salmo Secundo
The Magic Art: An Instrumental Masque Drawn From the Works of Henry Purcell
Making Ends Meet
Mannheim 87.87.87
Mass
A Message to Denmark Hill
Missa Brevis
Movement for Wind Quintet
Movers and Shakers
Music for Orchestra
Musica Duarum Partium Ecclesiastica

Natural Fantasy
Nature's Concord
New York Notes

O Filii Filiae
Octet
On Alligators
On the Raft
Orchestral and Electronic Exchanges

Percussion Duo
Percussion Symphony

Piano Concerto No. 1
Piano Concerto No. 2
Piano Concerto No. 3
Piano Sonata No. 1
Piano Sonata No. 2
Piano Sonata No. 3
Piano Trio
Piano Variations
The Politics of Harmony
The Prayer of Jonah
Prelude and Fugue for 4 Percussionists
Prelude to Kullervo
Psalm 39

A Reliquary for Igor Stravinsky
Rhapsody for Violin and Orchestra
Ringing Changes

Salve Regina: John Bull
Scherzo
Self-Similar Waltz
Short Suite
6 Pieces for Violin and Piano
Six Songs for Two Voices
Sonata for Flute and Piano
Sonata for Piano
Sonata for Violin and Piano
Sonatina for Woodwind Quartet
Song and Dance
A Song to the Lute in Musicke
Spectrum
Speculum Speculi
Spinoff
String Quartet
String Quartet No. 1
String Quartet No. 2
String Quartet No. 3
String Sextet
String Trio
Subversion
Summer Music
Super Salutem
Symphonia Sacra
Symphony No. 1 (Symphony In One Movement)
Symphony No. 2 (Symphony II)
Symphony No. 3

Tashi (Chamber Version)
Tashi (Orchestral Version)
Te Decet Hymnus
Three Cadenzas for the Mozart Concerto in C Major for Oboe and Piano
3 Mass Movements
Three Pieces for String Quartet
Three Prepositions for Piano
3 Songs for Tenor and Piano
Tiento Sobre Cabézón
Time's Encomium
Trio Concertante
Trio for Bass Instruments
Trio [No. 1 for Flute, Cello, and Piano]
Trio No. 2 for Flute, Cello, and Piano
Trio No. 3 for Flute, Cello, and Piano
Triptych
Trombone Trio
Turetzky Pieces
Twang
Twelve Short Pieces
Two-Part Symphony
Two Tranquil Pieces

Variations à deux
Violin Variations

The W. of Babylon
Wandering in this Place
Wind Quintet (1977)
Wind Quintet No. 1
Wind Quintet No. 2
The Winds
A Winter's Tale

Index

Index entries refer to page or entry numbers. Numbers prefaced by a lower-case *p* indicate a page number; numbers with an upper-case *W* refer to entries in the *Works and Performances* section; entries with an upper-case *D* refer to the *Discography*; entries with an upper-case *B* refer to entries in the *Writings About Wuorinen* and *Writings by Wuorinen* sections. Titles of newspaper articles are not indexed; titles of journal articles are indexed. All other titles, including titles of events, e.g., concert programs, concert series, and music festivals, are italicized.

About the Author

RICHARD D. BURBANK is Music Catalog Coordinator and Associate Professor of Library Administration at the University of Illinois at Urbana-Champaign. He is author of *Twentieth Century Music: Orchestral, Chamber, Operatic and Dance Music, 1900-1980* (1984), editor (with Steven L. Goulden) of *Day by Day: The Forties* (1977), and has written scholarly articles and book reviews for several library science and music journals.